Corgi Juniors and Husky Models

A Complete Identification and Price Guide

Bill Manzke

Schiffer Publishing Ltd

4880 Lower Valley Road, Atglen, PA 19310 USA

Dedication

To Helena and Steven.

Disclaimer

Corgi Toys, Corgi Classics, Husky Models, Corgi Juniors, Super Juniors, Whizzwheels, Corgi Rockets, Growlers, and the names of various features which appear on the models included in this book are trademarks of Mettoy Ltd. PLC and/or its successors Corgi Toys Ltd. and Corgi Classics Ltd. Hot Wheels, Auto-City, Haulers and Holiday Hot Wheels are trademarks of Mattel Inc. The names and external appearance of the prototypes for the various models produced that appear in this book are the trademarks of the manufacturers of the original vehicles as licensed to Mettoy Ltd. PLC, its successors, or Mattel Inc. Other brand names and trademarks referenced in this book are the property of the original manufacturer and/or their successors.

Photographs of models appearing in this book that are not part of the author's collection are used with the permission of the owners of the models and/or photographs. Images from the Internet or other public domain sources were not used in the creation of this book. The author retains all rights to the content of this book, its text and/or images.

Published by Schiffer Publishing Ltd.
4880 Lower Valley Road
Atglen, PA 19310
Phone: (610) 593-1777; Fax: (610) 593-2002
E-mail: Info@schifferbooks.com
Please visit our web site catalog at
www.schifferbooks.com
We are always looking for people to write books on new and related subjects. If you have an idea for a book, please contact us at the above address.

This book may be purchased from the publisher.
Include $3.95 for shipping.
Please try your bookstore first.
You may write for a free catalog.

In Europe, Schiffer books are distributed by
Bushwood Books
6 Marksbury Avenue
Kew Gardens
Surrey TW9 4JF England
Phone: 44 (0) 20 8392 8585
Fax: 44 (0) 20 8392 9876
E-mail: Bushwd@aol.com
Free postage in the UK. Europe: air mail at cost.

Acknowledgments

Where do I start to thank the many, many people that have made this book possible? Through my many contacts through e-mail, chat rooms, Internet web sites, and correspondence the list of those who have helped is indeed long. There are some that I know I will miss, so please forgive my oversight.

Three individuals have contributed greatly to the new material in the book, and I want to thank them personally here. First, Gary Hirst in the UK has opened my eyes to a wide range of promotional and UK only models from the Corgi Toys Ltd. and early Corgi Classics Ltd. time periods. With luck, I have done likewise for his interest in Hot Wheels. Our similar collecting styles and cross-ocean interests have broadened both of our collections and our knowledge of our subjects. Thank you for your support and friendship.

Second, Wolfgang Ghert of Germany has provided many photos for this book out of his fantastic collection of early Husky Models and Corgi Juniors. Many of Wolfgang's models are unique prototype or pre-production models. His generous contributions of photos and background information have given a unique insight into the early days of development and production of these models.

Third, Ricardo Caruso of Brazil has helped me discover the world of Kiko Corgi and Kiko Corgi Junior models. His friendship and knowledge from his unique Brazilian perspective has broadened my understanding of how Corgi Toys are viewed in the rest of the world. Ricardo also publishes a hobby magazine, to which I am proud to say I have contributed articles. Thank you for your help and wisdom.

I would like to thank Dr. Ed Force for his kind permission to include and expand upon the variation listing first published in his book *Corgi Toys,* and later updated in my book *The Unauthorized Encyclopedia of Corgi Toys*. This book is an offspring of these earlier works.

A number of friends from the Matchbox Collectors Community Hall have contributed material, data, and background information. I am grateful to Mark Curtis for hosting what must be the best diecast web site anyone could ask for on the Web. The members truly are a community, and they provide endless support and encouragement. (Here is a hint. If new information is found, it is usually reported there first.) Thanks must go to Brian "Poorvanner" Walker for his incredibly detailed notes on his van collection from which many new variations have been discovered. His collection of Corgi vans is unequaled. Thanks also go to Eric Gibbons, whose passion for Husky Models uncovered many new details that were not noticeable at first glance. A large packet of information from Steve Masson, with hundreds of variation reports, was greatly appreciated. Additional models from Dave Rogers were a great help in filling in some details. Other members, such as Christian Falkensteiner, Doug Breithaupt and Steve Beckett, have their own web sites that have provided much additional information.

Susan Pownall at the Corgi Collector Club has provided assistance and encouragement on numerous occasions. So, too, has Richard Walker at Corgi Classics Inc. in Chicago. Some of the new information that appears in this book was first shown in my articles for the *Corgi Collector* Club magazine.

Numerous contributors of information and materials wished not to have their specific contributions pointed out. Some sources were personally contacted, while others corresponded via the Internet. I would like to thank the following people for their invaluable help: Stephen Apps, Wilf Bainbridge, Henk van Brakel, Tony Buller, Ian Cousins, John M Dean, John Eio, Mark Foster, Keith Good, Tom Hammel, Andreas Held, Tony Howden, Michael Hylton, Dana Johnson, Anton Khropochnik, Mike Krull, Alex Lakhtman, Tom Larson, Munish Madan, Andy Pena, Simon Phillips, Bob Porcja, Chris Potter, Karen Preece, Martin Raynor, Derk Riesthuis, Steve Ryan, Vince Sclafani, Todd Sweeney, George Taylor, Will Turner, and Frank Wright. Thanks also to those of you who responded with information using the Variation Report Form in Ed Force's earlier book *Corgi Toys,* and in my book *The Unauthorized Encyclopedia of Corgi Toys.*

Finally, I wish to truly thank my wife, Maggie, who once again put up with the rantings of her husband during the creation of this book, not to mention the occasional unexpected boxes of little toy cars in the mailbox. Not only has she been my "in-house pre-editor," she also has supported me without wavering through some of the tough times we have been through together. I look forward to making return payment in kind with interest!

—Bill Manzke

Foreword

Welcome to *Corgi Juniors and Husky Models: A Complete Identification and Price Guide,* the first of what I hope will become a series of companion books covering Corgi Toys and related products from various eras. Actually, the initial book in the planned series could be considered Ed Force's book *Corgi Toys,* which was first published in 1984. Since then, his book has been updated only for those products produced by Mettoy until the company's closure in October 1983. Corgi products produced after that date were left for my larger book *The Unauthorized Encyclopedia of Corgi Toys.*

Until now, there haven't been any other books published that focus specifically on Husky Models, Corgi Juniors and Corgi Rockets. These smaller companions are often mentioned in books about larger scale Corgi Toys, but usually as an afterthought to round out the text. In my wanderings at toy shows and on the Internet, I have often been asked two questions: first, why isn't there a book on the smaller models, and second, why haven't I written one myself. With this book, I hope to address both questions.

I have included images of almost every model available to me for this book. My own collection is large and growing. It is not all-inclusive, though. Time and money act as a tag-team to ensure that fact. I am able to state that the listings in the back of the book ARE comprehensive, and include every variation issued as uncovered by my research. Certainly, there are bound to be some uncommon models I have missed. Promotional and regional models can be notoriously difficult to find.

I must sound a note of caution about values. Recession, terrorist attacks, and war have thrown a chill across the entire economy of much of the western world in recent years. The result has been a drop in collectable toy values in the short term. Values are recovering and will eventually exceed those of the late 1990s, but how soon and how fast are not yet known. Values quoted in this book must be viewed in the context of the publication date and world events of the time. The world has and will continue to change in unexpected ways. All we can do is look to the future and hope for the best.

Enjoy your Corgi Juniors, Corgi Rockets and Husky Models.

—Bill Manzke

Contents

History

Concept and Development

Husky Models, and later Corgi Juniors, may never have existed were it not for a request from an outside company. Woolworth, a major chain store in Britain and many other countries, wanted to market their own private brand of small diecast model vehicles to compete with the popular "Matchbox Series" by Lesney. The draw of an exclusive product was meant to attract customers away from other stores. In this way, they could get customers "in the door," where they would naturally do some of their other shopping too. To make this marketing plan effective, the new line of vehicles needed to have features that were better than the competition, be fairly priced, and be of high quality. In order to fulfill these needs, Woolworth turned to Mettoy, maker of the phenomenally popular Corgi Toys.

Mettoy was faced with the challenge, or golden opportunity, to create an entirely new, small, diecast product line all at once. The models in the product line needed to be good enough to do to Lesney's "Matchbox Series" what the original Corgi Toys did to Hornby's "Dinky Toys" in the late 1950s. Since the new product line would not be distributed through all Corgi Toys vendors, Mettoy was also faced with creating an entirely new brand name for the new small series. Keeping with the dog theme used with Corgi Toys, Mettoy chose the Husky Models name. The new name would be both easy to remember and also infer that the models were sturdy and well built. Mettoy chose mostly British vehicles to model in the initial line, with a few American and European cars to interest those markets.

The initial development work for the first models was done very quickly. Most would have vacuum plated plastic baseplates that incorporated a leaf spring action not found on other brands at the time. The scale of the models was variable depending upon the size of the prototype, though all would look about right on an "OO" scale train layout. This sliding scale formula had worked successfully with the larger Corgi Toys range, and was similar to what was being done by Lesney. Much of the initial product line was proportionally similar to the equivalent "Matchbox Series" models of the time.

The final brand name to be used for the new product line was still in question almost up to the time that the line was to be introduced. The first pre-production sample models presented to Woolworth's for approval actually had no name at all on their baseplates. The first choice of naming the new line was "Husky Toys." Initial packaging mock-ups carried this name for presentation purposes. Mettoy soon discovered, however, that "Husky Toys" was a trademarked name used by a company in Canada for their line of stamped steel toy trucks. The official name of the new line was quickly changed to "Husky Models" to avoid any potential conflict with the other manufacturer's products. (Today, many collectors still wrongly refer to the small diecast Mettoy products as Husky Toys.)

Woolworth's had a full product line in-place by the end of 1964, with new models added monthly. The full range listing could be found printed on the backs of the cards on which the models came. An early brochure actually shows the vehicles in the colors worn by the original pre-production models rather than the released products. (This has caused many collectors to search for non-existent variations!) Unlike Lesney with their boxes, Husky Models came packaged from the start on cards with plastic see-through bubbles. This type of packaging eliminated the need for a separate showcase to display models, and also reduced damage to stock caused when models fell out of their boxes. With everything ready, Woolworth's unveiled "Husky Models" just in time for the 1964 Christmas shopping season.

The initial "Husky Toys" prototypes. Note the light gray wheels. *Photo Courtesy of Wolfgang Gehrt / Goodies Old Toys.*

Prototypes have no wording at all on the base. *Photo Courtesy of Wolfgang Gehrt / Goodies Old Toys.*

The Jaguar Fire Chief Car in prototype form. *Photo Courtesy of Wolfgang Gehrt / Goodies Old Toys.*

Prototype of the Shell-BP Tanker. *Photo Courtesy of Wolfgang Gehrt / Goodies Old Toys.*

Prototype of the Milk Tanker. *Photo Courtesy of Wolfgang Gehrt / Goodies Old Toys.*

Prototype and released versions of the Volkswagen Pick-up. *Photo Courtesy of Wolfgang Gehrt / Goodies Old Toys.*

Husky Models

The initial reaction to Husky Models was very positive, and sales were strong even with the highly restricted distribution network. Mettoy, through Woolworth's stores, had raised the bar of customer expectations in the small diecast model field. Lesney and its many competitors quickly scrambled to upgrade their lines with more features to keep up with Husky Models. A war of new feature introductions quickly escalated much as it had earlier between Corgi Toys and Dinky Toys in the larger scales. One of the first things to occur was a creeping increase in the scale of the models from all brands to make them appear worth more than the earlier competition. Many of the initial Husky Models offerings would last only two or three years, quickly being replaced by larger models with more features. Lesney issued its first car with suspension with a diecast baseplate to hide the workings. Mettoy soon followed suit, reworking some models into a larger scale while adding the baseplate, thereby killing two birds with one stone. Less popular models were dropped in favor of new replacements in the larger size. Mettoy also learned from their design errors, improving the manufacturability of the new offerings. Trucks and construction vehicles, while not rapidly replaced like the cars, saw evolutionary changes made to the dies to reduce breakage and improve quality. Such changes were invisible to the average buyer, but helped keep production costs down.

By 1966, Husky Models had made major inroads in the markets where Woolworth's stores were present. However, other markets were also clamoring for the little models. Around 1967, after concluding discussions with Woolworth over the issue, Mettoy began marketing Husky Models through some of its regular distribution network. This was strictly limited to only those markets where Woolworth's stores were not present. Also at this time, Woolworth's requested that packaging in specific markets be pre-printed with pricing for that market. In order to track which models were going where, some models bound for the American market were packaged with numbers 50 higher than usual. For example, the #39 Jaguar XJ6 could also be found as #89, and so on. Some of the Husky Extras models would actually end up with three different numbers, depending on where it was sold. This situation would quickly become a logistics nightmare, especially considering the steady rise in popularity of Husky Models. Mettoy knew that the Woolworth's stores contract was severely restricting the growth of sales for their popular little models. By 1969, Mettoy and Woolworth's stores had negotiated an end to their contract, freeing Mettoy to distribute the product line wherever it chose.

1-A and 1-B Jaguars variations. *Photo Courtesy of Wolfgang Gehrt / Goodies Old Toys.*

More Jaguar color variations. *Photo Courtesy of Wolfgang Gehrt / Goodies Old Toys.*

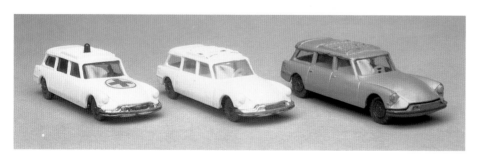

2-A and 2-B Citroen Safari (missing boats) with 6-A Ambulance.

3-A Mercedes-Benz 220 Saloon.

7-A Buick Electra with two shades of 9-A Buick Police Cars.

4-A and 4-B Jaguar Fire Cars.

8-A Ford Thunderbird Convertible.

Baseplate differences between early and later Jaguars.

8-A and 8-B Ford Thunderbirds.

17-A and 17-B Guy Warrior Milk Tankers.

14A Shell-BP Tanker and 14-B Shell Tankers.

10-A Guy Warrior Coal Truck with later Corgi Juniors version.

15-A Aveling-Barford Dump Truck with plow blade.

18 Plated Jaguar.

19-A Commer "Walk-Thru" Vans including white prototype model. *Photo Courtesy of Wolfgang Gehrt / Goodies Old Toys.*

14-B European promotional versions. *Photo Courtesy of Wolfgang Gehrt / Goodies Old Toys.*

20-A Ford Thames Vans (missing yellow ladders and antennas.)

Uncommon red version of the Zephyr Estate.

23-A Guy Warrior Army Tanker.

24-A Ford Zephyr Estate.

14-B Shell and Esso Tanker variations.

25-A S. & D. Refuse Wagon.

28-A Ford F350 Wrecker.

29-A ERF Cement Mixer Truck.

26-A Sunbeam Alpine.

30-A Studebaker Ambulance with unnumbered civilian version.

Color and wheel variations. *Photo Courtesy of Wolfgang Gehrt / Goodies Old Toys.*

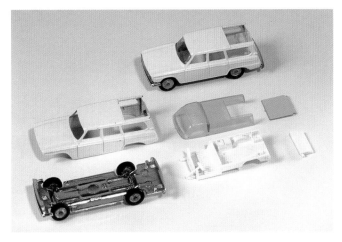

Disassembled view of a Studebaker. *Photo Courtesy of Wolfgang Gehrt / Goodies Old Toys*

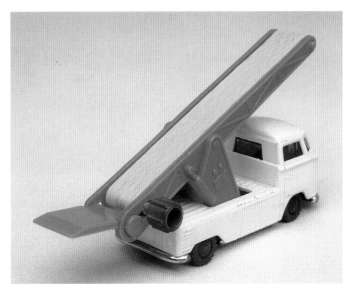

32-A Volkswagen Luggage Elevator.

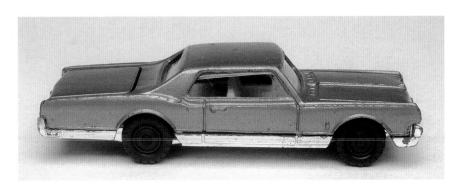

31-A Oldsmobile Starfire.

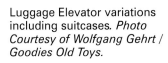

Luggage Elevator variations including suitcases. *Photo Courtesy of Wolfgang Gehrt / Goodies Old Toys.*

Oldsmobile Starfire variations.

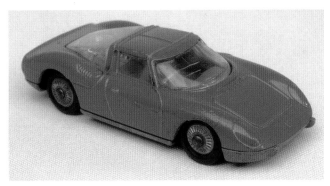

6-B Ferrari 250GT.

Prototype Yellow Cards. *Photo Courtesy of Wolfgang Gehrt / Goodies Old Toys.*

3006-A Service Station minus some of its vehicles.

35-A Ford F350 Camper in different colors.

2001-A Four Car Garage.

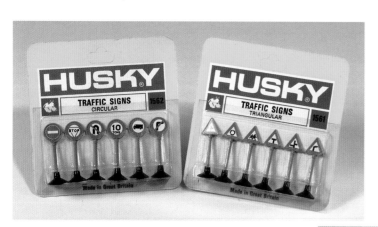

Husky Street Signs. *Photo Courtesy of Wolfgang Gehrt / Goodies Old Toys.*

36-A Simon Snorkel Fire Engine variations.

Husky Figures made in both Gt. Britain and Hong Kong. *Photo Courtesy of Wolfgang Gehrt / Goodies Old Toys.*

39-A Jaguar XJ6. (Also found as 89 in the USA.)

Variations of 22-B Aston Martin DB6 with a Corgi Juniors version.

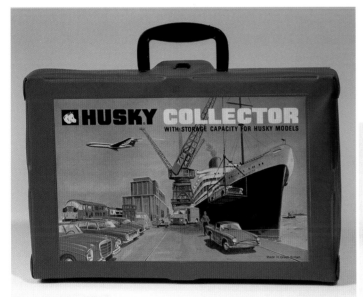

1580-A Husky Collector Case. *Photo Courtesy of Wolfgang Gehrt / Goodies Old Toys.*

21-B Jaguar E-Type 2+2.

9-B Cadillac Eldorado with a Corgi Juniors version. *Photo Courtesy of Wolfgang Gehrt / Goodies Old Toys.*

The Eldorado lasted into the Whizzwheels era.

Wheel Variations on the 3-B Volkswagen Police Car. *Photo Courtesy of Wolfgang Gehrt / Goodies Old Toys.*

Unusual Polizei version of the 3-B, thought to be a pre-production model.

43-A Massey Ferguson 3303 Tractor with Blade.

7-B Duple Vista 25 Coach.

More variations of the Willys Jeep. *Photo Courtesy of Wolfgang Gehrt / Goodies Old Toys.*

12-B Ford F350 Tower Truck.

40-A Ford Thames Walter Martin Caravan.

5-B Willys Jeep with later military version.

A selection of Thames Caravan colors. *Photo Courtesy of Wolfgang Gehrt / Goodies Old Toys.*

38-A Rice Beaufort Horse Box Trailer with much later set version.

The happy Potts family.

1206-A / 1006-A Chitty-Chitty-Bang-Bang.

Prototype and released versions of the 1201-A / 1001-A James Bond Aston Martin. *Photo Courtesy of Wolfgang Gehrt / Goodies Old Toys.*

37-A NSU RO 80 with later Corgi Juniors versions. *Photo Courtesy of Wolfgang Gehrt / Goodies Old Toys.*

1203-A / 1003-A Batboat packaging trials. *Photo Courtesy of Wolfgang Gehrt / Goodies Old Toys.*

1204-A / 1004-A Monkeemobile with a later version.

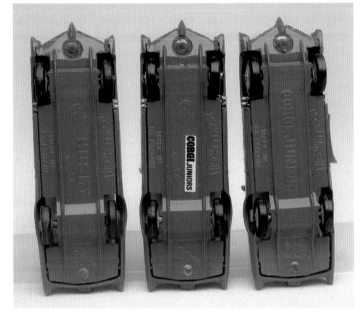

An example of baseplate evolution.

1205-A / 1005-A *The Man from U.N.C.L.E.* car.

Factory error (missing figures in car). *Photo Courtesy of Wolfgang Gehrt / Goodies Old Toys*

More Monkeemobile variations. *Photo Courtesy of Wolfgang Gehrt / Goodies Old Toys.*

Corgi Rockets

Never did the introduction of a range of diecast toy cars shake up the market more than the introduction of Mattel's Hot Wheels vehicles and sets. Overnight, boys around the world changed how they thought of model cars. What had at one moment been a way to play imitating real life and real vehicles turned into a high-speed fantasy blur of racing and tricks. It was late 1967. Mattel had made a phenomenal hit in the United States with their new Hot Wheels product line, and had their sights set on expanding into Europe. Every manufacturer of diecast models was bracing for the onslaught, and scrambling to come up with a competitive product line of their own. At the time, Mettoy was getting their first taste of success against Lesney's Matchbox Series with their Husky Models. Mettoy's major investments in tooling were soon being threatened by the upstart Mattel, much as Corgi Toys had threatened Dinky Toys in the 1950s. For once, Mettoy products were not the crest of the wave in the market.

Mattel's Hot Wheels cars actually were not much of a development. Mattel hadn't even tried to produce detail on their models that would come close to the state-of-the-art then produced by Lesney, Mettoy, and others. Instead, Hot Wheels were more an impression of the real vehicles they represented. Lack of fidelity was masked with flashy paint and trim. Even the slick plastic wheels on piano wire axles to reduce friction weren't novel. Where Mattel did have a novel product, with patents to protect it, was in the track systems. Diecast cars had never been used in such an acrobatic and fast paced manner. It was the track systems that made the cars popular.

Mettoy was used to competitors introducing new features, and was well practiced in responding in kind. Engineering efforts soon were focused on developing a competitive response as quickly as possible. Fortunately, Mettoy had Husky Models in production at the time. New models planned for the Husky Models line were diverted into what would become the Corgi Rockets program. Mettoy responded to the challenge with their "one-up the competition" style that had served them well in the past. Corgi Rockets cars would have more than fast wheels. They were designed to have interchangeable chassis parts that could be snapped on and off with a special key. The diecast bodies would be riveted to a diecast sub-plate where the plastic chassis would attach. Paint jobs would initially have the same candy-apple effect used by Mattel on the Hot Wheels cars. Mettoy coined the name "Solarbrite" for their finish, which was essentially a silver coating followed by a transparent color tint. Five of the initial seven cars released would have this type of paint job during the first year of production. New low friction "Whizzwheels" would be fitted and be a strongly pushed marketing feature.

Mettoy was also determined to one-up Mattel in their track sets. A unique-to-Corgi track profile was developed similar to the Hot Wheels track. Numerous accessories were designed including a Power Booster that shot any car entering it out the other end at great speed. The expected loops and jumps appeared, as well as starting tracks, lap counters, finish line flags and hairpin turns. There was even a tall Skypark parking garage that could be connected to the tracks. One ominous accessory was also released, an adapter that allowed Rockets track to be connected to "other brands."

Mattel had done their homework, though, and had a good group of lawyers. Once Corgi Rockets, Matchbox Superfast, and other me-too brands hit the market, Mattel went on the offensive in court charging patent infringement. The charges were not aimed at the cars others produced, but rather the track sets. Without their own track sets, Mattel knew the competition would be crippled. Unfortunately for Mettoy and others, Mattel won the case. Corgi Rockets track sets, along with those of the competition, were to stop production immediately. Existing stocks were allowed to be sold off, but no new production would be permitted.

It was now late 1969, and Mettoy was left in a tight spot. The complex removable chassis of their Rockets vehicles without the track systems looked just like an overly complicated, costly to produce car that simply ran on Hot Wheels tracks. Having just broken free from the Woolworth's stores contract for their Husky Models earlier in the year, Mettoy now had two competing lines of small diecast cars. A crash program had already been underway changing the brand name Husky Models to Corgi Juniors. (Described in the next section.) Now, further changes and consolidation were needed. The Rockets name was quickly dropped as existing stocks of the cars were sold off. The "Whizzwheels" feature was moved to the Corgi Juniors product line, causing even more chaos with mold and die changes to accommodate them on models without the removable chassis. Mettoy lost money heavily on all of the unusable product development costs and subsequent product design changes. A factory fire late in 1969 also dealt a heavy blow financially, but most of the product lost was in the larger Corgi Toys line.

Among the more interesting products lost due to the Mattel lawsuit was a little-known offshoot of the Rockets product line that was called "Electro-Rockets." This line was one of the first uses of Ni-Cad rechargeable batteries in a small toy car, being introduced soon after Mattel's "Hot Wheels Sizzelers." The cars were charged by a battery operated charging station that was sold individually or with one of the cars. Only two vehicles were ever released in this range. One of them, an Alfa Romeo Montreal, was unique and never reappeared in the Corgi Juniors product line. These models are highly prized by collectors, but can be difficult to find in mint condition due to a slow chemical reaction between the batteries and the finish on the cars. It is possible, though not certain, that Mettoy was required to surrender the Ni-Cad technology to Mattel as part of the lawsuit settlement. In any event, the "Electro-Rockets" were only offered for a very brief time and in such low quantities that they have remained unknown to many collectors.

One final note in regard to the Corgi Rockets product line. No track or accessory products appearing in the Corgi Rockets catalog were ever produced again. Mattel's initial patent on the track sets has long since lapsed, yet no former Rockets parts have reappeared. Speculation was widespread through the 1970s and 1980s. However, it is known that around 1970, Mettoy dumped a large number of dies into Swansea harbor, thus destroying them. It is quite likely that the majority of what was disposed of in that way was related to the Rockets program. The action was likely to fulfill an order by a court to destroy any production capability that infringed on Mattel's patent. Somewhere at the bottom of Swansea harbor rests a piece of Corgi history, and there are probably some still around today that know just what is lying down there.

Original Corgi Rockets dealer display. *Photo Courtesy of Wolfgang Gehrt / Goodies Old Toys.*

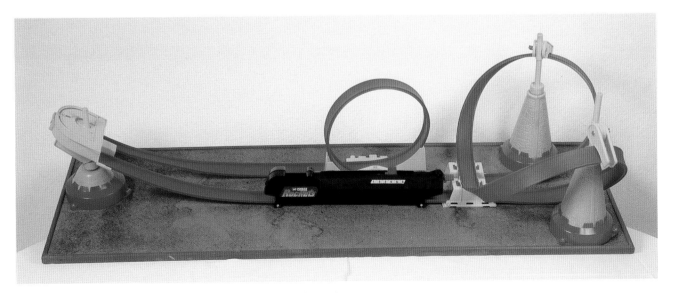

Corgi Rockets track set. *Photo Courtesy of Wolfgang Gehrt / Goodies Old Toys.*

903-A Mercedes-Benz 280 SL variations. *Photo Courtesy of Wolfgang Gehrt / Goodies Old Toys.*

905-A Volvo P1800 with larger Corgi Toys version.

902-A Jaguar XJ6.

904-A Porsche Carrera 6 with Corgi Juniors version.

View of the removable Rockets chassis.

906-A Jensen Interceptor with Corgi Juniors version.

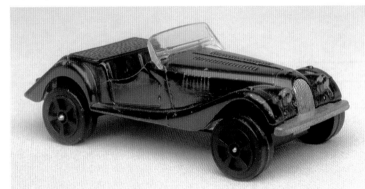

921-A Morgan Plus 8.

919-A Todd Sweeney Stock Car.

1970 Corgi Rockets catalog.

918-A Ital Design Bizzarini Manta variations. *Photo Courtesy of Wolfgang Gehrt / Goodies Old Toys.*

Corgi Juniors Conversion

Toward the end of 1969, Mettoy was embroiled in a number of programs at once. Corgi Rockets had just come to market, with the massive expenditure on tooling associated with the track sets and cars. Mattel's "Hot Wheels" products were making major inroads into the market, and hopes were still pinned on the Rockets to counter them. Lesney's "Matchbox Series" was reigning as king of the small diecast market. Woolworth's had agreed to release Mettoy from the exclusive contract for Husky Models, possibly to gain access to the Rockets line. Making matters worse, a warehouse fire at the Swansea, Wales, plant had wiped out much of the Corgi Toys product on-hand. The smaller Husky Models and Corgi Rockets, however, were produced in the Northampton, England, plant and were not effected by the blaze. Mettoy was left with a series of small vehicles still not associated with the popular Corgi Toys product line by consumers, but with little else available to sell. Something had to be done quickly.

In a crash program, the name of the complete Husky Models product line was changed to Corgi Juniors. The idea was to both ride the coat tails of the popular Corgi Toys name, as well as provide shops with stock while the company recovered from the fire. Dies were quickly modified to eliminate the Husky name on baseplates. To save time and get the models in production, small paper labels were produced with the new "CORGI JUNIORS" name and were applied to the otherwise brand-less baseplates. At least three different sizes of these small labels were produced to cover the various needs of the different models. This was a stopgap program aimed at quickly converting the product line and getting it out the door.

Some of the newer models under development at the time of the conversion would never be released as Husky Models, even though they had been announced. These models were reworked immediately to carry the new Corgi Juniors lettering on their baseplates. Models like the Porsche Carrera 6 and Mangusta would never carry the Husky logo or name.

A clever marketing strategy was developed for the new Corgi Juniors line. Models would be packaged with a pre-printed collector's card printed on the packaging. A special card book was issued so that owners could cut out the card from the model packaging and mount it in the book. A special promotion in the United States was also used to heighten the product's visibility. A grouping of the standard Corgi Juniors models were offered by City Service (later Citgo) gasoline stations that got customers a free model when they bought a full tank of fuel. Many new American collectors were introduced to the new Corgi Juniors in that way.

The crash program to convert Husky Models to Corgi Juniors was just about complete when another had to be undertaken by Mettoy. Again, it was Mattel's Hot Wheels products that were the cause, but this time it was their patents rather than their products driving the change. The Corgi Rockets product line that was developed to counter Mattel's Hot Wheels was to be phased-out due to the loss of the track sets as the result of a patent infringement case lost to Mattel. Mettoy's new Corgi Juniors would now need to be fitted with the Rockets' "Whizzwheels" as quickly as possible in order to be competitive. The "regular wheel" Corgi Juniors would appear only briefly before they too would be replaced. The toy car market demanded it.

Tan Husky and yellow Corgi Juniors Volkswagens.

Corgi Juniors label on the Volkswagen's base.

E8-C Tipping Farm Trailer.

E38-A NSU RO-80.

Label on the NSU's base.

E3005-B Leisure Time Set. *Photo Courtesy of Wolfgang Gehrt / Goodies Old Toys.*

Mercedes variations.

E1001-A James Bond Aston Martin.

E3009-A Service Station Set. *Photo Courtesy of Wolfgang Gehrt / Goodies Old Toys.*

E1006-A Chitty-Chitty-Bang-Bang.

Label on Chitty's base.

E45-A Mercedes-Benz 280SL.

E9-B Cadillac Eldorado.

Label on E1005-A base.

Rare label base twin pack.
*Photo Courtesy of Wolfgang
Gehrt / Goodies Old Toys.*

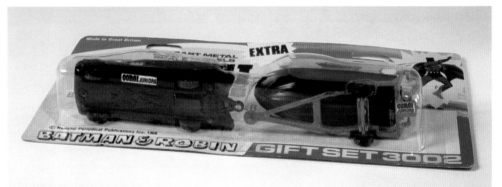

E2002-A Hoynor
Car Transporter.

Whizzwheels Conversion

Mattel had very carefully protected their track systems with patents. Waiting until Mettoy, Lesney, and others had introduced their own versions of track sets, Mattel went to work in the courts charging patent infringement. Making the story short, Mattel won the cases. This turn of events left Mettoy in a bad position. Without their own track sets, Corgi Rockets would appear to be overly complex models that still needed Mattel's track to run upon. Assembly costs for the Rockets were much higher than the competition. Corgi Juniors, on the other hand, were saddled with the old style wheels that wouldn't work on the popular tracks. Something had to be done right away (again).

Mettoy decided to withdraw the Corgi Rockets car line and concentrate on the more varied Corgi Juniors. The Whizzwheels feature would be moved to the Juniors line as fast as possible so market share could be saved. This posed quite a problem in the short term. The baseplates of most models could easily accept the smaller diameter wire axles, but the Rockets' Whizzwheels were much thicker than the old design. Mettoy quickly came up with an interim thin version of the Whizzwheels wheel that was in effect a simplified nylon wheel made to the old style wheel's dimensions. These thin Whizzwheels were quite wobbly, but the reworked product could be sent to stores quickly. Packaging in the short term was unchanged except for the addition of a small sticker announcing the addition of the Whizzwheels feature. This time period would see many short runs of interim model variations, as the factory decided on color and decoration changes just before or just after the conversion. Baseplates would also be reworked to add the Whizzwheels logo. For some models, this would be the second baseplate change within a year.

It quickly became apparent that the thin Whizzwheels were considered inferior by customers, with Mattel no doubt supporting the perception. Die makers were kept hard at work either revising baseplate dies, or creating completely new ones to accommodate the wider Rockets style of Whizzwheels. Some models would end-up sitting much higher off the ground, giving them quite an awkward appearance. Mettoy chose this route to avoid reworking the bodies of the models with larger wheel openings. In doing so, the models could stay in production with the old baseplate until the new one was ready. Models like the James Bond Aston Martin would take on a comical look. The Ford F350 Camper went from a plastic base to an elevated diecast base, giving it an off-road look long before such things were popular.

Models in the Corgi Juniors line would receive other modifications to make them more attractive to kids. Mettoy would increasingly make use of tinted windows in various colors. Indeed, the tinting color was often changed in production whenever the preferred color material was in short supply. Tinted windows had been in use to some extent in earlier models to hide internal features when no interior was present. Mettoy soon learned that tinted windows could be used to alter the appearance of a vacuum plated interior to a "mod" appearance. Tinted windows also eliminated the need for a separate part for a colored dome lamp on police, fire and towing vehicles.

Mettoy began to recover from the series of crash conversion programs once the 1970s were well underway. Corgi Juniors that just didn't look right with the Whizzwheels conversion were phased-out of the product line. New models designed from the start for Whizzwheels took their place, also changing the focus of the line in the process. Models that had originally been Corgi Rockets were also phased in to the Corgi Juniors line, rapidly expanding the range. The legacy of the period, though, would be the great number of interim variations for collectors to enjoy.

Whizzwheels E3-B with earlier version.

E37-A with Whizzwheels.

E72-A Mercedes-Benz C111 window color variations.

Variations of the E41-A Porsche Carrera 6. *Photo Courtesy of Wolfgang Gehrt / Goodies Old Toys.*

Variations of the NSU RO-80. *Photo Courtesy of Wolfgang Gehrt / Goodies Old Toys.*

E64-A Morgan Plus 8.

Whizzwheels E30-A Ambulance with earlier version.

Variations of the E45-A Mercedes-Benz. *Photo Courtesy of Wolfgang Gehrt / Goodies Old Toys.*

E7-B Duple Vista Coach variations.

E78-A Ole MacDonald's Truck.

Early Whizzwheels Corgi Juniors catalog.

Whizzwheels E13-A Sand Truck with similar Husky 10-A.

E14-B variations.

E1017-A Ford Holmes Wrecker.

Wheel variations on E1001-A. *Photo Courtesy of Wolfgang Gehrt / Goodies Old Toys.*

Salesman's display case from the era. *Photo Courtesy of Wolfgang Gehrt / Goodies Old Toys.*

More James Bond variations. *Photo Courtesy of Wolfgang Gehrt / Goodies Old Toys.*

E28-A Ford F350 Wrecker with earlier versions.

E3009-A Service Station Set. *Photo Courtesy of Wolfgang Gehrt / Goodies Old Toys.*

The Early 1970s: Change and Growth

The market for diecast toys in the 1970s was changing rapidly. Once Mattel's Hot Wheels had made their initial mark, kids began to think about toy cars differently. Fast wheels were no longer an innovation, they were a demanded feature. Fantasy play would grow ever farther from reflections of Mom and Dad's world. Reality was out. Wild cars and speed were in. The sales of the time would show this truth. Ever-wilder designs of fantasy vehicles greatly outsold more accurate models of real cars. Of the real car types, only exotic sports cars or racers left the shelves. Most sedans (saloons) and trucks remained unsold.

Mettoy had to react to this paradigm shift in their customers. Unwilling at first to go the way-out fantasy route, many new models cars were introduced of actual custom show vehicles. Most of these models had real life counterparts, though only as fuel for dreams by kid's fathers. The Corgi Juniors versions of these dream wheels would sell much better than the older products, but still not as well as the competition's complete fantasies. Eventually, even Mettoy would create a few unreal looking models, but by then the market was moving on yet again.

The disaster that was the Corgi Rockets program was to have one positive effect for Mettoy. The Rockets product line was full of the types of custom car designs that were just what was needed in the Juniors line-up. Mettoy quickly set out to create new simplified baseplates for many of the Rockets models. In some cases, the existing baseplate tooling was reworked to eliminate features used to hold the removable plastic chassis. These models appear to have a bulge in the same shape as the chassis cavity in the old Rockets versions. Other models were re-tooled with a completely new baseplate casting since the old one was not a suitable starting point. The conversion program would eventually see most but not all of the former Rockets assimilate into the Corgi Juniors product line. Some planned models out of the Rockets range would never reappear, even though they were shown in catalogs.

After the flurry of new and revised product introductions in 1970 and 1971, the release of entirely new Corgi Juniors slowed to a trickle from 1972 through 1974. The economy worldwide was experiencing a recession and Mettoy sales were down. This would be a period of product line consolidation and refocusing. Some new models were still introduced, and many old ones ended their production during this time. Models like the ERF Simon Snorkel Fire Engine and the Daimler Fleetline Bus would continue for well over two decades. Others like the Futura and ERF Tipper Truck would only have a brief time on the shelves. Most of the reworked Rockets models would also make their last appearance during this time. The Corgi Juniors range was able to establish itself as the number two or number three brand in popularity in most markets by mid-decade. However, competition was fierce and the battle for sales would rage on through the 1970s.

E11-B Austin Healey LeMans.

E21-C B.V.R.T. Vita-Mini.

E26-B and E26-C
ERF Fire Tender.

E33-B and E39-B
Jaguar E-type
2+2 variations.

E31-B Land Rover Wrecker variations.

E48-A ERF Tipper Truck.

E32-B Lotus Europa.

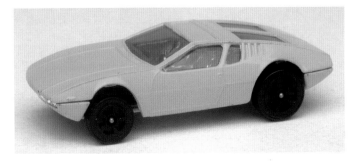

E6-C Mangusta DeTomaso.

E2006-A Mack Esso Tanker.

E2011-A Mack Army Tanker.

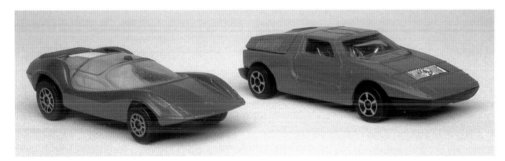

E52-A Adams Probe 16 with
E72-A Mercedes-Benz C111.

E16-B and E79-A Land Rovers.

E47-A Scammell Cement Truck.

E94-A Porsche 917.

E55-A Daimler Fleetline Bus. (First version.)

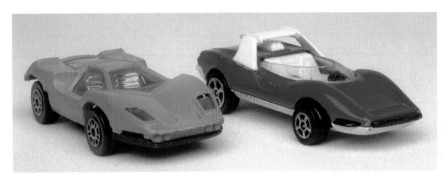

E60-A VW Double Trouble.

E71-A Marcos XP with E73-A Alfa Romeo Pininfarina.

E61-A Mercury Cougar Sheriff with E70-B Fire version.

E56-A Ford Capri Fire Chief.

E60-A color variations. *Photo Courtesy of Wolfgang Gehrt / Goodies Old Toys.*

Terex variations.

E42-B Terex Dumper.

E54-A Ford D-1000 Container Truck.

E67-A Capri Hot Pants Dragster.

E17-C Volkswagen 1300 variations with Japanese box.
Photo Courtesy of Wolfgang Gehrt / Goodies Old Toys.

E67-A Dragster with body opened.

E3021-A Emergency 999 Gift Set

E9-C Police Range Rover.

Playmat.

Two versions of the E42-C Rescue Range Rover.

E18-C Wigwam Camper.

E15-C Mercedes-Benz Bus including scorched version from late E3021-A Gift Set.

E22-C and E53-B Formula 1 Racers including Weetabix version.

E36-B Healer Wheeler, E99-A Jokermobile and Brazilian Fire version.

E28-B Hot Rodder with similar
E24-C Shazam Thunderbolt.

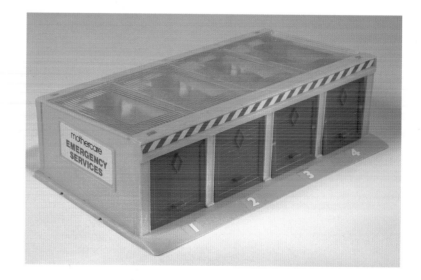

Mothercare version of the E2001-A Garage. *Photo Courtesy of Wolfgang Gehrt / Goodies Old Toys.*

E29-D ERF Simon Snorkel
with later versions.

E86-A Fiat X1/9
with later version.

E81-A Daimler Fleetline London Bus.

E82-A Crowder Can-Am Racer
with later E20-D Penguinmobile.

The late 1970s: Super Heroes and Trademark Licensing

By the mid 1970s, toy companies were rediscovering the potential of cross-marketing and name recognition. Television and movie tie-ins, once Corgi's strong suit in the 1960s, were again popular. Licenses for familiar characters like Batman and James Bond again got hot in the market. This trend was in an area Mettoy was already expert in exploiting, and they quickly moved to add such items to the Corgi "Juniors" line-up. In this section, "Juniors" will be in quotation marks due to Mettoy's decision to drop the word from the packaging during this period. (Strictly a marketing decision.) The line continued to be called "Juniors" within the factory, though, and continued to be referred to as such in correspondence.

One of the strongest product areas to be developed in the 1970s would be character models. Children's cartoon and comic book characters would be the hot properties. Corgi's Batman models, once associated with the live-action television show, would now be linked to the Saturday morning cartoon program. They were quickly joined by all manner of models for Superman, Spiderman, Scooby-Doo, The Flintstones, and others. Mettoy was able to develop new models quickly and inexpensively by simply reworking existing or discontinued products into character models. Models like the Hot Rodder became Shazam's Thunderbolt. The Can-Am Racer became the Penguinmobile. The Healer Wheeler became the Joker's car. The list of recycled castings would be long.

Mettoy didn't just rely on old castings to make their line of character vehicles. Indeed, two models that could have been reused were retooled instead. Two long-time favorites, the Batmobile and the James Bond DB5, would be introduced in completely new versions. This was done for two reasons. First, the older models had seen large production runs which probably left the dies in sad condition. Second, the new models were designed to be more economical to produce, keeping the flavor of the old without the extra expense of older design and fabrication methods. The new models were somewhat inferior to the originals, but they fit well into the product line of the time with comparable features and construction. As with the originals, these new versions would see very high production volumes due to their popularity. A number of other character models were introduced using entirely new castings as their basis. Superman was given a Supermobile space ship. Batman, Spiderman, and The Pink Panther would get racing cycles, and Batman and Spiderman also got helicopters.

Live-action television and movie characters also got a lot of attention in the Corgi "Juniors" line-up. Charlie's Angels would receive the first of many versions of a Chevrolet Van, theirs being the only one that was pink. Kojak would get a gold Buick Regal complete with off-center roof light. James Bond added a swimming Lotus and Space Shuttle to his fleet, while the bad guys got helicopters. The BBC show Blake's 7 got their "Starship Liberator." The American TV show Starsky and Hutch got their trademark Ford Torino, complete with the large white stripe over the roof and sides. A number of gift sets were also produced using the hero's cars or vans together with a specially decorated police car or helicopter. Special delivery vans were also produced.

Cartoon characters were not the only hot properties of the time. Models with real company logos were also popular. The Leyland Terrier Box Truck and Chevrolet Van would be used extensively to display corporate logos. The business for private issue promotional models was expanding, and Mettoy actively marketed their capabilities. Many companies came to Mettoy to have such models made. Unfortunately, such models were never publicly announced by Mettoy, so tracking them can be difficult. Other more public items like breakfast cereal promotions can still be difficult for collectors to find many years later. The variety of promotional items produced was extensive, and is more thoroughly described in a separate section of the book.

The decade would end well for Mettoy, at least as far as the "Juniors" range was concerned. However, storm clouds were on the horizon beginning in the 1980s as the market was about to go through another dramatic change. This time, Mettoy and its traditional competitors would all become the victims.

E26-B ERF Fire Engine with later version.

E48-B Shovel Loader.

E70-B Mercury Cougar Fire Chief car.

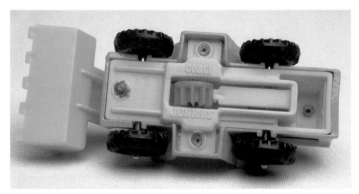

A view of the "Growlers" feature.

E20-C Cement Mixer.

E87-B and E74-B
Leyland Terriers.

E52-B Mercedes-Benz Taxi with similar civilian version.

Various Chevrolet and U.S. Vans.

E46-B Police Helicopter.

E51-B Volvo 245DL Estate.

Later version of E30-D Ford Cement Truck.

E55-B Refuse Truck with later Iveco model.

Uncommon versions of E62-B AMC Pacer.

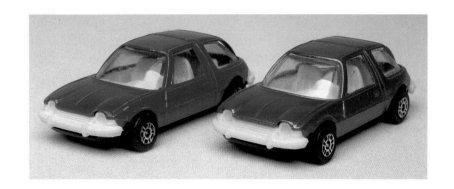

E7-C Quarry Dumper variations.

E10-C Triumph TR7.

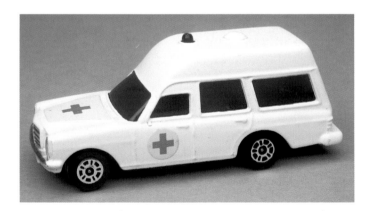

E1-E Mercedes-Benz Ambulance.

E68-A Kojak's Buick Regal.

More Buick Regal variations.

E28-C and E28-D Buicks.

E87-B and E95-A Leyland Terriers.

Many later Police versions of the Regal.

E70-D, E70-C and E45-B Ford Gran Torino.

E49-B Ford Tipper Truck.

E42-C Rescue Team Range Rover with later J59.

E97-B Leyland Terrier Tankers.

E53-A Fire Launch.

E98-B Mercedes-Benz Mobile Shop.

E59-B Mercedes-Benz 240D Polizei car.

E47-B Superman Supervan.

E90-A Fire Ball Van.

E11-C Superman Supermobile.

Color variations of E17-D Metropolis Police car.

E12-E Golden Eagle Jeep

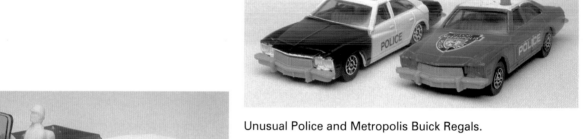

Unusual Police and Metropolis Buick Regals.

E69-A Batmobile with E78-B and E23-C.

One of many Carry Case versions.

E33-D Wonder Woman's car.

E99-A Jokermobiles.

Color Variations of the E50-B Daily Planet Truck.

Jokermobile window color versions.

E16-C Rover 3500 Police car.

E3040 City of Metropolis Set.

E131-A / E136-A Ferrari 308GTS.

Mettoy's Last Years

While the late 1970s were good times for Mettoy, the early 1980s would see hard times return. Market changes were again in the works, as home computers, computer games. and action figures arrived on the scene. Suddenly, the toy-buying world was infatuated with the plug-in computer games. While relatively crude, they were new and novel. Also, action figures became hot among boys as the "doll" stigma was successfully glossed-over by the industry. Suddenly, boys no longer had to imagine themselves as the hero in the toy cars. The action figures themselves became the focus of the play. Diecast toys were reduced to being accessories or props, rather than being the main focus of play. The kid market for diecast toys was being lost.

Mettoy reacted to the changing market by trying to develop their own home computer to play computer games and run rudimentary programs. This was a major departure from their main toy business, and major investments were made to develop the system. A separate division was set up to develop the new product, and a large percent of the company's budget went into its development. The end result was the Dragon computer. This Dragon, however, would end up slaying Mettoy in the end. Other companies were well ahead of Mettoy in the development and marketing of their products, and the Dragon had only limited success.

The main toy business at Mettoy suffered badly during this period due to the heavy diversion of funds to the Dragon. The company turned to changes in cosmetics on existing products to appeal to customers. The new Tampo printing process was used to redecorate models with more complex designs. While a number of new products continued to be introduced, the lean times would be more and more evident. Decorations over time were simplified. On occasion, "Juniors" with plated parts were produced unplated until the vacuum plating machine could be repaired. Toward the end, the lack of plating would be on purpose, with the formerly plated parts molded in gray or white plastic.

In the early 1980s, the American market grew to be a much bigger share of Mettoy's sales, especially in the "Juniors" range. American kids were now too young to remember Corgi's heyday in the 1960s, having been born after the first Hot Wheels were introduced. American kids wanted Hot Wheels-sized cars. Mettoy responded by expanding their offering of "Juniors" vehicles familiar to the American market. The sales growth that was started in the late 1970s with Batman and Spiderman would need to be sustained with other new products. Mettoy would also come to rely more heavily on the new large mass-market chain toy stores, which kept prices low by buying in bulk. Small toy stores would struggle to compete, since the wholesale price of "Juniors" in small quantities would often be more than the final sale price at the large chain stores.

One of the problems with selling to large chain toy stores would become controlling inventory and production. Mettoy's American distributor, Reeves International, needed to manage large stocks of product and have it ready to ship when the large stores requested it. The feast and famine nature of shipments from the warehouse caused logistical nightmares. In addition, the large chains like to dictate that their orders take priority over those of other customers. Reeves and Mettoy responded much as any other supplier would and produced "protection stock" to cover any shortages that occurred. In addition, production of a number of models intended for sale in the USA was subcontracted to a firm in Singapore. This relieved capacity problems at Mettoy's plants, and gave Reeves a supplier more convenient to the west coast of the USA.

A number of new models were introduced in the early 1980s. Most would appear in multiple colors as Mettoy attempted to keep their products looking fresh. Mettoy also tried packaging identically decorated Corgi Toys and Corgi "Juniors" models in "Little and Large" sets. New "Juniors" models often paralleled introductions in the larger Corgi Toys range in order to make these sets possible. The new Corgi Classics range of larger scale models would be echoed in the "Juniors" range with the introduction of a Mercedes-Benz 300SL Gullwing coupe, 1957 T-bird convertible, and 1957 Chevrolet convertible. The latter two would also have tie-ins to American TV shows.

New castings of British vehicles were coordinated to coincide with the introductions of real cars. These include a Rover 3500, Triumph TR7, Austin Mini Metro, Ford Capri 3.0, Ford Escort, and Ford Sierra. These models could be found in special promotional boxes as well as the standard product packaging. An Austin London Taxi finally joined the Daimler Fleetline bus. Older castings would also be redecorated and reappear as new models in rally trim. A number of models would also appear in "Royal Mail" trim in the very last days of Mettoy.

New European cars were also introduced. The French (Chrysler) Matra Rancho was introduced with "Made in England" on the base, the only model with this text. This may reflect that it was produced in the Northampton plant which actually is in England, not Wales as is the Swansea plant. It is also possible that an outside firm made the tooling on contract, since a number of the construction details are different than other models of the period. A Citroen 2CV6 was released to coincide with a James Bond movie. Other

European cars added to the range include a Renault 5 Turbo, Mercedes-Benz 240D and 350SL, and an Opel Corsa / Vauxhall Nova (depending on where it was sold.) Special versions of many models with regional graphics would be produced for many countries. Germany, France, Switzerland, Italy, and Saudi Arabia all received such special models.

A number of American cars were introduced during this period. Some, like the Dodge Magnum, did not last long in the product line. Others, like the Ford Mustang Cobra, Pontiac Firebird, and Chevrolet Corvette would be used extensively in many different paint schemes. Reeves International obtained licenses to produce a series of models representing different Major League Baseball, National Football League, and National Hockey League teams. The hope was that the familiar logos on the cars would increase sales of what were essentially standard line cars. Initial sales were a success, but they soon tapered off as the market became saturated. In addition, the distribution by the large chain toy stores was random at best. Models with home team graphics sold out quickly, while other team's cars sold slowly. Often, a simple redistribution of stock would have remedied the problem, but the large chains were not set up for the added expense, and the leftover stock often would need to be deeply discounted.

More licensed character vehicles appeared during this period. A Star Trek Enterprise and Klingon Battle Cruiser were issued to tie into the release of the movie "Star Trek II – The Wrath of Khan." Bugs Bunny got his own Beach Buggy. Yogi Bear, Scooby-Doo, and Woody Woodpecker got revamped old castings, too. The Flintstones got a number of their cars out of the cartoon series, as well as a gift set. An attempt to market a series of Wild West models would be short lived, with only a handful of models and sets released. The TV show Magnum P.I. got a Ferrari and Buick Regal Police Car. Other American and British TV show licenses were for Simon and Simon, and The Professionals.

Mettoy finally folded under its own weight on October 31, 1983. The ill-advised Dragon Computer project was too much of a drain for the rest of the company to support. The remaining stocks of toys were placed in the hands of receivers for liquidation. Quite a number of bizarre variations of Corgi "Juniors" were issued around this time as remaining inventories of parts were assembled into whatever could be sold. Under normal circumstances, this could have been the end of the Corgi "Juniors" story. Fortunately, a group of investors that included some of Mettoy's former managers convinced financial institutions to fund the start of a new company focused only on diecast toys. Happily, this new company would restart the Corgi product lines only five months after the close of Mettoy.

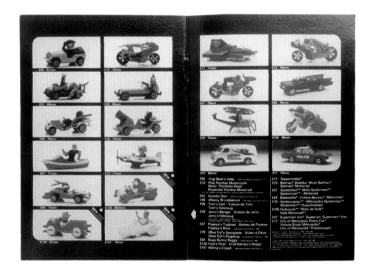

Typical models shown in the 1982 catalog.

E84-A Bugs Bunny Buggy.

E91-B Vantastic Van with later version.

E102-A Renault Turbo.

E93-B Dodge Magnum.

E104-A Ford Mustang Cobra
with Baseball versions.

E96-B Vega$ Thunderbird.

E105-A Ford Escort with
E127-A ADAC version.

E107-A Austin Mini Metro with later version.

E3111-A Wild West Railroad Set.

E125-A Ford Transit Dropside Pick-up.

E114-A Wild West Stage Coach.

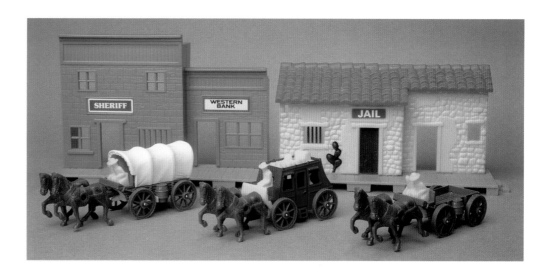

E3112-A Wild West Frontier Set.

E116-A and E117-A España '82 models.

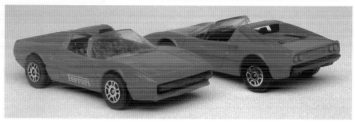

E131-A / E136-A Ferrari 308GTS.

E82-B Yogi Bear's Jeep.

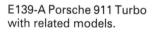

E137-A VW Polo Turbo with later versions.

E139-A Porsche 911 Turbo
with related models.

E124-A Mercedes-Benz 350SL.

Two Baseball Firebirds.

E152-A and E156-A 1957 Chevrolet.

E180-A Pontiac Firebird variations and later models.

All of the Baseball Firebird series.

Rare mis-matched spoiler and interior.

Baseball Firebird and Football Corvette.

E144-A British Gas Van.

E175-A Pipe Truck.

Poster from the cardback offer.

Vauxhall Nova / Opel Corsa variations.

E209-A, E120-A and E80-C.

E60-B James Bond Lotus Esprit
with later street version.

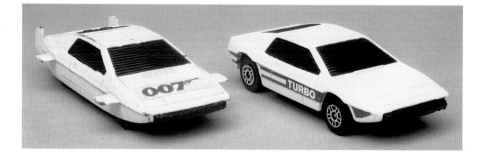

Color variations of E200-A.
Photo Courtesy of Wolfgang Gehrt / Goodies Old Toys.

E182-A Jeep Renegade 4x4.

E185-A Baja Off Road Van.

E200-A Hungry Hatchback Rover 3500.

Very late E31-B Land Rover Wrecker.

E184-A Range Rover.

Color variations of E3019-B set. *Photo Courtesy of Wolfgang Gehrt / Goodies Old Toys.*

Special 3 bus set with side label sheet. *Photo Courtesy of Wolfgang Gehrt / Goodies Old Toys.*

Porsche from the time of Mettoy's failure.

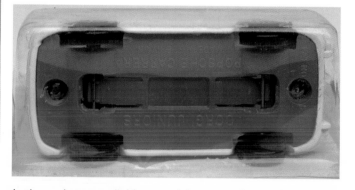

Two vehicle sets from around 1983.

In the end, any available material was used.

Two of the busses with labels applied.

Corgi Toys Ltd.

On March 29, 1984, a new company was formed from the Corgi portion of the old Mettoy PLC company. Corgi Toys Ltd. was founded by a group of former Mettoy managers and workers to resurrect the Corgi portion of the business. The initial days of the company were shaky, and the first products made were continuations of the old product line. However, the new company soon found its market and began to expand.

The focus of the larger scale Corgi products was shifted to the new adult collector market, a segment that had not existed earlier. The "Juniors" products (now the J-Series) would stay focused as the product line aimed at the younger customers. All of the manufacturers of diecast cars, including Mattel, had suffered from the market shift in the early 1980s. By the mid-1980s, the market for smaller scale models was being split into two competing camps. One camp, led by Mattel's Hot Wheels Vehicles, wanted their models to be wildly outlandish, the crazier, the better. The other camp wanted their models with high fidelity to prototype cars and trucks. Various European manufacturers were raising the bar for realism in these models, and that was the market that Corgi was targeting with its new J-Series product offerings.

One of the problems to be overcome by the new company was the loss of foreign markets and distributors when Mettoy collapsed. In many countries, most notably the United States, the flow of Corgi models was interrupted while new distribution arrangements were made. Large chain stores had to be courted to bring them back to Corgi. Some never returned, sighting unsold stocks of the final Mettoy products. Markets were rebuilt slowly. In many ways the distribution of Corgi products would be changed, as mass-market outlets diminished and specialty toy and hobby stores took their place.

Realism about the costs of developing new products was a constant concern for the new company. Fortunately, the diecast market of the time was developing a taste for collecting variations on themes. "Graphics Engineering" was used as a low cost way of releasing a wide variety of products to the market using a minimum number of castings. While some collectors scoffed at the explosion of different decorations, others happily paid for each new version. The adult collector market also crossed over into the smaller range, giving the J-series more than one target customer group.

Once the new company had its feet on the ground, new J-Series castings began to emerge. These new models are notable in that the scale again crept larger to match the offerings of European competitors. New models introduced during this period include a Volvo 760GLE, BMW 325i, Land Rover 110, and various trucks based on an Iveco cab and chassis. The Iveco truck would appear as a box truck, tanker, beverage truck, and refuse truck in many different graphics. Other vehicles would be reworked from older models. The Lotus Esprit lost its fins and became a road car, even though it still retained the slatted James Bond windows. (All production of licensed models stopped at the time of Mettoy's failure.) The Ford Capri 3.0 and BMW 325I would also grow Can-Am style air dams as racing versions. The Buick Regal would receive a jacked-up rear suspension as a hot rod, sadly spoiling the look of the police version. The Aston-Martin DB5 would appear in civilian clothing in many colors minus its ejector seat.

Many of the old models from the Mettoy days would continue for a time in the new J-Series. This helped fill the range with models, as well as provide continuity with the past. In some cases, large leftover stocks of models were in the company's warehouses. Some were partially completed models lacking only the tampo graphics for their original use. Many of these models would find their way to market to fill spaces in large sets. Others appeared on special low cost packaging in Europe. By the end of the 1980s, most of the older models would be out of production, though some would occasionally be produced in short batches to fill a special need if the dies were still in good condition. Corgi Toys Ltd. appears to have subscribed to the policy of bringing any model out of retirement if a sale could be made. The customer needed to purchase a production run of at least a set minimum quantity, which seems to have varied with the fortunes of the company at the time.

The 1980s saw a continuation of the brisk usage of Corgi models in both large and small scales as promotional products. Many companies became willing buyers of short runs of specially decorated models. Others simply had Corgi Toys Ltd. add a message to a standard model. This only served to increase the variety of the models offered, and thereby collector interest. Note that at about this time Corgi Toys, including the J-Series, were becoming something to be collected rather than played with by kids. The collector mindset was making its way from the adult collectors down through the younger generation. This was also true in the larger toy market. Consider the large collections of action figures, video games, etc. Collecting was becoming the end in itself, and manufacturers were quick to jump on the gravy train. Corgi Toys Ltd. would see strong growth in the 1980s. The company itself would soon become quite attractive to an old rival, Mattel Inc.

J3700C Coca-Cola Team Car and Transporter Set.

Royal Mail models from the period in receivership.

J10 Aston Martin DB6.

J1365 London Bus and Taxi Set.

J3158 London Scene Set.

J34 Rover 3500.

J3200H Hershey's Milk Chocolate Turbo Racing Team Set.

J18-A Jaguar XJS.

J46 Pontiac Firebird.

J200 Matra Rancho and Horsebox Set.

J32 Ferrari 308GTS.

J15-C Ford Transit Pick-up with cover.

Variations of J15-A. *Photo Courtesy of Wolfgang Gehrt / Goodies Old Toys.*

J15-A Lotus Esprit.

J36-A / J123-02 Ford Mustang.

J24 Ford Transit Wrecker with later versions.

J123-01 Ford Mustang.

J61/01 Team Racing Van with similar 90260 version.

J61 U.S. Custom Van.

J60 Buick Regal on red French card.

J81 Buick Regal N.Y.P.D. car.

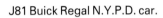

J21 Fiat X1/9.

J45/02 Chevrolet Corvette.

J122/01 Mercedes-Benz 300SL.

J62 Mercedes-Benz Mobile Shop.

J22/01 BMW 325i Rally car.

J29 and J29/01
Mercedes-Benz 500SL.

J5/02 Mercedes-Benz SAS Bus.

J30/01 BMW M3.

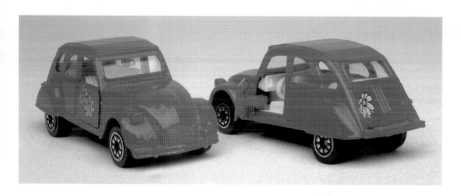

J27 Citroen 2CV.

J84 Volvo 760 Saloon.

J94 Mercedes-Benz 300TD Wagon.

J93 Jaguar XJ40 Saloon.

J89 Mercedes-Benz 2.3/16 Rally Saloon.

J41-B Jaguar XJ40 Police.

Red Transit Vans.

K5055 Alarm Blaster model. (Rebadged Maisto model.)

J44-B Renault Trafic Window Van.

Base showing Corgi logo in place of Maisto.

J97 Land Rover ONE TEN Fire Salvage.

Comparison of Land Rover castings.

J12-B BP Tanker with later Shell version.

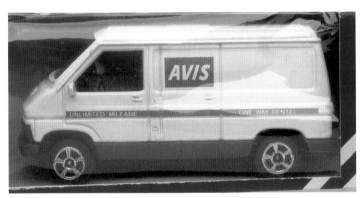

J25-B Renault Trafic Van.

J12-B Iveco Tanker with later versions.

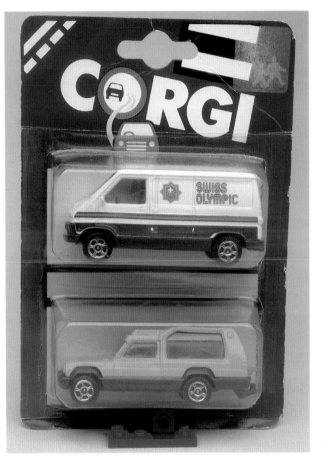

Promotional 2-pack with Renault Trafic and Matra Rancho.

J9/02 Iveco Box Truck.

J52 Iveco Refuse Truck.

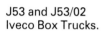
J53 and J53/02
Iveco Box Trucks.

J13/01 Iveco Beverage Truck.

J53 Iveco Fyffes Box Truck.

Mattel's Corgi Years

On December 18, 1989, Mattel Inc. would do something that would have been unthinkable in earlier times. They bought out Corgi Toys Ltd. Overnight, the large California based company went from being a rival to being the parent of the Corgi brand name. Mattel saw a number of reasons that the purchase of Corgi Toys Ltd. would be attractive. Corgi had a well-established distribution network in Europe, as well as farther-off countries like Australia, which Mattel desperately needed. The Corgi product identity was also firmly established in these markets, which was something Mattel could leverage. Mattel also saw opportunities to lower costs by moving production of Corgi products to the Far East. This was something the native Corgi Toys Ltd. management found difficult to do, since many of the employees of the company had been there since the Mettoy days.

The combination of the companies went smoothly for the most part. Corgi Toys Ltd. became a wholly owned subsidiary of Mattel Inc. This arrangement would serve both companies well. Corgi was now able to focus development efforts on the adult collectable market, utilizing Mattel's deeper pockets and existing manufacturing capability in the Far East. In return, Mattel was able to use Corgi's distribution network to increase its market share in Europe and Australia. Mattel moved Corgi's headquarters out of Swansea and closed down production there. The Corgi office was combined with Mattel's European headquarters in Leicester, although both still operated separately. This arrangement would work well for everything *except* the "Juniors" product line.

Mattel was now saddled with two competing ranges. Their mainstay Hot Wheels product line and the "Juniors" models were in uneasy competition with each other. In actuality, they did not compete for the same customers. Hot Wheels vehicles were less concerned with accuracy and more concerned with the "cool" factor. They were mostly designed around the tastes of young American buyers. "Juniors" were designed to more accurately reflect real vehicles and were made to a slightly larger scale. They were also centered on British and European vehicles, especially the later models. Unfortunately, Mattel was not comfortable with the distinction. One of the first items on their agenda was stopping the distribution of the "Juniors" range in the USA, in their mind protecting Hot Wheels vehicles' home market.

Under Mattel, only a few new models were introduced to the "Juniors" range. These models may have already been under development at the time Mattel purchased the company. This included a BMW 850csi, a Mercedes 500SL convertible, a Jaguar XJ9R Racer, Ferrari Testarossa, and a Ferrari 348TB coupe. All but the Jaguar would have duplicated existing Hot Wheels vehicles. A poor fidelity F1 Racer was also introduced as a Corgi product that did not live up to the fidelity of the other models. This may have been a cast-off from another Mattel project. An interesting, though ominous, situation occurred during Mattel's ownership of Corgi. In some circumstances, the lines between the Hot Wheels and Corgi "Juniors" ranges were blurred. The Hot Wheels Thunderstreak racer was redecorated and packaged in a Corgi box for a European promotion by Fuji Film. Hot Wheels Color Changers sets were sold in Europe as Corgi products with only the logo on the card changed. The cars in the package and the other card graphics were unchanged from their Hot Wheels roots.

In late 1993 or early 1994, the former Corgi "Juniors," "Turbos," and "Haulers" ranges were combined into a new Corgi Auto-City range. The range used all existing castings with no new offerings. The models were made in a fixed set of decorations that changed very little through the production run. These models were produced and distributed in the style of their Hot Wheels counterparts in large pre-configured assortments. Stores could not order individual models from the assortments. This kept Mattel's costs down by reducing the production variability to large lots instead of specific model runs. Packaging would also be distinct from the remainder of the Corgi product line. While the mainstream Corgi Classics and Superhaulers ranges reverted to the old Corgi dog logo in 1992, the Auto-City ranges continued with the Corgi skidding car logo for the remainder of Mattel's ownership. Foreshadowing the future, a number of sets were released in the range using Corgi castings but decorated with Hot Wheels Racing graphics and logos. Corgi Toys Ltd. involvement in the Auto-City range would be much less than before, with some control transferred to Mattel in California.

Mattel's ownership of Corgi came to an end in 1995. The two companies went their separate ways, taking their product lines with them. Unfortunately for collectors, the Auto-City (former "Juniors," "Turbos," and "Haulers") range would wind up on the wrong side of the fence.

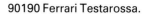

90190 Ferrari Testarossa.

93160 Emergency Super Set.

90361 Fuji Van and 90215 Fuji F1 Racer.

90076 BMW M3.

90317 Fuji Thunderstreak (Hot Wheels casting.)

90570a Mercedes-Benz 500SL with later versions.

90440 Porsche 935 and
94540b Porsche Targa.

93179 Mercedes-Benz 2.3 Taxi.

90571b Mercedes-Benz 500SL.

94220 Ferrari 348TB.

93234 Ford Transit Van - BP.

90420 Buick Police and 90035 Snorkel.

93177

90320 Iveco Refuse Recycling truck.

90505 Rescue Helicopter with earlier version.

Rebadged Hot Wheels models for the UK market.

Wrecker and Sierra from set 93425.

90580 Jaguar XJR9 Racer.

Various Ford Transit vans.

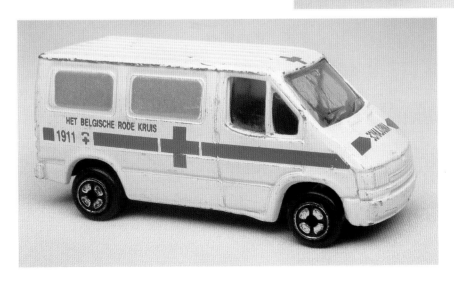

90018 Ford Transit Belgisch Rode Kruis.

Hot Wheels Postscript

The separation of the Corgi business from Mattel Inc. left the new Corgi Classics Ltd. without a small product line except for the Cameos series, which were mostly used for low-cost promotional releases. The tooling and stock for the former "Juniors" vehicles, "Turbos" cars, and "Haulers" trucks, all went to Mattel as part of the Auto-City range. The break between the two companies was clean, and no further interaction between their product lines would occur.

Mattel took possession of a large number of products that now carried an obsolete brand name in the tooling. In addition, there were numerous models that duplicated existing offerings in their core Hot Wheels product line. Some rationalization was needed. The Auto-City marketing name had been transferred to Mattel as part of the split. Mattel decided to retain the name as a separate part of the Hot Wheels line. Distribution would still be restricted to Europe. Packaging would remain unchanged in design, but with a revised Hot Wheels Auto-City graphic.

For a time, the Auto-City vehicles could be found with Corgi baseplates in Hot Wheels Auto-City packaging. This was slowly changed as the dies for each model were altered. The Corgi logo was replaced with the Hot Wheels flaming wheel logo. Production of the Auto-City range would end at the end of 1995. Other than the base text, no changes were made to the models or graphics during the brief two-year production life of the range.

In late 1995, Mattel began releasing former Corgi vehicles in sets. These models were not available individually, and were in unique body and interior colors. They also were equipped with Corgi style wheels. These sets continued to be introduced throughout 1996. Late in 1996, Mattel began introducing former Corgi models in the main Hot Wheels line-up. These models were fitted with Hot Wheels-style wheels and usually carried a printed Hot Wheels logo on the body or windows. Graphics were to a higher level than previously seen on the models as Corgi products, owing to the advancement in production techniques. The models were generally available in both North America and Europe, although there were packaging differences. Color or trim variations can also be found on a few models sent to the two markets. Former Corgi models also started appearing in special sets meant for adult collectors. These sets are usually intended to be premium models, and the level of decoration on them is high.

In 1998 everything changed again. Mattel purchased Tyco Toys Inc., mostly to gain access to their line of radio-controlled cars. In doing so, they also acquired the Matchbox line of diecast models. Tyco had previously purchased Universal Matchbox in 1992 and had promoted Matchbox heavily. Mattel now owned the former numbers one, two and three diecast product lines. Many vehicle designs were duplicated in all three product lines. Mattel needed to rationalize the product offerings quickly to avoid losing market share. One immediate result of the Tyco purchase was the removal of almost all former Corgi castings from production. Only one former Corgi model has remained in the line to-date. For some reason, Mattel continues to produce the old Porsche Carrera coupe. The casting dates back to the mid-1970s and is one of the least accurate of the former Corgi castings.

The future of the former Corgi dies owned by Mattel is presently in doubt. Whether Mattel plans to keep them, sell them, or dispose of them is unknown at this point. Only time will tell if they will ever be used to produce new models, or if collectors have seen the last of the Corgi "Juniors" line.

HWAC 93235
Ford Tipper and
90215 F1 Racer.

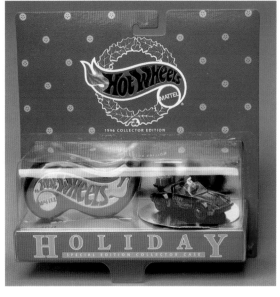

HW 16247-0910 Holiday Hot Wheels Targa.

HWAC 93147 and 93417 Sets.

HWAC 92401 Construction Set.

Taxi and Bus from F.A.O. Schwarz Set.

Unreleased Hot Wheels promotional BMW 850i.

Hot Wheels versions of the Jeep 4x4.

HW 16156 Surf Patrol Action Pack.

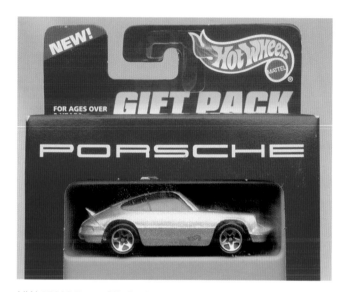

HW 15066 5-car Gift Pack with Porsche Carrera.

HW 95547 Mercedes 500SL on short European card.

HW 15113 Skip Loader Action Squad Set.

HW 95538 T-bird and HW 95540 Mustang Cobra.

HW 95522 Corvette and HW 16305 BMW 850i.

HW 95514 Ford Wrecker and HW 95528 Land Rover.

HW 15788 and HW 55015 Porsche Carrera.

Kroger and Rite-Aid 2-packs.

Corgi Classics Ltd.

After the split with Mattel in August of 1995, the new Corgi Classics Ltd. was formed to continue the Corgi-related business. The new company focused on the adult collector market initially, with a sideline in the promotional model market. All of the former Corgi Juniors, Turbos, and Haulers were gone. However, the new company did retain the Cameos and Superhaulers products. Mattel never found either of these lines useful to them, even though the Cameos were only slightly larger than a Hot Wheels model.

Fans of Corgi Juniors would not see much to encourage them for a number of years, except for an occasional article in the *Corgi Collector* Club magazine. Corgi Classics Ltd. would undertake a number of acquisitions in this period, as well as being acquired yet again by a larger company. Each time, it would change the mix of the product line. In 1996, the company would take over the assets of the failing Bassett Lowke Ltd. that had halted production. From this, Corgi gained an increased ability to include cast figures with their models. Soon afterward, Corgi would also acquire the assets of the failed Lledo PLC. This purchase happened in two phases, but eventually resulted in Lledo and Vanguards becoming part of the Corgi Classics Ltd. product line. This resulted in a general renumbering of all product lines to avoid conflicts.

During this same period, Corgi Classics Ltd. was itself acquired by Zindart Ltd. and became a subsidiary. Zindart is a contract manufacturer for many other companies. The combination resulted in the ability for Corgi and Johnny Lightning (produced by Playing Mantis, a Zindart customer) to share licensing agreements for products. Often, Corgi would produce a 1:43 scale version of a product with Johnny Lightning echoing it in 1:64 scale at the same time. The two companies also shared a line of 1:64 scale James Bond models for a time, with the baseplate text and packaging changed depending on the country of sale.

The long draught for fans of the old Corgi Juniors was broken in the late 1990s by the makers of Weetabix breakfast cereal. Weetabix came to Corgi with a request for a new run of the old Corgi Juniors Leyland Terrier Box Truck. The original version of this truck had been a very popular promotional item for Weetabix in the 1970s, and the promised new order more than justified creating a new set of dies. Corgi wisely created a new model that, while similar to the old, possesses a number of design improvements. The Weetabix promotion has been wildly success-ful, and a second customer, Eddie Stobart Ltd., also signed on with their own version of the model. While no additional versions have been made as of this writing, the casting is still available if needed.

A second Juniors-like model has also been produced. The fabulous old Chitty-Chitty-Bang-Bang from the late 1960s and early 1970s has been reproduced to coincide with a new stage play in London by the same name. Initially only available at the theater as a promotional model, it was later generally released. Once again, the model is based on the original design but with many improvements. It is sold in a clear plastic package to make the model look like it is flying.

Two new models that could be referred to as "son-of-Juniors" models have also been created by the company. In order to fill requests by London tourist business customers, Corgi created a 1:64 version of their larger New London TX1 Taxi. This model fills the slot of the old Juniors London Taxi in many gift sets. It is approximately the same size as the old model, but with the improved accuracy of modern manufacturing techniques. It will likely be used for promotional model customers and tourist sets for many years to come.

The second new model in the Corgi line is a totally new Ford Transit van casting in 1:64 scale. This model was created to be used in Ford introductory presentations for their new redesigned Transit vehicles. The new model is based on a larger vehicle weight prototype than was the old Juniors model, and is larger in length and height. It is more correct than the old model in proportions, however, with greater detailing. After the initial promotional uses for Ford, this van was released in the standard product line in many different paint schemes. It is marketed as a companion vehicle for Corgi's Superhaulers range. There also have been additional promotional uses of the model, and it continues to be available to customers as part of the standard product line.

To date, Corgi Classics Ltd. and Zindart have not released any additional Corgi Juniors sized models. This may be in part due to the ongoing contract Zindart holds with Playing Mantis Inc. to produce their Johnny Lightning vehicles. However, this situation could easily change after this book is published. Corgi has recently revived the Husky name for a small series of 1:43 scale model vehicles. By doing so, they have protected the name as a Corgi Classics trademark for the foreseeable future. With luck, we may yet see a new line of Husky Models or Corgi Juniors come to market for young and old alike to collect.

66101 TXI London Taxi and 56501 Weetabix Leyland Terrier.

TY87801 Chitty-Chitty-Bang-Bang.

56502 Eddie Stobart Ltd. Leyland Terrier.

66201 Eddie Stobart Ltd. Ford Transit Van.

66202 TNT Ford Transit Van.

66204 RAC Ford Transit Van.

66203 Royal Mail Ford Transit Van.

TY81703 AA Ford Transit Van.

Juniors from Brazil and Hungary

Corgi Toys and Corgi Juniors were already well established in the Brazilian market by the early 1980s, having been marketed in South America since the 1960s. About that time, the Brazilian government decided to impose a high tariff on manufactured goods imported into the country, including toys. The Brazilian importer of Corgi Toys, A. Kikoler, decided that in order to keep Corgi Toys and Corgi Juniors affordable in Brazil, he would need to set up a manufacturing plant there. It is unclear whether this occurred just before or just after the failure of Mettoy in 1983.

Kikoler and the management at Corgi formulated a plan to supply molds and dies that could be spared from the Mettoy production. They were shipped to Brazil where a production facility was obtained. The text on the baseplate dies was modified so that the new country of origin would be indicated. The Kiko product name was also added when possible. Designers in Brazil created new parts unique to that market to allow additional models to be added to the range. Kiko models also were equipped with their own unique wheel design. This was necessary since Corgi in the UK could not spare the heavily used molds for the wheels. The Brazilian-made parts were of inferior quality to the standard Corgi components and were not used on models other than the Brazilian products.

The range of Kiko Corgi Juniors was a good cross-section of the models available to the rest of the world. The range included models from the mid 1970s Corgi Juniors range, with some newer models included whenever Corgi had a spare set of dies available. Cars include the Ford Escort Mk. 1 sedan, Ford GT70, VW Polo, and Rover 3500. Trucks included the Mercedes-Benz Snack Truck, Ford Tipper and Cement Truck, and Range Rover Rescue Truck. A number of racers were also included in the line. Models from the earliest production in Brazil are decorated with paper labels. Later models would receive Tampo printed graphics. There were also a few examples of Kiko Corgi Juniors being used for promotional purposes.

At some point, all of the dies and molds were returned to Corgi Toys Ltd. The baseplate dies were changed back to the original text on the models still produced. However, the dies for models that were no longer in production in the UK were left in the state in which they were returned from Brazil. Unused dies and molds now in the possession of either Corgi Classics Ltd. or Mattel Inc. may still have these Kiko modifications. Any dies or molds that may eventually reenter production surely will be modified to remove them.

Distribution of the Kiko Corgi models was entirely within South America, and few collectors knew of their existence. With the advent of the Internet, information is now more generally available about the product line. Kiko models also occasionally find new homes through web auctions and international dealers.

There is an additional case of Corgi products being produced in another country. After the fall of the Iron Curtain across Europe, some older Corgi Juniors dies were sent to Metalbox GMK in Hungary. The models in this range were produced in some unique finishes, and the packaging carries both the Metalbox and Corgi logos. The circumstances leading up to their production and the range of models produced is not presently known, and will be the subject of further research.

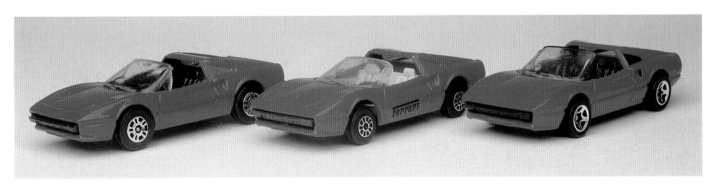

Juniors, Kiko, and Hot Wheels Ferrari 308 GTS from the same dies.

C16 Formula 1 Racer variations.

C32, C54, C59 and C72.

Example of a Kiko baseplate.

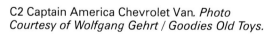

C63 and C69 Rover 3500 versions.

Examples of Kiko boxes.

C2 Captain America Chevrolet Van. *Photo Courtesy of Wolfgang Gehrt / Goodies Old Toys.*

C10, C13 and C34 vans.

Truck bodies.

C12, C37 and C8.

SACI Mercedes-Benz and Healer Wheeler.

Various Ford trucks.

Red Kiko Formula 5000 with yellow SACI copy.

Variations on the Mobil Crane.

Section 2
Background Topics

Numbering Systems

When Mettoy introduced Husky Models, they chose to number the models sequentially starting with "1." There was no publicly used series designation for the Husky series at the time. In this book, I will not use a prefix to designate Husky branded vehicles to distinguish them from other lines. Mettoy also had a system for a brief time that gave models different numbers depending upon the country in which the models were to be sold. Standard Husky Models vehicles can also be found with model numbers 50 higher than normal. Husky Extras, in a similar manner, could be found numbered in the 1000's, 1200's or 1400's. Mettoy's intention was to package the models pre-marked with the price for the local market, but the system quickly became unworkable. As new models entered the line, they would assume the model number of the models they replaced. This caused collectors to add a letter suffix to the model number to designate which model is being identified.

Corgi Rockets cars had their own unique 900 and up number series designated by the factory starting with the prefix "D" in some literature. I chose not to use that prefix since it can easily be confused with Corgi Classics numbering from the early 1980s. There was another series by Mettoy that carried an "R" prefix, but it is not easily confused with the Rockets line. Corgi Rockets were not produced long enough for one model to replace another, so an "A" suffix is only used to keep the numbering consistent with other Mettoy products.

Corgi Juniors inherited the Husky Models numbering system when the name change took place. Mettoy decided to standardize the numbering worldwide, so the extra market-oriented numbers disappeared. In fact, Corgi Juniors are considered an uninterrupted continuation of the Husky Models line, and appear so in the listings. Mettoy did, however, add an "E" prefix to the model number to differentiate the Juniors from the concurrent Rockets product line. The "E" prefix did not always appear in literature and on packaging, but it was in universal usage at the factory up until 1983. Again, the listings continue with the letter suffix system to designate differ-

ent models with the same number. The letter suffix was not used by the factory. Also note that the "Juniors" part of the name was dropped in the marketing and packaging of the line in the late 1970s, even though the line was still referred to as "Juniors" at the factory long afterward.

In 1983, just before the closure of Mettoy, Corgi "Juniors" was rearranged into a new numbering system starting with a "J" prefix. This was done due to the loss of control of the "E" series and the extreme number of foreign market special models being produced. The new "J" series would again start at "1," but did not progress very far when the factory closed. These few models are therefore lumped into the later listings for Corgi Toys Ltd. During the time between October 1983 and April 1984, Mettoy's receivers released many odd unnumbered models to clear existing parts inventories. While some multi-packs have no known number associated with them, the individual models are listed with the known models most closely associated with them. The listings in the back of the book will designate when models are from this transitional period.

Many collectors have noticed a five-digit number inside the packaging of many Mettoy Corgi Juniors and almost all later Corgi Toys Ltd. models. This number is a production number used internally at the factory and never described publicly. That is why it only appears in hidden locations. While there is some correlation between the publicized model number and this production number, they are not tracked in the listings. It is likely these numbers changed with packaging variations as well as model changes. Recording these numbers would often require opening a mint-on-card model to make it visible, which would destroy some of the value of such models.

At its start-up in April 1984, Corgi Toys Ltd. continued with the Mettoy era numbering systems and packaging designs of its predecessor. They did, however, make the "J" series letter prefix an official part of the model number. As the company grew and the product line stabilized, it soon became apparent that the numbering system was still flawed. It did not allow for multiple paint schemes on the same casting without again getting out of control. Around 1987, Corgi devised a suffix numbering system starting with

"/01" which gave them ninety-nine new sub-designations for the same model number. Castings being sold under multiple model numbers (due to their decorations) could then be consolidated under one number. This greatly simplified tracking, made necessary by the prolific use of Corgi and "Juniors" models for promotional purposes. This change resulted in the renumbering of some otherwise identical models over the short term. The listings for this period show each model listed under every number used when it was produced, with cross-referencing notes when possible.

Mattel purchased Corgi Toys Ltd. as a wholly owned subsidiary in late 1989. By 1990, the numbering system was again changed to be compatible with the Hot Wheels numbering system. Corgi products were assigned a five digit number starting with 9, (i.e.: 9xxxx) with similar models usually numbered together. Unfortunately, Mattel only considered their internal needs with this scheme, and many models released within a series were produced with only one model number for the complete series. Mattel had decided that inexpensive products could only be ordered by merchants in large groupings. The listings for Mattel era products at times contain a one or two letter suffix attached to the model number to designate different models. Corgi did not use this suffix system during this period. The "Juniors" name was also eliminated during this time from both formal and informal usage. Corgi briefly released models using the "Freeway" name, but that soon was replaced by the "Auto-City" name for the series. The "9xxxx" numbering series continued to be used by Mattel for the former "Juniors" models after the Corgi Classics Ltd. management buyout in August, 1995. Models produced after the split are considered Hot Wheels vehicles, and are in a separate section of the listings.

Since 1995, Corgi Classics Ltd. has only dabbled in the "Juniors" scale of models. These models appear in a revised 5-digit numbering system used by Corgi Classics. In this system, the first three numbers designate the casting number and the last two numbers the variation. Since the time that Mattel took all of the original "Auto-City" tooling, only two models have been retooled in the "Juniors" size. So far, a Leyland Terrier Box Truck and Chitty-Chitty-Bang-Bang have been produced. New tooling from a New London Taxi now takes the place of the original casting. A new Ford Transit Van is also being made, but it represents a larger prototype vehicle than the original "Juniors" Transit and is more accurate than older models.

In 2001, a two-letter prefix was added as a designation for the series of any given model. This was made necessary by Corgi Classics Ltd.'s purchase of the Lledo product line when Lledo PLC collapsed. Most numbers were also assigned a new casting number series rather than continuing the old one. At the time of the publication of this book, Corgi Classics Ltd. had no other plans to reenter the small diecast market. They have, however, issued larger scale models using the Husky brand name partly to renew the copyright of that brand for possible future use. In addition, Corgi Classics and the smaller Johnny Lightning from Playing Mantis of the USA frequently share licensing agreements on various movie and television trademarked properties. This is beneficial to both companies, since Corgi's parent company, Zindart, is the subcontract manufacturer of many Johnny Lightning products.

Husky Models number on a red card.

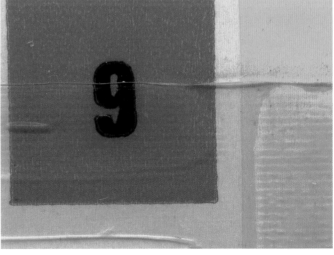

Husky number on a yellow card.

"JB" model number used on American cards.

Corgi Juniors model number on an early card.

Early Corgi Toys Ltd. "J" model number.

Late Mettoy "E" model number.

Corgi Rockets number on a Tune-Up Key.

Added version number in late "J" series.

Brazilian Kiko Corgi Juniors number series.

Initial 5-digit Corgi Classics Ltd. number series.

66202
TNT Transit Van

90020

FORD TRANSIT VAN

"9xxxx" number used during Mattel ownership.

TY81703
AA Transit Van

Modified Corgi Classics Ltd. "TY" number series

Wheel Types

When Husky Models first were introduced in 1964, Mettoy looked to the then-current practices of their largest competitor, Lesney, to create a similar standard wheel design. Since Husky Models were so small at the start, a simple one-piece plastic wheel design was developed that was identical on both faces. With a two-sided design, Mettoy would avoid production slowdowns caused when one-sided wheels are improperly assembled backward. The new wheels would be made in a number of standard sizes from which product designers could select when developing a new model. At the beginning, these wheels would be made in a medium gray color similar to Lesney's "Matchbox Series" models but darker. Over time, these wheels would be made progressively darker until they became fully black near the end of the decade.

Not long into Husky Models' production, new model designs started specifying a more premium wheel. A new wheel design was created using a diecast wheel with a hard black plastic tire. The new diecast wheel would also be two-sided in design for assembly ease. Two different standard patterns were developed. A version with radial fins that resembled wire wheels was created for sports cars and the premium Husky Extras line. A second version with five perimeter slots would be used on commercial vehicles and some cars where wire wheels would not have looked appropriate. A thicker plastic tire was also made available for use on models like the Willys Jeep. Both of these wheel designs would continue to be used into the first years of Corgi Juniors production.

The shortcomings of the original one-piece wheel soon became apparent when they were placed beside the diecast wheels. The diecast wheels in production were not small enough to replace the smallest of the one-piece wheels. To improve on the appearance of the small wheeled models in the product line, Mettoy developed a replacement black plastic wheel that used a vacuum plated insert to represent a hub cap. This greatly improved the wheel's appearance, but caused production problems due to its one-sided design. It would be used in some models up to the time of the Whizzwheels crash program. In other models, it would be replaced briefly with a third type of diecast wheel with a two-sided dished profile. This rather rare wheel was only used on some pre-Whizzwheels Corgi Juniors models of 1970 and 1971. Surprisingly, it can also be found under much later character vehicles of the early 1980s that, in theory, would not have wheels otherwise.

Mettoy's Corgi Rockets would be introduced with a totally new low friction wheel designed for a small diameter wire axle. These wheels would be made from low friction nylon material rather than the hard plastic of earlier Husky Models vehicles. These wheels would be named Whizzwheels to promote their fast rolling capability. The initial design was made with a deeply dished five-spoke design that was more realistic looking than Mattel's red line wheels. Once these wheels were introduced, however, Mettoy quickly learned that boys were more attracted to Mattel's brightly decorated wheels – realistic design was not a selling point. The deeply dished design on Corgi Rockets also meant that the wheels did not lend themselves to decoration in an automated process.

Within the first year of Rockets production, Mettoy designed replacement wheels, also called Whizzwheels, that would be phased into production as the different sizes became available. The new design possessed a flat protruding pattern that could easily be decorated in a foiling machine. This process fuses a vacuum plated foil material onto the surface of the wheel using a hot plate. The result is a shiny metallic surface in the shape of the protruding pattern. The resulting wheel gives the impression of metal spokes in its appearance. The first of the foiled Whizzwheels were made with a simple five spoke (5-spoke) and ring design. This design would be used on the last Corgi Rockets, as well as some later Corgi Juniors equipped with Whizzwheels.

Meanwhile, back at Mettoy, a crash program was again underway due to the Mattel patent infringement lawsuit blocking other manufacturers from making track sets. The market for regular-wheeled models was collapsing quickly, and Mettoy scrambled to fit faster wheels to the Corgi Juniors line. As a stopgap measure, a narrow version of the Whizzwheels design was developed as a direct replacement for the diecast and plated insert wheels. These wheels, while quite wobbly, bought time for the company to make the extensive die changes needed for the thicker Whizzwheels. Some models designed before the Whizzwheels conversion started could not accommodate the thicker wheels. These models would remain in the product line only briefly. The narrow Whizzwheels would only appear on models from 1970 through 1972. However, on most models, their appearance would be brief. In any given month as they appeared on one group of models they were being replaced by wide Whizzwheels on others.

Designers at Mettoy were soon dissatisfied with the simple 5-spoke foiled design on the early wide Whizzwheels. Mattel's wheels on their Hot Wheels vehicles looked more like the wheels on many racing and custom cars of the time. To improve the appearance of Corgi Juniors, Mettoy created a new pattern using a five double-spoked (5-dblspk) pattern. While essentially still a simple design, the new pattern would give a more realistic impression from a distance. Mettoy soon was using versions of this wheel across the product line. It would continue to be used through the 1970s and into the 1980s.

Here is a point where many collectors get confused. Mettoy, having two different wheel patterns to choose from in the early 1970s, would specify a "preferred" wheel type for each model. However, on occasions where stocks of the desired wheel type were not available, production was allowed to substitute different wheels as long as they were the same diameter. This avoided line stoppages while the correct wheels were obtained. Wheel types as a rule were never mixed on one model, the exception being when the front and rear wheels were different diameters. This substitution practice was rare in the early and mid 1970s, but became more and more common in the late 1970s and early 1980s as Mettoy slowly descended into bankruptcy.

Not all Corgi Juniors of the 1970s would be fitted with Whizzwheels. Models like the Rough Terrain Truck and various other construction and military vehicles would be produced with a large diameter, thin knobby black plastic wheel somewhat resembling a farm tractor wheel. This wheel was molded in black and would continue to be used as long as these models were in production. They were also made in at least two different diameters. Some models produced as late as 1996 were still using this wheel type.

The toy market of the early 1980s reflected what was going on in the real world. To model the progressively wilder off-road vehicles found in the real world, Mettoy and later Corgi Toys Ltd. created a series of larger and larger "off-road" Whizzwheels designs. Introduced in 1983 by Mettoy, the first of the designs were slightly larger than the standard wheels, and had a mild off-road tread design around the perimeter. The center of the wheel had a concentric ring pattern with four tabs facing outward from the inner ring and four more tabs facing inward from the outer ring. Corgi Toys Ltd. replaced this wheel with an even larger second type in 1985. This wheel had a larger diameter, deep treads extending across the tire, and a deeply recessed hub with five bumps representing lug nuts. This wheel was usually made in plain black since it was not easily decorated. By the early 1990s, while under Mattel ownership, the second design was replaced by an even larger design with deeper treads and a revised center pattern that could be bright foiled. Mattel has since used this pattern on their own Hot Wheels Castings.

When Corgi Toys Ltd. began production again in 1984, production practices were initially much the same as with Mettoy. Usage of the 5-spoke design would be rare, however, and it would essentially disappear by the late 1980s. Two new wheel patterns would be introduced in 1985, both designed with a greater area of bright foil. These two patterns are a series of teardrop shapes with either eight divisions (8-div) or four divisions (4-div) while being otherwise similar to the earlier wheels. The 8-div wheels would see a great amount of usage along with the 5-dblspk pattern through the end of the 1980s. Substitutions from one to the other in production would be frequent. The 5-dblspk wheel fell out of favor around the time Mattel bought Corgi Toys ltd. in 1989.

When production of the "Juniors" product line was moved to China in 1990, most models would thereafter be made with either the 8-div or 4-div wheel pattern. This continued through Mattel's ownership and the product line name change to Corgi Auto-City until Mattel and Corgi parted ways in August of 1995. At that point, the new Corgi Classics Ltd. lost all access to the former "Juniors" tooling. Mattel briefly continued the line as Hot Wheels Auto-City vehicles, mostly to use up existing stock. The former Corgi castings began to be used in mainstream Hot Wheels Sets, still with their 4-div or 8-div wheels. In 1996, a number of former Corgi castings appeared briefly in the main Hot Wheels product line, refitted with Hot Wheels type wheels. Most of the former Corgi castings went out of production when Mattel purchased Tyco and their Matchbox product line. (By that time, Matchbox had been through a series of owners.) Most of the former Corgi castings were regarded as unneeded duplications of either Hot Wheels or Matchbox models.

An interesting story must be waiting to be told about how Corgi Juniors came to be manufactured in Brazil as Kiko Corgi products. While the tooling for the models was transferred briefly to Brazil, the tooling for the wheels was not. Instead, Kiko Corgi Juniors were produced with a cheaper wheel design intended for use with crimped axle ends. There were exceptions to this practice, though, on models not fitted with Whizzwheels. (Rough Terrain Truck, Mobile Crane, etc.) It is the Kiko pattern wheel design that has survived into the present to be used on most small scale Corgi Classics Ltd. models. While the wheels may be made from a new set of dies, the pattern used is mostly unchanged.

Gray plastic wheel in two diameters.

Diecast wheel with radial fins.

Jaguars comparing gray plastic wheel
with diecast wheel with 5 perimeter slots.

Black plastic wheel with vacuum plated insert.

Early smooth diecast wheel with
diecast wheel with five perimeter slots.

Dished diecast wheel with black plastic tire.

Chrome foiled 5-spoke and 5-dblspk Whizzwheels.

Dished 5-spoke Whizzwheels with flat black 5-spoke Whizzwheels.

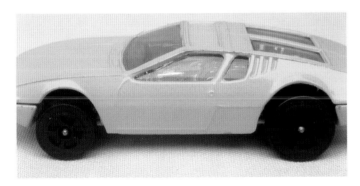

Two diameters of flat black 5-spoke Whizzwheels.

Black construction vehicle wheel.

Wheel evolution on the Guy Tanker.

Chrome foiled 5-spoke Whizzwheels in two diameters.

Chrome foiled 8-division and 4-division wheels.

Early off-road wheel.

Late chrome foiled off-road wheel.

Intermediate off-road wheel.

Brazilian Kiko wheel.

Corgi Classics Ltd. wheel.

Packaging Types

Husky Models, Corgi Rockets, and Corgi Juniors progressed through a series of packaging styles that were dictated by the marketing of the time. This section is an overview of the main packaging themes from each period, including some specific examples and variations. It is not, however, a complete listing, since many special packaging graphics were used over time to promote specific models in specific markets. Mettoy was also in the habit of responding to special requests by large customers and distributors with variations in packaging graphics. The topic deserves an entire book of its own to cover it thoroughly.

As seen in an earlier chapter, the initial 1964 packaging for Husky Models was a red and white card with a listing of the available models on the back. Some changes in text occurred over time to the face of the card, and later versions had graphics showing working features. Mettoy also preprinted the price of the model in some markets. The back of the card was revised frequently as models were introduced into the range. This list was printed in blue ink. At one time, deleted models were blocked-out. Later, the model number was either left blank or skipped entirely. Husky Extras were initially marketed as a distinct premium sub-range. They were packaged on distinctive blue and white cards. Husky Majors would share this design for a time, as would small sets.

By 1968, Husky packaging was looking very dated. A new yellow and red design was introduced to increase sales appeal in store displays. The word "models" was also dropped at this time, roughly corresponding to the dropping of the word "toys" from the larger Corgi line. As with the earlier packaging, added graphics were often used to promote working features. In some cases, these were the very same graphics used earlier. During this period, different model numbers were being used in different markets to allow Woolworth's to continue preprinting prices on the cards. The backs of the yellow cards had a printed traffic scene and slogan in European markets, but were blank in the American market. Larger sets would appear in shrink-wrapped boxes when necessary, but the Extras and Majors were still on cards whenever possible.

Corgi Rockets were introduced with their own unique series packaging. Large cards were used for the individual cars so that the special "Tune-up Key" could be displayed beside it. Sets were mostly boxed since each contained numerous track pieces. Extra track pieces and accessories were often sold in a clear bag with a card stapled to the top. The short-lived Electro-Rockets range had its own unique packaging unlike other products. Corgi Rockets were withdrawn from the market before any noticeable packaging variations could develop.

An entirely new card size with entirely new graphics was developed for the introduction of Corgi Juniors. Initial vehicle cards were tall with a collector card printed in the upper portion. The card was meant to be cut out and placed in a special collector book, which also served as a catalog. The old Husky Majors were renamed Corgi Super Juniors and shared similar graphics with preprinted collector cards. Packaging for sets remained mostly unchanged except for the graphics. Some sets briefly shared the "Technocrats" marketing seen briefly on the larger Corgi Toys products. The backs of the cards were arranged to provide data on the cutout collector card at this point.

The collector card packaging would be modified with the rapid introduction of Whizzwheels to Corgi Juniors. At first, an added label was placed on the card that sometimes overlapped the collector card. Graphics would soon be modified to add a Whizzwheels banner across the face of the card. By 1973, the height of the card had shrunk to allow more models to be displayed in the available shelf space. Some large customers also had their price labels preprinted on the face of the card. The collector card idea had run its course, and drawings of new models started to appear on the back.

Packaging graphics were changed in 1974 to a totally new design. Corgi Juniors would appear on orange, blue, or red cards. These cards possessed a flowing multi-colored racing stripe in contrasting colors. Eventually, almost every model could be found on each of the differently colored cards. This same generic graphics style was used on Super Juniors and sets, although Super Juniors would be packaged in window boxes with a card-hanging feature. A variation would also appear with the introduction of the "Growlers" models. Card backs would show drawings of other models in the Corgi Juniors product line. These drawings rotated through different groupings so identical models made at the same time often had different models shown on the back.

A new "Corgi Junior" (singular) bulls-eye graphics theme appeared in 1977. Colors initially varied on the packaging, but this soon settled on an orange / yellow / red effect. Special graphics would appear on super-hero and comic theme models with the bulls-eye shown smaller in the corner. A plain half-tone black version appeared on the back of the cards. This theme carried through larger models and sets, and there were many special versions created for individual models. The "Junior" part of the name was dropped from packaging in 1979, never to appear again.

By 1982, Mettoy decided to drop the bulls-eye graphics. Packaging graphics would be changed to a number of market-specific designs. American market cards would be white with bold diagonal lettering and sometimes show a photo of a real vehicle. This American packaging would continue through Mettoy's failure in 1983. British packaging was more thematic, with scenes of London or of a rural setting. Racing models would have a racing scene. By 1983, when the company was failing, British packaging changed to a blank yellow card with the Corgi name at the top. This allowed over-printing for promotional purposes and 2-pack production using the same generic card. Packaging would go through uncontrolled changes as Mettoy went under and leftover stock was sold. In the end, anything that could be put together for shipment would go out the door.

The new Corgi Toys Ltd. spent 1984 reusing Mettoy's final graphics style, although J-series "Juniors" models would briefly appear in European markets in a reverse-window card design. By 1985, the new company had devised an entirely new product image with a new "skidding car" logo. "Juniors" packaging would be either in standard cards with the new graphics theme or in a new hanging window box. This new window box could be nested one into the other for shipment but were not initially popular in the American market. Larger sets would essentially continue in the former packaging design redecorated in the new graphics. New larger multiple car sets would also appear on larger versions of the card design. Promotional models would appear in a simple box design. Some of these boxes were plain white with black printing. Others were printed with special designs requested by the customer. Graphics and packaging remained essentially unchanged through the 1980s. A short-lived attempt was made to reintroduce "Juniors" to the American market on cards with unique "Freeway" packaging, but the attempt saw only limited success.

By the beginning of the 1990s and Mattel ownership, the hanging window box was revised to have square ends. The card style of packaging was abandoned with the effective loss of the American market for Corgi Juniors. Graphics evolved through a number of designs and color variations. While the larger Corgi models returned to the dog logo and graphics in 1992, the "Juniors" line stayed with the "Skidding Dog" logo and graphics.

Mattel completely reorganized the "Juniors" products into the new Corgi Auto-City range in 1994. This range was not available in the American market. The range appeared in card style packaging that did not identify individual models. Small and medium sets also appeared on cards, with only the larger sets packaged in boxes. When Corgi and Mattel split in 1995, the graphics were changed to Hot Wheels Auto-City without any changes to the packaging style. Hot Wheels Auto-City models would only be issued for one year. By late 1996, former Corgi casting would appear in the main Hot Wheels product packaging.

Packaging of the Brazilian Kiko Corgi Juniors initially reflected contemporary Corgi models. These models were sold in a simple box design with a version of the bulls-eye graphics. This graphics design would persist throughout the Brazilian production. It is also notable that Brazilian production continued under license even when Mettoy was in bankruptcy.

Corgi Classics Ltd. has only dabbled in the Juniors 1:64 scale model size to-date. Initial offerings had unique promotional packaging. However, with the wide popularity of the new Transit Van, a standard card format has been found that seems to be persisting. With luck, the success of the Transit Van will continue and spawn additional similar models in the line.

First and second Husky Toys card variations. *Photo Courtesy of Wolfgang Gehrt / Goodies Old Toys.*

Husky Toys shipping box. *Photo Courtesy of Wolfgang Gehrt / Goodies Old Toys.*

Red and yellow Husky cards with graphics.

Prototype cards. *Photo Courtesy of Wolfgang Gehrt / Goodies Old Toys.*

Late Husky and early Corgi Juniors card backs.

Examples of early Husky Toys card backs.

H5-B on various card styles. *Photo Courtesy of Wolfgang Gehrt / Goodies Old Toys.*

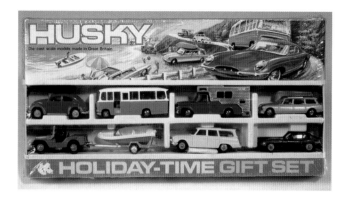

Husky Gift Set packaging. *Photo Courtesy of Wolfgang Gehrt / Goodies Old Toys.*

Corgi Juniors cards. *Photo Courtesy of Wolfgang Gehrt / Goodies Old Toys.*

Early and late collector card style packaging.

Husky Service Station packaging. *Photo Courtesy of Wolfgang Gehrt / Goodies Old Toys.*

Husky card style packaging for some sets. *Photo Courtesy of Wolfgang Gehrt / Goodies Old Toys.*

Corgi Juniors card backs.

Early Corgi Juniors Gift Set packaging.

Mid-70s Corgi Juniors card style.

Technocrats Gift Set packaging. *Photo Courtesy of Wolfgang Gehrt / Goodies Old Toys.*

Card color variations.

Comparison of card sizes.

"Growlers" card variation.

Mid-70s Gift Set packaging. *Photo Courtesy of Wolfgang Gehrt / Goodies Old Toys.*

Mid-70s card backs.

Card design after "Junior" was removed.

Late 70s card types.

Early 80s background scene card.

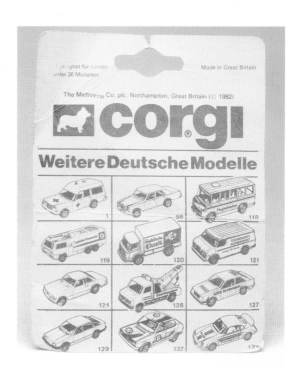

German market card back.

German market card style.

Another card style.

Late 70s Super packaging.

Special Mothercare stores packaging. *Photo Courtesy of Wolfgang Gehrt / Goodies Old Toys.*

72 Jaguar XJS

Final Mettoy UK market card style.

Final Mettoy USA market card style.

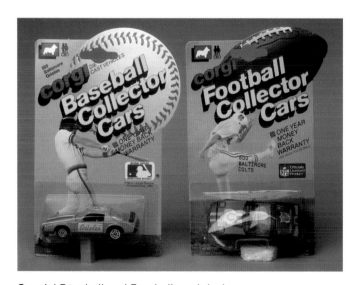

Special Baseball and Football card designs.

Double packaging from the time of Mettoy's failure.

One of many special offers. *Photo Courtesy of Wolfgang Gehrt / Goodies Old Toys.*

Special packaging for the USA market.

1985 hanging window box.

Corgi Toys Ltd. reverse window card.

Special USA box graphics from 1985.

Twin-pack card from 1985.

Red French market card from the mid 1980s.

Large card design used with some sets. *Photo Courtesy of Wolfgang Gehrt / Goodies Old Toys.*

Green Italian market card from the mid 1980s.

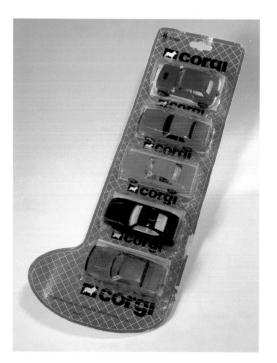

A special Christmas Stocking set card. *Photo Courtesy of Wolfgang Gehrt / Goodies Old Toys.*

The USA market Freeway card.

Late 1980s box style.

Hot Wheels Auto-City card design.

Early 1990s box style.

Short European and tall USA Hot Wheels card styles.

Corgi Auto-City card design.

Corgi Classics Ltd. packaging design.

Similar packaging for a promotional model.

New Transit Van promotional card style.

Standard card style for the New Transit Van.

Brazilian Kiko Corgi
Juniors packaging.

Catalogs and Literature

Catalogs and other literature for Husky Models, Corgi Rockets and Corgi Juniors date back to the very beginnings of each of these product lines. However, not every year of production in each range has its own corresponding catalog. Availability also varied from country to country, especially in the early years.

At the initial introduction of Husky Models in 1964, Mettoy made a foldout leaflet available showing all of the initial models. This brochure is noteworthy because it shows some of the models in colors that were on pre-production models rather than as they were released. This has caused many collectors to search for non-existent colors. Fortunately, most of the pre-production models still exist in private collections for verification. Unfortunately, a copy of this leaflet wasn't available to photograph at the publication date of this book.

As the Husky Models product line became established, Mettoy created more traditional catalog booklets for distribution in markets where they seemed desirable. These were in the more familiar format of a stapled booklet similar to the catalogs made for the larger Corgi Toys of the time. As had happened with the larger Corgi Toys products, a few of the new or "AVAILABLE LATER" models were shown in prototype colors that were later changed for production. In addition, at least the Porsche Carrera 6, if not other models, would be shown in the last Husky Models catalog but not released until the line had changed to Corgi Juniors. This was understandable when viewed together with the Rockets crash development program having been quickly followed by the Corgi Juniors name change crash program.

The rapid development and short product life of Corgi Rockets would leave time for the release of only one Rockets catalog. Other literature would be supplied in sets, but not released separately. Electro-Rockets would not appear in catalogs at all. Soon after the Mattel lawsuit, the Rockets name would appear very briefly in reference to the leftover track sets without mention of the cars.

Mettoy was keen to publicize the newly renamed Corgi Juniors in every way possible upon their introduction in 1970. An interesting scheme was developed where a "collector card" was printed into the card back for each model. Upon cutting the card from the packaging, buyers could mount it into a special booklet itself designed as a collectible item. It was also a catalog that displayed the models not yet in the buyer's collection. Naturally, all of the models needed to be purchased in order to fill the book, which became a goal in itself. The packaging changes for the Whizzwheels also created new versions of the cards, although no new spaces were provided in the booklet. The scheme was not extended to the larger sets, which suffered through the "Technocrats" marketing used by the larger Corgi Toys of the time.

By 1971, the novelty of the booklet idea had run its course. A new colorful large format color catalog was released that highlighted the new Whizzwheels feature on many models. This would be followed with newer versions for the next several years. Many of the converted older castings would appear for the last time in these catalogs, appearing very dated and out-of-place next to the new offerings. In addition, some the former Rockets castings would appear as Corgi Juniors in the catalogs. A few would never be released as such, leading to much speculation among collectors. Corgi Juniors would also be shown for the first time on the last page of the 1971-72 Corgi Toys catalog, taking the place of Corgi Rockets that had appeared the year before. This last page advertisement would continue into the mid-1970s.

In the 1974 Corgi Juniors catalog, Mettoy got away with an interesting ruse. They were developing a Juniors size model of the new Leyland Terrier to be introduced along with the unveiling of the real truck. (A promotional model was made for Leyland's advertising.) However, Mettoy still wanted to show that they were introducing a Coca-Cola delivery truck model later in the year. In order to maintain the secrecy for Leyland's product launch, Mettoy reworked a then current Matchbox Mercedes-Benz Girder Truck into a Coca-Cola Box Truck and photographed it for the catalog. Many collectors have searched for examples of this truck, which only existed as a prototype. Fortunately, Lesney did not make an issue of the ruse publicly and may have overlooked the matter at the time.

Another large format Corgi Juniors catalog was issued in 1977. It contained large clear photos of the product line, including sets. As usual, some prototype models were also shown, which had become an unfortunate habit by then. The 1977 Corgi Toys pocket catalog was the first of many to devote the entire rear of the catalog to a full listing of the Juniors line. This made a separate Corgi Juniors catalog unnecessary through the remainder of the Mettoy years. Corgi Juniors gradually merged into the mainstream product line. By the 1979 Corgi catalog, Mettoy dropped the "Juniors" name from advertising and packaging, even though the small line was still referred to as "Juniors" unofficially. By the 1983 catalog, Mettoy's last, the hard economic times were showing in the catalog's layout. The slick marketing and photography of previous years gave way to bland group shots with large blank areas on the page. Even the late boom in Corgi Juniors sales couldn't save Mettoy. Many models would be sold by Mettoy's receivers in all kinds of strange combinations that would never be cataloged.

The first Corgi Toys Ltd. catalog in 1984 would not be very different from the previous year. The layout was improved, and shows a photographic representation of the short-lived reverse-window card around every model. The catalog was shot with side views of the models, which were a mixture of leftover and new designs. By the 1985 catalog, the new company had established their new Corgi "skidding car" logo. The "J Series" was still called "Juniors" on the top corners of the pages, but nowhere else. The catalog itself was the same size as the previous pocket catalogs, only format-

ted vertically. The last year for the Pocket catalog format would be 1985, as Corgi Toys Ltd. turned its attention more to the adult collectibles market. Subsequent Juniors catalogs would be issued in a large full page format.

Mattel ownership brought an end to Juniors catalogs, since Mattel preferred to market their Hot Wheels product line. The renamed Auto-City line would appear in dealer catalogs, but these were not distributed to buyers. After the companies split, former Corgi Juniors castings would sometimes appear in the posters distributed for the main Hot Wheels product line, but this too would stop as soon as Mattel took ownership of the Matchbox brand product line.

1968 Husky catalog cover.

Husky Extras from the catalog.

Example page from the Husky catalog.

Sets in the Husky catalog.

1972 Corgi Juniors catalog.

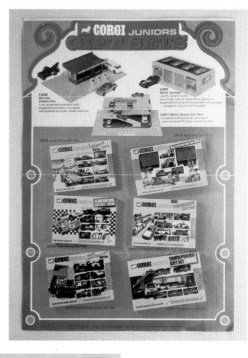

Gift Sets.

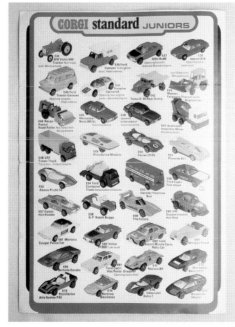

Example page from the Corgi Juniors catalog.

1974 Corgi Juniors catalog.

Extras, Super Juniors and Twin Packs.

Rear page showing the Mettoy logo.

Corgi Juniors advertised in the 1973 Corgi Toys catalog.

Corgi Junior section of the 1977 and 1978 Corgi Toys catalogs.

Corgi Juniors page from the 1975 Corgi Toys leaflet.

Corgi Junior section of the 1979 and 1980 Corgi Toys catalogs.

1977 Corgi Juniors catalog.

Corgi Junior section of the 1981 and 1983 Corgi Toys catalogs.

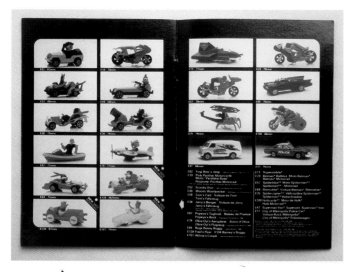

Vertical format of 1982 Corgi Catalog.

An issue of Corgi Collector Magazine showing "Juniors."

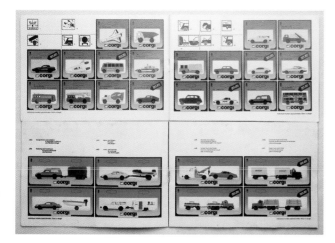

1984 Corgi Toys Ltd. catalog.

Example "Juniors" page.

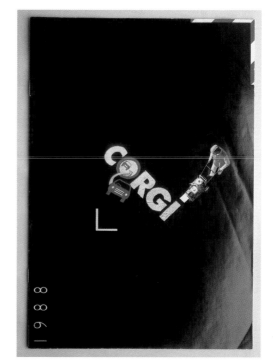

1988 Corgi Toys Ltd. catalog.

1985 Corgi Toys catalog.

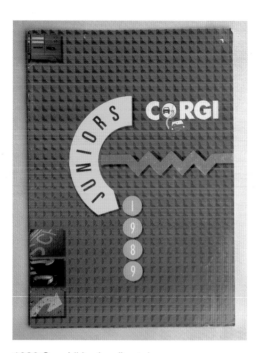

1989 Corgi "Juniors" catalog.

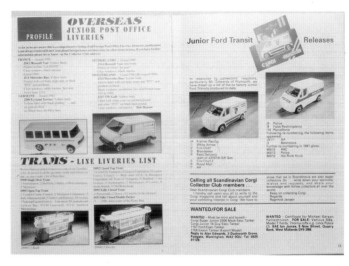

"Juniors" articles in Corgi Collector Magazine.

Catalog page showing dealer displays.

F.A.O. Schwarz Hot Wheels from Corgi dies.

Weetabix Cereal Advertisement.

Former Corgi Jeep used in a Little Debbies promotion.

Promotional Models and Regional Specials

Promotional models can be a collector's dream and nightmare all at once. Due to their nature, they tend to be known only to those few people that come into direct contact with them from the contracting company or the manufacturer. Some become known to the public through special offers or event giveaway programs. Many, however, are only used for in-house company promotions. This type is usually undocumented by the manufacturer and can be notoriously difficult for collectors to find. Determining the value of these models is even harder, and often is best left to an auction to decide.

Regional specials differ from promotional models in that they were available to the general public, but only in a limited area or country. Examples of these would be the many country-specific police, fire, and post office vehicles Corgi has produced over the years for its distributors in various countries. These models usually are requested by the distributor to enhance local sales by providing a recognizable market-specific model or group. It can sometimes be difficult for a person outside the original distribution area to determine if a model is a true promotional item or a regional special. For collecting purposes, they can be grouped together as hard-to-find items.

Through the Mettoy era, numerous promotional models were quietly produced. Most were never publicized, and collectors only know of them today through the detective work of other collectors. New discoveries continue to be made. Sometimes, only one example of a model is known which may not be in perfect condition. In other cases, only a photo or advertisement may be known without locating an example. A small number of any given model will eventually make their way onto the market. Often, however, sellers are not aware of the best locations in which to sell these items. Finding promotional models when they become available is the greatest challenge for any collector.

In the years following Mettoy's closure, Corgi production was full of promotional models and regional specials for every conceivable purpose. Initially, Corgi Toys Ltd. used special runs to help establish and stabilize the company. Fortunately, many of these special models were illustrated in the *Corgi Collector* magazine in the 1980s and early 1990s. Mattel further supported such programs when it purchased the company, as did the management of Corgi Classics Ltd. once they regained independence. Recently, the release of promotional models by Corgi Classics Ltd. has had less emphasis as the product line has grown. This probably does not reflect a loss of promotional sales, but rather the growth of the company overall.

A brief overview of some of the models produced through the years is presented in photos in this section. Some of these models have never appeared in the hobby press. The promotional models known to the author can be found throughout the Variation Listings in the back of this book. The total quantity of promotional items and regional specials produced by Corgi over the years could fill a small book, and just may someday. If any reader is lucky enough to discover any promotional model not described in the Variation Listings that follow, please send a report to the author with a full description including images if possible. The new find can then be added to the listings in any future editions.

One in a series of Dutch promotional tankers.

Later Shell promotional model.

Ready Brek Playbus.

Rear view of the tanker.

Hefty and Hilton promotional models.

Canadian Co-Op Tanker.

Hilton bus in its box. *Photo Courtesy of Wolfgang Gehrt / Goodies Old Toys.*

Mini Metro promo. *Photo Courtesy of Wolfgang Gehrt / Goodies Old Toys.*

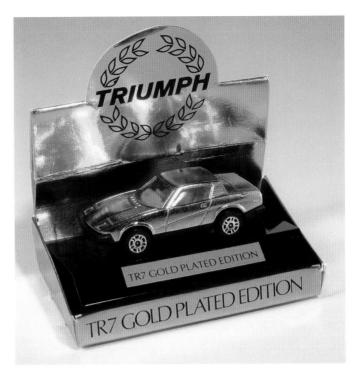

Presentation Triumph TR7. *Photo Courtesy of Wolfgang Gehrt / Goodies Old Toys.*

The first usage of the Leyland Terrier.

More promotional Terriers.

Unusual Terrier with full side labels.

Sierra models for a Ford dealer.

Motor Show Jaguar XJ-S.

Uni-Chem 2-pack.

Saudi Arabian Chubb.

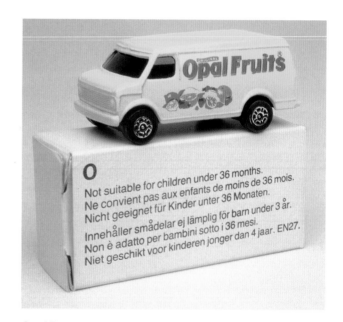

Opal Fruits promo U. S. Van.

Insurance company promo.

Red box BP Station models.

Yorkie car transporter. *Photo Courtesy of Wolfgang Gehrt / Goodies Old Toys.*

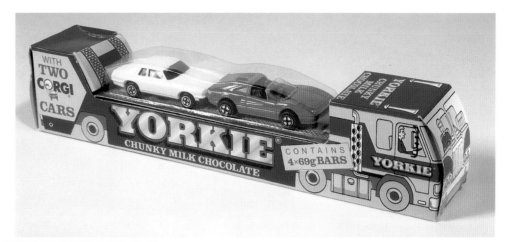

Blue box BP Station models.

Kellogg's Frosties models.

Models from a Weetabix promotion.

Box from a Saudi promotion. *Photo Courtesy of Wolfgang Gehrt / Goodies Old Toys.*

Avon Insurance Ford Transit.

More Iveco models.

Crayola Renault Trafic van.

Iveco for Batchelor's Peas.

Cutty Sark London Taxi.

Two additional Iveco Trucks.

Kwik Save model.

Specially decorated Hamleys models.

Hot Wheels Thunderstreak in Corgi packaging.

Chuck E. Cheese promotions.

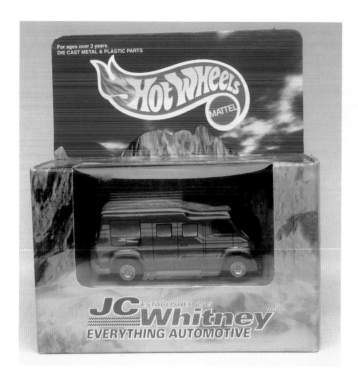

The Hot Rod Van as camper.

Eddie Stobart Terrier.

Chitty-Chitty-Bang-Bang.

Brazilian amusement park model.

Old and recent Weetabix Terriers.

Prototype and Pre-Production Models

Prototype and pre-production models are fascinating to most collectors. Such models are rarely seen by outsiders, and tend to be the subject of much speculation. Finding these types of models are like finding buried treasure in some ways. They are rare and usually unique. Most differ in some way from the resulting released model they represent. Others represent models that never made it to production at all.

For this section, we examine some of the prototype and pre-production models that were once part of the collection of Marcel Van Cleemput, one of the principle figures in the old Mettoy PLC. He was intimately involved with all facets of the development of Corgi Toys, and is the author of *The Great Book of Corgi* where some of these models have been shown before. Some of the early prototypes from the development of Husky Models have already been shown in earlier sections. The models here are from the early 1970s through the factory closure in 1983. This turbulent time in product development is best shown by the many ideas that were considered and eventually rejected. The story of the Corgi Juniors product line could have been much different had any of these prototype models made it into production.

Collectors can only speculate on what the reasons had been when models were rejected by the design team. In some cases, the company may have considered producing models around a common theme that did not develop as hoped. Sometimes, a design or construction issue may have been determined to be too costly to produce. At other times, the marketing team may have decided to turn down a model to preserve a balance in the product line. Market pressures, such as new models introduced by competitors, also shaped the decisions to produce any given model.

Pre-production models serve a slightly different purpose. When new models are developed, many decisions about finish and decorations must be considered. Often, a series of pre-production models will be created to determine which color or graphics is the most appealing. Sometimes such models are used to gain approval from a customer whose trademarks are to be used. Pre-production models can also be used for quality testing, manufacturing process development, and market studies. Once they are no longer needed, most pre-production models are thrown away. However, many eventually find their way into the hands of employee's children as presents at a company function.

This book makes no attempt to value prototype and pre-production models. They are also not included in the Variation Listings at the back of the book unless there is some question as to the released status of the model. Due to their unique nature, these models are best bought and sold in an auction or web-auction. The prices realized will vary widely depending on the desire of the bidders present. The range of collectors interested in prototypes and pre-production models is only a small section of the group of model collectors.

The models shown in this section are now in the collection of good friend Wolfgang Gehrt. The author is grateful for the chance to share them with other collectors through this book, and for the intercontinental friendship and support.

A proposed Husky driving school car. *Photo Courtesy of Wolfgang Gehrt / Goodies Old Toys.*

Wooden mock-up for the Volkswagen 1300. *Photo Courtesy of Wolfgang Gehrt / Goodies Old Toys.*

Wooden mock-up for the Austin-Healey LeMans. *Photo Courtesy of Wolfgang Gehrt / Goodies Old Toys.*

Body mock-up for the Ford Capri. *Photo Courtesy of Wolfgang Gehrt / Goodies Old Toys.*

A proposal for a futuristic theme. *Photo Courtesy of Wolfgang Gehrt / Goodies Old Toys.*

Futuristic car proposal. *Photo Courtesy of Wolfgang Gehrt / Goodies Old Toys.*

Some sort of space vehicle. *Photo Courtesy of Wolfgang Gehrt / Goodies Old Toys.*

Swamp buggy with six wheels. *Photo Courtesy of Wolfgang Gehrt / Goodies Old Toys.*

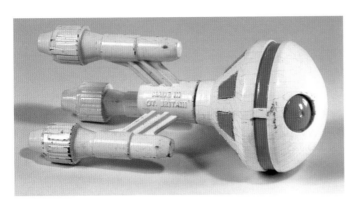

Space ship that looks a bit like the Blake's 7 Liberator. *Photo Courtesy of Wolfgang Gehrt / Goodies Old Toys.*

Superman cycle. (What's the point?) *Photo Courtesy of Wolfgang Gehrt / Goodies Old Toys.*

Off-road cycle proposal. *Photo Courtesy of Wolfgang Gehrt / Goodies Old Toys.*

Rejected color trial models. *Photo Courtesy of Wolfgang Gehrt / Goodies Old Toys.*

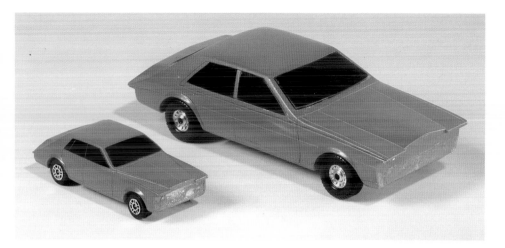

A proposed Cadillac Seville.
Photo Courtesy of Wolfgang Gehrt / Goodies Old Toys.

Proposed 1982 Chevrolet Camaro.
Photo Courtesy of Wolfgang Gehrt / Goodies Old Toys.

Wooden bus mock-up. *Photo Courtesy of Wolfgang Gehrt / Goodies Old Toys.*

AA Services Transporter. *Photo Courtesy of Wolfgang Gehrt / Goodies Old Toys.*

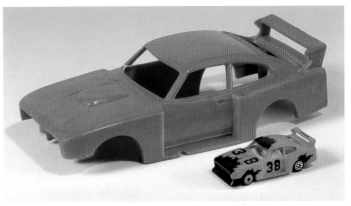

Body mock-up for the Can-Am Capri. *Photo Courtesy of Wolfgang Gehrt / Goodies Old Toys.*

Proposed promotional models. *Photo Courtesy of Wolfgang Gehrt / Goodies Old Toys.*

Additional proposals for the truck casting. *Photo Courtesy of Wolfgang Gehrt / Goodies Old Toys.*

Sports team busses that never were. *Photo Courtesy of Wolfgang Gehrt / Goodies Old Toys.*

Proposed ice cream van. *Photo Courtesy of Wolfgang Gehrt / Goodies Old Toys.*

Prototype Iveco box truck.

Iveco Esso tanker prototype.

Prototype Pepsi truck with production version.

Section 3
Variation Listings

About Values

The values given for models in the following Variation Listings were set at a time of great economic uncertainty and geopolitical unrest. At the time of this book's writing, world events and a persistent recession in the United States have suppressed values of all collectibles temporarily. While the author's crystal ball is out-of-order, values must be presumed to be recovering to their late 1990s levels in the short term. The values quoted in this book make this assumption. Time will tell whether it will be true. The best advice is to study the market conditions and use the values in this book as a way to set the relative value of one model versus another.

As mentioned so often in previous books, readers must consider condition heavily in valuing a model. These rules must be kept in mind:

1. Values in this book are quoted for *mint flawless models in mint flawless packaging*, unopened if sealed.

2. Values in this book are quoted for the most common variation(s) unless otherwise noted.

3. Scarce or high value models may be marked AUCTION due to volatility in prices realized for models recently sold.

4. Recent models are not assigned values since these models are still available from the original retailers.

5. Models that were announced but not produced, prototypes, and pre-production models are not assigned values.

6. Standard models in packaging that displays film or TV characters may be of higher value than those models in standard packaging *only* while sealed in the package. Opened or loose examples of these models may not have a higher value.

7. Models of other brand names using Corgi dies are not assigned values. Values for these models should be determined from the appropriate value guide for that brand.

8. Values quoted for models are for estimation purposes only, and are not a guarantee that the quoted value will be realized for any given transaction. Neither the author nor the publisher offer any item for sale, nor offer to purchase any item, in conjunction with the publication of this book and value guide.

Husky Models and Corgi Juniors
The Mettoy Years
1956 - 1983 Factory Closure

This section contains the variation listing for models produced from the introduction of Husky Models in 1964 through the failure of Mettoy on November 1, 1983. This section in its original form appeared as part of Ed Force's book *Corgi Toys,* and the data is used with his kind permission. It has been extensively reviewed and updated for this book, including new data uncovered since the publication of *The Unauthorized Encyclopedia of Corgi Toys*. In some cases, the order of variations listed for a specific model has been changed to properly reflect the order in which each variation was produced. The format of this section of the variation listing has been preserved for ease of use for those familiar with the previous books.

Note: values shown are in US dollars ($US) for mint-in-mint package condition as of May 2003. As a general rule, subtract 35-40% for mint loose, 50-60% for excellent, 60-70% for vg/chipped.

Husky Models (1964-1969)
Corgi Juniors (1970-1983)

Models produced between 1964 and 1969 were called Husky Models and were sold exclusively at Woolworth's stores. In 1970 the name of the series was changed to Corgi Juniors and distribution was expanded to all Corgi Toys sales outlets. In the late 1970s, the word Juniors was dropped from the packaging even though the range was still referred to as Corgi Juniors in correspondence. Models are listed under their Corgi Juniors number where different from Husky number, if known. Some Husky Models were issued under more than one number, depending upon manufacture date and country of sale. This was often made necessary to avoid duplication with model numbers in new large scale Corgi ranges.

1-A   Jaguar Mark X   66mm 1964-1967 $30-40

Small casting, yellow interior, clear windows, vacuum plated plastic base, gray plastic wheels.

1. Dark non-metallic blue body.
2. Light metallic blue body.
3. Medium metallic aqua-blue body.
4. Medium metallic blue body.
5. Red body. (Same color as H4-A but without roof beacon or side label.)

1-B   Jaguar Mark X   71mm 1967-1969

| | Pale Yellow | $60-100 |
| | Other Colors | $30-40 |

Larger casting, yellow interior, clear windows, unpainted diecast base. (Also found as Husky 51 in USA market.)

1. Dark non-metallic blue body, gray plastic wheels.
2. Light metallic blue body, gray plastic wheels.
3. Medium metallic blue body, gray plastic wheels.
4. Red body, gray plastic wheels. (Same color as H4-B but without roof beacon or side label.)
5. Dark non-metallic blue body, diecast wheels with five perimeter slots and black tires.
6. Light metallic blue body, diecast wheels with five perimeter slots and black tires.
7. Medium metallic blue body, diecast wheels with five perimeter slots and black tires.
8. Pale yellow body, diecast wheels with five perimeter slots and black tires.

1-C   Reliant TW9 Pickup   66mm 1970-1972

| | Orange | $15-20 |
| | Tan | $25-35 |

No interior, green tinted windows, unpainted diecast base, three wheels, gray track clip attaches to front bumper.

1. Light tan (almost ivory) body, thin black Whizzwheels.
2. Orange body, thin black Whizzwheels.
3. Orange body, thin chrome Whizzwheels.

1-D   Grand Prix Racer   75mm 1973-1976 $10-12

White interior, black diecast base, Whizzwheels, number 32 and American Flag labels.

(Note: Prototype shown in white in 1974 Corgi Juniors catalog, but not released in that color.)

1. Metallic green and white body.

1-E   Mercedes-Benz 220D Ambulance   76mm 1977-10/1983 $4-6

No interior, rear windows have frosted effect, black plastic base, Whizzwheels.

1. All white body, silver headlamps, silver grill and bumper, purple tinted windows, red cross labels on hood and doors.
2. All white body, silver headlamps, silver grill and bumper, blue tinted windows, red cross labels on hood and doors.
3. All white body, silver headlamps, silver grill and bumper, blue tinted windows, red cross labels on hood and doors, Corgi name blanked-out on base.
4. All white body including headlamps, grill and bumper, blue tinted windows, red cross labels on hood and doors.
5. Off-white body with red roof, body color headlamps, grill and bumper, blue tinted windows, red cross labels on doors only.

2-A   Citroen Safari   64mm 1964-1967 $30-40

Small casting, yellow interior, clear windows, vacuum plated plastic base, gray plastic wheels, tan plastic boat on roof.

1. Light yellow body.

2-B   Citroen Safari   70mm 1967-1969, 1970-1973

| | Regular wheels | $30-40 |
| | Whizzwheels | $20-30 |

Larger casting, yellow interior unless noted, clear windows, unpainted metal base, boat on roof.

1. Metallic green body, tan boat, gray plastic wheels, Husky base; 1967
2. Lime gold body, tan boat, gray plastic wheels, Husky base; 1967-1968
3. Lime gold body, blue boat, gray plastic wheels, Husky base; 1969-1969
4. Lime gold body, blue boat, vacuum plated wheels with tires, Husky base; 1969-1969
5. Dark Metallic blue body, white boat, vacuum plated wheels with tires, Corgi Juniors label; 1970.
6. Dark Metallic blue body, white boat, black Whizzwheels, Corgi Juniors label; 1970.
7. Yellow body, white boat, tan interior, black Whizzwheels, Corgi Juniors base.
8. Yellow body, white boat, yellow interior, black Whizzwheels, Corgi Juniors base.

9. Yellow body, white boat, tan interior, chrome Whizzwheels, Corgi Juniors base.
10. Yellow body, white boat, yellow interior, chrome Whizzwheels, Corgi Juniors base.
11. Metallic purple body, white boat, chrome Whizzwheels, Corgi Juniors base.
12. Blue body, white boat, chrome Whizzwheels?, Corgi Juniors base.
13. Lime gold body, white boat, chrome Whizzwheels, diecast Corgi Juniors base.

2-C   Blakes 7 Liberator   74mm 1980-1981 $20-30

Spacecraft, no interior, green tinted windows, white diecast base, no wheels. (also see 44-B.)

1. White and gold body.

3-A   Mercedes-Benz 220 Sedan   64mm 1964-1968 $30-40

Opening trunk, yellow interior, clear windows, vacuum plated plastic base, gray plastic wheels.

1. Light blue body.
2. Yellow body. (Believed to be a pre-production model. Need clarification.)

3-B   Volkswagen 1200 Police Car   66mm 1968-1969, 1970-1974

	Regular wheels	$30-40
	Whizzwheels	$20-30
	Polizei	$AUCTION

Modified 20-B casting with body color headlamps, red interior unless noted, clear windows unless noted, blue dome light, unpainted diecast base, "POLICE" labels unless noted.

1. White and black body, smooth diecast wheels with black tires, Husky base, "POLICE" in tall font on door decals; 1968.
2. White and black body, yellow interior, smooth diecast wheels with black tires, Husky base, "POLICE" in tall font on door decals; 1968.
3. White and black body, smooth diecast wheels with black tires, Husky base, "POLIZEI" in tall font on door decals; 1968. (Possibly a preproduction model intended for the German market.)
4. White and black body, diecast wheels with five perimeter slots and black tires, Husky base, "POLICE" in tall font on side labels; 1968-1969 (also packaged as Husky 53.)
5. White and black body, diecast wheels with five perimeter slots and black tires, Corgi Jr. label base, "POLICE" in standard font on side labels; 1970.
6. White and black body, diecast wheels with five perimeter slots and black tires, Corgi Jr. cast into base, "POLICE" in standard font on side labels; 1970-1971
7. White and black body, black Whizzwheels, modified base, "POLICE" in standard font on side labels; 1972-1973.
8. All white body, black Whizzwheels, modified base, "POLICE" in standard font on side labels; 1973-1974.

3-C   Volkswagen 1300 Police Car   68mm 1975-1976 $10-12

Modified 17-C casting with silver color headlamps, blue tinted widows and dome light, unpainted diecast base, Whizzwheels, "POLICE" labels.

1. White body, red interior.
2. White body, yellow interior.

3-D   Stromberg's Jet Ranger Helicopter   75mm 1977-1979 $20-30

Plastic interior, base, skids, and rotors, clear windows, no wheels, fish emblem.

1. Black and yellow body, yellow plastic interior, base, skids and rotors.
2. Black and yellow body, red plastic interior, base, skids and rotors. (Found in set.)

4-A   Jaguar Mark X Fire Chief's Car   66mm 1964-1967 $30-40

Modified 1-A casting, yellow interior, clear windows, vacuum plated plastic base, gray plastic wheels, red and white Fire decals, turning chrome siren on roof.

1. Red body.

4-B   Jaguar Mark X Fire Chief's Car   71mm 1967-1969 $30-40

Modified 1-B casting, yellow interior, clear windows, unpainted diecast base, red and white Fire labels, turning chrome siren on roof.

1. Red body, gray plastic wheels. (Same red color as H4-A.)
2. Dark red body, gray plastic wheels.
3. Dark red body, diecast wheels with five perimeter slots and black tires.

4-C   Zetor 5511 Farm Tractor   56mm 1970-1979 $10-12

Diecast base includes body parts, black plastic interior, no windows, black plastic wheels of two sizes. (May be found with yellow plastic disk harrow out of Agricultural Set.)

1. Orange main body, red base.
2. Metallic green main body, white base.

5-A   Lancia Flaminia   63mm 1964-1968

| | Blue | $30-40 |
| | Red | $100-120 |

Yellow interior, clear windows, vacuum plated plastic base, gray plastic wheels, opening hood.

1. Deep Red body.
2. Light blue body.

5-B   Willys Jeep   62mm 1968-1969, 1970-1973

Cast wheels	$20-30
Whizzwheels	$15-25

Brown interior unless noted, no windows, unpainted diecast base, folding plastic windshield frame.

1. Metallic green body, yellow interior, yellow windshield, smooth diecast wheels with knobby black tires, Husky base; 1968. (May be pre-production model.)
2. Metallic green body, brown interior, yellow windshield, smooth diecast wheels with knobby black tires, Husky base; 1968.
3. Metallic green body, gray windshield, smooth diecast wheels with knobby black tires, Husky base; 1968.
4. Metallic green body, gray windshield, diecast wheels with five perimeter slots and black tires with molded sidewalls and tread, Husky base; 1969.
5. Metallic green body, gray windshield, diecast wheels with five perimeter slots and black tires with molded sidewalls and tread, Corgi Juniors label; 1970.
6. Light tan body, gray windshield, diecast wheels with five perimeter slots and black tires with molded sidewalls and tread, Corgi Juniors label; 1970.
7. Yellow body with side step plate removed, gray windshield, wide black Whizzwheels, modified Corgi Juniors Whizzwheels base.
8. Light tan body with side step plate removed, gray windshield, wide black Whizzwheels, modified Corgi Juniors Whizzwheels base.
9. Light tan body with side step plate removed, gray windshield, chrome Whizzwheels, modified Corgi Juniors Whizzwheels base.
10. Orange body with side step plate removed, gray windshield, wide black Whizzwheels, modified Corgi Juniors Whizzwheels base.
11. Orange body with side step plate removed, gray windshield, chrome Whizzwheels, modified Corgi Juniors Whizzwheels base.
12. Red body with side step plate removed, gray windshield, brown interior, chrome Whizzwheels, modified Corgi Juniors Whizzwheels base.
13. Red body with side step plate removed, gray windshield, yellow interior, chrome Whizzwheels, modified Corgi Juniors Whizzwheels base.
14. Red body with side step plate removed, gray windshield, white interior, chrome Whizzwheels, modified Corgi Juniors Whizzwheels base.
15. Purple body with side step plate removed, gray windshield, yellow interior, chrome Whizzwheels, modified Corgi Juniors Whizzwheels base. (May be faded red model. Need verification.)

5-C   NASA Space Shuttle   70mm 1980-10/1983 $20-30

Opening hatches, gold interior, no windows, black diecast base, plastic wheels, American Flag on left wing, "U.S.A." on right wing. (Casting also used for E41-B James Bond Space Shuttle.)

1. White upper and black lower body, packaged as Enterprise. (The real Shuttle Enterprise was the first Shuttle atmospheric drop test vehicle and never flew into orbit. It is now part of the collection of the Smithsonian Institute in Washington, DC.)
2. White upper and black lower body, packaged as Columbia. (The real Shuttle Columbia was the first NASA Space Shuttle to be launched into orbit. It was destroyed during re-entry in 2003 with the loss of all aboard.)

6-A   Citroen Safari Ambulance   64mm 1964-1967 $30-40

Modified 1-A casting, blue interior, roof light and rear windows, clear front windows, vacuum plated plastic base, gray plastic wheels, red cross decal on hood.

1. White body.
2. Off-white body.

6-B   Ferrari Berlinetta 250GT   69mm 1967-1969 $30-40

Red interior unless otherwise noted, clear windows, vacuum plated plastic engine, diecast lower body-base same color as upper body.

1. Maroon body and base, smooth diecast wheels with black tires.
2. Maroon body and base, diecast wheels with radial fins and black tires.
3. Red body and base, diecast wheels with radial fins and black tires.

6-C   DeTomaso Mangusta   70mm 1970-1973 $15-25

Vacuum plated plastic interior and grilles, diecast lower body-base same color as upper body.

1. Yellow-green body and base, green tinted windows, black Whizzwheels.
2. Yellow-green body and base, amber tinted windows, black Whizzwheels.
3. Yellow-green body and base, amber tinted windows, silver 5-spoke Whizzwheels.
4. Metallic purple body, amber tinted windows, black Whizzwheels.
5. Metallic purple body, amber tinted windows, silver 5-spoke Whizzwheels.

6-D   Daily Planet Helicopter   75mm 1979-1980 $20-30

White plastic interior, base, skids, and rotors, clear windows, red and white "DAILY PLANET" labels.

1. Red main body.

7-A   Buick Electra Sedan   69mm 1964-1968 $30-50

Yellow interior, clear windows, vacuum plated plastic base, gray plastic wheels.

1. Orange-red body.

7-B   Duple Vista 25 Coach   76mm 1968-1969, 1970-1973

Regular wheels	$15-20
Whizzwheels	$12-15

Yellow interior, green tinted windows, white plastic upper body, diecast base same color as lower body, unpainted diecast grille and bumpers.

1. Turquoise lower body, gray plastic wheels, Husky base; 1968.
2. Turquoise lower body, black plastic wheels with vacuum plated inserts, Husky base; 1969.
3. Dark red lower body, black plastic wheels with vacuum plated inserts, Corgi Juniors base label; 1970.
4. Yellow lower body, black Whizzwheels, modified Corgi Juniors Whizzwheels base.
5. Light purple lower body, black Whizzwheels, modified Corgi Juniors Whizzwheels base.
6. Light purple lower body, chrome Whizzwheels, modified Corgi Juniors Whizzwheels base.
7. Light purple lower body, chrome Whizzwheels, modified Corgi Juniors Whizzwheels base, Flat Black "scorching" on side. (From Gift Set E3021.)
8. Orange lower body, chrome Whizzwheels, modified Corgi Juniors Whizzwheels base.
9. Orange lower body, black Whizzwheels, modified Corgi Juniors Whizzwheels base.
10. Orange lower body, chrome Whizzwheels, modified Corgi Juniors Whizzwheels base, Flat Black "scorching" on side. (From Gift Set E3021.)

7-C   Dumper Truck   74mm 1976-10/1983 $4-6

Plastic base and operating tipper (same colors), no interior, grille label. (Prototype shown in 1976 catalog with Red chassis-cab, yellow tipper and base, but not produced in that color scheme.)

1. Dark Metallic Blue chassis-cab, yellow tipper and base, clear windows, black plastic wheels, white and black grill label with four headlamps and split diamond badge at center.
2. Dark Metallic Blue chassis-cab, yellow tipper and base, clear windows, black plastic wheels, yellow and black grill label with two headlamps and "CORGI" at top edge.
3. Light non-metallic blue chassis-cab, yellow tipper and base, clear windows, black plastic wheels, yellow and black grill label with two headlamps and "CORGI" at top edge.
4. Medium non-metallic blue chassis-cab, yellow tipper and base, clear windows, black plastic wheels, yellow and black grill label with two headlamps and "CORGI" at top edge.
5. Yellow chassis-cab, black tipper and base, no windows, 6point Whizzwheels, no grill label; 1980-1982.
6. Yellow chassis-cab, red tipper and base, no windows, black Whizzwheels, no grill label; 1983-10/1983.

8-A   Ford Thunderbird Convertible   66mm 1964-1966 $30-50

Yellow interior, clear windshield, vacuum plated plastic base and grille, gray plastic wheels.

1. Light red (dark pink) body, packaged with black removable tonneau cover.
2. Light red (dark pink) body, packaged without black removable tonneau cover.

8-B   Ford Thunderbird Hardtop   66mm 1966-1968 $30-50

Plastic detachable hardtop, otherwise as 8-A.

1. Yellow body, blue top.
2. Yellow body, black top.

8-C   Tipping Farm Trailer   69mm 1968-1969, 1970-? $12-15

Diecast tipper and chassis, black plastic hydraulic cylinder.

1. Red tipper, yellow chassis, "Husky" cast into bottom, smooth diecast wheels and black tires with rounded profile (implement tires.)
2. Red tipper, yellow chassis, "Husky" cast into bottom, diecast wheels with five perimeter slots and black tires with rounded profile (implement tires.)
3. Orange tipper, blue chassis, Corgi Juniors label on bottom, diecast wheels with five perimeter slots and black tires with rounded profile (implement tires.)
4. Red tipper, yellow chassis, "CORGI JUNIORS" cast into bottom, thin silver center Whizzwheels. (Also in set E2502-A.)
5. Yellow tipper, metallic green chassis, "CORGI JUNIORS" cast into bottom, thin black center Whizzwheels. (Only found in set E2516-A.)

8-D   Rover 3500 Sedan   77mm 1979-10/1983 $4-6

Clear windows unless noted, black plastic base, Whizzwheels, opening rear hatch.

1. Dark metallic blue body, yellow interior; 1979. (May or may not come in promotional box.)
2. Light metallic blue body, yellow interior; 1980-1981?
3. Light metallic blue body, red interior; 1981?
4. Bright yellow body, red interior; 1982?
5. Bright yellow body, white interior; 1982?
6. Bright yellow body, orange interior; 1982?
7. Bright yellow body, either white interior with yellow tinted windows or yellow interior with clear windows; 1982? (need clarification.)
8. Non-metallic red body, white interior; 1982?
9. Non-metallic red body, ??? interior, yellow tinted windows. 1982?
10. White body, red interior; 1983?
11. Non-metallic blue body, red interior; (Found in transitional era 2-pack, 1983-84.)
12. Non-metallic blue body, yellow interior; 1983?
13. Non-metallic blue body, yellow interior, yellow tinted windows; 1983?
14. Non-metallic maroon body, white interior; 1983?
15. Dark red body, red interior. (Found in set E2551-A.)
16. Silver body, yellow interior; 1983?

9-A   Buick Electra Police Car   69mm 1964-1968 $30-40

Modified 7-A casting, yellow interior, clear windows, red dome light, red and white Police decals, vacuum plated plastic base and grille, gray plastic wheels.

1. Dark blue body.
2. Royal blue body (darker shade of blue.)

9-B   Cadillac Eldorado   78mm 1968-1969, 1970-1971

| | **Regular wheels** | **$30-40** |
| | **Whizzwheels** | **$20-30** |

Red interior, clear windows, unpainted diecast base unless noted, opening hood, detailed engine. (Note: Drawing shown in 1968 Husky catalog with dark blue body, but not released in that color scheme. Pre-production model known with purple body and yellow interior.)

1. Bright blue body, black plastic wheels with vacuum plated inserts, tow hook, Husky base; 1968-1969.
2. Bright blue body, black plastic wheels with vacuum plated inserts, tow hook, Corgi Juniors label over cast Husky Models logo on base; 1970.
3. Metallic green body, black plastic wheels with vacuum plated inserts, tow hook, Corgi Juniors label on base with blank center; 1970.
4. Metallic blue body, dished diecast wheels with black plastic tires, tow hook, Corgi Juniors label on base; 1970. (Short run, may be out of Gift Set.)
5. Metallic green body, narrow black Whizzwheels, modified base, tow hook.
6. Metallic green body, narrow black Whizzwheels, modified base, no tow hook.
7. White body with gloss black hood, narrow black Whizzwheels, modified base, no tow hook.
8. White body with dull black hood, narrow chrome Whizzwheels, modified silver painted base, no tow hook.

9-C   Police Range Rover   69mm 1973-1980 $4-8

Dome lights, Whizzwheels, Police labels.

1. White body, yellow interior, blue tinted windows, chrome plastic base, rectangular labels with blue crown over blue outlined red stripe with white "POLICE" on doors only.
2. White body, yellow interior, blue tinted windows, black plastic base, rectangular labels with blue crown over blue outlined red stripe with white "POLICE" on doors only.
3. White body, yellow interior, blue tinted windows, black plastic base, long thin labels with black outline, day-glow orange background and black "POLICE" text on doors.
4. White body, white interior, blue tinted windows, black plastic base, long thin labels with day-glow orange-red background and "POLICE" in dark blue printed block.
5. White body, yellow interior, blue tinted windows, black plastic base, long thin labels with day-glow orange-red background and "POLICE" in dark blue printed block.
6. White body, red interior, blue tinted windows, long thin labels with day-glow orange-red background and "POLICE" in dark blue printed block.
7. White body, yellow interior, blue tinted windows, black plastic base, long thin labels that do not extend beyond wheels with red background and white "EMERGENCY" text on doors. (Possibly from set E3021-A or E3026-A. Need clarification.)

10-A   Guy Warrior Coal Truck   70mm 1964-1969, 1970-1972? $25-35

Blue tinted windows, no interior, vacuum plated plastic base, black plastic coal load.

1. Red body, gray plastic wheels, open rear corner windows in cab, Husky base.
2. Red body, gray plastic wheels, closed rear corner windows in cab, Husky base.
3. Red body, black plastic wheels with vacuum plated inserts, closed rear corner windows in cab, Husky base.
4. Orange body, gray plastic wheels, open rear corner windows in cab, Husky base.
5. Orange body, black plastic wheels with vacuum plated inserts, closed rear corner windows in cab, Husky base.
6. Orange body, black plastic wheels with vacuum plated inserts, closed rear corner windows in cab, Corgi Juniors label base.
7. Orange body, black plastic wheels with vacuum plated inserts, closed rear corner windows in cab, Corgi Juniors cast into base. May have black plastic base. (Possibly confused with last version of E13-A which is red but with Whizzwheels.)

10-B   Ford GT 70   73mm 1973-1975 $15-20

Vacuum plated plastic interior and detailed engine, unpainted opening rear hatch, unpainted diecast base, Whizzwheels. (Note: Prototype shown in 1974 Corgi Juniors catalog with pink body with blue tinted windows, but not released in that color scheme.)

1. Bright orange body, clear windows.
2. Bright orange body, blue tinted windows.

10-C   Triumph TR7   77mm 1977-10/1983

	Standard versions	**$4-6**
	Plated base versions	**$5-8**
	Gold plated promotional	**$AUCTION**

Yellow interior unless noted, blue tinted windows unless noted, black plastic base unless noted, Whizzwheels, tow hook. (Prototype shown in 1980 Corgi catalog with white and blue body with vacuum plated bumpers and base, but not released in that color scheme.)

1. White and blue body, number 3 and TR7 label on hood, orange and red painted taillamps.
2. White and blue body, number 3 and TR7 label on hood, unpainted taillamps.
3. White and blue body, number 3 and TR7 label on hood, unpainted taillamps, red interior.
4. White and dull black body, number 3 and TR7 label on hood, unpainted taillamps, yellow interior.
5. White and dull black body, number 3 and TR7 label on hood, unpainted taillamps, black interior.
6. White and dull black body, no label on hood, black interior.
7. White and dull black body, "Castrol" logo label on hood, unpainted taillamps, 5-dblspk wheels. (May have been a promotional model for Castrol.)
8. Silver and red body, number 3 and TR7 label on hood.
9. Silver body, number 3 and TR7 label on hood, yellow interior.
10. Silver body, no label on hood, white interior.
11. Red body, dark blue lower sides, number 7 and British Airways labels.
12. Red body, dark blue lower sides, number 7 and British Airways labels, yellow interior, vacuum plated base and bumpers.
13. Red body including lower sides, number 7 and British Airways labels.
14. Red body including lower sides, number 7 and British Airways labels, , yellow interior vacuum plated base and bumpers.
15. Red body including lower sides, number 7 and British Airways labels, yellow interior.
16. Red body including lower sides, number 7 and British Airways labels, white interior.
17. Red body including lower sides, number 7 and British Airways labels, white interior, clear windows.
18. Red body including lower sides, number 7 and British Airways labels, yellow tinted windows.
19. Red body, yellow interior, no labels. (Sold in special Union Jack box.)
20. Orange body, red interior, no labels.
21. Orange body, yellow interior or white interior with yellow tinted windows, no labels. (Need clarification.)
22. Yellow body, red interior, no labels.
23. Yellow body, red interior, clear windows, no labels.
24. Yellow body, tan interior, clear windows, no labels. (Possibly from a later period.)
25. Dark green body, white interior, no labels.
26. Green body, black interior, no labels.
27. Metallic green body, clear windows, red interior, no labels.
28. Black body, clear windows, white interior, no labels.

29. Black body, clear windows, white interior, no labels.

30. Black body, clear windows, red interior, no labels.

31. Black body, clear windows, yellow interior, no labels. (Transitional era model.)

32. Black body, clear windows, yellow interior, no labels, gray base and bumpers. (Transitional era model.)

33. Black body, amber tinted windows, white interior, no labels.

34. Brown body, amber tinted windows, white interior, no labels.

35. Blue body, clear windows, white interior, no labels.

36. Metallic copper body, clear windows, red interior, no labels.

37. Cream body, clear windows, white interior, no labels.

38. Gold plated body, white interior, clear windows, display platform (plinth) and special gold presentation box. (Qty: 250. Promotional model for British Leyland at product launch of real car.)

11-A   Forward Control Land Rover   66mm 1964-1969 $30-40

Removable plastic rear cover, blue tinted windows, no interior, gray plastic wheels. (Also see H21-A.)

1. Non-metallic medium green body including base, tan plastic rear cover, small rear corner windows in cab, no suspension, front bumper part of body.

2. Non-metallic medium green body, black plastic base with suspension, tan plastic rear cover, small rear corner windows in cab, front bumper part of base.

3. Non-metallic medium green body, black plastic base with suspension, tan plastic rear cover, no corner windows, front bumper part of base.

4. Metallic aqua-green body, black plastic base with suspension, light olive plastic rear cover, no corner windows, front bumper part of base.

11-B   Austin Healey LeMans Sprite   68mm 1970-1974 $15-20

Amber tinted windows and headlights, diecast base, number 50 labels pre-applied to doors, sheet of additional labels supplied in package.

1. Red body, light blue interior, black Whizzwheels, charcoal gray base.

2. Red body, yellow interior, chrome Whizzwheels, charcoal gray base.

3. Red body, yellow interior, chrome Whizzwheels, black base.

11-C   Supermobile   76mm 1979-10/1983 $20-30

Striking fists, clear canopy, red interior and jet, red and yellow "S" emblem labels, three small black plastic wheels.

1. Light blue upper and lower body-base castings with silver striker housings, silver vacuum plated striking fists, painted Superman head.

2. Medium blue upper and lower body-base castings with silver striker housings, silver vacuum plated striking fists, painted Superman head.

3. Medium blue upper and lower body-base castings including striker housings, silver vacuum plated striking fists, unpainted Superman head.

4. Medium blue upper and lower body-base castings including striker housings, red striking fists, unpainted Superman head.

12-A   Volkswagen Tower Truck   60mm 1964-1967 $30-40

Red plastic telescopic tower, blue tinted windows, no interior, vacuum plated plastic base, gray plastic wheels.

1. Yellow body.

12-B   Ford F-350 Tower Truck   71mm 1968-1969 $30-40

Red plastic telescopic tower, blue tinted windows, no interior, vacuum plated plastic Husky base.

1. Yellow body, gray plastic wheels.

2. White body, gray plastic wheels.

3. White body, black plastic wheels with vacuum plated inserts.

12-C   Reliant-Ogle Scimitar   73mm 1970-1973

	White	$20-30
	Metallic blue	$15-20

Yellow interior, amber tinted windows, unpainted metal base.

1. White body, black Whizzwheels.

2. Metallic blue body, black Whizzwheels.

3. Metallic blue body, chrome Whizzwheels.

12-D   Ford GT 70   73mm 1975-1976 $8-12

Modified 10-B casting, Growler, unpainted diecast opening rear hatch, vacuum plated plastic interior, blue tinted windows, black plastic base, Whizzwheels.

1. Metallic green body.

2. Bright orange body.

12-E   Golden Eagle Jeep   68mm 1979-1981 $4-6

Yellow interior, clear windshield, detachable plastic top, silver diecast base, Whizzwheels. (Prototype shown in 1979 Corgi catalog having yellow body with black roof and interior, but not produced in this color scheme.)

1. Metallic brown body, white top.

2. Metallic brown body, tan top, eagle label on hood.

13-A   Guy Warrior Sand Truck   70mm 1964-1969, 1970-1972 $25-35

Same castings as 10-A, blue tinted windows, no interior, tan plastic sand load.

1. Bright yellow body, gray plastic wheels, open rear corner windows in cab, chrome plastic Husky base.

2. Bright yellow body, gray plastic wheels, closed rear corner windows in cab, chrome plastic Husky base.

3. Blue body, gray plastic wheels, open rear corner windows in cab, chrome plastic Husky base.

4. Blue body, gray plastic wheels, closed rear corner windows in cab, chrome plastic Husky base.

5. Blue body, black plastic wheels with vacuum plated inserts, closed rear corner windows in cab, chrome plastic Husky base.

6. Blue body, black plastic wheels with vacuum plated inserts, closed rear corner windows in cab, chrome plastic base with Corgi Juniors label.

7. Blue body, dished diecast wheels with black plastic tires, closed rear corner windows in cab, chrome plastic base with Corgi Juniors label.

8. Red body, Whizzwheels, closed rear corner windows in cab, modified black plastic Corgi Juniors Whizzwheels base.

13-B   Rough Terrain Truck   68mm 1976-1978 $6-10

Main body-base and white cab castings, plastic interior-grille-stripe, plastic tow hook, clear windows, black plastic wheels.

1. Red main body and base, black interior. (Also used in set E3022-A1.)

2. Blue main body and base, black interior. (Also used in set E3023-A1.)

3. Blue main body and base, red interior.

13-C   Buck Rogers Starfighter   72mm 1980-10/1983 $5-8

Blue interior and jets, yellow retracting wings, stripe labels, no wheels.

1. White body and base.

14-A   Guy Warrior Tanker   70mm 1964-1966

	Shell-BP	$40-60
	Shell	$30-40

Rounded tank, separate casting forms rear of tank, blue tinted windows, no interior, vacuum plated plastic base and grille, white decals with red and yellow Shell emblems, gray plastic wheels.

1. Yellow body, "Shell-BP" decals form white panels on tank sides and rear, open rear quarter windows in cab.

2. Yellow body, "Shell" decals form white panels on tank sides and rear, open rear quarter windows in cab.

3. Yellow body, "Shell" decals form white panels on tank sides and rear, filled-in rear quarter windows in cab.

14-B   Guy Warrior Tanker   73mm 1966-1969, 1970-1974

	Promotional versions	$50-100
	Shell and Esso regular wheels (non-promotional versions)	$30-40
	Esso with Whizzwheels	$12-15

Larger casting, squarish tank, no separate rear casting, blue tinted windows, no interior, unpainted diecast base and grille unless noted.

1. Yellow body, Shell decals on sides only with white stripe toward rear from logo, Husky base, gray plastic wheels.

2. Yellow body, Shell decals on sides only with white stripe toward rear from logo, Husky base, diecast wheels with five slots and black tires.

3. White body, Esso decals, Husky base, gray plastic wheels.

4. White body, Esso decals, Husky base, diecast wheels with five slots and black tires; 1969.

5. White body, Esso labels, Husky base, diecast wheels with five slots and black tires; 1969.

6. White body, Esso labels, Corgi Juniors label on base, diecast wheels with five slots and black tires; 1970.

7. White body, Esso labels, Corgi Juniors label on base, black plastic wheels with vacuum plated inserts; 1970.

8. White body, Esso labels, Corgi Juniors label on base, dished diecast wheels without slots, black tires; 1970-71.

9. White body, Esso labels, Corgi Juniors Cast into base, dished diecast wheels without slots, black tires; 1971.

10. White body, Esso labels, Corgi Juniors Cast into white painted base, dished diecast wheels without slots, black tires; 1971.

11. White body, Esso labels, white modified diecast base with added "Whizzwheels" text, wide 5-spoke Whizzwheels which protrude beyond the fenders.

12. White body, ljsselstreek N.V. labels, Husky base, gray plastic wheels; (Netherlands promotional.)

13. Yellow body, Shell logo and "termo plan" on side labels, Husky base, gray plastic wheels; (Netherlands promotional for Royal Dutch Shell.)

14. Yellow body, "Eindhovense Olie Centrale" and telephone number on clear side labels, rounded clear Shell label on back of the tank, Husky base, gray plastic wheels. (Netherlands promotional for local oil distributor. Possibly Code 2.)

15. Yellow body, "Van Staveren - Nieuw-Vennep" and telephone number on clear side labels, rounded clear Shell label on back of tank, Husky base, gray plastic wheels. . (Netherlands promotional for local oil distributor. Possibly Code 2.)

16. Yellow body, "Oliehandel von Aalst" and telephone number on clear side labels, rounded clear Shell label on back of tank, Husky base, gray plastic wheels. . (Netherlands promotional for local oil distributor. Possibly Code 2.)

17. Yellow body, "Fa. Marees & Kistemaker Schoolweg 68 Julianadorp" on clear side labels, square clear Shell label on back of tank, Husky base, gray plastic wheels. . (Netherlands promotional for local oil distributor. Possibly Code 2.)

18. Yellow body, revised Shell labels with red "Shell" toward rear sides from logo, Shell logo on rear of tank, Corgi Juniors Cast into white painted diecast base, dished diecast wheels without slots and black tires; 1971. (Shell service station promotional in northern Europe. Special red card packaging. Further background data needed.)

| 14-C | Guy Warrior Esso Tanker | 73mm 1975-1976 | $8-12 |

Black plastic base including headlights, blue tinted windows, no interior, red-white-blue Esso labels, Whizzwheels.
1. White body, plastic base.

| 14-D | Buick Regal Taxi | 70mm 1977-1980 | $8-12 |

Vacuum plated plastic interior, amber tinted windows and roof sign, white and black Taxi labels, chrome grille and bumpers, black plastic base with suspension, Whizzwheels.
1. Yellow-orange to dark yellow body. (Shade varies and may fade when exposed to sunlight.)

| 15-A | Volkswagen Pickup Truck | 60mm 1965-1967 | $30-40 |

Removable tan plastic rear top, blue tinted windows, no interior, vacuum plated plastic base, gray plastic wheels.
1. Light green body.

| 15-B | Studebaker Wagonaire TV | 76mm 1967-1969, 1970-1971 | $30-40 |
| | Camera Car | | |

Clear front and bluish-purple rear tinted windows, turning TV camera and man in rear hatch.
1. Dark yellow body, vacuum plated plastic Husky base-grille, gray plastic wheels.
2. Dark metallic blue body, vacuum plated plastic Husky base-grille, gray plastic wheels.
3. Dark metallic blue body, vacuum plated plastic Husky base-grille, diecast wheels with five perimeter slots and black tires.
4. Light yellow body, vacuum plated plastic Husky base-grille, diecast wheels with five perimeter slots and black tires.
5. Metallic medium blue body, vacuum plated plastic Husky base, diecast wheels with five perimeter slots and black tires.
6. Metallic medium blue body, unpainted diecast Husky base, diecast wheels with five perimeter slots and black tires.
7. Metallic turquoise body, unpainted diecast Husky base, diecast wheels with five perimeter slots and black tires.
8. Metallic turquoise body, unpainted diecast Corgi Juniors base, diecast wheels with five perimeter slots and black tires.
9. Bright yellow body, unpainted diecast Corgi Juniors base, narrow black Whizzwheels.
10. Metallic green body, unpainted diecast Corgi Juniors base, black Whizzwheels. (Body shade varies.)
11. Metallic green body, unpainted diecast Corgi Juniors base, chrome Whizzwheels. (Body shade varies.)

15-C	Mercedes-Benz Bus	74mm 1973-10/1983	
		Standard versions	$4-6
		Scorched version from set	$5-8

Black plastic base, and grille, Whizzwheels. (Prototype shown in 1982 Corgi catalog with yellow body and black "AUTOBUS" graphics, but not produced with that those graphics.) **[[Do you mean to say ...with those graphics. I.e. take out the "that?" Please confirm.]]**
1. Metallic blue body, yellow circle "School Bus" text with red outlined white stripe labels, red interior, clear windows.
2. Metallic blue body, yellow circle "School Bus" text with red outlined white stripe labels, yellow interior, amber tinted windows.
3. Dark yellow (almost orange) body, 2 black stripes and horizontal "School Bus" text labels with text through lower stripe only, yellow interior, amber tinted windows.

4. Light yellow body, "School Bus" labels with text through lower stripe only, yellow interior, amber tinted windows.
5. Light yellow body, "School Bus" labels with text through lower stripe only, red interior, amber tinted windows.
6. Light yellow body, "School Bus" labels with text through both stripes, yellow interior, amber tinted windows.
7. Light yellow body, "School Bus" labels with text through both stripes, yellow interior, clear windows.
8. Light yellow body, "School Bus" labels with text through both stripes, no interior, opaque windows.
9. Light yellow body, "School Bus" labels with text through both stripes, no interior, faces at windows, no labels; 1982.
10. Light yellow body, no labels, no interior, clear windows with printed cardboard passenger scene (as found on E-116.) 1983.
11. Light yellow body, no labels, no interior, opaque black windows; 1983.
12. Bright red body, no labels, no interior, opaque black windows; 1983-10/1983.
13. Bright green body, no labels, no interior, opaque black windows; 1983-10/1983.
14. Green body, white side stripe and "Holiday Inn" text, no interior, opaque black windows. (1983-10/1983. May be found packaged as J5.)
15. Metallic blue body, no labels, flat black "scorch marks" on sides, amber tinted windows. (Found only in late versions of E3021 Emergency 999 Gift Set.)

| 16-A | Aveling-Barford Dump Truck | 79mm 1965-1969 | $30-40 |

Vacuum plated plastic snowplow and base, no windows or interior, gray plastic wheels including dual wheels on rear.
1. Yellow chassis-cab, red tipper.
2. Red chassis-cab, gray tipper.
3. Red chassis-cab, yellow tipper.

| 16-B | Land Rover Pickup Truck | 71mm 1971-1976 | $10-15 |

No interior, black plastic base and tow hook, Whizzwheels. Baseplate type given when known.
(Note: Prototype shown in 1972 Corgi Juniors catalog in set E2503 with dark blue body, but not released in that color scheme.)
1. Metallic olive body, clear windows, smooth baseplate with patent application number.
2. Metallic olive body, amber tinted windows, smooth baseplate with patent application number.
3. Metallic spring green body, amber tinted windows, baseplate with patent number and suspension.
4. Non-metallic olive body, amber tinted windows.
5. Non-metallic medium green body, dark windows.
6. Non-metallic spring green body, clear windows.
7. Metallic light blue body, amber tinted windows.
8. Metallic light purple (lilac) body, amber tinted windows.

| 16-C | Rover 3500 Police Car | 77mm 1980-10/1983 | $4-6 |

Modified 8-D casting, opaque blue roof bar, opening rear hatch, Police labels on sides and hatch, black plastic base and tow hook, Whizzwheels.
1. White body, clear windows, red interior.
2. White body, clear windows, yellow interior.
3. White body, amber tinted windows, yellow interior.

| 17-A | Guy Warrior Milk Tanker | 70mm 1965-1968 | $30-40 |

Same castings as 14-A, rounded tank with "Milk" decals, blue tinted windows, no interior, vacuum plated plastic base and grille, gray plastic wheels.
1. White body, open rear quarter windows in cab.
2. White body, filled-in rear quarter windows in cab.

17-B	Guy Warrior Milk Tanker	73mm 1968-1969	
		Promotional versions	$50-100
		Milk	$30-40

Same casting as 14-B, squarish tank with "Milk" decals unless noted, blue tinted windows, no interior, unpainted diecast base and grille.
1. White body, gray plastic wheels.
2. Cream body, gray plastic wheels.
3. Cream body, diecast wheels with five slots and black tires.
4. Cream body, diecast wheels with five slots and black tires, "Milk" paper labels instead of decals.
5. White body, gray plastic wheels, "LS OLJAN" and "RYDBERG & STREIFFERT A-A TEL. 13 24 61" decals. (Promotional for Danish market, possibly Code 2.)

| 17-C | Volkswagen 1300 | 68mm 1972-1977 | $15-20 |

Clear windows, unpainted metal base, Whizzwheels, flower labels on roof and doors, sheet of additional labels supplied in earlier packaging versions.
1. Metallic olive body, yellow interior.

2. Metallic olive body, red interior.

3. Metallic turquoise body, yellow interior.

17-D   Buick City of Metropolis Police Car 76mm 1979-10/1983 $20-30

Vacuum plated plastic interior, bumpers, and grille unless noted, amber tinted windows unless noted, opaque red roof light, black plastic base, Whizzwheels, "CITY OF METROPOLIS POLICE" shield label on hood, white "POLICE" on blue label on sides.

1. Metallic dark blue body, white roof, amber tinted windows.

2. Non-metallic medium blue body, white roof, amber tinted windows.

3. Non-metallic medium blue body, white roof, unplated gray interior and bumpers, amber tinted windows. (Produced when vacuum plating equipment not functional.)

4. Non-metallic medium blue body, white roof, clear windows.

5. Non-metallic medium blue body including roof, unplated gray interior and bumpers, ??? windows. (Produced near time of Mettoy failure 1983.)

18-A   Jaguar Mark X (Plated)   66mm 1965-1967 $30-40

Same casting as 1-A, yellow interior, clear windows, vacuum plated plastic base, gray plastic wheels.

1. Light gold plated body.

18-B   Jaguar Mark X (Plated)   71mm 1967-1969 $30-40

Same castings as 1-B, yellow interior, clear windows, unpainted metal base. (Note: Shown in 1968 Husky catalog using Jaguar E-Type casting, but not released in that design.)

1. Silver vacuum plated body, gray plastic wheels.

2. Darker gold vacuum plated body, gray plastic wheels.

3. Darker gold vacuum plated body, diecast wheels with five perimeter slots and black tires.

4. Silver vacuum plated body, diecast wheels with five perimeter slots and black tires.

18-C   Wigwam Camper Van   77mm 1973-1975 $10-15

Detailed interior, amber tinted windows, black plastic base, Whizzwheels.

1. Metallic magenta (red) body.

2. Dark blue body.

3. Medium blue body.

4. Purple body.

18-D   AMF Ski-Daddler Snowmobile   1977-19?? $20-30

Black upper and lower body, yellow center section / seat / skis. (Same casting as used in front half of set E2506-A. Prototype shown in 1978 Corgi catalog with brown driver.)

1. Driver with all-over blue snowsuit, white helmet without goggles, black Whizzwheels.

2. Driver with all-over blue snowsuit, white helmet with goggles, silver foiled Whizzwheels.

3. Driver with all-over blue snowsuit and helmet with goggles, black Whizzwheels.

19-A   Commer "Walk-Thru" Van   64mm 1965-1969 $30-40

No interior, blue tinted windows, sliding side door, diecast base, gray plastic wheels.

1. Lime green body, red sliding door, light gray base.

2. Lime green body, red sliding door, unpainted base.

3. Lime green body, red sliding door, Combopost logo, other details not known, Netherlands promotional.

4. Red body and sliding door, unpainted base.

19-B   Sport Boat on Trailer   5mm 1969-1970, 1970-1973

Standard wheels	$15-20
Whizzwheels	$10-15
Bond Set version (loose)	$20-30

Cream deck, red hull unless noted, blue tinted windshield unless noted, blue outboard motor unless noted, diecast trailer.

1. Gold trailer, black plastic wheels with vacuum plated inserts, "Husky" lettering on hull; 1969.

2. Blue trailer, black plastic wheels with vacuum plated inserts, no lettering on hull, Corgi Juniors label on trailer; 1970.

3. Blue trailer, dished diecast wheels with black plastic tires, no lettering on hull, Corgi Juniors label on trailer; 1971. (Need verification on lettering and label.)

4. Gold trailer, black Whizzwheels, "Corgi Juniors" lettering on hull.

5. Blue trailer, narrow black Whizzwheels, "Corgi Juniors" lettering on hull.

6. Blue trailer, light blue motor, narrow chrome Whizzwheels, "Corgi Juniors" lettering on hull.

7. Metallic blue trailer, narrow chrome Whizzwheels, "Corgi Juniors" lettering on hull.

8. Blue trailer with wider fenders, light blue motor, wide chrome Whizzwheels, "Corgi Juniors" lettering on hull, blue tinted windshield.

9. Blue trailer with wider fenders, light blue motor, wide chrome Whizzwheels, "Corgi Juniors" lettering on hull, purple tinted windshield.

10. White deck, black hull, silver trailer, chrome Whizzwheels, "Corgi Juniors" lettering on hull. (Found only in James Bond Spy Who Loved Me Gift Set E3030-A1.)

11. Red deck, white hull, white trailer with wider fenders, black motor, wide chrome Whizzwheels, "Corgi Juniors" lettering on hull, clear windshield. (From sets E2553-A and later J205.)

19-C   Pink Panther Motorcycle   68mm 1980-1982 $20-30

Pink Panther figure, black spoked plastic wheels.(Prototype shown in 1980 Corgi catalog yellow shroud, but not released in that color scheme.)

1. Unpainted metal and red plastic motorcycle.

20-A   Ford Thames Van   61mm 1965-1969 $30-40

Yellow interior, antenna and ladder, opening rear doors, clear windows, vacuum plated plastic base and grille, gray plastic wheels.

1. Red body, including plastic opening doors.

20-B   Volkswagen 1300   66mm 1968-1969, 1970-1971

Regular wheels	$30-40
Whizzwheels	$20-30

Clear windows, unpainted diecast base, plastic luggage on roof.

1. Blue body, black luggage, yellow interior, diecast wheels with five perimeter slots and black tires, Husky base; 1968-1969.

2. Aqua body, brown luggage, yellow interior, diecast wheels with five perimeter slots and black tires, Husky base; 1968-1969.

3. Tan body, black luggage, yellow interior, diecast wheels with five perimeter slots and black tires, Husky base; 1969.

4. Yellow body, black luggage, yellow interior, diecast wheels with five perimeter slots and black tires, Husky base; 1969.

5. Yellow body, brown luggage, red interior, diecast wheels with five perimeter slots and black tires, Corgi Juniors label on base; 1970.

6. Yellow body, brown luggage, yellow interior, diecast wheels with five perimeter slots and black tires, Corgi Juniors label on base; 1970.

7. Red body, black luggage, yellow interior, black wide Whizzwheels, modified base; 1971.

8. Orange body, black luggage, yellow interior, black wide Whizzwheels, modified base; 1971.

20-C   Cement Mixer Trailer   45mm 1976-1977 $10-15

Amber plastic cover raises, gold engine, red plastic barrel, wheel and tow bar, black plastic wheels. (Shown in 1976 catalog with yellow body, but not produced in this color scheme.)

1. Plated diecast body.

20-D   Penguinmobile   73mm 1979-1981 $20-30

Same body casting as 82-A but without "Growler" feature in baseplate, "The Penguin" driver with top hat, black plastic base, Whizzwheels.

1. White body, blue engine behind driver, "Penguin" label on spoiler, umbrella label on hood with copyright at bottom edge.

2. White body, blue engine behind driver, "Penguin" label on spoiler, umbrella label on hood without copyright at bottom edge.

3. White body, red engine behind driver, "Penguin" label on spoiler, umbrella label on hood without copyright at bottom edge.

4. White body, yellow engine behind driver, "Penguin" label on spoiler, umbrella label on hood without copyright at bottom edge.

5. White body, black engine behind driver, "Penguin" label on spoiler, umbrella label on hood without copyright at bottom edge.

21-A   Military Forward Control Land Rover 66mm 1965-1968 $30-40

Blue tinted windows, no interior, olive plastic removable rear cover, white star decal on cab roof, gray plastic wheels. (Also see H11-A.)

1. Olive drab body including integral base, small rear corner windows in cab, no suspension, front bumper part of body.

2. Olive drab body, black plastic base with suspension, small rear corner windows in cab, front bumper part of base.

3. Olive drab body, black plastic base with suspension, no corner windows, front bumper part of base.

21-B   Jaguar E Type 2+2   69mm 1968-1969 $30-40

Yellow interior, clear windows, diecast wheels with radial fins and black tires, diecast Husky lower body-base.

1. Metallic maroon body and base. (Also packaged as Husky 71.)

21-C   B.V.R.T Vita-Mini 1300 Mini-Cooper S 55mm 1970-1974 $15-20

Vacuum plated plastic interior and engine, blue tinted windows, unpainted diecast base and grille, Whizzwheels, number 73 and other racing labels.

1. Metallic purple body.

21-D   Chevrolet Charlie's Angels Van   68mm 1977-1980 $20-30

No interior, transparent windows unless noted, black plastic base, Whizzwheels, side labels with "Charlie's Angels" logo and mock window. (Note: Shade of pink may vary from pale to medium.)

1. Pink body, blue tinted windows, "Chevrolet Van" lettering on base, circular window on side labels.

2. Pink body, amber tinted windows, "Chevrolet Van" lettering on base, circular window on side labels, light ribs on roof.

3. Pink body, blue tinted windows, "U.S. Van" lettering on base, circular window on side labels, light ribs on roof.

4. Pink body, blue tinted windows, "U.S. Van" lettering on base, rectangular window on side labels, light ribs on roof.

5. Pink body, amber tinted windows, "U.S. Van" lettering on base, rectangular window on side labels, heavy ribs on roof.

6. Pink body, amber tinted windows, "Chevrolet Van" lettering on base, rectangular window on side labels, heavy ribs on roof.

7. Pink body, red tinted windows, "U.S. Van" lettering on base, rectangular window on side labels.

22-A   Citroen Safari Military Ambulance   64mm 1965-1968 $30-40

Modified 2-A casting, blue interior, blue tinted rear windows and dome light, clear front windows, red cross decal on hood, vacuum plated plastic base, gray plastic wheels.

1. Olive drab body.

22-B   Aston Martin DB6   73mm 1968-1969, 1970 $30-40

Yellow interior, vacuum plated plastic base and grille unless noted. (Later Husky versions also found packaged as Husky 72 for the US market. This is not the James Bond version.)

1. Metallic bronze body, clear windows, gray plastic wheels, Husky base; 1968.

2. Metallic purple body, clear windows, gray plastic wheels, Husky base; 1968.

3. Metallic purple body, clear windows, diecast wheels with five perimeter slots and black tires, Husky base; 1969.

4. Metallic purple body, blue tinted windows, diecast wheels with five perimeter slots and black tires, Husky base; 1969.

5. Metallic purple body, clear windows, diecast wheels with five perimeter slots and black tires, Corgi Juniors label over "HUSKY" on base; 1970. (Produced during transition to Corgi Juniors product name.)

6. Metallic purple body, blue tinted windows, diecast wheels with five perimeter slots and black tires, Corgi Juniors label over "HUSKY" on base; 1970. (Produced during transition to Corgi Juniors product name.)

7. Metallic olive body, blue tinted windows, diecast wheels with five perimeter slots and black tires, Husky base; 1969.

8. Metallic olive body, blue tinted windows, diecast wheels with five perimeter slots and black tires, Corgi Juniors label over "HUSKY" on base; 1970. (Produced during transition to Corgi Juniors product name.)

9. Metallic olive body, blue tinted windows, diecast wheels with five perimeter slots and black tires, Corgi Juniors label over blank area on base; 1970.

22-C   Formula 1 Racer   74mm 1973-1978 $10-15

Gold diecast engine, roll bar and windshield, white driver, unpainted diecast base, Whizzwheels.

1. Dark yellow body, Union Jack and number 3 labels.

2. Dark yellow body, Weetabix labels; promotional model.

22-D   Paramedic Emergency Unit   68mm 1981-1982 + Sets $4-6

Chevrolet van casting, no interior, transparent windows unless noted, red and black graphics on white side labels unless noted, black plastic base unless noted, Whizzwheels.

1. White body, blue tinted windows, "U.S. VAN" on base, heavy ribs on roof.

2. White body, blue tinted windows, "U.S. VAN" on base, light ribs on roof.

3. White body, amber tinted windows, "U.S. VAN" on base, light ribs on roof.

4. White body, blue tinted windows, "CHEVROLET VAN" on base, light ribs on roof.

5. White body, amber tinted windows, "CHEVROLET VAN" on gray plastic base, light ribs on roof.

6. White body, amber tinted windows, "U.S. VAN" on blue plastic base, heavy ribs on roof.

7. White body, amber tinted windows, "U.S. VAN" on red plastic base, heavy ribs on roof.

8. White body, opaque black windows, "U.S. VAN" on blue plastic base, light ribs on roof.

9. White body, opaque black windows, blank plastic base, heavy ribs on roof.

10. White body, opaque black windows, "U.S. VAN" on base, heavy ribs on roof.

11. White body, opaque black windows, "U.S. VAN" on base, heavy ribs on roof, side graphics tampo printed on sides.

12. White body, opaque black windows, blank base, light ribs on roof, side graphics tampo printed on sides.

13. White body, clear windows, blank base, light ribs on roof, side graphics tampo printed on sides.

23-A   Guy Warrior U.S. Army Tanker   70mm 1965-1967 $30-40

Same castings as 14-A and 17-A, blue tinted windows, no interior, vacuum plated plastic base and grille, white star and U.S. Army decals, gray plastic wheels.

1. Olive drab body, open rear quarter windows in cab.

2. Olive drab body, filled-in rear quarter windows in cab.

23-B   Loadmaster Shovel   78mm 1967-1969, 1970-1974 $30-40

No interior, working shovel, large knobby black plastic wheels.

1. Dark orange body, green tinted windows, vacuum plated plastic shovel and Husky base with four rivet locations; 1967-1968.

2. Yellow body, green tinted windows, vacuum plated plastic shovel and Husky base with four rivet locations; 1968-1969.

3. Yellow body, clear windows, vacuum plated plastic shovel and Husky base with side rivet locations blanked; 1968-1969.

4. Yellow body, clear windows, modified diecast shovel, vacuum plated plastic Husky base with side rivet locations blanked; 1969.

5. Modified yellow body with modified rear fender shape and other differences, clear windows, modified diecast shovel, modified diecast Corgi Juniors base; 1970-1974. (Made from different die set incorporating many minor changes.)

23-C   Batbike   68mm 1979-10/1983 $20-30

Batman figure, black plastic five-spoke wheels.

1. Unpainted diecast and black plastic motorcycle, black cowl with black and yellow bat label.

2. Unpainted diecast and black plastic motorcycle, black cowl without label.

24-A   Ford Zephyr Estate Car   61mm 1966-1969

                                                Red $50-75

                                                Blue $30-40

Yellow interior, clear windows, vacuum plated plastic base and grille, gray plastic wheels, opening hatch. (Drawn with white body in early catalog, but not released in that color.)

1. Metallic blue body.

2. Metallic dark red body.

24-B   Aston Martin DBS   73mm 1971-1973 $15-20

White interior, clear windows, unpainted diecast base and grille, opening black hood, detailed engine, Whizzwheels. (Note: Prototype shown in 1973 Corgi Toys catalog with tan body, but not released in that color scheme. Different prototype shown in 1974 Corgi Juniors catalog with dark blue body and white base, but not released in that color scheme.)

1. Light yellow-green body, black hood.

24-C   Shazam Thunderbolt   77mm 1979-1980 $20-30

Same casting as 28-B, amber windshield, driver, vacuum plated plastic engine and exhaust pipes, red-yellow-black labels, white diecast base, Whizzwheels.

1. Yellow body.

25-A   S. & D. Refuse Wagon   69mm 1966-1969, 1970-1972 $30-40

Blue tinted windows, no interior, vacuum plated plastic base and tipping rear body.

1. Light blue chassis-cab, poorly defined cab roof ribs and step at rear edge of body casting, gray plastic wheels, Husky base, no ribs on roof of rear hinged section.

2. Light blue chassis-cab, well defined cab roof ribs, no step at rear edge of body casting, gray plastic wheels, Husky base, ribs on roof of rear hinged section.

3. Red chassis-cab, well defined cab roof ribs, no step at rear edge of body casting, gray plastic wheels, Husky base, ribs on roof of rear hinged section.

4. Red chassis-cab, well defined cab roof ribs, no step at rear edge of body casting, black plastic wheels with vacuum plated inserts, Husky base, ribs on roof of rear hinged section.

5. Orange chassis-cab, well defined cab roof ribs, no step at rear edge of body casting, black plastic wheels with vacuum plated inserts, Corgi Juniors label on base, ribs on roof of rear hinged section. 1970-1971.

6. Orange chassis-cab, well defined cab roof ribs, no step at rear edge of body casting, dished diecast wheels with black tires, Corgi Juniors cast into base, ribs on roof of rear hinged section. 1971-1972.

25-B   Captain America's Porsche 917   72mm 1979-1980 $20-30

Same body casting as 51-A and 94-A, vacuum plated plastic interior, red tinted windows, vacuum plated plastic engine, black plastic base, smaller front and larger rear Whizzwheels, red-white-blue Captain America labels.

1. Metallic dark blue body, matching spoke pattern on front and rear wheels.

2. Metallic medium blue body, mismatched spoke pattern on front and rear wheels.

26-A   Sunbeam Alpine   61mm 1966-1969 $30-40

Blue (almost black) plastic top, clear windows, yellow interior, vacuum plated plastic base. (Drawn with light blue body in early catalog, but not released in that color.)

1. Metallic cooper body, gray plastic wheels.

2. Red body, gray plastic wheels.

3. Red body, black plastic wheels with vacuum plated inserts.

26-B   ERF Fire Tender   76mm 1970-1974 $10-15

Yellow ladder, blue tinted windows and dome lights, no interior, silver diecast base, grille and body panels, Whizzwheels.

1. Red body.

26-C   ERF Fire Tender   76mm 1975-1980, 1982-10/1983 $4-6

Yellow ladder, no interior, black plastic base, headlights and rear panel. Grille is now part of body casting. Whizzwheels.

1. Red body, blue tinted windows and dome light.

2. Red body, opaque black windows and dome light. (1983)

27-A   Bedford TK 7-Ton Lorry   72mm 1966-1969, 1970-1971

                                Maroon, Red, Orange $30-40

                                Dark Green $AUCTION

No interior or windows, diecast bucket and swinging arms, vacuum plated plastic base. (Also found as Husky 77 in the USA market.)

1. Dark green body, unpainted bucket and arms, gray plastic wheels, Husky base.

2. Maroon body, unpainted bucket and arms, gray plastic wheels, Husky base.

3. Red body, silver bucket and arms, gray plastic wheels, Husky base.

4. Red body, silver bucket and arms, black plastic wheels with vacuum plated inserts, Husky base.

5. Red body, silver bucket and arms, black plastic wheels with vacuum plated inserts, Corgi Juniors label on base; 1970.

6. Red body, yellow diecast bucket, silver arms, dished diecast wheels with black plastic tires, Corgi Juniors cast into base; 1971.

7. Orange-red body, yellow diecast bucket, silver arms, dished diecast wheels with black plastic tires, Corgi Juniors cast into base; 1971.

27-B   Formula 5000 Racing Car   74mm 1973-1981 $4-6

Gold engine and windshield, plastic driver, diecast base, Whizzwheels. (Note: Prototype shown in 1977 Corgi Juniors catalog with dark blue body, but not released in that color scheme.)

1. Black body, white driver, gold radiators, number 4 with blue and white stripe labels, white base.

2. Red body, yellow driver, number 4 with blue and white stripe labels, unpainted base. Casting changed to eliminate radiators.

3. Red body, yellow driver, number 8 with yellow and silver stripe labels, unpainted base. Casting changed to eliminate radiators.

4. Red body, white driver, number 8 with yellow and silver stripe labels, unpainted base. Casting changed to eliminate radiators.

28-A   Ford F-350 Wrecker   78mm 1966-1969, 1970-1971

                                Regular wheels $30-40

                                Whizzwheels $20-30

Blue-green tinted windows, no interior, vacuum plated plastic boom, framing, and base-grille unless noted. (Drawn with red body in early catalog, but not released in that color.)

1. Light blue body, gray plastic wheels, vacuum plated plastic Husky base; 1966-1967

2. Light blue body, black plastic wheels with vacuum plated inserts, vacuum plated plastic Husky base; 1967-1968

3. Medium blue body, black plastic wheels with vacuum plated inserts, vacuum plated plastic Husky base; 1968-1969.

4. Dark blue body, black plastic wheels with vacuum plated inserts, vacuum plated plastic base with Corgi Juniors label; 1970.

5. Dark blue body, thin black Whizzwheels, modified vacuum plated plastic base with "CORGI JUNIORS" and "WHIZZWHEELS" text, "FORD F350 TRUCK" text moved to rear of base and "PAT APP 3396/69" added to front of base; 1970.

6. Pale green body, thin black Whizzwheels, modified vacuum plated plastic base with "CORGI JUNIORS" and "WHIZZWHEELS" text, "FORD F350 TRUCK" text moved to rear of base and "PAT APP 3396/69" added to front of base; 1970.

7. Turquoise green body, black Whizzwheels, silver painted diecast Corgi Juniors base; 1971.

28-B   Hot Rodder   77mm 1973-1976 $15-18

Vacuum plated plastic interior, engine, and exhaust pipes, amber tinted windshield, white diecast base, red and blue stripe labels with white stars, Whizzwheels.

(Prototype shown in 1974 Corgi catalog with lime green body, but not released in this color scheme.)

1. Yellow body.

28-C   Buick Regal Police Car   76mm 1977-1979 $8-12

Vacuum plated plastic interior, bumpers and grille, amber tinted windows, red roof light, black plastic base with suspension, Whizzwheels, white and black Police labels.

1. White body, black roof, red taillights.

2. White body, black roof, white taillights.

28-D   Buick Regal Sheriff's Car   76mm 1980-1980 $8-12

Same casting and details as 28-C except for black and white Sheriff labels, base with suspension.

1. Black body, white roof, amber tinted windows.

2. Black body, white roof, clear windows.

29-A   ERF Cement Mixer Truck   70mm 1966-1969 $25-35

Green tinted windows, no interior, red plastic barrel, turning chute, vacuum plated plastic base.

1. Yellow body with corner cab windows, chrome plastic chute, gray plastic wheels.

2. Yellow body without corner cab windows, chrome plastic chute, gray plastic wheels.

3. Yellow body without corner cab windows, unpainted diecast chute, gray plastic wheels.

4. Yellow body without corner cab windows, unpainted diecast chute, black plastic wheels with vacuum plated inserts.

29-B   ERF Simon Snorkel Fire Engine   79mm 1970-1971 $15-20

Same casting as 36-A, no interior or windows, vacuum plated plastic upper and lower snorkel arms, basket, mounting, and baseplate.

1. Dark red body, diecast wheels with five perimeter slots and black plastic tires, Corgi Juniors label on vacuum plated plastic base; 1970.

2. Dark red body, black Whizzwheels, Corgi Juniors base.

29-C   ERF Simon Snorkel Fire Engine   76mm 1972-1973 $10-15

New casting with longer cab, blue tinted windows, no interior, amber-yellow plastic upper and lower snorkel arms, basket and mounting, unpainted diecast base, Whizzwheels.

1. Dark red body, deep basket.

29-D   ERF Simon Snorkel Fire Engine   76mm 1974-10/1983 $4-6

Same body casting as 29-C, no interior, new type snorkel with shallow basket and other changes, plastic base color matches booms, Whizzwheels.

1. Dark red body, gray plastic booms and base. (need verification)

2. Bright red body, amber-yellow plastic booms and base, blue tinted windows.

3. Bright red body, yellow plastic booms and base, blue tinted windows.

4. Bright red body, yellow plastic booms and base, opaque black windows.

5. Bright red body, amber-yellow plastic booms and base, opaque black windows, blanked text at rear of base. (1982)

6. Bright red body, yellow plastic booms and base, opaque black windows, blanked text at rear of base. (Early 1983 as E29, number later changed to J8.)

30-A   Studebaker Wagonaire   75mm 1966-1969, 1970-1971

     Ambulance   Ambulance $30-40

                           Civilian (loose from set) $40-50

White interior, blue tinted windows, sliding rear roof panel, removable stretcher, opening tailgate.

1. White body, red cross decal on hood, vacuum plated plastic base, gray plastic wheels.

2. White body, red cross decal on hood, vacuum plated plastic base, diecast wheels with five perimeter slots and black tires.

3. White body, red cross label on hood, diecast Corgi Juniors base, diecast wheels with five perimeter slots and black tires; 1970.

4. White body, red cross label on hood, diecast Corgi Juniors base, narrow black Whizzwheels; 1970.

5. Light yellow body, white seats, blue tinted windows, white tailgate, no stretcher, diecast wheels with five perimeter slots and black tires, vacuum plated plastic Husky base. (Found in H3005-A/B Holiday/Leisure Time Gift Set only.)

6. Beige (cornflower yellow) body, white seats, blue tinted windows, white tailgate, no stretcher, diecast wheels with five perimeter slots and black tires, vacuum plated plastic Husky base. (Found in H3005-A/B Holiday/Leisure Time Gift Set only.)

7. Beige (cornflower yellow) body, white seats, blue tinted windows, white tailgate, no stretcher, diecast wheels with five perimeter slots and black tires, diecast Husky base. (Found in H3005-A/B Holiday/Leisure Time Gift Set only.)

30-B   Studebaker Wagonaire Ambulance   75mm 1971-1972 $25-35

Modified casting with cast-in tailgate and braces, ridged blue tinted rear windows and roof panel permanently half open, white interior with stretcher, diecast base, black Whizzwheels, red cross label on hood. (Also found in E3021 Emergency 999 Gift Set.)

1. White body.

30-C   Studebaker Wagonaire Ambulance 75mm 1972-1973? $20-30
Modified casting with two sirens on roof, blue dome light, modified base with smaller 'Whizzwheels' lettering and "Pat App" at rear axle, otherwise as 30-B. (Also found in E3021 Emergency 999 Gift Set.)
1. White body.

30-D   Ford Mobile Cement Mixer73mm 1976-1980, 1982-10/1983 $4-6
Plastic rotating barrel and base including barrel support, no interior, Whizzwheels. (Prototype shown in 1980 Corgi catalog with brick red body, opaque windows, silver barrel and black rear support. But not produced in that color scheme.)
1. Metallic olive green body, yellow barrel and base, amber tinted windows; 1976-1979.
2. Metallic olive green body, yellow barrel and base, opaque black windows; 1979?
3. Non-metallic green body, yellow barrel and base, amber tinted windows.
4. Non-metallic green body, white barrel and base, opaque black windows.
5. Red body, silver barrel, black base, tinted windows? 1980?
6. Red body, white barrel, white bracket and base, opaque black windows.
7. Yellow body, red barrel and base, opaque black windows.
8. Blue body, white barrel and base, blue tinted windows.
9. Blue body, black barrel, white bracket and base, opaque black windows; 1983.
10. Blue body, white barrel, tan bracket and base, opaque black windows; 1983.
11. Blue body, white barrel and base, opaque black windows; 1983.
12. Blue body, tan barrel and base, opaque black windows; (Found in 1983-84 transitional period 2-pack to sell-off existing stock. May not have been sold separately.)
13. Orange body, black barrel and base, clear windows; 1982.
14. Orange body, white barrel and base, opaque black windows. (Found in 1983-84 transitional period 2-pack to sell-off existing stock. May not have been sold separately.)

31-A   Oldsmobile Starfire   76mm 1966-1969 $30-40
Yellow interior, clear windows, opening trunk, vacuum plated plastic base-grille.
1. Light metallic blue body, gray plastic wheels.
2. Dark metallic blue body, gray plastic wheels.
3. Dark metallic olive green body, gray plastic wheels.
4. Medium metallic olive green body, gray plastic wheels.
5. Medium metallic olive green body, black plastic wheels with vacuum plated inserts.

31-B   Land Rover Wrecker   73mm 1970-1980
    Standard versions $10-15
    Promotional $15-20
Amber tinted windows and dome light unless noted, plated diecast hook, black plastic base, Silver trimmed Whizzwheels unless otherwise noted. Baseplate type given when known.
1. Metallic purple body, "Wrecker Truck" labels, smooth baseplate with patent application number and clip for hook.
2. Red body, "Wrecker Truck" labels, smooth baseplate with patent application number and clip for hook.
3. Red body, "Wrecker Truck" labels, smooth baseplate with patent application number and blank rear tab without clip feature.
4. Red body, "Wrecker Truck" labels, baseplate with patent number and visible suspension.
5. Metallic blue body, "24 HOUR Crash Service" labels, black Whizzwheels.
6. Metallic blue body, "24 HOUR Crash Service" labels.
7. Metallic blue body, no labels, baseplate with patent number and visible suspension.
8. Metallic dark blue body, "24 HOUR Crash Service" labels on clear plastic backing, baseplate with patent number and visible suspension.
9. Non-metallic light blue body, "24 HOUR Crash Service" labels on blue paper backing, black Whizzwheels.
10. Non-metallic light blue body, "24 HOUR Crash Service" labels on blue paper backing.
11. Non-metallic medium blue body, "24 HOUR Crash Service" labels on blue paper backing, baseplate with patent number and visible suspension.
12. Red body, black plastic baseplate with patent number without suspension, amber tinted windows, no labels, shorter silver hook.
13. Red body, black plastic baseplate with patent number without suspension, red tinted windows, no labels, shorter silver hook. (May be from after Mettoy closure.)
14. Red body, black plastic baseplate with patent number without suspension, blue tinted windows, no labels, shorter silver hook.

15. Matte olive green body, "RECOVERY" label, black Whizzwheels. (Found in Military Set E3029-A.)
16. Metallic dark blue body, "Motor Trader" labels on sides. (Promotional for Motor Trader magazine.)
17. Red body, black plastic base, blue tinted windows, "M1 BREAKDOWN" on doors. (May be from set around or after Mettoy closure.)

32-A   Volkswagen Luggage Elevator Truck 78mm 1966-1969 $30-40
Same casting as 12-A, blue tinted windows, no interior, light blue conveyor frame and ramp, rubber conveyor belt turned by unpainted diecast knob, gray plastic wheels, vacuum plated plastic base, packaged with loose light blue luggage on sprue.
1. White body, yellow conveyor belt.
2. White body, red conveyor belt.
3. Red body, red conveyor belt.

32-B   Lotus Europa   71mm 1970-1974 $15-20
Clear windows, silver diecast lower body-base, Whizzwheels, Union Jack label on one side only.
1. Dark metallic green body, yellow interior and opening rear hatch.
2. Dark metallic green body, orange-yellow interior and opening rear hatch.
3. Light non-metallic green body, yellow interior and opening rear hatch.

32-C   The Saint's Jaguar XJS   76mm 1978-1981 $15-18
Same casting as 72-B, clear windows, black plastic base, Whizzwheels.
1. White body, red interior, black Saint figure label on hood.
2. White body, yellow interior, black Saint figure label on hood.

33-A   Farm Livestock Trailer   69mm 1967-1969, 1970-1970 $25-35
Opening diecast tailgate, four tan plastic calves and base, yellow plastic wheels with tires, bottom of body casting forms base, no axle between wheels. (Drawn in yellow in the 1966 Husky Models catalog, but not produced in that body color.)
1. Olive green body and tailgate, Husky name on base, tires without edge bead (implement tires.)
2. Olive green body and tailgate, Husky name on base, tires with edge bead.
3. Turquoise body and tailgate, Husky name on base, tires without edge bead (implement tires.)
4. Turquoise body and tailgate, Husky name on base, tires with edge bead.
5. Orange or Turquoise body and tailgate, Corgi Juniors label on base, tires with edge bead. (Need verification as to which body color exists.)
6. Orange body and tailgate, Corgi Juniors name cast into base, tires with edge bead.
7. Orange body and tailgate, Corgi Juniors name cast into base, tires without edge bead (implement tires.)

33-B   Jaguar E-Type 2+2   71mm 1970-1975+ $10-15
Raising hood, detailed engine part of body casting, clear windows, silver diecast base, Whizzwheels. (Later revised to E39-B.)
1. Yellow body, red interior.
2. Yellow body, yellow interior.
3. Blue body, red interior.
4. Blue body, yellow interior.
5. Blue body, white interior.
6. Red body, white interior.

33-C   Chevrolet Ambulance Van   (1977?)   N/A
Not issued. (See E22-D.)

33-D   Wonder Woman's Wonder Car   62mm 1979-1980 $20-30
Same castings as 74-A, black interior with driver, interior forms black stripe around model's front and sides, white diecast base, Whizzwheels.
1. Orange upper body, amber windshield, Wonder Woman hood label.
2. Orange upper body, blue windshield, Wonder Woman hood label.

34-A   Volvo 400 Farm Tractor 54mm 1967-1969, 1970-1974 $25-35
Diecast base same color as body, unequally sized yellow plastic wheels with black farm implement tires front and black tractor tires rear (unless noted,) silver grille and headlamps.
1. Red body and base including engine, black exhaust stack, Husky base.
2. Red body and base including engine and stack, Husky base.
3. Red body and base including engine and stack, Corgi Juniors label on base.
4. Red body and base including engine and stack, Corgi Juniors cast into base, front tires with beaded edge.

34-B   Stinger Army Helicopter   70mm 1975-1978 $10-15
Plastic interior, parts, skids and rotors, clear canopy.
1. Olive drab body, black interior, skids and rotors, white "Army" labels.
2. White body, light blue interior, skids and rotors, "SEARCH" labels. (Found in Rescue Set E3023-A1.)

3. White body, light blue interior, skids and rotors, no labels. (Found in Rescue Set E3023-A1.)

34-C   Chevrolet Hertz Rental Van   68mm 1980-10/1983 $4-6
No interior, black plastic base unless noted, Hertz Truck Rental side labels, Whizzwheels.
1. Yellow body, "CHEVROLET VAN" base, clear windows, ??? ribs on roof.
2. Yellow body, "CHEVROLET VAN" base, blue tinted windows, light ribs on roof.
3. Yellow body, "CHEVROLET VAN" base, amber tinted windows, light ribs on roof.
4. Yellow body, "CHEVROLET VAN" base, amber tinted windows, heavy ribs on roof.
5. Yellow body, "U.S. VAN" base, amber tinted windows, light ribs on roof.
6. Yellow body, "U.S. VAN" base, opaque black windows, ??? ribs on roof.
7. Yellow body, "U.S. VAN" on yellow plastic base, opaque black windows, ??? ribs on roof. (Transitional era 2-pack with Coca-Cola truck to clear existing stock.)

35-A   Ford F-350 Camper   78mm 1967-1969, 1970-1972 $30-40
Plastic camper with interior, diecast pickup with windows but no interior. (Later Husky versions also packaged as Husky 85.)
1. Dark yellow pickup, vacuum plated camper body with smooth roof and yellow door, yellow interior, green tinted windows, vacuum plated plastic Husky base, gray plastic wheels.
2. Dark yellow pickup, vacuum plated camper body with smooth roof and yellow door, yellow interior, blue tinted windows, vacuum plated plastic Husky base, gray plastic wheels.
3. Dark metallic blue pickup, vacuum plated camper body with smooth roof and yellow door, yellow interior, blue tinted windows, vacuum plated plastic Husky base, gray plastic wheels.
4. Dark metallic blue pickup, vacuum plated camper body with smooth roof and yellow door, yellow interior, blue tinted windows, vacuum plated plastic Husky base, black plastic wheels with vacuum plated inserts.
5. Dark metallic blue pickup, vacuum plated camper body with ribs on roof and yellow door, yellow interior, blue tinted windows, vacuum plated plastic Husky base, black plastic wheels with vacuum plated inserts.
6. Turquoise pickup, vacuum plated camper body with ribs on roof and yellow door, yellow interior, green tinted windows, vacuum plated plastic Husky base, black plastic wheels with vacuum plated inserts; 1969.
7. Turquoise pickup, vacuum plated camper body with ribs on roof and yellow door, yellow interior, green tinted windows, vacuum plated plastic base with Corgi Juniors label, black plastic wheels with vacuum plated inserts; 1970.
8. Turquoise pickup, vacuum plated camper body with ribs on roof and yellow door, yellow interior, green tinted windows, vacuum plated plastic base with Corgi Juniors label, dished diecast wheels with black tires; 1970.
9. Turquoise pickup, vacuum plated camper body with ribs on roof and yellow door, yellow interior, green tinted windows, silver painted diecast base, black Whizzwheels, modified wheel wells on pickup.
10. Red pickup, white camper body with ribs on roof, yellow door and interior, green tinted windows, silver painted diecast base, black Whizzwheels, modified wheel wells on pickup.
11. Red pickup, white camper body and interior with ribs on roof, green tinted windows, silver painted diecast base, black Whizzwheels, modified wheel wells on pickup.
12. Red pickup, white camper and interior with ribs on roof, green tinted windows, silver painted diecast base, chrome 5-spk pattern Whizzwheels, modified wheel wells on pickup.

35-B   Air Bus Helicopter   70mm 1975-1979 $8-12
Left and right body castings, black plastic rotors and base with landing gear, base also forms interior, clear windows. (Casting also used for E40-B Army Red Cross Helicopter. Prototype shown in 1975 Corgi Juniors catalog with white body and blue rotors, but not produced in that color scheme.)
1. Orange body, White "A" with black "AIRBUS" graphics.
2. Metallic blue body, White "A" and "AIRBUS" graphics.

35-C   Tipper Truck   71mm 1983-10/1983 $4-6
Same casting and tipper as 49-B, clear windows, no interior, black plastic base, Whizzwheels, unpainted tailgate.
1. Silver body, blue tipper?
2. Red body, tan tipper.
3. Red body, white tipper.

36-A   Simon Snorkel Fire Engine   79mm 1967-1969 $25-35
No windows or interior, vacuum plated plastic upper and lower snorkel arms, basket, mounting and base. (Also found as H86 in USA.)
1. Dark red body, gray plastic wheels.

2. Dark red body, diecast wheels with five perimeter slots and black plastic tires.
3. Medium red body, diecast wheels with five perimeter slots and black tires.

36-B   Healer Wheeler   76mm 1973-1977 $10-15
Black plastic base with "HEALER WHEELER" text, Whizzwheels, black-white-red hood triangle label. (Casting also used for E99-A.)
1. White body, round red cross labels behind doors, clear windows, blue tinted interior and roof light.
2. White body, side labels with black "Ambulance" and red cross, clear windows, blue tinted interior and roof light.
3. White body, side labels with black "Ambulance" and red cross, blue tinted windows and roof light, transparent blue interior.
4. White body, side labels with black "Ambulance" and red cross, purple tinted windows and roof light, transparent purple interior.
5. White body, side labels with black "Ambulance" and red cross, blue tinted windows and roof light, no interior.

36-C   Chevrolet Coca-Cola Van   68mm 1979-1980+ $10-12
Blue tinted windows unless noted, no interior, black plastic base, Whizzwheels with vacuum plated center pattern unless noted.
1. Red body, red and white Coca-Cola logo side labels, "CHEVROLET VAN" base, light ribs on roof.
2. Red body, red and white Coca-Cola logo side labels, "U.S. VAN" base, light ribs on roof.
3. Red body, red and white Coca-Cola logo side labels, "U.S. VAN" base, heavy ribs on roof.
4. Red body, red and white Coca-Cola logo side labels, "U.S. VAN" base, light ribs on roof, black wheels.
5. Red body, red and white Coca-Cola logo side labels, "U.S. VAN" base, heavy ribs on roof, black wheels.
6. Red body, red and white Coca-Cola logo side labels, "U.S. VAN" base with Corgi Juniors blanked-out, heavy ribs on roof.
7. Red body, red and white Coca-Cola logo side labels, "U.S. VAN" base, heavy ribs on roof, opaque black windows.
8. Red body, red and white Coca-Cola logo side labels, blank base, ??? ribs on roof, opaque black windows.
9. Red body, red and white Coca-Cola logo Tampo printed on sides, "U.S. VAN" base, heavy ribs on roof, opaque black windows.
(Note: Versions with tampo printed sides also exist from the Corgi Toys Ltd. era, and may have started production prior to Mettoy's closure.)

37-A   NSU RO 80   70mm 1969-1970, 1970-1973 $30-40
Opening hood, vacuum plated plastic engine, interior, bumpers and grille. (Note: Drawn in 1968 Husky catalog with pale yellow body, but not released in that color scheme or that year.)
1. Metallic aqua body, clear windows, blue diecast Husky base, black plastic wheels with vacuum plated inserts; 1969.
2. Metallic medium blue body, clear windows, blue diecast Husky base, black plastic wheels with vacuum plated inserts; 1969.
3. Metallic dark blue body, blue tinted windows, dark blue diecast base with Corgi Juniors label in large blank area, black plastic wheels with vacuum plated inserts; 1970.
4. Metallic light purple body and diecast Corgi Juniors base, green tinted windows, black dished 5-spoke Whizzwheels; 1971.
5. Metallic light purple body and diecast Corgi Juniors base, purple-blue tinted windows, black dished 5-spoke Whizzwheels; 1971. (Similar to window color found on early E41-A Porsche.)
6. Metallic dark purple body and diecast Corgi Juniors base, green tinted windows, black dished 5-spoke Whizzwheels; 1971.
7. Magenta (pink) body and Corgi Juniors base, black hood, green tinted windows, black flat 5-spoke Whizzwheels; 1972.
8. Magenta (pink) body and Corgi Juniors base, black hood, green tinted windows, Whizzwheels; 1972.
9. Magenta (pink) body and Corgi Juniors base, black hood, clear windows, Whizzwheels; 1972.
10. Magenta (pink) body and Corgi Juniors base, black hood, yellow tinted windows, Whizzwheels; 1972.
11. Metallic bronze body and Corgi Juniors base, black hood, amber tinted windows, Whizzwheels; 1973.
12. Metallic bronze body and Corgi Juniors base, black hood, clear windows, Whizzwheels; 1973.
13. Non-metallic blue body and Corgi Juniors base, black hood, ??? tinted windows, Whizzwheels; 1973.

14. White body, Black Corgi Juniors base, black hood, blue tinted windows, Whizzwheels; 1973. (May have been part of a set.)

37-B   Porsche Carrera Police Car   74mm 1976-1980

Police	$4-6
Polizei	$10-15

Blue tinted windows and dome lights, black plastic base, Whizzwheels, Police labels. (Note: Similar model without roof lights is from after Mettoy closure.)

1. White body, red interior, large white background door labels with tall blue "POLICE" over blue outlined red stripe.

2. White body, yellow interior, large white background door labels with tall blue "POLICE" over blue outlined red stripe.

3. White body, yellow interior, small white background door labels with short blue "POLICE" under blue outlined red stripe.

4. White body, red interior, low florescent orange background door labels with short blue "POLICE" over blue outlined stripe which is the background color.

5. White body with green hood , green "Polizei" labels on doors, red interior. (German issue.)

38-A   Rice Beaufort Horse Trailer69mm 1968-1969, 1970-1971 + SETS

Regular Wheels	$15-20
Whizzwheels	$10-15

Body color diecast opening tailgate unless noted, horse figure, body casting includes base. (Note: drawing shown in 1968 Husky catalog with tan body, but not released in that color scheme.)

1. Turquoise body, black plastic wheels with vacuum plated inserts, Husky base; 1968-1969.

2. Metallic green body, black plastic wheels with vacuum plated inserts, Husky base; 1969.

3. Metallic green body, black plastic wheels with vacuum plated inserts, Corgi Juniors label on base.

4. Red body, black plastic wheels with vacuum plated inserts, Corgi Juniors label on base.

5. Red body, dished diecast wheels with rounded black plastic tires, Corgi Juniors label on base.

6. Red body, black Whizzwheels, Corgi Juniors base, unpainted tailgate.

7. Metallic copper body, chrome Whizzwheels, Corgi Juniors base, unpainted tailgate.

8. Bright green body, chrome Whizzwheels, Corgi Juniors base, green tailgate. (Set E2550-A.)

9. Metallic gold body (not copper.) (Shown in 1978 Corgi catalog as part of set E2503-B and again in 1983 Corgi catalog as part of set E2550-A. Possibly a prototype model. Was it produced?)

38-B   Jerry's Banger   75mm 1980-10/1983 $20-30

Body with swept fenders, short fat green plastic cannon, red cannonballs, brown figure, vacuum plated plastic engine and exhaust pipes, vacuum plated plastic grille, Whizzwheels. (Completely different casting from earlier E1014-A, which looks more like a motorized roller skate.)

1. Orange body with vacuum plated base.

2. Yellow body with vacuum plated base. (Possibly out of sets.)

3. Orange body with green base matching cannon color. (1983)

4. Yellow body with green base matching cannon color. (Possibly out of sets.)

39-A   Jaguar XJ6 4.2   75mm 1968-1969, 1970-1973 $20-30

Opening trunk, clear windows, unpainted diecast base, plastic interior and tow hook.

1. Bright yellow body, red interior, diecast wheels with five perimeter slots and black tires, Husky base; 1968-1969. (Also found packaged as Husky #89.)

2. Bright yellow body, red interior, diecast wheels with five perimeter slots and black tires, Corgi Juniors label on base.

3. Metallic silver body, red interior, narrow black Whizzwheels, Corgi Juniors base.

4. Metallic silver body, red interior, narrow chrome Whizzwheels, Corgi Juniors base.

5. Metallic maroon body, yellow interior, narrow chrome Whizzwheels, Corgi Juniors base.

6. Metallic copper body, yellow interior, narrow chrome Whizzwheels, Corgi Juniors base.

39-B   Jaguar E Type 2+2   71mm 1975-1977 $8-12

Growler, similar body casting to 33-B using same opening hood and window molding, modified baseplate with noise maker, vacuum plated engine and interior, clear windows, black plastic base, Whizzwheels.

1. Brick red body.

2. Metallic Purple body.

39-C   Chevrolet Pepsi-Cola Van   68mm 1979-1980 $10-12

No interior, black plastic base, Whizzwheels.

1. White body, red / white / light blue / dark blue Pepsi-Cola side labels, blue tinted windows, "CHEVROLET VAN" base, light ribs on roof.

2. White body, red / white / light blue / dark blue Pepsi-Cola side labels, blue tinted windows, "CHEVROLET VAN" base, heavy ribs on roof.

3. White body, red / white / light blue / dark blue Pepsi-Cola side labels, amber tinted windows, "CHEVROLET VAN" base, light ribs on roof.

4. White body, red / white / light blue / dark blue Pepsi-Cola side labels, amber tinted windows, "U.S. VAN" base, light ribs on roof.

5. White body, red / white / light blue / dark blue Pepsi-Cola side labels, blue tinted windows, "U.S. VAN" base, light ribs on roof.

6. White body, red / white / light blue / dark blue Pepsi-Cola side labels, blue tinted windows, "U.S. VAN" base, heavy ribs on roof.

40-A   Ford Transit Martin   65mm 1968-1969, 1970-1971 $20-30
**   Walter Caravan**

Diecast opening rear door, diecast unpainted base, first base type fits inside body. (Also found packaged as Husky Models 90. Note: Drawing shown in 1968 Husky catalog with white body, but not released in that color scheme.)

1. Red body, white door and interior, clear windows, Husky base, black plastic wheels with vacuum plated inserts.

2. Lime green body, white door and interior, clear windows, Husky base, black plastic wheels with vacuum plated inserts.

3. Lime green body, white door and interior, clear windows, Husky base, cast wheels with 5 perimeter slots and black tires.

4. Turquoise body and door, white interior, clear windows, Husky base, cast wheels with 5 perimeter slots and black tires.

5. Yellow body, unpainted door, blue interior, clear windows, Corgi Juniors label on base, black plastic wheels with vacuum plated inserts.

6. Yellow body, unpainted door, white interior, clear windows, Corgi Juniors base, black Whizzwheels.

7. Blue body, unpainted door, white interior, clear windows, Corgi Juniors base , black dished 5-spoke Whizzwheels.

8. Blue body, unpainted door, white interior, clear windows, Corgi Juniors base , black flat 5-spoke Whizzwheels.

9. Blue body, unpainted door, white interior, clear windows, Corgi Juniors base , chrome Whizzwheels.

10. Metallic light blue body, unpainted door, white interior, clear windows, Corgi Juniors base , chrome Whizzwheels.

11. Metallic light blue body, unpainted door, white interior, amber tinted windows, Corgi Juniors base , chrome Whizzwheels.

12. Metallic gray body, unpainted door, white interior, clear windows, Corgi Juniors base, chrome Whizzwheels.

13. Metallic light blue body, unpainted door, white interior, clear windows, black plastic Corgi Juniors base, chrome Whizzwheels.

40-B   Army Red Cross Helicopter   70mm 1977-1978 $8-12

Same casting and details as 35-B.

1. Olive drab body, "ARMY" and red cross labels.

40-C   James Bond Aston Martin   72mm 1979-10/1983 $20-30

Red interior and figures, opening roof hatch, Whizzwheels. (Note: Body sits higher off of ground than regular wheel E1001-A, but lower than Whizzwheels E1001-A.)

1. Metallic silver body, vacuum plated plastic base-grille, clear windows.

2. Metallic grainy silver body, vacuum plated plastic base-grille, clear windows.

41-A   Porsche Carrera 6   69mm 1970-1973

Regular Wheels	$20-30
Whizzwheels	$10-15

Opening rear hood, vacuum plated plastic interior and engine, red front hood paper label with "19" number unless noted, white diecast lower body-base. (Note: Drawing shown in 1968 Husky catalog, but not released as a Husky Models product.)

1. White body with red decal on hood, clear cockpit and aqua engine cover windows, black plastic wheels with vacuum plated inserts, "CORGI JUNIORS" cast into base without pat app number.

2. White body with red decal on hood, aqua tinted cockpit and engine cover windows, black plastic wheels with vacuum plated inserts, "CORGI JUNIORS" cast into base without pat app number.

3. White body with red decal on hood, blue tinted cockpit and engine cover windows, black plastic wheels with vacuum plated inserts, "CORGI JUNIORS" cast into base without pat app number.

4. White body with red decal on hood, blue tinted cockpit and engine cover windows, "CORGI JUNIORS WHIZZWHEELS" cast into base with pat app number, narrow black Whizzwheels.

5. White body, blue tinted cockpit and engine cover windows, "CORGI JUNIORS WHIZZWHEELS" cast into base with pat app number, narrow black Whizzwheels.

6. White body, green tinted cockpit and engine cover windows, "CORGI JUNIORS WHIZZWHEELS" cast into base with pat app number, narrow black Whizzwheels.

7. White body, purple tinted cockpit and engine cover windows, "CORGI JUNIORS WHIZZWHEELS" cast into base with pat app number, narrow black Whizzwheels.

8. White body, purple tinted cockpit and engine cover windows, "CORGI JUNIORS WHIZZWHEELS" cast into base with pat app number, wide chrome foiled 5-spoke Whizzwheels.

9. White body, blue tinted cockpit and engine cover windows, "CORGI JUNIORS WHIZZWHEELS" cast into base with pat app number, wide chrome foiled 5-spoke Whizzwheels.

10. White body, round blue label with white "9" on hood, blue tinted cockpit and engine cover windows, "CORGI JUNIORS WHIZZWHEELS" cast into base with pat app number, wide chrome foiled 5-spoke Whizzwheels.

41-B   James Bond Space Shuttle   70mm 1979-1981 $20-30
Same castings as 5-C with different labels.
1. White body, black base, yellow labels on wings with black "6" on left wing and Drax logo on right wing.

42-A   Euclid 35 Ton Rear Dump Truck 70mm 1969, 1970-1971 $15-20
Body, tipper and metallic charcoal gray base castings, no interior or windows.
1. Dark yellow cab-chassis, red tipper, black plastic wheels, Husky base.
2. Dark yellow cab-chassis, red tipper, black plastic wheels, Corgi Juniors label on base.
3. Dark yellow cab-chassis, red tipper, black Whizzwheels, Corgi Juniors base.

42-B   Terex R35 Rear Dump Truck   70mm 1972-1975? $10-15
Diecast charcoal gray baseplate (unless noted) with new lettering, Whizzwheels (chrome spokes unless noted), otherwise as E42-A.
1. Red chassis-cab, dark yellow tipper, black Whizzwheels.
2. Red chassis-cab, dark yellow tipper, unpainted base.
3. Blue chassis-cab, yellow plastic tipper.
4. Blue chassis-cab, silver tipper.
5. Blue chassis-cab, dull beige plastic tipper.

42-C   Rescue Range Rover   69mm 1977-1980

Rescue Team	$4-6
Other versions	$10-15

Blue tinted windows and dome lights, black plastic base unless noted, Whizzwheels. (Prototype shown in 1980 Corgi catalog as part of set E3013 with red body and yellow side labels with "COAST GUARD" lettering, but not produced in that color combination.)
1. Red body, red interior, pale yellow full-length side stripe labels with "RESCUE TEAM" lettering, 5-spoke wheels.
2. Red body, yellow interior, deep yellow full-length side stripe labels with "RESCUE TEAM" lettering, may have 5-spoke or 5-dblspk wheels.
3. Red body, white interior, vacuum plated base, shorter yellow side stripe labels with rounded ends and black "RESCUE TEAM" lettering, may have 5-spoke or 5-dblspk wheels.
4. Red body, yellow interior, white side labels with red "CRASH TENDER" lettering. (Only issued in set E3028-A.)
5. Red body, red interior, white side labels with red "CRASH TENDER" lettering. (Only issued in set E3028-A.)
6. Red body, yellow interior, yellow rectangular side labels with "RESCUE" lettering. (Only issued in set E3103-A.)
7. Orange body, yellow interior, vacuum plated base, yellow rectangular side labels with "RESCUE" lettering. (Only issued in sets E3101-A and E3103-A.)
8. Light Blue body, yellow interior, white side labels with "COASTGUARD" lettering. (Only issued in set E3023-A.)
9. Medium Blue body, red interior, white side labels with "COASTGUARD" lettering. (Only issued in set E3023-A.)

43-A   Massey Ferguson 3303 Tractor 74mm 1969, 1970-1980
with Blade

Husky base	$25-35
Corgi Juniors base	$10-15

Plastic interior and exhaust stack, lifting diecast blade and arms, black plastic wheels, unpainted diecast base.
1. Yellow body and blade, red interior, Husky base.
2. Yellow body and blade, red interior, Corgi Juniors label on base.

3. Yellow body, red blade and interior, Corgi Juniors cast into base.
4. Lighter yellow body, red blade and interior with filled-in gap on arms, Corgi Juniors cast into base. (Also in set E2502-A.)
5. Orange body, black blade, yellow interior, Corgi Juniors cast into base; 1980.

44-A   Raygo Rascal 600 Road Roller   74mm 1970-1978 $10-15
Body, roller housing and base castings, gray plastic roller, seat and engine, two black plastic wheels. Roller housing pivots on body.
1. Blue body, orange housing and base, Corgi Juniors label on base.
2. Corgi Juniors cast into base, otherwise as type 1.

44-B   Starship Liberator   75mm 1979-1980 $20-30
Same casting as 2-C, yellow plastic parts, green tinted windows, white turbine.
1. Metallic silver blue body, gold diecast collar.
2. Metallic medium blue body, silver diecast collar.
3. Metallic silver blue body, silver diecast collar. (No blue tint at all.)

45-A   Mercedes-Benz 280SL   70mm 1970-1974 $15-20
Opening doors, clear windows, diecast base-grille.
1. Metallic silver body, red interior, unpainted base, black plastic wheels with vacuum plated inserts.
2. Metallic silver body, red interior, unpainted base, thin black Whizzwheels.
3. Metallic light blue body, red interior, unpainted base, thin black Whizzwheels.
4. Yellow body, red interior, unpainted base, black Whizzwheels.
5. Yellow body, red interior, white painted grill and base, black Whizzwheels.
6. Metallic red body, white interior, unpainted base, black Whizzwheels.
7. Metallic red body, white interior, unpainted base, chrome Whizzwheels.
8. Metallic red body, yellow interior, unpainted base, chrome Whizzwheels.
9. Blue body, yellow interior, chrome base, chrome Whizzwheels.
10. Blue body, off-white interior, chrome base, chrome Whizzwheels.

45-B   Starsky and Hutch Ford Gran Torino 75mm 1977-10/1983 $15-20
Opaque black windows, no interior, red roof light, Whizzwheels. Casting also used for E70-C and E70-D.
1. Red body, vacuum plated plastic base-grille with "STARSKY & HUTCH" in center block, white trim label, red plastic roof light.
2. Red body, vacuum plated plastic base-grille with blank center block, white trim label, red plastic roof light.
3. Red body, vacuum plated plastic base-grille with blank center block, white trim label, diecast roof light part of body.
4. Red body, unplated gray plastic base-grille with blank center block, white trim label, diecast roof light part of body.
5. Red body, unplated white plastic base-grille with blank center block, white trim label, diecast roof light part of body.

46-A   Jensen Interceptor   73mm 1970-1973 $20-30
Opening doors, yellow interior, unpainted diecast base-grille.
1. Metallic maroon body, yellow interior, green tinted windows, "CORGI JUNIORS" cast into baseplate, black plastic wheels with vacuum plated inserts.
2. Metallic maroon body, yellow interior, green tinted windows, "CORGI JUNIORS WHIZZWHEELS" cast into baseplate, narrow black center Whizzwheels.
3. Metallic maroon body, red interior, clear windows, "CORGI JUNIORS WHIZZWHEELS" cast into baseplate, narrow black center Whizzwheels.
4. Orange body, yellow interior, green tinted windows, "CORGI JUNIORS WHIZZWHEELS" cast into baseplate, narrow chrome center Whizzwheels.
5. Light metallic aqua body, yellow interior, green tinted windows, "CORGI JUNIORS WHIZZWHEELS" cast into baseplate, wide chrome center Whizzwheels.
6. Light metallic aqua body, yellow interior, clear windows, "CORGI JUNIORS WHIZZWHEELS" cast into baseplate, wide chrome center Whizzwheels.
7. Light metallic green body, yellow interior, clear windows, "CORGI JUNIORS WHIZZWHEELS" cast into baseplate, wide chrome center Whizzwheels.

46-B   Police Helicopter   75mm 1976-1979, 1983-10/1983

Standard	$4-6
Kojak Set (loose)	$8-10

Clear canopy, plastic interior-base-skids and rotors, dashboard and Police labels.
1. White body, blue interior and rotors, Police and stripe labels.
2. White body, red interior and rotors, Police and stripe labels.
3. Metallic blue body, white interior and rotors, "CITY OF NEW YORK POLICE" labels. (Found in Kojak set E2527-A.)
4. Blue body, red interior and rotors, no labels. 1983.
5. Red body, white interior and rotors, no labels. 1983.

47-A   Scammell Concrete Mixer   72mm 1971-1976 $10-15
Upper and lower body-base castings, red plastic barrel, no interior, Whizzwheels.
1. White upper and blue lower body, amber tinted windows.
2. White upper and blue lower body, blue tinted windows.

47-B   Chevrolet Superman Supervan   68mm 1978-10/1983

	Silver	$15-20
	Red	$30-40

Superman figure on side labels with either "SUPERMAN" or "SUPERVAN" lettering , black plastic base, Whizzwheels. (Prototype shown in 1978 Corgi catalog with added "POW!" balloon around Superman's forward fist, but not produced with that side label.) Note: A number of different variations were produced at the same time by Mettoy due to two slightly different sets of tooling in use.

Known feature differences are as follows:

a. Two different body castings were produced at the same time and are identified by the weight of the ribs on the roof.

b. Two different baseplate texts seem to have been in production at the same time, although the "Chevrolet" baseplate started earlier and the "U.S." baseplate stayed in production longer. This also applies to other Chevrolet Van / U. S. Van variants. The "Chevrolet" was also modified for production in Brazil for the Kiko Corgi products there.

c. Two different window colors were used interchangeably.

d. Side labels may have changed with planned country of sale due to licensing and trademark issues.

Verified variations identified at the time of publication are as follows:

1. Silver body with heavy roof ribs, silver "SUPERMAN" side labels with "©DC 1978" in top rear corners, amber tinted windows, "Chevrolet Van" base lettering.

2. Silver body with thin roof ribs, silver "SUPERMAN" side labels with "©DC 1978" in top rear corners, amber tinted windows, "Chevrolet Van" base lettering.

3. Silver body with thin roof ribs, silver "SUPERMAN" side labels with "©DC 1978" in top rear corners, blue tinted windows, "Chevrolet Van" base lettering.

4. Silver body with thin roof ribs, silver "SUPERMAN" side labels with tiny "©DC 1978" at bottom under city, blue tinted windows, "Chevrolet Van" base lettering.

5. Silver body with heavy roof ribs, silver "SUPERMAN" side labels with tiny "©DC 1978" at bottom under city, blue tinted windows, "Chevrolet Van" base lettering.

6. Silver body with heavy roof ribs, silver "SUPERMAN" side labels with tiny "©DC 1978" at bottom under city, amber tinted windows, "U.S. Van" base lettering.

7. Silver body with thin roof ribs, silver "SUPERMAN" side labels with tiny "©DC 1978" at bottom under city, amber tinted windows, "U.S. Van" base lettering.

8. Silver body with thin roof ribs, silver "SUPERMAN" side labels with tiny "©DC 1978" at bottom under city, blue tinted windows, "U.S. Van" base lettering.

9. Silver body with thin roof ribs, silver "SUPERVAN" side labels, blue tinted windows, "Chevrolet Van" base lettering.

10. Silver body with thin roof ribs, silver "SUPERVAN" side labels, amber tinted windows, "Chevrolet Van" base lettering.

11. Silver body with thin roof ribs, silver "SUPERVAN" side labels, amber tinted windows, "U.S. Van" base lettering.

12. Silver body with heavy roof ribs, silver "SUPERVAN" side labels, blue tinted windows, "U.S. Van" base lettering.

13. Silver body with heavy roof ribs, silver "SUPERMAN" side labels with tiny "©DC 1978" at bottom under city, opaque black windows, "U.S. Van" base lettering with brand name blanked.

14. Red body with heavy roof ribs, silver "SUPERMAN" side labels with "©DC 1978" in top rear corners, opaque black windows, "U.S. Van" base lettering without Corgi Juniors text, black Whizzwheels. (Found in Superman set E3081-A.)

48-A   ERF Tipper Truck   75mm 1970-1973 $20-30

Cab, tipper, tailgate and chassis castings, amber tinted windows, no interior, Whizzwheels.

1. Red cab, silver tipper and tailgate, metallic charcoal gray chassis.

2. Red cab, silver tipper and tailgate, unpainted chassis.

3. Blue cab, yellow tipper, unpainted tailgate, metallic charcoal gray chassis.

4. Blue cab, yellow tipper, unpainted tailgate, unpainted chassis.

5. Blue cab, tan tipper, unpainted tailgate, unpainted chassis.

6. Blue cab, yellow tipper, unpainted tailgate, black chassis.

48-B   Shovel Loader   78mm 1975-1979 $8-12

Yellow plastic interior, engine, stack, base and working shovel, clear windows, knobby black plastic wheels. (Prototype shown in 1980 Corgi catalog with red body and vacuum plated shovel, but not produced in that color scheme.)

1. Red body, black Growler gear in base.

2. Red body, red Growler gear in base.

3. Orange body, red Growler gear in base.

4. Red body, modified base without Growler gear.

5. Orange body, modified base without Growler gear. (also found in set E2007-A1.)

49-A   Pininfarina Modulo   72mm 1971-1973 $15-20

Maroon interior and stripe between upper and lower body castings, clear windows, Whizzwheels, red and black rear roof label.

1. Yellow upper and lower body.

49-B   Ford Tipping Lorry   73mm 1977-1979 $8-12

No interior, unpainted diecast tailgate, black plastic base, Whizzwheels.

1. Silver chassis-cab, light blue tipper, blue tinted windows.

2. Silver chassis-cab, light blue tipper, clear windows.

49-C   Woody Woodpecker's Car   70mm 1981-10/1983 $20-30

Modified 78-A casting, red interior with figure, red and white stripe labels, navy blue diecast base, Whizzwheels.

1. Yellow body.

50-A   Ferrari 512 S   71mm 1971-1974 $15-20

Clear windows, silver diecast base, Whizzwheels. (Later modified to E57-B.)

1. Metallic dark purple upper body, number 6 label, cream interior and engine cover.

2. Metallic dark red upper body, number 4 label, cream interior and engine cover.

3. Metallic dark red upper body, number 6 label, cream interior and engine cover.

4. Metallic dark red upper body, number 6 label, yellow interior and engine cover.

5. Metallic dark red upper body, number 6 label, white interior, narrow louvered engine cover. (1974)

50-B   Leyland Daily Planet Van   73mm 1979-1980 $15-20

Daily Planet labels, no interior, black plastic base, Whizzwheels.

1. Red body, opaque black windows.

2. Silver body, opaque black windows.

3. Silver body, transparent blue tinted windows.

51-A   Porsche 917   72mm 1971-1973 $15-20

Vacuum plated plastic interior and engine, clear windows, Whizzwheels, number 23 label.

(Note: Shown in 1972 Corgi Juniors catalog with non-metallic mustard yellow upper body, but not released in that color.)

1. Gold upper body, red lower body-base.

51-B   Volvo 245DL Estate Car   76mm 1976- 10/1983 $4-6

Opening rear hatch, black plastic base-grille, Whizzwheels.

1. Metallic green body, yellow interior, amber tinted windows.

2. Orange body, yellow interior, amber tinted windows.

3. Orange body, red interior, amber tinted windows.

4. Cream body, yellow interior, amber tinted windows.

5. Cream body, yellow interior, clear windows.

6. Cream body, orange interior, clear windows.

7. Light blue body, yellow interior, amber tinted windows.

8. Metallic charcoal gray body, yellow interior, amber tinted windows.

9. Metallic light blue body, ??? interior, clear windows.

10. Dark blue body, ??? interior, clear windows.

11. Bright White body, white interior, clear windows. (Possibly from transitional era 1983-84.)

12. Metallic purple body, yellow interior. (Shown in 1978 catalog. Possibly a prototype model.)

13. Yellow body, white interior, yellow tinted windows. (Shown in 1983 catalog. Was it produced?)

14. Tan body, red interior, yellow tinted windows. (Shown in 1983 catalog as part of set E2554-B. Was it produced?)

52-A   Adams Probe 16   72mm 1971-1973 $15-20

Blue tinted windows, cream interior, black plastic base, Whizzwheels.

1. Metallic purple body.

2. Metallic gold body.

52-B   Mercedes-Benz 240D Taxi   76mm 1976-1979 $8-12

Amber tinted windows and roof sign, yellow interior, black plastic base, Whizzwheels. (Shown in 1976 catalog with black body, gray interior, white "TAXI" on doors, but not produced in this color scheme.)

1. Cream body, black and white Taxi labels.

52-C   Scooby Doo Mystery Ghost Catcher 69mm 1982- 10/1983 $20-30

Dark green diecast lower body-base, black Whizzwheels, tan dog figure, hood label.

1. Medium green upper body.

53-A   Fire Launch   74mm 1977-1979 $8-12

Plastic hull, three black wheels, chrome diecast spotlight bar, vacuum plated plastic interior and water cannon, red-white-blue Fire and stripe labels.

1. Red diecast superstructure, light blue hull.

53-B   Formula 1 Racer   73mm 1980- 10/1983 $5-8

Same casting as 22-C, gold vacuum plated plastic engine and windshield, plastic driver, black and gold Corgi Special labels, unpainted diecast base, Whizzwheels.

1. Black body, yellow driver.
2. Black body, white driver.

54-A   Ford D-1000 Container Truck   73mm 1972-1978 $10-15
Plastic bucket and base, unpainted diecast swinging arms, transparent blue tinted windows unless noted, Whizzwheels. (Note: Prototype shown in 1972 Corgi Juniors catalog with dark green body and clear windows, but not released in that color scheme.)
1. Red cab-chassis, dark yellow bucket and base.
2. Red-orange cab-chassis, dark yellow bucket and base.
3. Red-orange cab-chassis, dark yellow bucket and base, opaque black windows.
4. Red-orange cab-chassis, white bucket and base.
5. Red cab-chassis, gray bucket and base.
6. Red cab-chassis, tan bucket and base. (Also found in 1983-84 transition period 2-pack to sell-off existing stock.)
7. Red cab-chassis, white bucket and base, no windows. (Also found in 1983-84 transition period Bumper set to sell-off existing stock. Continued by Corgi Toys Ltd. as J12.)
8. Orange cab-chassis, white bucket and base, no windows.
9. Green cab-chassis, white bucket and base, opaque black windows. (Shown in 1983 Corgi catalog. Was it released?)

55-A   Daimler Fleetline Double-decker Bus 77mm 1971-1973

Esso	$15-20
Promotional	$20-30

Yellow interior, no windows, red diecast base, 5-spoke Whizzwheels. (Casting later revised with windows but without interior as E81-A.)
1. Red body, red and blue "Esso UNIFLOW MOTOR OIL PROTECTS *FASTER*"" on white labels.
2. Red body, Union Jack and blue "GRAY LINE SIGHTSEEING VICTORIA B.C., CANADA" on white labels. (Canadian promotional.)

55-B   Refuse Truck   71mm 1976-1980, 1982- 10/1983 $4-6
Working two-piece refuse body, black plastic base, Whizzwheels, no interior, rear body section has vertical ribs unless noted. (Shown in 1976 catalog with yellow cab and red refuse body, but not produced in this color scheme.)
1. Dark metallic blue cab, yellow refuse body, faintly blue tinted windows.
2. Non-metallic medium blue cab, yellow refuse body, faintly blue tinted windows, no vertical ribs on rear body segment.
3. Gold cab, blue refuse body, green tinted windows.
4. Silver cab, blue refuse body, amber tinted windows.
5. Green cab, white refuse body, clear windows.
6. Non-metallic medium blue cab, yellow refuse body, opaque black windows.
7. Non-metallic medium blue cab, white refuse body, smoke tinted windows. (1982)
8. Orange cab, white refuse body, opaque black windows. (1983, may also be packaged as J13.)
9. Orange cab, gray refuse body, opaque black windows. (1983, may also be packaged as J13.)
10. Yellow cab, gray refuse body, opaque black windows. (1983, may also be packaged as J13.)

56-A   Ford Capri Fire Chief's Car   75mm 1971-1974

Fire Chief	$15-20
From Rockets Sets (loose)	$20-40
"Wall of Death" Set (loose)	$50-75

Blue tinted windows and dome light, white diecast base, Whizzwheels.
1. Red body, white hood, white interior, black "Fire Chief" lettering on white labels.
2. Red body, white hood, yellow interior, black "Fire Chief" lettering on white labels.
3. Red body, white hood, white interior, red "Fire" lettering on white labels.
4. Red body including hood, yellow interior, red "Fire" lettering on white labels.
5. Metallic teal body without roof light, clear windows, ??? interior, "8" labels. (Uses body casting as found on Rockets 922-A. Found only in Juniors Club Racing Gift Set E3020-A.)
6. Red body without roof light, clear windows, ??? interior, "8" labels. (Uses body casting as found on Rockets 922-A. Found only in Juniors Club Racing Gift Set E3020-A.)
7. White body without roof light, clear windows, yellow interior, plated "WHIZZWHEELS" base without tow hook, "WALL OF DEATH" labels with Batman Logo, 5-spk wheels. (From Rockets "Wall of Death Set" 2062-A. Model listed here due to usage in Rockets set but with Juniors Whizzwheels base.)

56-B   Chevrolet Spider-Van   68mm 1978-1980 $20-30
No interior, black plastic base, Whizzwheels, "Spider-Van" labels. Note: A number of different variations were produced at the same time by Mettoy due to two slightly different sets of tooling in use. (Prototype shown in 1978 Corgi catalog with Spiderman shown in different pose, but not produced with these labels.)
Known feature differences are as follows:
a. Two different body castings were produced at the same time and are identified by the weight of the ribs on the roof. All versions found to-date have "U.S. VAN" text on the baseplate unless noted.
b. At least two different window colors were used interchangeably.
c. Side labels may have changed with planned country of sale due to licensing and trademark issues.
Verified variations identified at the time of publication are as follows:
1. Dark blue body, blue tinted windows, light roof ribs, "©MGC" on side labels, "U.S. VAN" base.
2. Dark blue body, amber tinted windows, heavy roof ribs, "©MGC" on side labels, "U.S. VAN" base.
3. Dark blue body, blue tinted windows, light roof ribs, no "©MGC" on side labels, "U.S. VAN" base.
4. Dark blue body, blue tinted windows, light roof ribs, no "©MGC" on side labels, "CHEVROLET VAN" base.
5. Dark blue body, amber tinted windows, ??? roof ribs, no "©MGC" on side labels.
6. Medium blue body, blue tinted windows, ??? roof ribs, no "©MGC" on side labels.
7. Silver body, blue tinted windows, ??? roof ribs, silver background in web labels, ??? base. (One known example found to-date, possibly a pre-production model.)
(Note: A similar blue Spiderman van was produced in Brazil as a Kiko-Corgi Juniors model. See the description in that section.)

57-A   Cadillac Eldorado Hot Rodder   77mm 1971-1973

Pink	$15-25
Pale Blue	$30-40

Modified 9-B casting, protruding silver engine, clear windows, unpainted diecast base-grille, red / white / blue American flag-like roof and trunk lid stripe labels supplied on sheet in package, Whizzwheels.
1. Metallic hot pink body, red interior, black Whizzwheels, "CADDY HOT RODDER" label on sides.
2. Metallic hot pink body, red interior, silver 5-spoke Whizzwheels, "CADDY HOT RODDER" label on sides.
3. Metallic hot pink body, yellow interior, silver 5-spoke Whizzwheels, "CADDY HOT RODDER" label on sides.
4. Metallic pale blue body, red interior, silver 5-spoke Whizzwheels, "CADDY HOT RODDER" label on sides.

57-B   Ferrari 512S   71mm 1975-1977 $8-12
Same body casting as late 50-A, "Growlers" mechanism in modified baseplate, vacuum plated plastic interior and louvered engine cover, clear windows, number 6 label, black plastic base, Whizzwheels.
1. Light blue body, black base.

57-C   Spiderbike   74mm 1979- 10/1983 $20-30
Red and blue Spiderman figure, black five-spoke plastic wheels.
1. Unpainted diecast and red plastic motorcycle.

58-A   GP Beach Buggy   61mm 1971-1977 $15-20
Chrome diecast base, Whizzwheels. (Similar to Rockets 910-A but without roll bar and removable chassis. Body later used for E84-B Bugs Bunny Buggy.)
1. Metallic dark red body, clear windshield, off-white interior.
2. Metallic copper body, clear windshield, off-white interior.
3. Metallic purple body, clear windshield, off-white interior.
4. Metallic dark red body, clear windshield, yellow interior.
5. Metallic dark red body, amber tinted windshield, yellow interior.

58-B   Tom's Go-Cart   69mm 1980- 10/1983 $20-30
Red plastic exhaust pipe, steering wheel and headrest, gray figure, Whizzwheels. (Completely different casting from earlier E1013-A which has cover over Tom's head.)
1. White chassis-fenders, vacuum plated plastic engine cover with label on front.
2. Light Yellow chassis-fenders, vacuum plated plastic engine cover with label on front.
3. Dark Yellow chassis-fenders, vacuum plated plastic engine cover with label on front.

59-A   The Futura   75mm 1971-1973 $15-20
No interior, black diecast base, Whizzwheels, Futura labels.
1. Orange body, blue tinted windows.
2. Orange body, green tinted windows.

59-B   Mercedes-Benz 240D Police Car   76mm 1977-1980 $8-12
Blue tinted windows and dome lights, yellow interior, black plastic base, Whizzwheels.

1. White body, green and white Polizei labels.

59-C   Mercedes-Benz 240D   76mm 1982- 10/1983
                                        Standard versions $4-6
                                        James Bond Version $20-30

Clear windows unless noted, black plastic base, Whizzwheels.

1. Dark blue body, tan interior.
2. Dark blue body, black interior.
3. White body, brown interior.
4. Red body, white interior.
5. Silver body, tan interior. (used in set E1380-A.)
6. Black body, yellow interior, gray paint splatter on hood, windshield and roof. (Only found in James Bond Moonraker Set E3030-A1.)
7. Dark teal blue body, white interior.
8. Light blue body, yellow interior.
9. Medium blue body, black interior.
10. Medium blue body, red interior.
11. Medium blue body, white interior. (Found in transitional era 2-pack 1983-84.)
12. Metallic blue body, yellow interior.
13. Metallic blue body, white interior, amber tinted windows. (Found in set E2518-B.)
14. Metallic blue body, yellow interior, amber tinted windows.
15. Medium green body, black interior.
16. Medium green body, tan interior.
(Other combinations probably exist.)

60-A   VW Double Trouble Hot Rod   74mm 1971-1973 $20-30
Vacuum plated plastic interior and engines, blue tinted windows, black diecast base with "CORGI JUNIORS WHIZZWHEELS" text, Whizzwheels. (Note: Color varies widely within each variation and may appear different under different types of light. Same casting also issued as E160-A in different colors and modified base text.)
1. Metallic platinum rose body. (Can be found with 5-spoke front and 5-dblspk rear wheels.)
2. Metallic nail polish pink body.
3. Metallic copper body.

60-B   James Bond Lotus Esprit   75mm 1977- 10/1983 $15-20
Opaque black windows, no interior, black plastic base, black Whizzwheels.
1. White body, red 007 on white paper backed label on hood (bonnet.)
2. White body, red 007 Tampo printed on hood (bonnet.) 1983.

61-A   Mercury Cougar XR7 Sheriff's Car   75mm 1971-1975 $20-30
Blue tinted windows and dome lights, unpainted diecast base, Whizzwheels, Sheriff labels on doors.
1. White body, black top, yellow interior.
2. White body, black top, white interior.
3. White body, black top, red interior.

61-B   Buick Regal Sheriff's Car   76mm 1979-1980 $8-12
Casting and details as 28-D. (May be catalog number error.)
1. White and black body.

61-C   Ford Capri 3.0 S   76mm 1980-1981, 10/1983
                                        Standard versions $4-6
                                        Promotional version $10-15

Blue tinted windows unless noted, black plastic base-grille, Whizzwheels. (Also see E64-B The Professional's Capri.)
1. Red body, yellow interior, black trim.
2. Red body, yellow interior, no trim, amber tinted windows.
3. Red body, vacuum plated interior, no trim. (also found in "Always Efficient" Ford promotional box.)
4. Blue body, yellow interior, no trim.
5. Blue body, yellow interior, no trim, amber tinted windows.
6. Green body, black interior, no trim. (1983, possibly a Corgi Toys Ltd. model from a set.)
7. Silver body, black interior, no trim.
8. Silver body, black interior, black "SUPERCHARGE" graphics. (Promotional for BP Supercharge card customers. May be from after Mettoy's closure.)
9. Silver body, red plastic base-grill, clear windows, yellow interior, no trim. (Produced during or after the time of Mettoy's closure to use excess parts inventory, 1983.)
10. White body, red plastic base-grill, clear windows, red interior, no trim. (Produced during or after the time of Mettoy's closure to use excess parts inventory, 1983.)
11. White body, black plastic base-grill, clear windows, red interior, no trim. (Produced during or after the time of Mettoy's closure to use excess parts inventory, 1983.)

12. White body, black plastic base-grill, clear windows, black interior, no trim. (Produced during or after the time of Mettoy's closure to use excess parts inventory, 1983.)
13. Yellow body, black plastic base-grill, clear windows, red interior, segmented black stripe on lower sides. (From Little/Large set 1373-A, 1983.)
14. Yellow body, black plastic base-grill, clear windows, red interior, no graphics. (1983.)

62-A   Volvo P-1800   71mm 1971-1973 $25-35
Clear windows, unpainted diecast base-grille with tow hook, Whizzwheels. (Also found in set E3025-A.)
1. Red body, blue interior, black hood.
2. Red body, cream interior, black hood.
3. Red body, yellow interior, black hood.

62-B   AMC Pacer   74mm 1976-1980 $4-6
Vacuum plated plastic interior and bumpers unless noted, black plastic base, Whizzwheels. (Note: Colors vary widely and are described as closely as possible. Earlier models have "CORGI JUNIORS" text on baseplate, later models have "corgi" text. Unplated interior versions produced during times of known factory production problem with vacuum plating machine.)
1. Metallic dark maroon body, blue tinted windows.
2. Metallic dark maroon body, clear windows.
3. Metallic red body, amber tinted windows.
4. Metallic red body, clear windows.
5. Metallic royal blue body, blue tinted windows.
6. Metallic royal blue body, amber tinted windows.
7. Metallic medium blue body, blue tinted windows.
8. Metallic medium blue body, clear windows.
9. Metallic medium blue body, amber tinted windows.
10. Metallic medium blue body, clear windows, unplated white interior and bumpers.
11. Metallic medium turquoise body, clear windows, unplated white interior and bumpers.
12. Metallic light aqua body, clear windows, unplated white interior and bumpers.
13. Metallic light aqua body, amber tinted windows, unplated white interior and bumpers.
14. Metallic baby blue body, clear windows, unplated white interior and bumpers.
15. Metallic dark navy blue body, clear windows, unplated white interior and bumpers.
16. Metallic dark navy blue body, amber tinted windows, unplated white interior and bumpers.
17. Non-metallic light blue body, clear windows. (late production.)
18. Non-metallic medium blue body, amber tinted windows, unplated white interior and bumpers.
19. Non-metallic royal blue body, amber tinted windows, unplated white interior and bumpers. (Found in transitional era 2-pack 1983-84.)

63-A   Ford Escort Rallye   69mm 1971-1975 $20-30
Clear windows, unpainted diecast base-grille, Whizzwheels, label sheet provided in package.
1. Metallic blue body, red interior, red and black stripes and number 32 labels.
2. Metallic blue body, white interior, red and black stripes and number 32 labels.
3. Metallic blue body, yellow interior, red and black stripes and number 32 labels.
4. Metallic blue body, red interior, no stripes or labels. (Found in set E3025-A without label sheet.)

63-B   Surf Rescue Helicopter   75mm 1977-1979 $10-15
White interior, base, pontoons and rotors, blue and white Surf Rescue labels, clear windows. (Prototype shown in 1978 catalog with yellow body and black lettering, but not produced in this color scheme.)
1. Metallic dark blue body.

64-A   Morgan Plus 8   67mm 1971-1973 $20-30
Black interior, clear windshield, unpainted diecast base-grille, Whizzwheels.
1. Yellow body, black and white "20" number label on door.
2. Yellow body, no label on door.
3. Red body, black and white "20" number label on door.
4. Red body, blue and white "20" number label on door.

64-B   The Professionals' Ford Capri   76mm 1980- 10/1983 $25-40
Same casting as 61-C, black plastic base-grille, Whizzwheels.
1. Metallic silver body with sunroof, blue tinted windows, vacuum plated interior.
2. Metallic silver body with sunroof, blue tinted windows, yellow interior.
3. Silver body with sunroof, blue tinted windows, yellow interior.
4. Silver body without sunroof, blue tinted windows, yellow interior.

5. Silver body without sunroof, clear windows, red interior.

65-A Bertone Carabo   **75mm 1971-1973**   **$20-30**
Amber tinted windows, light green lower body-base casting, Whizzwheels.
1. Metallic purple upper body, cream interior and grilles.
2. Metallic purple upper body, red interior and grilles.

65-B Caravan Trailer   **75mm 1976-1980**   **$4-6**
Light blue interior, base and opening door, clear windows, black hitch, Whizzwheels.
1. White body, light blue door and interior.
2. Cream body, butterscotch door and interior. (Found in set E2518-B.)
3. Tan body, red door and interior. (Found in set E2554-A.)

66-A Centurion Tank   **68mm 1976-1978**   **$8-12**
Black plastic base, rotating turret and raising gun barrel, three black wheels.
1. Olive drab body.

66-B Ice Cream Van   **Not Produced**   **N/A**
Shown in 1980 catalog but not issued. May be confused with Brazilian Kiko-Corgi model.

67-A Ford Capri Dragster   **73mm 1971-1973**   **$30-40**
Similar body casting to 56-A, red and silver interior with engine, roll bars and rear seat, white diecast base, Whizzwheels, Union Jack and "Hot Pants" labels.
1. Yellow body.

67-B Road Roller   **68mm 1976-1978**   **$4-6**
Plastic rollers, body panels and steering wheel; body casting includes base.
1. Orange body, black plastic parts.
2. Orange body, gray plastic parts.

67-C Popeye's Tugboat   **77mm 1980- 10/1983**   **$20-30**
Plastic hull, yellow deck, red superstructure and hull, Popeye figure, Spinach can label.
1. Three black wheels.
2. 3 bumps on bottom (No wheels).

68-A Kojak's Buick Regal   **76mm 1977-1980**   **$10-15**
Amber tinted windows, vacuum plated plastic interior, bumpers and grille, red roof light, black plastic base with suspension, Whizzwheels.
1. Metallic copper body.

69-A Batmobile   **75mm 1976- 10/1983**   **$50-80**
Blue tinted canopy, red interior, driver, bat label, black plastic base, Whizzwheels.
1. Black body, painted figure, no tow hook.
2. Black body, unpainted figure, no tow hook.
3. Black body, unpainted figure, tow hook. (From sets.)
4. Black body, unpainted figure, tow hook, narrow bat label on deck. (From sets.)

70-A U.S. Racing Buggy   **73mm 1971-1974**   **$15-25**
White interior with driver, vacuum plated plastic engine and exhaust pipes, white diecast base, Whizzwheels, red-white-blue stars and stripes labels.
1. Light blue body.

70-B Mercury Cougar XR7 Fire Chief's Car **75mm 1975-1977**   **$10-15**
Same casting as 61-A, blue tinted windows and roof lights, yellow interior, unpainted diecast base-grille, Whizzwheels, red and yellow Fire Dept. Chief labels.
1. Red body.

70-C Ford Gran Torino Fire Chief's Car   **75mm 1977-1982**   **$5-8**
Same casting as 45-B, opaque black windows, no interior, roof light. (Prototype shown in 1982 Corgi catalog with yellow "FIRE CHIEF" tampo printed on doors, but not produced with that decoration.)
1. Red body, vacuum plated plastic base-bumpers with "STARSKY & HUTCH" text in the center, red plastic roof light, yellow "Fire Chief Dept." labels with small chief over red and white shield, blue upper and lower label edges.
2. Red body, vacuum plated plastic base-bumpers without "STARSKY & HUTCH" text in the center, red plastic roof light, yellow "Fire Chief Dept." labels with small chief over red and white shield, blue upper and lower label edges.
3. Red body, vacuum plated plastic base-bumpers, diecast roof light part of body, "Fire Chief" labels with shield in black center block.
4. Red body, unplated gray plastic base-bumpers, diecast roof light part of body, "Fire Chief" labels with shield in black center block.
5. Red body, unplated white plastic base-bumpers, diecast roof light part of body, "Fire Chief" labels with shield in black center block.

70-D Ford Gran Torino   **75mm 1983- 10/1983**   **$4-6**
Same casting as 70-C, diecast roof light part of body, no labels or graphics.
1. Blue body, vacuum plated plastic base and grille.
2. Blue body, black plastic base and grille.
3. Blue body, gray plastic base and grille. (1983 near factory closure.)
4. Red body, gray plastic base and grille. (1983 near factory closure.)

5. Red body, white plastic base and grille. (1983 near factory closure.)

71-A Marcos XP   **69mm 1971-1975**   **$15-20**
Plated interior, amber tinted windows and headlamps, black diecast base, Whizzwheels.
(Note: Prototype shown in 1972 Corgi Juniors catalog with pale metallic gold body, but not released in that color scheme.)
1. Bright orange body, amber tinted windows and headlamps.
2. Bright orange body, clear windows and headlamps.
3. Creamy orange body, amber tinted windows and headlamps.

71-B Austin London Taxi   **72mm 1980- 10/1983**
                              Standard versions   **$4-6**
                              Promotional version   **$8-10**
Unpainted diecast base-grille, Whizzwheels. (Continued as J17 in 1984. Prototype shown in 1980 Corgi catalog with black interior, but not released in that color scheme.)
1. Black body, yellow interior, clear windows.
2. Black body, yellow interior, yellow tinted windows.
3. Black body, orange interior, yellow tinted windows.
4. Black body, yellow interior, yellow tinted windows, white "Black & White" text on roof. (Promotional model for the liquor company.)

72-A Mercedes-Benz C111   **74mm 1972-1977**   **$15-20**
Vacuum plated plastic interior, black plastic lower body-base, Whizzwheels.
(Note: Prototype shown in 1972 Corgi Juniors catalog with dark blue body, white base and clear windows, but not released in that color scheme. Different prototype shown in 1974 Corgi Juniors catalog with dark blue body and base with clear windows, but also not released in that color scheme.)
1. Red body, blue tinted windows.
2. Red body, yellow tinted windows.

72-B Jaguar XJS   **76mm 1979-1980, 1982- 10/1983**
                              Standard versions   **$4-6**
                              Motor Show version   **$5-8**
Plastic base, Whizzwheels.
1. Navy blue body, white interior, clear windows, vacuum plated plastic base.
2. Navy blue body, white interior, clear windows, black base.
3. Red body, white interior, clear windows, black base.
4. Red body, yellow interior, clear windows, black base.
5. Red body, opaque black windows, black base, white Motor Show lettering; 1982. (Supplied from factory in open yellow vacuum-formed tray of 12 cars. Known to have been made in either 5-spoke or 5-dblspk wheel types. Not individually packaged.)
6. Red body, opaque black windows, black base; 1983.
7. Red body, opaque black windows, yellow base; 1983. (Produced from leftover Hockey Car parts after Mettoy factory closure.)
8. Medium blue body, opaque black windows, no interior, black base.
9. Light blue body, opaque black windows, no interior, black base.
10. Metallic Copper body, yellow interior, clear windows, black base.
11. Metallic Copper body, white interior, clear windows, black base.
12. Maroon body, no interior, opaque black windows, black base.
13. White body, opaque black windows, no interior, black base.
14. Silver body, opaque black windows, no interior, black base.

73-A Pininfarina Alfa Romeo P33   **73mm 1971-1973**   **$15-20**
White plastic wing and seats, black dashboard, clear windshield, white diecast base, Whizzwheels.
(Note: Prototype shown in 1972 Corgi Juniors catalog with mirrored purple body, but not released in that color scheme. Different prototype shown in 1973 Corgi Toys catalog with yellow body and red wing, but not released in that color scheme)
1. Non-metallic blue body.

73-B Drax Airlines Helicopter   **75mm 1979-1979**   **$20-30**
Yellow plastic interior, base, skids and rotors, amber tinted windows, Drax Airlines labels.
1. White body.

74-A Bertone Runabout Barchetta   **62mm 1972-1975**   **$15-20**
White diecast lower body-base, plastic interior and stripe between castings, Whizzwheels.
(Note: Prototype shown in 1972 Corgi Juniors catalog with light metallic green body, but not released in that color scheme.)
1. Orange upper body, black interior and stripe, amber tinted windshield.
2. Orange upper body, black interior and stripe, clear windshield.
3. Orange upper body, red interior and stripe, clear windshield.

74-B Leyland Ryder Rental Truck   **73mm 1977-1980**   **$8-12**
No interior, black plastic base, Whizzwheels.

1. Yellow body, blue tinted windows, "Ryder Truck Rental" side labels.

2. Yellow body, opaque black windows, "Ryder Truck Rental" side labels.

3. Yellow body, opaque black windows, reversed "Ryder Truck Rental" side labels. (Known factory error.)

75-A   Super Stock Car   69mm 1973-1975 $10-15

Red interior, diecast base, Whizzwheels, Union Jack label.

1. Silver body, yellow base.

2. Silver body, blue base.

75-B   Spidercopter   74mm 1977-1982 $20-30

Light red interior, parts and legs, clear canopy, spider labels, black rotor.

1. Metallic blue body.

76-A   Chevrolet Astro 1   Not Issued   N/A

Not issued. Shown in 1972 Corgi Juniors catalog with metallic red body. Intended to be Rockets Chevrolet Astro 1 without removable base feature.

76-B   U.S. Army Jeep   62mm 1974-1978 $10-15

Silver gray plastic folding windshield, brown interior and driver, white star label, olive diecast base, black Whizzwheels.

1. Olive drab body and base.

76-C   (Chrysler) Matra Rancho   73mm 1980- 10/1983 $4-6

White interior, clear windows, opening hatch with black diecast hinge plate, body color diecast tailgate, black plastic base-grille, Whizzwheels. (Casting also used for E210-A and E-223-A. Prototype shown in 1980 Corgi catalog with silver body, but not produced in that color scheme.)

1. Metallic light brown (gold) body.

2. Metallic light green body.

3. Red body.

4. Orange body. (Also found in Little-Large Set 1355-A.)

5. Non-metallic green body.

6. Non-metallic blue body. (From transitional era 2-pack.)

77-A   Ital Design Bizzarini Manta   72mm 1971-1973 $15-20

Cream interior, clear windows, black diecast base, Whizzwheels.

(Note: Prototype shown in 1972 Corgi Juniors catalog with metallic dark blue body, but not released in that color scheme.)

1. Metallic hot pink body.

2. Non-metallic hot pink body.

3. Non-metallic lime green body.

4. Metallic copper body.

5. Metallic aqua-blue body.

6. Metallic red body.

77-B   Excavator   73mm 1977-1980 $10-15

Plastic interior, diecast chassis-base, black plastic wheels.

(Note: Prototype shown in 1977 Corgi Juniors catalog with yellow body and chassis, but not released in that color scheme.)

1. Yellow turning body, blue chassis-base, white plastic interior, vacuum plated arm and scoop.

2. White turning body, metallic blue chassis-base, red plastic interior, red plastic arm and scoop.

3. Yellow turning body, black chassis-base, white plastic interior, white plastic arm and scoop. (Possibly out of a set or from a later era.)

78-A   Ole Macdonald's Truck   63mm 1971-? $20-30

Unpainted diecast base-grille-engine with front fenders, Whizzwheels. (Similar to 931-A, but with revised base casting.)

1. Red cab, tan interior and rear body.

2. Red cab, brown interior and rear body.

78-B   Batcopter   76mm 1978-1981 $15-20

Red plastic interior, skids, base and rotors, blue canopy.

1. Black body, red bat shape labels with yellow "BAT MAN" text.

2. Black body, red bat shape labels without text.

79-A   Land Rover Military Ambulance   71mm 1975-1976

	Olive Drab	$10-15
	White and light blue (loose)	$15-20

No interior, plastic rear cover, black Whizzwheels. (Same body casting as E16-B.)

1. Olive drab body and rear cover, smooth black plastic baseplate with patent application number, amber tinted windows, red cross labels.

2. Olive drab body and rear cover, black plastic baseplate with patent number and suspension, amber tinted windows, red cross labels.

3. Olive drab body and rear cover, black plastic baseplate with patent number and suspension, blue tinted windows, red cross labels.

4. Olive drab body and rear cover, black plastic baseplate with patent number and suspension, clear windows, red cross labels.

5. White body, Light blue rear cover, black plastic baseplate with patent number and suspension, red cross labels. (Only found in Coast Guard Set E3022-A1.)

79-B   Olive Oyl's Aeroplane   68mm 1980- 10/1983 $20-30

Red propeller, vacuum plated plastic parts, black seat with figure, black plastic base, two Whizzwheels, labels on wings.

1. Yellow body.

80-A   Porsche Carrera   74mm 1974-1975 $8-12

Black plastic base, Whizzwheels, number 4 and red-white-blue stripe labels.

1. White body, clear windows, yellow interior.

2. White body, clear windows, red interior.

3. White body, amber tinted windows, yellow interior.

80-B   Fiat X1/9   73mm 1978-1978 $5-8

Same castings as 86-A, black plastic base and interior, chrome engine, clear windows, number 4 and red-white-blue labels, Whizzwheels.

1. White body.

80-C   Leyland Marvel Comics Van   73mm 1979-1980 $20-30

Green tinted windows, no interior, black plastic base, Whizzwheels.

1. Dark green body, Marvel Comics logo labels.

81-A   Daimler Fleetline Double-decker Bus 76mm 1974- 10/1983

Standard versions	$4-6
Coca-Cola & promotional versions	$10-15

Black plastic base, Whizzwheels (chrome unless noted), no interior.

1. Red body, faces in windows, "Visit Britain—Visit London" labels.

2. Red body, faces in windows, "Enjoy Coca-Cola" labels.

3. Red body, faces in windows, "See more London" labels.

4. Red body, black windows, "See more London" labels, black Whizzwheels; 1982.

5. Red body, black windows, "See more London" labels; 1982.

6. Red body, black windows, "BTA Welcome to Britain" labels; (Possibly a tourist shop special.)

7. Green body, black windows, interchangeable labels; 1982. (From unnumbered 3-pack.)

8. Cream body, black windows, interchangeable labels; 1982. (From unnumbered 3-pack.)

9. Dark blue body, black windows, interchangeable labels; 1982. (From unnumbered 3-pack. Also found in transitional era 2-pack without labels 1983-84 packed with random Juniors car.)

10. Red body, black windows, no labels or graphics; 1983-10/1983. (Excess stock sold-off by Corgi Toys Ltd. in unmarked 1985 style card.)

11. Red body, faces in windows, "Ready Brek PLAYBUS" labels. (Late 1970s UK breakfast cereal promotional model, exact date not known.)

12. Red body, faces in windows, "Hefty New Year's Eve in LONDON" labels, special gold foil box. (Late promotional model, exact date or promotion details not known.)

13. Red body, faces in windows, "Sugar Puffs" labels. (1976 U.K breakfast cereal promotional model.)

14. Red body, faces in windows, "Stay at Kensington Hilton" labels. (Hotel promotional model.)

15. Red body, black windows, "MECMAN" labels, mounted on stand with award plaque. (Promotional for Mecman, other details not known.)

82-A   Can-Am Racer   73mm 1974-1978 $8-12

Growler mechanism in base, off-white driver and engine, number 9 and stripe labels, black plastic base, Whizzwheels. (Casting also used for E20-D Penguinmobile.)

1. Metallic blue body.

2. Metallic purple body.

3. Metallic blue body, red "Growler" gear in base.

82-A   Yogi Bear's Jeep   61mm 1981- 10/1983 $20-30

Green interior with Yogi Bear figure, diecast base same color as body, Whizzwheels.

1. Dark yellow body and base, "Jellystone Park" hood label.

83-A   Commando V100 Armored Car   73mm 1974-1977 $8-12

Black plastic rotating turret, white "COMMANDO V100" labels, black plastic wheels, diecast lower body-base same color as upper body.

1. Olive drab body and base.

83-B   Goodyear Blimp   77mm 1980-1981 $4-6

Red and blue plastic fins, blue gondola, red engines and parts.

1. Chrome finish, Goodyear and Corgi graphics.

84-A   Daimler Scout Car   62mm 1974-1978 $8-12

Brown figure with gun moves sideways, black plastic base and wheels.

1. Olive drab body, red-white-olive rear label.

84-B   Bugs Bunny Buggy   70mm 1980- 10/1983

	Orange	$20-30

| | Copper-orange | $25-35 |
| | Red | $40-50 |

Bugs Bunny figure, carrot label on hood, unpainted diecast base with grille and headlights, Whizzwheels. (Body from E58-A Beach Buggy.)

1. Copper-orange body, red plastic dash and engine.
2. Copper-orange body, yellow plastic dash and engine.
3. Orange body, yellow plastic dash and engine.
4. Orange body, lighter red plastic dash and engine.
5. Red body, yellow plastic dash and engine.

85-A   Skip Dumper   58mm 1974-1978, 1980-10/1983 $4-6

Plastic tipper, black plastic seat and steering wheel, black plastic wheels.

1. Yellow body, red tipper.
2. Yellow body, red tipper, black plastic tow hook captured by rear axle.
3. Metallic dark green body, yellow tipper.
4. Non-metallic pale green body, yellow tipper.
5. Red body, yellow tipper. (Found in 1983-84 transitional period 2-pack to sell-off existing stock. May not have been sold separately.)

86-A   Fiat X1/9   73mm 1974-1978, 1980- 10/1983 $4-6

Black plastic "CORGI JUNIORS" base unless noted, vacuum plated plastic engine, clear windows unless noted, Whizzwheels. (Prototype shown in 1974 Corgi Juniors catalog with yellow body, but not produced in that color scheme. Different prototype shown in 1980 Corgi catalog with silver body and "9 FIAT" labels, but not produced in that color scheme.)

1. Apple green body, no labels, black interior.
2. Apple green body, no labels, red interior.
3. Light yellow body, number 4 and stripe labels, red interior.
4. Light yellow body, number 9, Fiat and stripe labels, red interior.
5. Light yellow body, no labels, Fiat and stripe labels, red interior.
6. Gold body, number 4 and stripe labels without Fiat name, black interior; 1980.
7. Gold body, number 9 labels, black interior.
8. Gold body, number 4, Fiat and stripe labels, black interior; 1981.
9. Gold body, number 9 and Fiat labels, black interior; 1981.
10. Gold body, number 9 and Fiat labels, red interior; 1981.
11. Orange body, number 9 and Fiat labels, red interior; 1981.
12. Orange body, no labels, red interior; 1981. (Also see E203-A.)
13. Metallic blue body, number 9 and Fiat labels, red interior. (Also found in Little-Large set 1356-A.)
14. Metallic blue body, number 9 and Fiat labels, black interior. (Also found in Little-Large set 1356-A.)
15. White body, no labels, black interior, revised "corgi" text on base.
16. White body, no labels, black interior, yellow tinted windows, revised "corgi" text on base.
17. White body, no labels, red interior, revised "corgi" text on base.
18. White body, number 4 and stripe labels, black interior, revised "corgi" text on base.
19. Metallic dark gray body, no labels, black interior, revised "corgi" text on base; 1983. (May be from transitional era after Mettoy closure.)
20. Non-metallic dark blue body, no labels, black interior, revised "corgi" text on base; 1983. (May be from transitional era after Mettoy closure.)
21. Non-metallic dark blue body, no labels, red interior, base with brand blanked; 1983. (May be from transitional era after Mettoy closure.)
22. Non-metallic medium blue body, no labels, red interior, revised "corgi" text on base; 1983. (May be from transitional era after Mettoy closure.)
23. Yellow body, no labels, black interior, revised "corgi" text on base; 1983. (May be from transitional era after Mettoy closure.)
24. Yellow body, no labels, red interior, revised "corgi" text on base; 1983. (May be from transitional era after Mettoy closure.)
25. Tan body, no labels, black interior, revised "corgi" text on base; 1983. (May be from transitional era after Mettoy closure.)

87-A   Mercedes-Benz Coca-Cola Truck   Not Released   N/A

Not Issued. Assigned 87-A for clarity due to appearance of prototype in catalog. (Note: The Mercedes Coca-Cola Lorry prototype shown in the 1974 Corgi Juniors catalog, and the second box van prototype shown in the 1975 Corgi Juniors catalog, were never produced. All production models were made using the Leyland Terrier casting.)

87-B   Leyland Terrier Delivery Van   73mm 1975-1980+

	Standard Coca-Cola and	
	Pepsi Versions	$10-12
	Promotional Versions	$15-40

No interior, black plastic base unless noted, Whizzwheels.

1. Red body, white roofs, red and white Coca-Cola labels, blue tinted windows; 1975-1976.
2. White body, clear windows, red and blue Pepsi-Cola logo; 1975-1980.
3. White body, blue tinted windows, red and blue Pepsi-Cola logo; 1975-1980.
4. White body, black opaque windows, red & blue Pepsi-Cola labels (1983?)
5. Dark yellow body, blue tinted windows, Weetabix labels. (1979 promotional for Weetabix.)
6. Orange body, opaque black windows, W. H. Smith logo. (1980 promotional for W. H. Smith.)
7. White Body, white labels with "Caledonian Autominologists" and dates, blue tinted windows, black plastic base. (Promotional model for club, 1976.)
8. Red body, opaque black windows, black plastic base, "Gamleys" logo on white labels, 5dblspk Whizzwheels. (Promotional issue for Gamley's Toyshop.)
9. White body, pink-black-white "Advance" labels, 5dblspk Whizzwheels, opaque black windows. (Promotional issue for Advance Laundry.)
10. White body, orange "Treetex HORIZON" labels, 5dblspk Whizzwheels, opaque black windows. (Promotional issue for Treetex Horizon.)
11. White Body, white labels with "THINK BIGGEST" and "LEYLAND TERRIER" text and company logo, blue tinted windows, black plastic base. (Promotional model for Leyland, 1975.)
12. White body, opaque black windows, large "BCL bioflo REAGENTS FOR AUTOMATION" labels on sides extending down to rainbow-like arch around wheel openings, ordering information on box roof. (Promotional for BCL bioflo, possibly only 50 made.)

88-A   Mobile Crane   68mm 1975-1980 $4-6

No interior, black plastic wheels and hook. (Prototype shown in 1975 Corgi Juniors catalog with yellow body and red booms, but not produced in that color scheme.)

1. Light red body, yellow plastic upper and lower crane booms, mounting and base, amber tinted windows and dome lights.
2. Yellow body, vacuum plated plastic lower crane boom, black plastic base, black plastic upper crane boom and mounting, blue tinted windows and dome lights. (Found in set E3100-A.)
3. Yellow body, white plastic lower crane boom and base, black plastic upper crane boom and mounting, blue tinted windows and dome lights. (Example found in Mexico, possibly available elsewhere.)

89-A   Citroen Dyane   76mm 1975-1982 $4-6

Opening hatch, clear windows unless noted, black plastic base, Whizzwheels.

1. Dark metallic yellow (gold) body, black roof, red interior.
2. Lighter metallic yellow body, black roof, red interior.
3. Lighter metallic yellow body and roof, red interior.
4. Metallic green body, black roof, red interior.
5. Metallic purple body, yellow interior.
6. Metallic purple body, yellow interior, yellow tinted windows.
7. Non-metallic yellow body and roof, red interior.
8. Orange body, red interior.
9. Metallic dark blue body, red interior.
10. Metallic light blue body, yellow interior.

90-A   Chevrolet Fire Ball Custom Van   68mm 1977-1979 $4-6

No interior, black plastic base, Whizzwheels.

1. Black body with thin roof ribs, "CHEVROLET VAN" base, clear windows, "FIRE BALL" side labels.
2. Black body with thin roof ribs, "CHEVROLET VAN" base, blue tinted windows, "FIRE BALL" side labels.
3. Black body with thin roof ribs, "CHEVROLET VAN" base, amber tinted windows, "FIRE BALL" side labels.
4. Black body with heavy roof ribs, "CHEVROLET VAN" base, blue tinted windows, "FIRE BALL" side labels.
5. Black body with thin roof ribs, "U.S. VAN" base, amber tinted windows, "FIRE BALL" side labels.
6. Black body with heavy roof ribs, "U.S. VAN" base, blue tinted windows, "FIRE BALL" side labels.
7. Black body with heavy roof ribs, "U.S. VAN" base, amber tinted windows, "FIRE BALL" side labels.

91-A   Chevrolet Golden Eagle Van   68mm 1977-1979 $4-6

No interior, black plastic base, Whizzwheels.

1. Orange body with thin roof ribs, amber tinted windows, "CHEVROLET VAN" base, "Golden Eagle" labels with detailed mountain lake scene and eagle with claws forward, label has dark colors.
2. Orange body with thin roof ribs, amber tinted windows, "CHEVROLET VAN" base, "GOLDEN EAGLE" all upper case on side labels, lighter color mountain lake scene with eagle claws down.

3. Orange body with thin roof ribs, blue tinted windows, "CHEVROLET VAN" base, "GOLDEN EAGLE" all upper case on side labels, lighter color mountain lake scene with eagle claws down.

4. Orange body with thin roof ribs, amber tinted windows, "U.S. VAN" base, "GOLDEN EAGLE" all upper case on side labels, lighter color mountain lake scene with eagle claws down.

5. Orange body with thin roof ribs, blue tinted windows, "U.S. VAN" base, "GOLDEN EAGLE" all upper case on side labels, lighter color mountain lake scene with eagle claws down.

91-B   Vantastic Custom Van   69mm 1980-1981 $4-6

Customized Dodge Van body casting with raised rear roof, blue tinted windows, no interior, unpainted diecast base with exhaust pipes and "Hot Rod Custom Van" lettering, Whizzwheels.

1. Black body, yellow and orange Vantastic labels.

92-A   VW Polo   73mm 1977-1981 $4-6

Opening doors, amber tinted windows, black plastic base, Whizzwheels, no body graphics.

1. Metallic lime green body, yellow interior.

2. Metallic medium green body, yellow interior.

3. Metallic medium green body, orange interior.

4. Metallic medium green body, red interior.

5. Non-metallic pale green body, yellow interior.

6. Tan body, red interior.

93-A   Tug Boat   75mm 1977-1979 $4-6

Orange plastic superstructure, yellow plastic hull, three black plastic wheels.

1. Metallic dark green deck.

93-B   Dodge Magnum   72mm 1980-1981 $4-6

Opaque black windows, no interior, unpainted diecast base, Whizzwheels, opening hood, vacuum plated plastic engine, grille and bumpers.

1. Yellow body.

94-A   Porsche 917   72mm 1974-1977 $8-12

Vacuum plated plastic interior and engine, amber tinted windows, black plastic base with Growler gear, Whizzwheels; same casting as 51-A. (Prototype shown in 1975 Corgi Juniors catalog with metallic maroon body, but not produced in that color scheme.)

1. Metallic silver body.

94-B   Chevrolet Adidas Van 68mm 1978-1981, 1983-10/1983

Adidas and blank versions	**$4-6**
Promotional	**$10-15**

No interior, black plastic base, white "adidas" and logo on blue side labels unless noted.

1. Medium blue body, "Chevrolet Van" base, blue tinted windows, chrome spoke Whizzwheels.

2. Medium blue body with thin ribs on roof, "U.S. Van" base, blue tinted windows, chrome spoke Whizzwheels.

3. Medium blue body with heavy ribs on roof, "U.S. Van" base, blue tinted windows, chrome spoke Whizzwheels.

4. Medium blue body with thin ribs on roof, "U.S. Van" base, amber tinted windows, chrome spoke Whizzwheels.

5. Medium blue body with heavy ribs on roof, "U.S. Van" base, amber tinted windows, chrome spoke Whizzwheels.

6. Medium blue body, ??? base, clear windows, black Whizzwheels.

7. Medium blue body with thin ribs on roof, "U.S. Van" base, opaque black windows, chrome spoke Whizzwheels.

8. Medium blue body with heavy ribs on roof, "U.S. Van" base, opaque black windows, chrome spoke Whizzwheels.

9. Medium blue body with heavy ribs on roof, "U.S. Van" base, opaque black windows, chrome 5dblspk Whizzwheels, "adidas" and logo tampo printed. (1983-10/1983, excess stock later sold in unmarked Corgi Toys Ltd. card.)

10. Light blue body with thin ribs on roof, ??? base, blue tinted windows, chrome spoke Whizzwheels. (Body color is noticeably lighter than label background. Possibly a paint color substitution at the factory due to a shortage.)

11. White body, medium blue roof with heavy ribs, "U.S. Van" base, opaque black windows, chrome foiled Whizzwheels, "adidas" and logo tampo printed. (1983, assembly error using Gas van bodies to use up inventory.)

Non-Adidas versions without their own unique model number:

(No officially assigned model number. Listed here for closest matching cataloged item.)

12. Medium blue body with heavy roof ribs, blank base, opaque black windows, chrome Whizzwheels, no decorations or logos. (Found in 1983-84 transitional period 2-pack to sell-off existing stock.)

13. Medium green body with heavy roof ribs, "U.S. VAN" base, opaque black windows, black Whizzwheels, no decorations or logos. (Found in 1983-84 transitional period 2-pack to sell-off existing stock.)

14. Medium green body with heavy roof ribs, blank base, clear windows, chrome Whizzwheels, no decorations or logos. (Found in 1983-84 transitional period 2-pack to sell-off existing stock.)

15. Red body with light roof ribs, blank base, opaque black windows, chrome Whizzwheels, no decorations or logos. (Found in 1983-84 transitional period 2-pack to sell-off existing stock.)

16. Maroon body with light roof ribs, blank base, opaque black windows, chrome Whizzwheels, no decorations or logos. (Found in 1983-84 transitional period 2-pack to sell-off existing stock.)

17. Yellow body with light roof ribs, "U.S. VAN" base, opaque black windows, chrome Whizzwheels, no decorations or logos. (Found in 1983-84 transitional period 2-pack to sell-off existing stock.)

18. Yellow body with light roof ribs, "CHEVROLET VAN" base, blue tinted windows, chrome Whizzwheels, no decorations or logos. (Found in 1983-84 transitional period 2-pack to sell-off existing stock.)

19. Dark yellow body with heavy roof ribs, blank base, opaque black windows, chrome Whizzwheels, no decorations or logos. (Found in 1983-84 transitional period 2-pack to sell-off existing stock.)

20. Black body with light roof ribs, "CHEVROLET VAN" base, blue tinted windows, chrome Whizzwheels, no decorations or logos. (Found in 1983-84 transitional period 2-pack to sell-off existing stock.)

21. Pink body with light roof ribs, "U.S. VAN" base, blue tinted windows, chrome Whizzwheels, no decorations or logos. (Found in 1983-84 transitional period 2-pack to sell-off existing stock.)

22. White body with heavy roof ribs, blank base, opaque black windows, chrome Whizzwheels, no decorations or logos. (Found in 1983-84 transitional period 2-pack to sell-off existing stock.)

23. White body, "U.S. Van" base, amber tinted windows, chrome 5dblspk Whizzwheels, white rectangular label with red "POLICE" on sides. (Probably transitional period model or out of unknown set.)

24. White body with heavy ribs on roof, "U.S. Van" base, opaque black windows, chrome Whizzwheels, side labels with "WIMPY" and character on sides. (From Wimpy promotional set. May be from later era.)

25. White body with heavy ribs on roof, blank base, opaque black windows, chrome Whizzwheels, side labels with "WIMPY" and character on sides. (From Wimpy promotional set. May be from later era.)

26. White body, green side labels with Arabic writing and yellow sail shape. (Arabian issue.)

27. White body with thick roof ribs, opaque black windows, black plastic "U.S. VAN" base, Whizzwheels, green and black "UniChem" labels with clear plastic backing. (Promotional model for UniChem, also found in 2-packs.)

28. White body with thick roof ribs, clear windows, black plastic "U.S. VAN" base, Whizzwheels, green and black "UniChem" labels with clear plastic backing. (Promotional model for UniChem, also found in 2-packs.)

29. Silver body with heavy ribs on roof, "U.S. VAN" base, amber tinted windows, chrome Whizzwheels, silver "Jaws Telephone Service" side labels. (Found in James Bond Gift Sets E3030-A and E3082-A.)

30. Silver body with light ribs on roof, "CHEVROLET VAN" base, amber tinted windows, chrome Whizzwheels, silver "Jaws Telephone Service" side labels. (Found in James Bond Gift Sets E3030-A and E3082-A.)

31. White body with light ribs on roof, "U.S. Van" base, opaque black windows, chrome Whizzwheels, silver "Jaws Telephone Service" side labels. (Found in James Bond Gift Sets E3030-A and E3082-A.)

32. White body with light ribs on roof, "U.S. Van" base, amber tinted windows, chrome Whizzwheels, silver "Jaws Telephone Service" side labels. (Found in James Bond Gift Sets E3030-A and E3082-A.)

33. Vans without a unique model number with other body colors and combinations of features exist but have not yet been reported.

95-A   Leyland Coca-Cola Van   73mm 1977-1982 $15-20

Same casting as 87-B, black plastic base, Whizzwheels. (87-B1 has white roof.)

1. All red body, blue tinted windows, red and white Coca-Cola logo side labels.

2. All red body, opaque black windows, red and white Coca-Cola logo side labels.

3. All red body, opaque black windows, no side labels. (Transitional era model from 1983-84 used in 2-packs to clear excess inventory.)

96-A   Field Gun and Soldiers   80mm 1975-1978 $8-12

Chassis and raising gun barrel castings, two black plastic wheels, brown plastic accessory piece with two soldiers.

1. Olive drab gun, white star and "U.S. Army" label.

96-B   Ford Thunderbird 1957   72mm 1980-10/1983

Standard including red	$5-8
Red with Vega$ card	$20-30
White with Vega$ card	$120-150

Opening hood, detailed engine, clear windshield, black interior, vacuum plated plastic grille, bumpers and spare wheel cover, unpainted diecast base, Whizzwheels.
1. Red body; Vegas$ packaging; 1980-1981.
2. White body; Vegas$ packaging; 1980-1981.
3. Red body; standard packaging; 1982-1983.
4. Cream body; 1982-1983.
5. Green body, 1983.

97-A   Guy Exxon Tanker   73mm 1975-1976

Exxon	$8-12
Co-op	$20-30

Same casting as 14-C, no interior, black plastic base and headlights, Whizzwheels, red-white-blue Exxon labels.
1. White body, blue tinted windows.
2. White body, purple tinted windows.
3. White body, blue tinted windows, "CO-OP 100% CANADIAN OWNED" labels. (Canadian promotional model.)

97-B   (Leyland) Petrol Tanker   75mm 1977-10/1983 $4-6

No interior, black plastic lower body-base, Whizzwheels.
1. Metallic silver body, silver background paper labels with "Shell" and red-orange-white Shell logo, opaque black windows.
2. Metallic silver body, silver background paper labels with "Shell" and red-orange-white Shell logo, blue tinted windows.
3. Metallic silver body, silver background paper labels with "Shell" and red-orange-white Shell logo, amber tinted windows.
4. Light red body, red-white-black Texaco logo, amber tinted windows.
5. White body, red and green BP labels with shield to rear, amber tinted windows, black Whizzwheels.
6. White body, red and green BP labels with shield to front, amber tinted windows, black Whizzwheels.
7. White body, red and green BP labels with shield to rear, amber tinted windows, chrome Whizzwheels.
8. White body, red and green BP labels with shield to front, amber tinted windows, chrome Whizzwheels.
9. White body, red and green BP labels with shield to front, opaque black windows, chrome Whizzwheels.
10. White body, red and green BP labels with shield to front, amber tinted windows, chrome Whizzwheels, Corgi Juniors name removed from baseplate.
11. White body, red and green BP tampo printed with shield to front, opaque black windows, chrome Whizzwheels.
12. White body, Total labels, possibly not released. (Shown in 1982 Corgi catalog.)
13. Medium blue body, no labels or graphics, opaque black windows. (Transition period model made during loss of trademark licensing to sell-off existing stock.)
14. Yellow body, no labels or graphics, opaque black windows, black Whizzwheels. (Transition period model made during loss of trademark licensing to sell-off existing stock.)
15. Medium green body, no labels or graphics, opaque black windows. (Transition period model made during loss of trademark licensing to sell-off existing stock.)

98-A   Marcos XP   71mm 1975-1977 $8-12

Growler, modified E71-A casting with cast headlamps, vacuum plated plastic interior and engine, black plastic base with black growler gear, Whizzwheels.
1. Metallic Amber body, amber tinted windows.
2. Non-metallic orange body.

98-B   Mercedes-Benz Mobile Shop   72mm 1977-1979 $5-8

Clear windows, yellow front interior, grocery store printed scene on folded cardboard insert, black plastic base, Whizzwheels. (Prototype shown in 1978 Corgi catalog with orange body, but not produced in this color scheme.)
1. Medium blue body. (Exact shade varies from darker blue through light blue.)

98-C   Police Jet Ranger Helicopter   77mm 1980-1980 $4-6

Red interior, base, pontoons and rotors, clear windows, Police labels.
1. White body.

99-A   Jokermobile   76mm 1979-1981 $20-30

Same casting as 36-B, no interior, black plastic base, Whizzwheels, "JOKER" labels.

1. White body, blue tinted windows and roof light, "CORGI JUNIORS" text on base, blanked area on base where former model name had been, no copyright on labels.
2. White body, blue tinted windows and roof light, "corgi" text on base, "© DC COMICS INC 1979" in blanked area on base, "©DC 1979" on right side label, no copyright on front or left side labels.
3. White body, amber tinted windows and roof light, "corgi" text on base, "© DC COMICS INC 1979" in blanked area on base, "©DC 1979" on right side label, no copyright on front or left side labels.
4. White body, clear windows and roof light, "corgi" text on base, "© DC COMICS INC 1979" in blanked area on base, "©DC 1979" on right side label, no copyright on front or left side labels.

100-A   Hulkcycle   63mm 1981- 10/1983 $20-30

Green plastic seat with Incredible Hulk figure, three red plastic wheels.
1. Black body.

101-A   Leyland Punch and Judy Show Van 73mm 1983-10/1983 $20-30

Blue tinted windows, no interior, black plastic base, Whizzwheels.
1. Red body, colorful "Kasperl-Theater" labels; German issue.

102-A   Renault 5 Turbo   70mm 1981- 10/1983 $4-6

Red interior, grille, bumpers and lower body stripe, clear windows, vacuum plated plastic mirrors, black plastic base, Whizzwheels. (Prototype shown in 1981 Corgi catalog with opaque black windows, but not produced with this feature.)
1. Yellow body with orange tint, black roof, black and white "9 MICHELIN" and "RENAULT elf" labels.
2. Yellow body with green tint, black roof, black and white "9 MICHELIN" and "RENAULT elf" labels.
3. Yellow body with orange tint, black roof, no labels. (Found in set E3115-A.)

103-A   Ford Transit Wrecker   72mm 1981- 10/1983 $4-6

No interior, red plastic boom and roof bar, black plastic base and hook, red-white-black "24 hour service" labels, Whizzwheels.
1. White body, blue tinted windows.
2. White body, amber tinted windows.
3. White body, smoke tinted windows.
4. White body, opaque black windows.

104-A   Ford Mustang Cobra   74mm 1981- 10/1983 $5-8

Opening hatch, Whizzwheels. (Also see E140-A. Prototype shown in 1981 Corgi catalog with silver body and black base, but not released in this color scheme.)
1. Orange body, white interior, clear windows, black plastic base, no labels.
2. Orange body, white interior, clear windows, orange plastic base, no labels.
3. Orange body, yellow interior, amber tinted windows, black plastic base, no labels.
4. Orange body, white interior, clear windows, black plastic base and grille, red/orange/black "Mustang" labels.
5. Yellow body, yellow interior, amber tinted windows, black plastic base and grille, red/orange/black "Mustang" labels.
6. White body, yellow interior, amber tinted windows, black plastic base, no labels, "CHAMPIONS" box. (Issued in UK only.)
7. Metallic steel blue body, white interior, clear windows, black plastic base, no labels.
8. Red body, yellow interior, amber tinted windows, black plastic base, no labels, "CHAMPIONS" box. (Issued in UK only.)

105-A   Ford Escort   75mm 1981- 10/1983 $4-6

Opening doors, clear windows, black plastic base, black painted grille, Whizzwheels.
1. Metallic green body with red tail lamps, light brown interior.
2. Metallic green body with body color tail lamps, light brown interior.
3. Metallic light blue body, light brown interior.
4. Non-metallic blue body, light brown interior.
5. Non-metallic blue body, black interior.

107-A   Austin Mini Metro   75mm 1981- 10/1983

Standard	$4-6
Promotional	$15-20

Opening doors, clear windows, black plastic base and grille, Whizzwheels. (Prototype shown in 1981 Corgi catalog with gold body, but not produced in this color scheme.)
1. Metallic dark blue body, light tan interior. (Also issued in Union Jack box.)
2. Bright blue body, light tan interior.
3. Bright blue body, red interior.
4. Bright blue body, white interior. (Also issued in "CHAMPIONS" box.)
5. Silver body, red interior. (Also issued in "CHAMPIONS" box.)
6. Red body, tan interior. (Also issued in "THE BEST OF BRITISH" box.)

7. Red body, white interior. (Found in 1353A Little and Large Set.)

8. White body without graphics, black interior, "Longbridge Family Day Souvenir" and "MG Metro Turbo" on special window box. (Promotional model for Austin Rover.)

(Note: Special "Royal Mail" versions of the Austin Mini Metro produced during the last months of Mettoy but marketed after Mettoy's closure are listed in the Corgi Toys Ltd. listings. They were never publicly assigned a Mettoy era model number.)

108-A   Railroad Locomotive   76mm 1981- 10/1983 $4-6
Black plastic boiler, yellow cowcatcher, base and parts, unpainted diecast smokestack top and headlight, black plastic railroad wheels.
1. Red cab and chassis.

111-A   Railroad Passenger Coach   75mm 1981- 10/1983 $4-6
Yellow plastic body, Union Pacific labels, black plastic railroad wheels.
1. Red chassis.

112-A   Railroad Goods Wagon   75mm 1981- 10/1983 $4-6
Green plastic body, red sliding door, black plastic railroad wheels.
1. Red chassis, "Buffalo Bill's Circus" labels.
2. Red chassis, "Wild West Show" labels.

113-A   Paddle Steamer   75mm 1982- 10/1983 $4-6
White plastic lower superstructure, stacks, sternwheel and front roller.
1. Yellow upper superstructure, blue hull, "St. Louis Queen" labels.

114-A   Stage Coach   80mm 1981- 10/1983 $4-6
Light brown horses, tongue and spoked wheels, yellow interior, driver and roof.
1. Red body.

115-A   James Bond Citroen 2CV6   74mm 1981- 10/1983 $25-35
Opening doors, red interior, clear windows, black plastic base, Whizzwheels.
1. Dark yellow body, black grille.
2. Pale yellow body, black grille.

116-A   Mercedes-Benz España '82 Team Bus 74mm 1981- 10/1983 $5-8
Amber tinted windows with faces, soccer team labels, black plastic base and grille, Whizzwheels.
1. Red body, white label panels.

117-A   Chevrolet España '82 Team Van 68mm 1981- 10/1983 $5-8
No interior, black plastic base, Whizzwheels.
1. White body with thin roof ribs, "CHEVROLET VAN" base, blue tinted windows, "Naranjito ESPAÑA 82" labels.
2. White body with thin roof ribs, "CHEVROLET VAN" base, yellow tinted windows, "Naranjito ESPAÑA 82" labels.
3. White body with thin roof ribs, "U.S. VAN" base, blue tinted windows, "Naranjito ESPAÑA 82" labels.
4. White body with thin roof ribs, "U.S. VAN" base, yellow tinted windows, "Naranjito ESPAÑA 82" labels.
5. White body with heavy roof ribs, "U.S. VAN" base, blue tinted windows, "Naranjito ESPAÑA 82" labels.

118-A   Mercedes-Benz Airport Bus   74mm 1983- 10/1983 $15-20
Opaque black windows, black plastic base and grille, Whizzwheels.
1. Orange body, black stripes, white "Flughafenbus" graphics on sides. German issue.

119-A   Chubb Airport Crash Tender   74mm 1983- 10/1983 $15-20
Same casting as 123-A, clear windows, yellow interior, roof panels and nozzle, black plastic base, six Whizzwheels.
1. Red body, number 9 and "Flughafen-Feuewehr" labels. German issue.

120-A   Dan Dare Car   (1981)   N/A
Not issued. Prototype shown in 1981 Corgi catalog.

120-B   Leyland Ice Cream Truck   73mm 1983- 10/1983 $15-20
Blue tinted windows, no interior, black plastic base, Whizzwheels.
1. White body, "Frohliche Eiszeit" labels, German issue.

121-A   Chevrolet Technical Service Van 68mm 1983- 10/1983 $15-20
Tinted windows, no interior, black plastic base, Whizzwheels.
1. Blue body, white "Technischer Kundendienst" labels, amber tinted windows. German issue.
2. Blue body, white "Technischer Kundendienst" labels, blue tinted windows. German issue.

122-A   Covered Wagon   75mm 1982- 10/1983 $4-6
Light brown horses, tongue and spoked wheels, yellow figures and front base.
1. Green body, removable white plastic top.

123-A   Chubb Airport Crash Tender   74mm 1982- 10/1983 $4-6
Clear windows, black plastic base, six Whizzwheels.
1. Red body, yellow interior, roof panels and nozzle, black and white "AIRPORT RESCUE" and number 8 labels.

2. Red body, cream interior, roof panels and nozzle, black and white "AIRPORT RESCUE" and number 8 labels.

124-A   Mercedes-Benz 350 SL   75mm 1982- 10/1983 $4-6
Clear windows, tan interior, black plastic base and tow hook, Whizzwheels.
1. Metallic light green body, silver grille.
2. Red body, silver grille.
3. Red body, no accent painting.

125-A   Ford Transit Dropside Truck 72mm 1982- 10/1983 $4-6
Opaque black windows unless noted, no interior, black plastic base, Whizzwheels.
1. Yellow body, black Wimpey graphics on doors. (similar to 146-A.)
2. Yellow body, no graphics.
3. Yellow body, amber tinted windows, no graphics.
4. Yellow body, blue tinted windows, no graphics.
5. Medium blue body, no graphics.
6. Medium blue body, clear windows, no graphics.
7. Medium green body, no graphics.
8. Medium green body, no graphics, amber tinted windows.
9. Medium green body, no graphics, blue tinted windows.
10. White body, no graphics.
11. Red body, no graphics.
12. Red body, no graphics, blue tinted windows.
13. Brown body, no graphics.
14. Light green body, no graphics. (Also used in set E3114-A.)

126-A   Ford Transit Wrecker   72mm 1983- 10/1983 $15-20
Same casting as 103-A, opaque black windows, red plastic boom and roof bar, black plastic base and hook, Whizzwheels.
1. Bright yellow body, "Abschleppdienst hilft Tag und Nacht" labels. German issue.

127-A   Ford Escort ADAC
**   Road Service Car   75mm 1983- 10/1983 $15-20**
Tan interior, clear windows, black plastic base, Whizzwheels.
1. Yellow body, black "ADAC-Strassenwacht" and "ADAC" graphics. German issue.

128-A   Fred Flintstone's Flyer   69mm 1982- 10/1983 $20-30
Fred Flintstone figure, tan plastic front wheels and rear log roller.
1. Orange body.

129-A   Ford Sierra 2.3 Ghia   75mm 1983- 10/1983
Standard	$4-6
Ford promotional packaging	$5-8
Dealer promotional graphics	$8-10

Opening doors, clear windows, plastic lower body-base, Whizzwheels.
1. Yellow body, red interior and taillights, light brown lower body-base.
2. Yellow body, red interior and taillights, black lower body-base. (Shown in 1983 Corgi catalog as part of set E2551-A. Was it released?)
3. Metallic silver brown body, brown interior, reddish taillights, brownish gray lower body-base.
4. Metallic silver body, yellow interior, yellow taillights, gray lower body-base. (Packaged with dinghy in set E2551-B.)
5. Metallic Silver body, black interior, red taillights, gray base. (packaged in promotional Ford box.)
6. Metallic Silver body, brown interior and taillights, gray base. (packaged in promotional Ford box.)
7. Blue body, red interior and taillights, gray base. (also packaged in promotional Ford double-wide card.)
8. Blue body, tan interior and taillights, gray base.
9. Blue body, tan interior and taillights, black base.
10. Red body, red interior and taillights, light gray lower body-base, white "O&M" on hood. (Promotional issue by Ford dealer, possibly Code 2 by Ford.)
11. Red body, brown interior and taillights, light brown lower body-base, "AIRFLOW" on hood. (Promotional issue by Ford dealer, possibly Code 2 by Ford.)

131-A   Magnum PI Ferrari 308 GTS   75mm 1982- 10/1983 $4-6
Identical to 136-A, clear windshield, white seats, black dashboard, grille, vents and base, Whizzwheels.
1. Dark red body.
2. Bright red body.

133-A   Magnum PI Buick Regal
**   Police Car   75mm 1982- 10/1983 $4-6**
Identical to E150-A, vacuum plated plastic interior, grille and bumpers unless noted, offset round red roof light, black plastic base with suspension unless noted, Whizzwheels. (Note: It is not possible to distinguish between E150-A and E133-A once they have been removed from their packaging. All variations have been listed for both. Similar cars with a full width lightbar on the roof are later J60 produced by

Corgi Toys Ltd. Prototype for both E133-A and E150-A shown in 1980 catalog with dark blue ends, but not produced in that color scheme.)

1. Black front and rear, white center of body, amber tinted windows, black "POLICE" on small white door labels.

2. Black front and rear, white center of body, amber tinted windows, black "POLICE" on small white door labels, unplated gray interior, grill and bumpers. (Produced at a time when the vacuum plating machine had broken-down.)

3. Black front and rear, white center of body, clear windows, black "POLICE" on large white door labels.

4. Black front and rear, white center of body, clear windows, white "POLICE" on large blue door labels. (Same labels as used on E17-D Metropolis Police Car.)

134-A   Barney's Buggy   69mm 1982- 10/1983 $20-30
Tan interior, grille and base, Flintstones character driver, black plastic wheels.

1. Red body with brown wheel markings.

135-A   Austin Metro Datapost   70mm 1982- 10/1983 $4-6
Same casting as 107-A, opening doors, clear windows, black plastic base and tow hook, Whizzwheels.

1. White body, blue roof and hood, clear plastic "77 HEPOLITE" hood label, "Tricentral 77 Datapost" side label with paper backing, tan interior. (Label prevents doors from opening.)

2. White body, blue roof and hood, clear plastic "77 HEPOLITE" hood label, "Tricentral 77 Datapost" side tampo printing, tan interior.

3. White body, blue roof and hood, clear plastic "77 HEPOLITE" hood label, "Tricentral 77 Datapost" side tampo printing, red interior.

136-A   Ferrari 308 GTS   75mm 1982- 10/1983
                                    Standard Release $4-6
                                    Promotional $10-15
Casting and details as 131-A.

1. Bright red body, otherwise 131-A.

2. Black body, tan seats, no graphics.

3. Black body, ivory seats, yellow hood panel with "FERRARI" and horse logo. (Promotional model packaged in special box for W. H. Smith Ltd. Listed under this number for documentation purposes only.)

137-A   VW Polo Turbo   73mm 1982- 10/1983 $4-6
Same castings as 92-A, opening doors, clear windows unless noted, black plastic base and tow hook, Whizzwheels.

1. Cream body, red interior, red and orange trim and number 6 graphics.

2. Cream body, yellow interior, red and orange trim and number 6 graphics.

3. White body, red interior, red and orange trim and number 6 graphics.

4. White body, red interior, red and orange trim and number 6 graphics, no graphics on sides.

5. White body, red interior, blue and green trim and number 6 graphics.

138-A   Rover 3500 Triplex   75mm 1982- 10/1983 $4-6
Same casting as 8-D, clear windows, red interior, opening hatch, black plastic base and tow hook, Whizzwheels.

1. White body, blue roof and hood, red interior, number 12 and Triplex graphics.

2. White body, blue roof and hood, white interior, number 12 and Triplex graphics.

3. White body, blue roof and hood, yellow interior, number 12 and Triplex graphics.

4. White body, blue roof and hood, tan interior, number 12 and Triplex graphics.

139-A   Porsche Carrera Turbo   74mm 1982- 10/1983 $4-6
Same casting as 80-A, clear windows, black plastic base, Whizzwheels.

1. Black body, yellow interior, gold name and stripe graphics.

2. Black body, white interior, gold name and stripe graphics.

140-A   Ford Mustang Cobra   73mm 1982- 10/1983 $4-6
Same casting as 104-A, Whizzwheels.

1. Bright yellow body, black plastic grille-lower body-base with tow hook, amber tinted windows, red interior, red /orange / black "MUSTANG" hood graphic, red / orange swish side graphics.

2. Bright yellow body, yellow plastic grille-lower body-base with tow hook, amber tinted windows, yellow interior, red /orange / black "MUSTANG" hood graphic, red / orange swish side graphics.

3. Bright yellow body, orange plastic grille-lower body-base with tow hook, clear windows, yellow interior, red /orange / black "MUSTANG" hood graphic, red / orange swish side graphics.

4. Bright yellow body, orange plastic grille-lower body-base with tow hook, clear windows, white interior, red /orange / black "MUSTANG" hood graphic, red / orange swish side graphics.

5. Orange body, orange plastic grille-lower body-base with tow hook, clear windows, white interior, no body graphics.

6. Red body with white base and interior, yellow tinted windows. (Shown in 1983 catalog as part of set E2553-A. Was it produced?)

141-A   Ford Capri 3.0 S   75mm 1982- 10/1983 $4-6
Same casting as 61-C, opening hood, Whizzwheels.

1. White body, black bumpers, grille and base, yellow interior, red and green stripes, red "8," green "Alitalia."

2. White body, black bumpers, grille and base, red interior, red and green stripes, red "8," green "Alitalia."

3. White body, red bumpers, grille and base, red interior, red and green stripes, red "8," green "Alitalia."

143-A   Leyland Royal Mail Van   73mm 1983- 10/1983 $4-6
No interior, plastic base, Whizzwheels.

1. Bright red body, transparent blue tinted windows, yellow "Royal Mail Parcels" on red labels, black base.

2. Bright red body, transparent smoked windows, yellow "Royal Mail Parcels" on red labels, blue base.

3. Bright red body, opaque black windows, yellow "Royal Mail Parcels" on red labels, black base.

4. Bright red body, opaque black windows, yellow "Royal Mail Parcels" on red labels, yellow base.

5. Bright red body, opaque black windows, yellow "Royal Mail Parcels" on red labels, red base.

144-A   Chevrolet British Gas Van   68mm 1983- 10/1983 $4-6
Chevrolet van casting with possible tooling variations, no interior, Whizzwheels.

1. White body, medium blue roof, opaque black windows, paper label side graphics as follows: dark blue lower sides with small "British Gas" and flame symbol along bottom, progressive medium and light blue stripes above, light blue "Gas" in upper rear corners of sides, black plastic "U.S. Van" base.

2. White body, medium blue roof, opaque black windows, paper label side graphics as follows: dark blue lower sides with small "British Gas" and flame symbol along bottom, progressive medium and light blue stripes above, light blue "Gas" in upper rear corners of sides, gray plastic "U.S. Van" base.

3. White body, medium blue roof, opaque black windows, tampo printed side graphics as follows: dark blue lower sides with small "British Gas" and flame symbol along bottom, progressive medium and light blue stripes above, light blue "Gas" in upper rear corners of sides, black plastic "U.S. Van" base.

4. White body, medium blue roof, amber tinted windows, tampo printed side graphics as follows: dark blue lower sides with small "British Gas" and flame symbol along bottom, progressive medium and light blue stripes above, light blue "Gas" in upper rear corners of sides, blank black plastic base.

(Also see Corgi Toys Ltd. era J37.)

145-A   Chevrolet British Telecom Van   68mm 1983- 10/1983 $4-6
No interior, black plastic "U.S. VAN" base, Whizzwheels.

1. Dark yellow body, blue tinted windows, blue "British TELECOM" and phone cord logo side labels on clear plastic backing.

2. Dark yellow body, amber tinted windows, blue "British TELECOM" and phone cord logo side labels on clear plastic backing.

3. Dark yellow body, opaque black windows, blue "British TELECOM" and phone cord logo side labels on clear plastic backing.

(Also see Corgi Toys Ltd. era J38.)

146-A   Ford Transit Dropside Truck   72mm 1983- 10/1983 $4-6
Same casting as 125-A, blue tinted windows, black plastic base, Whizzwheels.

1. Dark yellow body, black Wimpey graphics on hood. (Otherwise identical to 125-A1. Note: BTS Tyre Service version is from later Corgi Toys Ltd. era.)

147-A   Leyland Roadline Van   73mm 1983- 10/1983 $4-6
Green tinted windows, no interior, plastic base, Whizzwheels.

1. Bright green body, Roadline logo on white labels, black base.

2. Bright green body, Roadline logo on white labels, gray base.

3. Bright green body, Roadline logo on white labels, blue base.

148-A   USS Enterprise   70mm 1982- 10/1983 $20-30
Star Trek spacecraft, diecast and plastic body, black NCC-1701 label.

1. White body.

149-A   Klingon Warship   75mm 1982- 10/1983 $20-30
Star Trek spacecraft, single casting plus white plastic cabin.

1. Metallic dark blue body, yellow and black K labels.

2. Medium non-metallic blue body, yellow and black K labels.

150-A   Simon and Simon Buick Regal   75mm 1982- 10/1983 $8-15
          Police Car
Identical to E133-A, vacuum plated plastic interior, grille and bumpers unless noted, offset round red roof light, black plastic base with suspension unless noted, Whizzwheels. (Note: It is not possible to distinguish between E150-A and E133-A once they have been removed from their packaging. All variations have been listed

for both. Similar cars with a full width lightbar on the roof are later J60 produced by Corgi Toys Ltd. Prototype for both E133-A and E150-A shown in 1980 catalog with dark blue ends, but not produced in that color scheme.)

1. Black front and rear, white center of body, amber tinted windows, black "POLICE" on small white door labels.

2. Black front and rear, white center of body, amber tinted windows, black "POLICE" on small white door labels, unplated gray interior, grill and bumpers. (Produced at a time when the vacuum plating machine had broken-down.)

3. Black front and rear, white center of body, clear windows, black "POLICE" on large white door labels.

4. Black front and rear, white center of body, clear windows, white "POLICE" on large blue door labels. (Same labels as used on E17-D Metropolis Police Car.)

5. Black front and rear on top surfaces only, white center of body including entire sides, amber tinted windows, white "POLICE" on large blue door labels. (May be from production problem.)

151-A   Wilma's Coupe   **70mm 1982- 10/1983**   **$20-30**
Tan plastic base and rear panel, Wilma Flintstone figure, black Whizzwheels hidden under bottom.

1. Yellow body.

152-A   Simon and Simon 1957
          Chevrolet Convertible   **74mm 1982- 10/1983**   **$20-30**

Clear windshield, red interior, vacuum plated plastic grille and bumpers, black plastic base, Whizzwheels.

1. Black body with white upper rear fenders.

153-A   DeLorean DMC 12   **(1982)**   **N/A**
Not issued. Prototype shown in 1982 catalog.

156-A   1957 Chevrolet Convertible   **74mm 1982- 10/1983**   **$5-8**
Same casting as 152-A, clear windshield, red interior, vacuum plated plastic grille and bumpers, black plastic base, Whizzwheels.

1. White body, red and yellow flame trim.

2. White body, no graphics or trim. (1983)

3. Black body, white trim. (left-over stock of 152-A1, 1983.)

157-A   Army Jeep   **68mm 1983- 10/1983**   **$4-6**
Same casting as 12-E, clear windshield, yellow interior, no cover, black diecast base, Whizzwheels.

1. Olive drab body, white star on hood.

158-A   Centurion Army Tank   **70mm 1983- 10/1983**   **$4-6**
Same casting as 66-A, turning black plastic turret with raising gun barrel, black plastic base, three black plastic wheels.

1. Olive drab body.

159-A   Commando V100 Armored Car   72mm 1983- 10/1983   **$4-6**
Same casting as 83-A, turning black plastic turret, black plastic wheels.

1. Olive drab upper and lower body, white star and lettering labels.

160-A   VW Hot Rod   **73mm 1982- 10/1983**   **$4-6**
Same body casting as 60-A, vacuum plated plastic engines and interior, clear windows, black diecast base with "corgi" text, Whizzwheels.

1. Non-metallic orange body.

2. Non-metallic red body.

3. Shown in 1983 Corgi catalog with non-metallic red body and white painted base. (Was it produced?)

161-A   Opel Corsa 1.3SR   **71mm 1983- 10/1983**   **$???**
Prototype shown in 1983 Corgi catalog with golden yellow body, opaque black windows, black plastic base and grille. Was it produced?

163-A   Opel Corsa 1.3SR   **71mm 1983- 10/1983**   **$4-6**
Clear windows, black plastic base and grille, Whizzwheels.

1. Red body, white interior.

2. Red body, yellow interior.

170-A   Vauxhall Nova Hatchback   **71mm 1983- 10/1983**   **$4-6**
Clear windows, white interior, opening hatch, black plastic lower body-base-grille, Whizzwheels.

1. Red body.

2. Dark Blue body.

174-A   Quarry Truck   **74mm 1983- 10/1983**   **$4-6**
Plastic tipper, vacuum plated plastic grille, exhaust stacks and windows, black plastic base, six Whizzwheels.

1. Light yellow chassis-cab, red tipper.

2. Dark yellow chassis-cab, orange tipper.

175-A   Pipe Truck   **74mm 1983- 10/1983**   **$4-6**

Plastic flatbed with gray pipe load, vacuum plated plastic grille, stacks and windows, black plastic base, six Whizzwheels.

1. Red chassis-cab, yellow flatbed.

2. Red chassis-cab, black flatbed.

3. Green chassis-cab, yellow flatbed.

4. Green chassis-cab, white flatbed.

176-A (?) Flatbed Truck   **74mm 1983?**   **$6-10**
Plastic flatbed without load, vacuum plated plastic grille, stacks and windows, black plastic base, six Whizzwheels.

1. Blue chassis-cab, yellow flatbed, no load. (May not have been released separately. Found in unnumbered five truck set.)

177-A   Chemco Tanker   **75mm 1983- 10/1983**   **$4-6**
Light blue plastic tank, vacuum plated plastic fillers, hoses, grille, stacks and windows, black plastic base, six Whizzwheels.

1. Dark blue chassis-cab, Corgi Chemco graphics on tank.

(Note: Similar Shell version is from Corgi Toys Ltd. era and has a different model number.)

178-A   Container Truck   **74mm 1983- 10/1983**   **$4-6**
Plastic container on flatbed body, vacuum plated plastic grille, stacks and windows, black plastic base, six Whizzwheels.

1. Green chassis-cab, cream to white container on light green flatbed body, yellow and black "Corgi" graphics on container sides.

2. Green chassis-cab, cream to white container on medium green flatbed body, yellow and black "Corgi" graphics on container sides.

3. Green chassis-cab, cream to white container on black flatbed body, yellow and black "Corgi" graphics on container sides.

4. Red chassis-cab, red container with white top, red flatbed body, "Coca-Cola" graphics on container sides. (May be a transitional era model or may have a different model number.)

179-A   Chevrolet Corvette   **72mm 1983- 10/1983**   **$5-8**
Clear roof and windows, red interior, black dash and engine, opening hood, red taillights, black plastic base, Whizzwheels. (May come packaged as '83 Corvette or '84 Corvette.)

1. Cream body with low side vents, '83 Corvette card text. (Note: Error text, no prototype 1983 Corvette was ever produced.)

2. White body without low side vents, '84 Corvette card text. (Note: Side vents removed from die to allow side graphics on Football versions.)

3. Silver body without low side vents, no graphics.

4. Silver body without low side vents, clear plastic label on hood with blue "YOU'RE IN THE RACE" and logo. (Insurance company promotional, possibly Code 2.)

5. Yellow body, no graphics. (Shown in 1983 Corgi catalog. Was it produced?)

6. Pale metallic blue body, no graphics. (Shown in 1983 Corgi catalog. Was it produced?)

7. Black body, no graphics. (Possibly a transitional era model from 1983-84.)

180-A   Pontiac Firebird   **73mm 1983- 10/1983**   **$5-8**
Plastic spoiler, grille and interior, clear windows, black plastic base, Whizzwheels.

1. Red body, black seats & spoiler.

2. Black body, tan seats & spoiler.

3. Black body, white seats, tan spoiler. (Known lot where factory used-up excess spoiler moldings.)

4. Black body, white seats & spoiler.

5. Black body, black seats & spoiler.

6. Black body, black seats & spoiler, red area between headlamps. (Similar to a Firebird in a popular American TV show, but not licensed to use the trademarks.)

7. Blue body, black seats and spoiler. (Possibly a transitional period model or from the Bumper set E3035-A.)

181-A   Mercedes-Benz 300SL   **72mm 1983- 10/1983**   **$4-6**
Opening gullwing doors, clear windows, chrome plastic base and bumpers, 5dblspk Whizzwheels.

1. Red body, white interior.

2. Red body, tan interior.

3. Red body, yellow interior.

4. Red body, black interior, racing number on hood.

182-A   4x4 Renegade Jeep   **?mm 1983- 10/1983**   **$4-6**
Clear windshield, red interior and roll bar, black base, black off-road Whizzwheels with spare on rear. (Prototype shown in 1983 Corgi catalog with different wheels and graphics, but not produced with these features.)

1. Yellow body, blue / red / orange striped graphic on hood with black "5" in white box.

183-A   Renegade Jeep with Hood   66mm 1983- 10/1983 $4-6

White plastic roof, interior, black base, black off-road Whizzwheels with spare on rear. (Prototype shown in 1983 Corgi catalog with different wheels and graphics, but not produced with these features.)

1. Deep navy blue body, red / yellow / white striped graphic on hood with black "5" in white box.

184-A   Range Rover – Open Top   74mm 1983- 10/1983 $4-6

Clear windshield, black plastic grille and base, Whizzwheels.

1. Maroon body, tan interior.
2. Maroon body, white interior.
3. Red body, tan interior.
4. Red body, white interior.
5. Metallic green body, white interior including added driver figure. (May be preproduction model or from set, further details needed.)

185-A   Baja Off Road Van   69mm 1983- 10/1983 $4-6

Same casting as 91-B, black diecast base and grill, Whizzwheels.

1. Yellow body with flat black front, opaque black windows, red / white / black side labels with "4WD" side labels.

190-A   Buick Regal

**   Arabian Police Car   75mm 1983(?) - 10/1983 $15-20**

Same casting as 68-A, red roof light, black plastic base without suspension, Whizzwheels. (Produced for the Arabian market.)

1. White body, vacuum plated interior, grille and bumpers, amber tinted windows, black Arabic writing on white labels on front doors.
2. White body, vacuum plated interior, grille and bumpers, clear windows, black Arabic writing on white labels on front doors.
3. White body, light gray interior, grille and bumpers, clear windows, black Arabic writing on white labels on front doors.
4. White body, light gray interior, grille and bumpers, smoke tinted windows, black Arabic writing on white labels on front doors.

191-A   Leyland Arabian

**   Pepsi-Cola Truck   73mm 1983- 10/1983 $15-20**

Clear windows, no interior, black plastic base, Whizzwheels.

1. White body, red-white-blue-light blue Pepsi logo with Arabic lettering. Arabian issue.

192-A   Mercedes-Benz

**   Arabian Ambulance   74mm 1983- 10/1983 $15-20**

Same casting as 1-E, blue tinted windows and dome light, no interior, black plastic base, Whizzwheels.

1. White body, red crescent, Ambulance and Arabic door labels, Arabian issue.

193-A   Chubb Arabian Airport

**   Crash Tender   74mm 1983- 10/1983 $15-20**

Same casting as 123-A, black plastic base, six Whizzwheels.

1. Red body, clear windows, vacuum plated interior, panels and nozzle, black trim and white Arabic lettering labels. Arabian issue.
2. Red body, blue tinted windows, white interior, panels and nozzle, black trim and white Arabic lettering labels. Arabian issue.

194-A   Mercedes-Benz 240D

**   Arabian Taxi   75mm 1983- 10/1983 $15-20**

Clear windows, white interior, black plastic base and tow hook, Whizzwheels.

1. Red body, red door labels with white Arabic lettering. Arabian issue.

195-A   Leyland Arabian Bottle Truck   73mm 1983- 10/1983 $15-20

No interior, black plastic base, Whizzwheels.

1. White body, orange and green Arabic logo on white labels, smoke tinted windows. Arabian issue.
2. White body, orange and green Arabic logo on white labels, opaque black windows. Arabian issue.

196-A   Police Tactical Force Van   69mm 1983- 10/1983 $4-6

Same casting as 91-B, opaque black windows, unpainted diecast base, Whizzwheels.

1. White body, "POLICE TACTICAL FORCE" with blue and red stripe on side labels.

200-A   Pencil Eater (Hungry Hatchback) 77mm 1983- 10/1983 $10-15

Pencil sharpener based on 8-D Rover 3500, special black base with "PENCIL EATER" text, special interior with pencil sharpener accessed through rear opening hatch, 5Dblspk wheels, special "HUNGRY HATCHBACK" double wide card.

1. Blue body, off-white interior.
2. Red body, white interior.

201-A   Leyland Schat Bottle Truck   73mm 1983- 10/1983 $15-20

Arabian issue.

1. Details not known.

202-A   Leyland 7-Up Bottle Truck   73mm 1983- 10/1983 $15-20

Arabian issue.

1. Details not known.

203-A   Fiat X1/9   72mm 1983- 10/1983 $4-6

Same casting as 86-A, red interior and grille, black base, Whizzwheels.

1. Orange body.

204-A   Renault 5 Turbo   68mm 1983- 10/1983 $4-6

Same casting as 102-A, clear windows, black plastic base, vent and tow hook, Whizzwheels.

1. Medium blue body, red interior, grille, bumpers and lower body stripe, vacuum plated mirrors.
2. Medium blue body, red interior, grille, bumpers and lower body stripe, red mirrors.
3. Light blue body, white interior, grille, bumpers and lower body stripe, vacuum plated mirrors.
4. Medium blue body, black interior, light blue bumpers and lower body stripe, vacuum plated mirrors, (Shown in 1983 Corgi catalog. Was it released?)

205-A   Porsche Carrera 911   73mm 1983- 10/1983

**   Standard $4-6**

**   Arabian $15-20**

Same casting as 80-A, clear windows, black plastic base unless noted, Whizzwheels.

1. Black body, red interior, silver painted headlamps and front bumper, black hood label with two gold stripes and "turbo" text, black side labels with two unequal width stripes and "PORSCHE" text. (Also see similar models numbered J35 produced by Corgi Toys Ltd.)
2. Metallic light green body, other details not known.
3. Yellow body, red interior, no graphics.
4. Medium blue body, black interior, no graphics. (Transitional era model found in two-packs and sets, no official model number.)
5. White body, yellow interior, blue baseplate, no graphics. (Transitional era model found in two-packs and sets, no official model number.)
6. Red body, cream interior, Arabic writing on hood. (Correct model number not known at time of publication. Produced for Saudi market.)

206-A   Buick Regal   75mm 1983- 10/1983 $4-6

Civilian version of 68-A, vacuum plated plastic interior, grille and bumpers unless noted, black plastic base with "CORGI JUNIORS" text and suspension unless noted, clear windows unless noted, Whizzwheels. (Used in many sets in late 1970s and early 1980s prior to individual release. Also used in many transition era sets in 1983 and 1984. Note: The Mettoy era model does not have a jacked-up hot-rod rear axle like later Corgi Toys Ltd. models.)

1. Red body, yellow tinted windows.
2. Darker red body, yellow tinted windows.
3. Bright red body.
4. Yellow body.
5. Bright green body.
6. Medium blue body.
7. Light blue body.
8. Metallic dark blue body. (Similar to Metropolis police car but without roof light or second color.)
9. White body, no suspension, black plastic base with revised "CORGI" without Juniors text.
10. Tan body, other details not known.
11. Black body, no suspension, black plastic base with revised "CORGI" without Juniors text.
12. Black body, unplated white interior and bumpers, suspension, black plastic base with 4 rivets and with blanked-out brand name area.
13. Green body, unplated gray interior and bumpers, black plastic base with suspension but with brand name blanked-out.
14. Green body, unplated black interior and bumpers, no suspension, black plastic base with revised "CORGI" without Juniors text.
15. Green body, unplated gray interior and bumpers, no suspension, black plastic base with revised "CORGI" without Juniors text.
16. Medium blue body, no suspension, black plastic base with revised "CORGI" without Juniors text.
17. Medium blue body, unplated white interior and bumpers, no suspension, black plastic base with revised "CORGI" without Juniors text.
18. May exist with lavender body. Other details not known.

207-A   Ford Sierra German Police Car   75mm 1983- 10/1983 $10-15

Red interior, blue tinted windows and dome lights, light red taillights, opening doors, black plastic base, Whizzwheels.

1. White body, green hood and stripe, white Polizei lettering. (German issue.)

2. White body, red hood and side stripes, black "POLIZEI" on hood and doors, "044 21" on roof with roof lights. (Swiss issue.)

208-A   Ford Sierra German Doctor's Car 75mm 1983- 10/1983 $10-15

Same casting as 207-A, blue tinted windows and dome lights, red interior, light red taillights, opening doors, black plastic base, Whizzwheels.

1. White body, red cross and trim and black Notarzt lettering. German issue.

209-A   Leyland German Mail Truck 73mm 1983- 10/1983 $10-15

Clear windows, no interior, black plastic base, Whizzwheels.

1. Dark yellow body, black "…und ab geht die Post" lettering on yellow side labels. German issue.

210-A   Safari Park Matra Rancho 73mm 1983- 10/1983 $5-8

Same casting as E76-C, clear windows, white interior, black plastic base, Whizzwheels.

1. Tan body, Safari graphics. German issue.

211-A   Ford Escort German Driving School Car 75mm 1983- 10/1983 $10-15

Same casting as 105-A, opening doors, clear windows, black plastic base, Whizzwheels.

1. Green body, white interior, white Fahrschule lettering. German issue.

2. Green body, tan interior, white Fahrschule lettering. German issue.

212-A   VW Polo Siemens Service Car 71mm 1983- 10/1983 $10-15

Same casting as 92-A, opening doors, clear windows, white interior, black plastic base and tow hook, Whizzwheels.

1. Blue body, white "Siemens Wartungsdienst" lettering. German issue.

214-A   Mercedes-Benz PTT Bus 74mm 1983- 10/1983 $10-15

Same casting as E15-C.

1. Yellow body, opaque black windows, yellow side labels with red stripe and black "PTT" with horn logo. (Swiss issue. Found in reverse window card.)

215-A   VW Polo PTT car 1983- 10/1983 $10-15

Same casting as E92-A.

1. Yellow body, clear windows, small door labels with "PTT" and cross logo. (Swiss issue. Found in reverse window card.)

216-A   Chevrolet Swissair Van 68mm 1983- 10/1983 $5-8

No interior, black plastic base, Whizzwheels. (Produced for the Swiss market.)

1. White body with heavy roof ribs, blue tinted windows, "U.S. VAN" base, brown lower side stripe and black "swissair" with red and white flag on side labels.

2. White body with heavy roof ribs, yellow tinted windows, "U.S. VAN" base, brown lower side stripe and black "swissair" with red and white flag on side labels.

3. White body with heavy roof ribs, smoke tinted windows, "U.S. VAN" base, brown lower side stripe and black "swissair" with red and white flag on side labels.

4. White body with heavy roof ribs, opaque black windows, blank base, brown lower side stripe and black "swissair" with red and white flag on side labels.

217-A   Leyland Ovomaltine Van 73mm 1983- 10/1983 $10-15

Standard Leyland box truck casting.

1. Orange body, opaque black windows, black "Ovomaltine" text on white / yellow / orange side labels. (Produced for the Swiss market.)

218-A   Leyland Swiss TV Van 73mm 1983- 10/1983 $10-15

Clear windows, no interior, blue plastic base, Whizzwheels.

1. Blue body, white "Schweizer Fernsehan" labels. Swiss issue.

219-A   Swiss Police Car 1983- 10/1983 $10-15

Details not known.

1. Swiss issue.

220-A   Ford Transit Dropside Truck 72mm 1983- 10/1983 $10-15

Same casting as E125-A.

1. Blue body, opaque black windows "HENNIEZ" labels on doors. (Swiss issue.)

221-A   Leyland Zweifel Chips Van 73mm 1983- 10/1983 $10-15

Labels on sides with Zweifel Pomy Chips and "Z" logo.

1. Yellow body, yellow plastic base. (Swiss issue.)

2. Yellow body, black plastic base. (Swiss issue. Need verification.)

222-A   Chevrolet Swissair Van 68mm 1983- 10/1983 $5-8

Appears to be British issue of 216-A.

1. Presumably same as 216-A.

223-A   Safari Park Matra Rancho 73mm 1983- 10/1983 $5-8

Same casting as 210-A.

1. Tan body, black chassis, white seats, brown mud splatters, black "SAFARI" on doors, lion head & arched "SAFARI PARK" on hood.

224-A   Chevrolet Rivella Van 68mm 1983- 10/1983 $15-20

Chevrolet van casting.

1. White body, opaque black windows, red side labels with wine glass and "rivella" text. (Swiss issue.)

225-A   Chubb Airport Crash Tender 74mm 1983- 10/1983 $15-20

Same casting as 123-A. (Also found as J225 in reverse window card.)

1. Red body with white roof nozzle, "Flughafen-Feuerwehr 9" side graphics. (Swiss issue.)

226-A   Ford Transit Wrecker 72mm 1983- 10/1983 $15-20

Same casting as 103-A.

1. Yellow body with red boom and black hook, red and black graphics. (Swiss issue.)

227-A   Swiss Mercedes-Benz Ambulance 76mm 1983- 10/1983 $15-20

Swiss issue, same casting as 1-E.

1. Details not known.

228-A   Leyland Papeterie Truck 73mm 1983- 10/1983 $15-20

White side labels with twisted pencil logo and "en route pour votre PAPETERIE" text. (Promotional issue for French company.)

1. Dark blue body, opaque black windows, blue plastic baseplate.

250-A   Simon Snorkel Fire Truck 76mm 1983- 10/1983 $15-20

Same casting as 29-B, yellow plastic snorkel parts and base, clear windows, Whizzwheels.

1. Red body, "BRANDBIL" lettering on snorkel; Danish issue.

251-A   ERF Fire Tender 76mm 1983- 10/1983 $15-20

Same casting as 26-C, yellow ladder, blue tinted windows and dome lights, black plastic headlights and base, Whizzwheels.

1. Red body, "FALCK" labels; Danish issue.

2. Red body, "FALCK" Tampo printed on body including rear panel; Danish issue.

252-A   Ford Transit Wrecker 72mm 1983- 10/1983 $15-20

Same casting as 103-A, clear windows, red plastic boom and roof bar, black plastic base and hook, Whizzwheels.

1. Red body, "FALCK" labels; Danish issue.

253-A   Mercedes-Benz Ambulance 76mm 1983- 10/1983 $15-20

Same casting as 1-E, blue tinted windows and dome light, black plastic base, Whizzwheels.

1. White body, red hood and window frames, "FALCK" labels; Danish issue.

254-A   Mercedes-Benz 240D Emergency Car 76mm 1983- 10/1983 $15-20

Same casting as 59-C, clear windows, white interior, black plastic base, Whizzwheels.

1. White body, red stripe and "FALCK" labels; Danish issue.

255-A   Chevrolet Emergency Van 68mm 1983- 10/1983 $15-20

Red body, opaque black windows, black plastic base, Whizzwheels.

1. White "FALCK" and logo on red side labels; Danish issue.

2. White "FALCK" and logo Tampo printed on sides, "FALCK" printed on front and rear; Danish issue.

Baseball Cars

All 1982 Baseball Trading Cars use the 104-A Ford Mustang Cobra with white body, amber tinted windows, yellow interior unless noted, Whizzwheels and plastic lower body-base in varying colors, Tampo printed graphics unless noted. The baseball team logo is on the hood and team name is on the roof.

400-A   Baltimore Orioles $8-10

1. Orange base, orange-white-black logo.

401-A   Boston Red Sox $8-10

1. Red base, red-white-blue logo.

402-A   California Angels $8-10

1. Red base, red-white-blue logo.

403-A   Chicago White Sox $8-10

1. Red base, blue-white-red logo.

404-A   Cleveland Indians $8-10

1. Blue base, red-white-blue logo.

405-A   Detroit Tigers $8-10

1. Blue base, yellow interior, orange-blue-white logo.

2. Blue base, red interior, orange-blue-white logo.

406-A   Kansas City Royals $8-10

1. Blue base, yellow interior, blue-white-gold logo.

2. Blue base, red interior, blue-white-gold logo.

407-A   Milwaukee Brewers $8-10

1. Yellow base, blue-yellow-white logo.

408-A   Minnesota Twins $8-10

1. Red base, blue-white-red logo.

409-A   New York Yankees $8-10

1. Red base, red-white-blue logo.

2. Orange base, red-white-blue logo. (may be factory error.)

410-A Oakland Athletics $8-10

1. Red base, yellow-green-white logo. (may be factory error.)
2. Yellow base, yellow-green-white logo.
3. Yellow base, yellow-green-white logo, graphics on paper labels instead of Tampo printed.

411-A Seattle Mariners $8-10

1. Yellow base, yellow-blue-white logo.

412-A Texas Rangers $8-10

1. Blue base, red-white-blue logo.

413-A Toronto Blue Jays $8-10

1. Blue base, blue-white-red logo.

414-A Atlanta Braves $8-10

1. Red base, blue-white-red logo.

415-A Chicago Cubs $8-10

1. Blue base, red-white-blue logo.

416-A Cincinnati Reds $8-10

1. Red base, red-white-black logo.

417-A Houston Astros $8-10

1. Orange base, orange-white-blue logo.
2. Red base, orange-white-blue logo. (May be factory error.)

418-A Los Angeles Dodgers $8-10

1. Red base, blue-white-red logo.

419-A Montreal Expos $8-10

1. Red base, blue-white-red logo.

420-A New York Mets $8-10

1. Orange base, orange-white-blue logo.

421-A Philadelphia Phillies $8-10

1. Yellow base, maroon and white logo.

422-A Pittsburgh Pirates $8-10

1. Yellow base, gold-white-black logo.

423-A St. Louis Cardinals $8-10

1. Red base, red-white-yellow logo.

424-A San Diego Padres $8-10

1. Yellow base, yellow-white-brown logo.

425-A San Francisco Giants $8-10

1. Orange base, orange and black logo.

Hockey Cars

The 1982-83 Hockey Trading Cars use either the 104-A Ford Mustang Cobra, 72-B Jaguar XJS, or 80-A Porsche Carrera. Colors, windows and bases vary. (Note: Prototype "COLORADO 5" white Porsche known to exist, but not produced.)

426-A Calgary Flames $8-10

1. White Jaguar, opaque black windows, red "14" and Flames logo.

427-A Boston Bruins $8-10

1. Yellow Mustang, black base, yellow interior, amber tinted windows, black "7" and black / white / yellow logo.

428-A Buffalo Sabres $8-10

1. White Jaguar, blue base, black windows, "11" with blue-white-yellow logo.

429-A Chicago Black Hawks $8-10

1. White Jaguar, red base, black windows, "18" and team logo Tampo printed.
2. White Jaguar, red base, black windows, "18" and team logo on white paper labels.

430-A Edmonton Oilers $8-10

1. White Mustang, orange base, yellow interior, amber tinted windows, "99" and team logo.

431-A Hartford Whalers $8-10

1. White Porsche, black base, red interior, clear windows, blue "5" and blue / green logo.

432-A Montreal Canadiens $8-10

1. White Mustang, red base, yellow interior, amber tinted windows, "23" with red-white-blue logo.
2. White Mustang, red base, red interior, amber tinted windows, "23" with red-white-blue logo.

433-A New York Islanders $8-10

1. White Mustang, blue base, yellow interior, amber tinted windows, "22" with orange-white-blue logo.
2. White Mustang, blue base, red interior, amber tinted windows, "22" with orange-white-blue logo.

434-A New York Rangers $8-10

1. White Porsche, black base, red interior, clear windows, blue "3" and red / white / blue logo.

435-A Philadelphia Flyers $8-10

1. White Mustang, orange base, yellow interior, amber tinted windows, "7" with orange and black logo.

436-A Quebec Nordiques $8-10

1. White Porsche, black base, yellow interior, clear windows, blue "26" and red / white / blue logo.
2. White Porsche, black base, red interior, clear windows, red "26" and red / white / blue logo.
3. White Porsche, black base, red interior, clear windows, red "26" and red logo.

437-A Toronto Maple Leafs $8-10

1. White Mustang, blue base, yellow interior, amber tinted windows, "21" with blue and white logo.

438-A Vancouver Canucks $8-10

1. Yellow Jaguar, black base and windows, "12" with red and black logo. (Note: Prototype known to exist with white body.)

439-A Winnipeg Jets $8-10

1. White Porsche, black base, red interior, clear windows, "10" with red-white-blue logo.

440-A Detroit Red Wings $8-10

1. White Mustang, red base, yellow interior, amber tinted windows, "28" with red and white logo.
2. White Mustang, red base, red interior, amber tinted windows, "28" with red and white logo.

441-A Minnesota North Stars $8-10

1. Yellow Mustang, green base, yellow interior, amber tinted windows, "20" with green-white-yellow logo.

442-A Pittsburgh Penguins $8-10

1. White Jaguar, black base and windows, "17" with black and yellow logo.

443-A St. Louis Blues $8-10

1. Yellow Jaguar, blue base, black windows, "1" with blue and yellow logo.

444-A Washington Capitols $8-10

1. White Jaguar, red base, black windows, "21" with blue and red logo.

445-A Los Angeles Kings $8-10

1. White Jaguar, yellow base, black windows, "16" with brown and white logo.

446-A National Hockey League $8-10

1. White Mustang, orange base, yellow interior, amber tinted windows, "NHL" orange and black logo.

448?-A New Jersey Devils $8-10

1. White Mustang, red base, amber tinted windows, yellow interior, "5" with red and black logo. (Model number not confirmed.)

1983 Baseball Cars

The numbers of the 1983 Baseball Trading Cars begin with 5 and correspond otherwise to the 1982 numbers. All models are based on the 180-A Pontiac Firebird and have black plastic interior, base and spoiler, clear windows and Whizzwheels. The logo is on the roof, hood and sides of the car. An unnumbered poster showing the entire series was available as an on-pack offer. Some of the cars shown on the poster are not as actually produced.

500-A Baltimore Orioles $8-10

1. Orange body, white-orange-black logo.

501-A Boston Red Sox $8-10

1. Red body, red-white-blue logo.

502-A California Angels $8-10

1. Dark blue body, red and white logo.

503-A Chicago White Sox $8-10

1. Red body, red-white-blue logo.

504-A Cleveland Indians $8-10

1. White body, red and blue logo.

505-A Detroit Tigers $8-10

1. Orange body, orange-white-blue logo.

506-A Kansas City Royals $8-10

1. Dark blue body, yellow-white-blue logo.

507-A Milwaukee Brewers $8-10

1. Yellow body, yellow-white-blue logo.

508-A Minnesota Twins $8-10

1. Red body, red-white-blue logo.

509-A New York Yankees $8-10

1. White body, red-white-blue logo with blue pinstripes.

510-A Oakland Athletics $8-10

1. Yellow body, yellow-white-green logo.

511-A Seattle Mariners $8-10

1. Yellow body, yellow-white-blue logo.

512-A	Texas Rangers	$8-10

1. White body, red-white-blue logo.

513-A	Toronto Blue Jays	$8-10

1. Dark blue body, red-white-blue logo.

514-A	Atlanta Braves	$8-10

1. White body, red-white-blue logo.

515-A	Chicago Bears	$8-10

1. Light blue body, red-white-blue logo.

516-A	Cincinnati Reds	$8-10

1. Red body, red-white-black logo.

517-A	Houston Astros	$8-10

1. Orange body, orange-white-blue logo.

518-A	Los Angeles Dodgers	$8-10

1. Dark blue body, red-white-blue logo.

519-A	Montreal Expos	$8-10

1. White body, red-white-blue logo.

520-A	New York Mets	$8-10

1. Orange body, orange-white-blue logo.

521-A	Philadelphia Phillies	$8-10

1. White body, brown logo.

522-A	Pittsburgh Pirates	$8-10

1. Yellow body, black-white-yellow logo.

523-A	St. Louis Cardinals	$8-10

1. Red body, red-white-blue logo.

524-A	San Diego Padres	$8-10

1. Yellow body, brown-white-yellow logo.

525-A	San Francisco Giants	$8-10

1. Orange body, black and white logo.

Football Cars

The 1983 Football Collector Cars are all based on the 179-A Chevrolet Corvette and have a red interior, black plastic base, clear windows and Whizzwheels. They are licensed by the National Football League, and each car bears the NFL emblem on its rear window. The helmet logo is on the hood, nose and doors of the car.

600-A	Baltimore Colts	$8-10

1. Dark blue body, white and blue logo.

601-A	Buffalo Bills	$8-10

1. Dark blue body, red-white-blue logo.

602-A	Cincinnati Bengals	$8-10

1. White body, orange and black logo.

603-A	Cleveland Browns	$8-10

1. White body, orange-white-brown logo.

604-A	Denver Broncos	$8-10

1. Orange body, orange-white-blue logo.

605-A	Houston Oilers	$8-10

1. White body, red-white-light blue logo.

606-A	Kansas City Chiefs	$8-10

1. White body, reddish orange-white-gold logo.

607-A	Miami Dolphins	$8-10

1. Orange body, orange-white-blue logo.

608-A	New England Patriots	$8-10

1. Red body, red-white-black logo.

609-A	New York Jets	$8-10

1. White body, green and white logo.

610-A	Oakland Raiders	$8-10

1. Black body, silver and black logo.

611-A	Pittsburgh Steelers	$8-10

1. Yellow body, black and white logo.

612-A	San Diego Chargers	$8-10

1. Yellow body, blue-white-gold logo.

613-A	Seattle Seahawks	$8-10

1. White body, blue-green-silver logo.

614-A	Atlanta Falcons	$8-10

1. Silver body, black-white-red logo.

615-A	Chicago Bears	$8-10

1. White body, orange-white-black logo.

616-A	Dallas Cowboys	$8-10

1. Dark blue body, silver-white-blue logo.

617-A	Detroit Lions	$8-10

1. White body, silver-white-blue logo.

618-A	Green Bay Packers	$8-10

1. White body, green-white-gold logo.

619-A	Los Angeles Rams	$8-10

1. Yellow body, blue-white-gold logo.

620-A	Minnesota Vikings	$8-10

1. Yellow body, purple and white logo.

621-A	New Orleans Saints	$8-10

1. Black body, gold-white-black logo.

622-A	New York Giants	$8-10

1. White body, red-white-blue logo.

623-A	Philadelphia Eagles	$8-10

1. Silver body, green-white-silver logo.

624-A	St. Louis Cardinals	$8-10

1. Maroon body, maroon-white-black logo.

625-A	San Francisco 49ers	$8-10

1. Red body, gold-white-red logo.

626-A	Tampa Bay Buccaneers	$8-10

1. Red body, red and white logo.

627-A	Washington Redskins	$8-10

1. Yellow body, maroon-white-black logo.

Corgi Rockets (10/1969-1971)

Corgi Rockets were produced from October 1969 through 1971. Each model had a removable chassis with a letter designation and ran on black or chrome Whizzwheels. Gold Rockets "Key" with model name and number included with individually packaged cars. Some models were reworked Husky Models castings. Early models were painted in a color tinted "Solarbrite" finish and color shades varied widely. They were intended to be used with Corgi Rockets Track Sets. Track set production ended due to a lawsuit by Mattel (maker of Hot Wheels Sets) and the dies and molds for the track and accessories were destroyed. Most models were later reworked to Corgi Juniors without the removable chassis.

NOTE: Wheel types are not associated with specific model variations due to the easily removable nature of the sub-chassis.

901-A	Aston Martin DB6	72mm 10/1969-1971	$40-70

Yellow interior, green tinted windows, "C" type chassis with black dished or flat 5-spoke Whizzwheels. (Prototype known with pink body but not released in that body color.)

1. "Solarbrite" dark gold body, base with beveled side sills.
2. "Solarbrite" dark gold body, base with non-beveled side sills.
3. "Solarbrite" light gold body, base with non-beveled side sills.
4. Bright orange body, base with non-beveled side sills.

902-A	Jaguar XJ6	72mm 10/1969-1971	$40-70

Clear windows, opening trunk, "C" type chassis with black dished or flat 5-spoke Whizzwheels. (Prototypes known in chrome vacuum plated body, but not released in that color.)

1. "Solarbrite" darker green body with slight yellow tint, red interior, base with small "CORGI" over "ROCKETS" text.
2. "Solarbrite" medium green body, red interior, base with small "CORGI" over "ROCKETS" text.
3. "Solarbrite" medium green body, white interior, base with large "CORGI" over "ROCKETS" text.
4. "Solarbrite" light aqua body, white interior, base with small "CORGI" over "ROCKETS" text.
5. "Solarbrite" light aqua body, white interior, base with large "CORGI" over "ROCKETS" text.
6. "Solarbrite" gold body, white interior, base with small "CORGI" over "ROCKETS" text.
7. Light lime green body, white interior, base with small "CORGI" over "ROCKETS" text.
8. Light lime green body, white interior, base with large "CORGI" over "ROCKETS" text.

903-A	Mercedes-Benz 280 SL	70mm 10/1969-1971	
		Common colors	$40-70
		"Solarbrite" copper	$200-400+

Clear windows, opening doors, "C" type chassis with black dished or flat 5-spoke Whizzwheels. (Prototype known in chrome vacuum plated body, but not released in that color.)

1. "Solarbrite" copper body, white interior, beveled side sills on base.
2. "Solarbrite" dark blue body, red interior, beveled side sills on base.

3. "Solarbrite" dark blue body, white interior, beveled side sills on base.

4. "Solarbrite" dark blue body, white interior, non-beveled side sills on base.

5. "Solarbrite" medium blue body, white interior, beveled side sills on base.

6. "Solarbrite" medium blue body, white interior, non-beveled side sills on base.

7. Florescent lime green body, white interior, non-beveled side sills on base.

8. Black body, red interior, "SPECTRE" labels on hood and doors. (From set 978-A1.)

904-A   Porsche Carrera 6   69mm 10/1969-1971 $35-50

Blue tinted windows, vacuum plated plastic interior and engine, opening rear, red hood decal or label with number 19, "A" type chassis with smaller diameter black dished or flat 5-spoke Whizzwheels, base same color as body.

1. Light orange/ yellow body and base, base with number on base under front axle rod.

2. Light orange/ yellow body and base, base without number on base under front axle rod.

905-A   The Saint's Volvo P-1800   68mm 10/1969-1971

Saint without tow hook	$35-50
Saint with tow hook	$100-150
Red from Sets (mint loose)	$60-100

Clear windows, "A" type chassis with smaller diameter black dished or flat 5-spoke Whizzwheels.

1. White body, blue hood label with white Saint figure, light blue interior, base without tow hook, narrow tabs at base front.

2. White body, blue hood label with white Saint figure, light blue interior, base without tow hook, wide tabs at base front.

3. White body, blue hood label with white Saint figure, light blue interior, base with tow hook.

4. Red body, yellow interior, base with tow hook. (from set 975-A1.)

5. Red body, white interior, base with tow hook. (from set 975-A1.)

906-A   Jensen Interceptor   74mm 10/1969-1971 $50-75

White interior, amber tinted windows, "C" type chassis with black dished or flat 5-spoke Whizzwheels. (Doors do not open like Corgi Juniors version. Prototype known with light green body, but not released in that color.)

1. "Solarbrite" red body, unpainted base with beveled side sills.

2. "Solarbrite" red body, unpainted base with non-beveled side sills.

3. "Solarbrite" red body, white base with non-beveled side sills.

4. Hot pink body, unpainted base with beveled side sills.

5. Hot pink body, unpainted base with non-beveled side sills.

907-A   Cadillac Eldorado   76mm 10/1969-1971 $50-75

White interior, clear windows, opening hood, "C" type chassis with black dished or flat 5-spoke Whizzwheels.

1. "Solarbrite" copper body including hood, based on 9-A casting, unpainted base with beveled side sills.

2. "Solarbrite" copper body including hood, based on 9-A casting, unpainted base with non-beveled side sills.

3. "Solarbrite" copper body, black hood, based on 9-A casting, unpainted base with non-beveled side sills.

4. "Solarbrite" copper and black body based on 57-A casting. (Need confirmation. May not exist.)

908-A   Chevrolet Astro 1   73mm 1970-1971 $40-70

Opening rear body, cream interior and hood triangle, clear windshield, "A" type chassis with flat chrome foiled 5-spoke Whizzwheels.

1. Metallic maroon body, pale gray base.

909-A   Mercedes-Benz C111   73mm 1970-1971 $40-70

Vacuum plated plastic interior hood panel and engine, blue tinted windows, opening rear hood, white lower body-base, "D" type chassis with flat chrome foiled 5-spoke Whizzwheels.

1. Metallic dark blue upper body.

2. Red upper body.

910-A   GP Beach Buggy   59mm 1970-1971 $35-50

Black interior, clear windshield, wire roll bar, "B" type chassis with larger diameter dished black 5-spoke Whizzwheels.

1. Hot pink body, base without patent number.

2. Hot pink body, base with patent number.

3. Light lime green body, base without patent number.

4. Light lime green body, base with patent number.

911-A   Marcos XP   69mm 1970-1971 $40-70

Vacuum plated plastic interior and engine, amber tinted windows, black base, "B" type chassis with flat chrome foiled 5-spoke Whizzwheels.

1. Gold body, red rear grille and taillights.

913-A   Aston Martin DBS   73mm 1970-1971 $40-70

Opening black hood, yellow interior, clear windows, "C" type chassis with dished or flat or dished black 5-spoke Whizzwheels.

1. "Solarbrite" blue body and hood, unpainted base.

2. "Solarbrite" blue body, black hood, unpainted base.

3. "Solarbrite" blue body, black hood, white painted base.

916-A   Carabo Bertone   75mm 1970-1971 $40-70

Amber tinted windows, black front and rear body panels, dull blue lower body-base, "C" type chassis with flat or dished black 5-spoke Whizzwheels.

1. "Solarbrite" green upper body, orange-red interior, front and rear grilles.

2. "Solarbrite" green upper body, white interior, front and rear grilles.

917-A   Pininfarina Alfa Romeo P33   73mm 1970-1971 $40-70

Black interior, white seats and wing, black front and rear grilles, white lower body-base, clear windshield, chrome foiled Whizzwheels.

1. "Solarbrite" dark purple upper body.

918-A   Ital Design Bizzarini Manta   72mm 1970-1971 $40-70

Cream interior, clear windows, "C" type chassis with flat chrome foiled 5-spoke Whizzwheels. (Prototype known with candy-apple red body, but not released in that color.)

1. Metallic dark blue body, red base.

2. Metallic dark blue body, black base.

3. Metallic light blue body, black base.

4. Metallic aqua body, black base.

919-A   Todd Sweeney Stock Car   69mm 1970-1971 $40-70

Yellow interior, orange chassis, name labels, "D" type chassis with larger diameter dished black or flat chrome foiled 5-spoke Whizzwheels.

1. Light purple body, red roof, no patent number on base under front axle.

2. Light purple body, red roof, patent number on base under front axle.

920-A   Derek Fiske Stock Car   70mm 1970-1971 $40-70

White cab with red roof, yellow interior, red chassis, name labels, "D" type chassis with dished black or flat chrome foiled 5-spoke Whizzwheels.

1. Silver hood, no patent number on base under front axle.

2. Silver hood, patent number on base under front axle.

921-A   Morgan Plus 8   67mm 1970-1971 $40-70

Black interior, clear windshield, silver headlights, unpainted grille and bumper, silver exhaust pipes, "D" type chassis with larger diameter flat 5-spoke Whizzwheels.

1. "Solarbrite" red body, unpainted grille and base, black wheels, no patent number on base.

2. "Solarbrite" red body, unpainted grille and base, black wheels, patent number on base.

3. "Solarbrite" red body, white painted grille and base, chrome foiled wheels.

922-A   Ford Capri   74mm 1970-1971

Standard versions	$40-70
Set Versions (mint loose)	$75-125

Clear windows, "C" type chassis with flat chrome foiled 5-spoke Whizzwheels unless noted. (Prototype known in metallic copper body, but not released in that color.)

1. Metallic light blue body, unpainted grille, cream interior.

2. Lime green body, rally version, black grill and base, white interior, "8" stickers on hood and sides.

3. Metallic dark purple body, unpainted grille, yellow interior. (From set 976-A1.)

4. Metallic light blue body, unpainted grille, yellow interior. (From set 976-A1.)

5. Metallic aqua body, unpainted grille, cream interior. (From set 976-A1.)

6. White body, unpainted grille, yellow interior, "6" and checked labels. (From set 978-A1.)

7. White body without roof light, clear windows, yellow interior, plated "WHIZZWHEELS" base without tow hook, "WALL OF DEATH" labels with Batman Logo, 5-spk wheels. (From Rockets "Wall of Death Set" 2062-A1. Model listed here due to usage in Rockets set but with Juniors Whizzwheels base. Model also listed under E56-A.)

923-A   Ford Escort 007 (James Bond)   70mm 1970-1971 $100-125

Red interior, clear windows with open forward side windows, blue, white and black "007" and "JAMES BOND SPECIAL AGENT" labels, stripe and number 7 labels, unpainted grille and lights, chrome foiled Whizzwheels.

1. White body, light blue stripes.

924-A   Mercury Cougar XR7 (James Bond) 79mm 1970-1971 $100-125

Yellow interior, clear windows, unpainted grille and bumpers, black hood label, "D" type chassis with flat chrome foiled 5-spoke Whizzwheels. (Also see 937-A)

1. Bright red body, black roof.

2. Bright red body, black roof, ski rack.

925-A   Ford Capri 007 (James Bond)   74mm 1970-1971 $100-125

Yellow interior, clear windows, number 6 stripe and checker labels, unpainted grille, bumpers and tow hook, "C" type chassis with dished black or flat vacuum plated 5-spoke Whizzwheels.

1. White body.

926-A   Jaguar Mk. II Control Car   74mm 1970-1971 $100-125

White interior, clear windows, light red sign on roof, two men on rear platform, emblem and lettering labels, unpainted grille and lights, "C" type chassis with dished or flat chrome foiled 5-spoke Whizzwheels.

1. Metallic gold body, painted figures in rear.

2. Metallic copper body, unpainted white figures in rear.

927-A   Ford Escort World Cup Rally Car   70mm 1970-1971 $40-70

Red interior, clear windows with closed forward side windows, black diecast base, grille shield and bars, silver headlights, rally labels supplied on sheet in package, chrome foiled Whizzwheels.

1. White body, red trim.

928-A   Mercedes-Benz 280SL S.P.E.C.T.R.E. 70mm 1970-1971 $100-125

Red interior, clear windows, S.P.E.C.T.R.E and wild boar labels, unpainted grille, "C" type chassis with flat chrome foiled 5-spoke Whizzwheels.

1. Black body.

930-A   Bertone Runabout Barchetta   64mm 1970-1971 $40-70

Light-red interior and body stripe, amber windshield, white lower body-base, "A" type chassis with large rear and small front flat chrome foiled 5-spoke Whizzwheels.

1. Metallic green upper body.

931-A   Ole Macdonald's Truck   63mm 1970-1971 $40-70

Brown plastic interior and rear body, unpainted engine, grille, headlights and exhaust pipes, no front fenders, "D" type chassis with two different diameter flat chrome foiled 5-spoke Whizzwheels.

1. Yellow cab.

932-A   The Futura   75mm Not Produced   N/A

Not produced.

933-A   Ford Holmes Wrecker   72mm 1970-1971

White cab	$75-125
Blue cab	$AUCTION

Gold diecast booms, red hooks and cradle, amber tinted windows and dome lights, red and yellow "Auto Rescue" labels, unique Rockets sub-frame with large diameter flat vacuum plated 5-spoke Whizzwheels. (Same upper casting used for E1017-A which is red and yellow.)

1. White cab and boom mountings, dark metallic blue chassis and rear body.

2. Medium blue cab and boom mountings, white chassis and rear body.

937-A   Mercury Cougar XR7   75mm 1970-1971 $40-70

Yellow interior and spoiler, unpainted grille and bumpers, "D" type chassis with flat vacuum plated 5-spoke Whizzwheels. (Prototype shown in early catalog with yellow body and black roof and spoiler, but not produced in this color scheme.)

1. Metallic dark gold body, clear windows.

2. Metallic dark gold body, yellow tinted windows.

975-A   Super Stock Gift Set No. 1   1971-1971 $200-400

Red Volvo P1800, yellow trailer, Todd Sweeney racer, 3 figures, Tune-up key.

1. Volvo with yellow interior.

2. Volvo with white interior.

976-A   Super Stock Gift Set No. 2   1971-1971 $200-400

Capri, trailer, Derek Fiske racer, Tune-up key.

1. Purple Capri with yellow interior, yellow trailer.

2. Metallic light blue Capri with yellow interior, metallic light blue trailer.

3. Metallic Aqua Capri with ivory interior. (May be confused with similar Juniors model from set E3020-A.)

977-A   Super Stock Gift Set No. 3   1971-1971 $200-400

Jaguar control car, Todd Sweeney racer, Derek Fiske racer, 3 figures, Tune-up key.

978-A   O.H.M.S.S. Gift Set   1971-1971 $AUCTION

White Escort, red Cougar with skis, white Capri and black Mercedes-Benz 280SL, see individual listings for details.

9xx-A   Corgi Rockets/Whizzwheels Trailer 1971-1971, 1971-1972

Corgi Rockets version	
(mint loose)	$30-50
Corgi Juniors Whizzwheels version	
(mint loose)	$20-40

Trailer from sets 975-A and 976-A, not sold separately. Later used in Corgi Juniors Club Racing Gift Set E2030-A with revised base text.

1. Yellow trailer body, "CORGI Rockets TRAILER" on base. (Used in 975-A and 976-A.)

2. Metallic dark blue trailer body, "CORGI Rockets TRAILER" on base. (Used in 976-A.)

3. Metallic dark blue trailer body, "CORGI WHIZZWHEELS TRAILER" on base. (Used in E2030-A.)

4. Metallic teal trailer body, "CORGI WHIZZWHEELS TRAILER" on base. (Used in E2030-A.)

Extras

The first Husky Extras, with 1000, 1200 or 1400 numbers, were added to the Husky line in 1967. The number used depended on the country of sale and date of production. In 1970, as Corgi Juniors, they were given 1000 numbers, which will be used here for the sake of continuity. The Extras remained in production through 1972. Later some models were reissued in the regular Corgi Juniors series, but with casting changes.

1001-A, 1201-A

James Bond Aston Martin (Husky)   73mm 1967-1969 $150-175

1001-A   James Bond Aston Martin (Corgi Jr.) 73mm 1970-1972 $125-150

Blue tinted windows, opening roof hatch, ejecting seat with passenger, interior with driver, vacuum plated plastic base, ejection trigger on right side of car.

1. Metallic silver gray body, brown interior, Husky base, gray plastic wheels, (1201, 1401).

2. Metallic silver gray body, red interior, Husky base, gray plastic wheels, (1201, 1401).

3. Metallic silver gray body, red interior, Husky base, diecast wheels with five perimeter slots and black tires, (1201).

4. Metallic silver gray body, red interior, base with Corgi Juniors label, diecast wheels with five perimeter slots and black tires.

5. Metallic silver body, red interior, modified diecast Corgi Juniors base with "WHIZZWHEELS" text, wide black dished 5-spoke Whizzwheels. (Note: Body height much higher than earlier versions but fender opening shape unchanged. Later E40-C has plastic baseplate and sat lower.)

6. Same as 1001-A5 except black flat 5-spoke Whizzwheels.

7. Same as 1001-A5 except chrome foiled 5-spoke Whizzwheels.

8. Same as 1001-A5 except chrome foiled 5-dblspoke Whizzwheels.

1002-A, 1202-A Batmobile (Husky)   77mm 1967-1969 $150-175

1002-A   Batmobile (Corgi Jr.)   77mm 1970-1972 $125-150

Blue canopy, red interior, two painted figures, vacuum plated plastic parts, red bat labels on doors.

1. Black body, Husky base with Batman figure, gray plastic wheels crimped on rear axle to drive pulsing flame, hitch hole, (Can be found packaged as Husky 1402, 1202, or 1002 depending on country of sale and date of manufacture.).

2. Black body, Corgi Juniors label on base with Batman figure, gray plastic wheels crimped on rear axle to drive pulsing flame, hitch hole.

3. Black body, diecast "Whizzwheels" base, black Whizzwheels, hitch pin.

4. Black body, diecast "Whizzwheels" base, chrome Whizzwheels, hitch pin.

1003-A, 1203-A Batboat on Trailer (Husky)   88mm 1968-1969 $100-125

1003-A   Batboat on Trailer (Corgi Jr.)   88mm 1970-1972+Sets $75-100

Boat with blue windshields, two figures unless noted, gold diecast trailer.

1. Black plastic boat with "Husky" name and "MADE IN GT. BRITAIN" molded into bottom, "BAT" and "BOAT" on rear of boat around smaller exhaust tube, yellow fin with bat labels, trailer with gray plastic wheels, hitch with pin. (Need confirmation. May have been a preproduction model.)

2. Black plastic boat with "Husky" name and "MADE IN GT. BRITAIN" molded into bottom, "BAT" and "BOAT" on rear of boat around smaller exhaust tube, red fin with bat labels, trailer with gray plastic wheels, hitch with pin.

3. Black plastic boat with "Husky" name and "BAT BOAT" molded into bottom, "MADE IN" and "GT. BRITAIN" on rear of boat around larger exhaust tube, red fin with bat labels, trailer with gray plastic wheels, hitch with pin.

4. Black plastic boat with "Husky" name removed from bottom and "CORGI JUNIORS" label applied, "BAT BOAT" molded into bottom, "MADE IN" and "GT. BRITAIN" on rear of boat around larger exhaust tube, red fin with bat labels, trailer with gray plastic wheels, hitch with pin.

5. Black plastic boat with "Corgi Juniors" name and "BAT BOAT" molded into bottom, "MADE IN" and "GT. BRITAIN" on rear of boat around larger exhaust tube, red fin with bat labels, trailer with chrome Whizzwheels, hitch with hole instead of pin, no figures. (Found in later sets.)

1004-A, 1204-A Monkeemobile (Husky)   76mm 1968-1969 $150-200

1004-A   Monkeemobile (Corgi Jr.)   76mm 1970-1972 $125-150

Yellow interior with four figures, vacuum plated plastic engine, white roof, yellow Monkees logo.

1. Red body, Husky base with two raised lines and cast "HUSKY models" on baseplate, diecast wheels with radial fins and black tires, "Monkees" decals on doors. (May be found packaged as either 1004 or 1204).

2. Red body, Husky base with two raised lines and cast "HUSKY models" on baseplate, diecast wheels with radial fins and black tires, "Monkees" labels on doors. (May be found packaged as either 1004 or 1204).

3. Red body, Husky base with two raised lines and "CORGI JUNIORS" label over cast "HUSKY models" on baseplate, diecast wheels with radial fins and black tires, "Monkees" labels on doors. (Need confirmation.)

4. May exist with "CORGI JUNIORS" label over blank area on base.

5. Red body, Corgi Juniors base with two raised lines and cast "CORGI JUNIORS" on baseplate, diecast wheels with radial fins and black tires, "Monkees" labels on doors.

6. Red body, flat Whizzwheels base, black dished 5-spoke Whizzwheels, "Monkees" labels on doors.

7. Red body, flat Whizzwheels base, black flat 5-spoke Whizzwheels, "Monkees" labels on doors surrounded by raised locator groove.

1005-A, 1205-A

The Man From U.N.C.L.E Car (Husky)	72mm 1968-1969	$150-175

1005-A

The Man From U.N.C.L.E Car (Corgi Jr.)	72mm 1970-1970	$200+

Vacuum plated plastic interior with two figures, clear windows, opening hood with rocket launcher, diecast wheels with radial fins and black tires, lower-body-base same color as upper body. (Also known factory error with passengers missing.)

1. Blue body and base, chrome stripe between castings, Husky base, (May be found packaged as either 1005 or 1205).

2. Blue body and base, chrome stripe between castings, Corgi Juniors label on Husky base.

3. Blue body and base, chrome stripe between castings, Corgi Juniors label on modified base with raised flat area where husky dog head and text had been.

1006-A, 1206-A

Chitty Chitty Bang Bang (Husky)	76mm 1969-1969	$150-175
1006-A Chitty Chitty Bang Bang (Corgi Jr.)	76mm 1970-1972	$125-150

Vacuum plated plastic hood and windshield, red interior with four figures, gold radiator and headlights, retractable side wings, front and rear wings, metallic charcoal gray fenders and base.

1. Copper body, gold diecast wheels with open spokes and black tires, Husky base, red side wings with yellow end wings. (1206).

2. Same as 1206-A1 except yellow side wings with orange end wings. (1206).

3. Same as 1206-A1 except orange side wings with yellow end wings. (1206).

4. Corgi Juniors label over Husky lettering on base, gold diecast wheels with open spokes and black tires, yellow side wings with orange end wings.

5. Corgi Juniors label over Husky lettering on base, gold diecast wheels with open spokes and black tires, orange side wings with yellow end wings.

6. Corgi Juniors label over blank area on base, gold diecast wheels with open spokes and black tires, orange side wings with yellow end wings.

7. Whizzwheels base, yellow side wings with orange end wings, black Whizzwheels.

1007-A Ironside Police Van	67mm 1971-1972	$125-150

Yellow interior and lever, clear windows, unpainted base, lifting rear door and lowering panel with figures, San Francisco Police emblem labels, Whizzwheels.
1. Blue body.

1008-A Popeye's Paddle Wagon	70mm 1971-1972	$150-175

Vacuum plated plastic grille and headlights, copper boiler and stack, figures of Popeye, Olive and Swee' Pea, decals on paddle boxes, front Whizzwheels, large black rear wheels.
1. Yellow body, light blue chassis.

1010-A James Bond Volkswagen	66mm 1971-1973	$175-200

Yellow interior, clear windows, number 5, stripe and lettering labels, unpainted diecast base, Whizzwheels.
1. Orange body.

1011-A James Bond Bobsled	73mm 1970-1972	$200-250

Gray plastic bumper, driver figure in light blue with yellow helmet, black and yellow checker and white 007 label, diecast base, black Whizzwheels.
1. Yellow body, silver painted base.
2. Yellow body, unpainted base.

1012-A S.P.E.C.T.R.E Bobsled	73mm 1970-1972	$200-250

Same casting and components as 1011-A, driver figure in brown with black helmet, black wild boar label.
1. Orange body, silver painted base.
2. Orange body, unpainted base.

1013-A Tom's Go Cat	68mm 1971-1972	$60-80

Chassis without fenders, dark red roof and dynamite case with yellow and red labels, red steering wheel, cat figure with gun, label on front, Whizzwheels. (Completely different casting from later E58-B which does not have cover over Tom's head. Note: this label says "Tom's Go Cat," that of the no. 58-B says "Tom's Go Cart.")

1. Yellow chassis, silver hood, silver top of roof, Tom with white boots up to knee.
2. Yellow chassis, silver hood, silver top of roof, Tom with white feet only.

1014-A Jerry's Banger	62mm 1971-1972	$60-80

Roller skate body without fenders, slender brass color cannon, light blue mounting, panniers of cannonballs and gunpowder, mouse figure, unpainted diecast base, Whizzwheels. (Completely different casting from later E38-B which has swept fenders and does not look like a roller skate.)
1. Red upper and silver lower body.

1017-A Ford Holmes Wrecker	93mm 1971-1972	$100-120

Similar to Corgi Rockets 933.
1. Yellow cab and boom support, red rear deck, silver booms, red hooks, transparent yellow tinted windows. (Also used in set E3021-A1.)

Little/Large Gift Sets

Models were first put on the market in 1982, but with one exception (1365 Routemaster Bus and London Taxi, in 1983) have not been shown in Corgi catalogs. Sets contained standard Corgi model plus matching (if possible) Corgi Jr. model. Most models were current at the time of release in standard production trim, except in cases where the juniors model was redecorated to match the larger one. All were introduced 1982 unless noted, and continued until factory closure in October, 1983. Some sets were briefly reissued in the French market by Corgi Toys Ltd. in the mid-1980s.

1352	Renault 5 Turbo 307-B and E102-A	1982-10/1983	$25-40

Standard colors and trim.

1353	Austin Metro 275-B and E107-A	1982-10/1983	$25-40

1. Blue bodies, white interior in 275-B, tan interior in E107-A.
2. Blue bodies, red interior in 275-B, red interior in E107-A.
3. Red bodies, white interiors in both cars.

1354	Texaco Special Racers 154-B2 & E53-B	1982-10/1983	$25-40

Standard colors and trim.

1355	Talbot Rancho 457-B and E76-C	1982-10/1983	$25-40

1. Red bodies on both models.
2. Orange bodies on both models.

1356	Fiat X1/9 306-B and E86-A	1982-10/1983	$25-40

Metallic blue bodies, black interiors, standard labels.

1357	Jeep Golden Eagle 441-B and E12-E	1982-10/1983	$25-40

Metallic brown bodies with eagle labels on hood, tan removable roof, standard trim.

1358	Citroen 2CV 346-A and E115-A	1982-10/1983	$25-40

Yellow bodies without trim, red interiors. (Shade of yellow varies, but both cars match.)
1. Large car is medium yellow 272-A, James Bond packaging.
2. Large car is lighter yellow 346-A, standard packaging.

1359	Ford Escort 334-B and E105-A	1982-10/1983	$25-40

1. Metallic light blue bodies on both cars, black interior in 334-B, ivory interior in E105-A.
2. Silver bodies on both cars, tan interior in both cars.

1360	Batmobile 267-A and E69-A	1982-10/1983	$40-80

Standard colors and trim, larger Batmobile has gold tow hook.

1361	James Bond Aston Martin 271-B and E40-C	1982-10/1983	$40-80

Standard colors and trim.

1362	James Bond Lotus Esprit 269-B and E60-B	1982-10/1983	$40-80

Standard colors and trim.

1363	Buck Rogers 647-A & E13-C	1982-10/1983	$40-80

Standard colors and trim.

1364	NASA Space Shuttle 648-A & E5-C	1982-10/1983	$25-40

Standard colors and trim.

1365	London Bus 469-A and London Taxi E71-A	1983-10/1983	$25-40

Standard colors and trim.

1371	VW Turbo 309-B and E137-A	1982-10/1983	$25-40

White bodies, red interiors, red racing stripes and numbers.

1372	Jaguar XJS (?) and (?)	1982-10/1983	$25-40

(Details not known at time of publication. Possibly a version for "The Saint.")

1373	Ford Capri 312-C and E61-C	1982-10/1983	$25-40

1. Silver bodies, red interior and black side stripes on 312-C, yellow interior in 61-C.
2. Yellow bodies, ??? interior and black side stripes on 312-C, red interior in 61-C.

1376	Starsky and Hutch Ford Torino 292-A and E45-B	1982-10/1983	$40-80

Standard colors and trim.

1378	Porsche 924 303-C & Juniors Carrera	1982-10/1983	$25-40

Black bodies with yellow interiors, gold trim on both.

1380	Mercedes-Benz 240D 285-A & E59-C	1982-10/1983	$25-40

Silver bodies, tan interiors, no graphics.

1382	Ford Mustang 370-A and E104-A	1982-10/1983	$25-40

Standard colors and trim.

1383	Mack Pumper 2029-A and Crash Tender E123-A	1982-10/1983	$25-40

Standard colors and trim.

1384	Ford Thunderbird 810-A and E96-B	1982-10/1983	$25-40

1. Cream bodies, red top on larger car.
2. Cream bodies, black top on larger car.

1385	Datapost Austin Metro 281-B & E135-A	1982-10/1983	$25-40

Standard colors and trim.

1387	Ferrari 308 GTS 298-A and E131-A/E136-A	1982-10/1983	$25-40

Red bodies, standard colors and trim.

1389	Ford Sierra 299-A and E129-A	1982-10/1983	$25-40

Standard colors and trim.

1390	Porsche 924 (black) 310-B and (E?)	1982-10/1983	$25-40

Black bodies, red interior and gold trim on 303-C, tan interior and no trim on Juniors Carrera.

1393	Jeep (open) 447-B and E182-A	1982-10/1983	$25-40

Standard colors and trim.

1394	Jeep (with hood) 448-B and E183-A	1982-10/1983	$25-40

Metallic copper brown bodies, tan tops, eagle graphics on hoods.

1395	Mazda Pick-up 495-A and Range Rover E184-A	1982-10/1983	$25-40

Standard colors and trim.

1396	Space Shuttles	1982-10/1983	$25-40

(May be identical to 1364)

1397	BMW M1 380-B and Mercedes E124-A	1982-10/1983	$25-40

Red BMW with BASF graphics, red Mercedes without graphics.

1401	Lotus Elite 382-B and Triumph TR7 E10-C	1982-10/1983	$25-40

Standard colors and trim.

1402	Giant Tipper (?) and Skip Truck E85-A	1983-10/1983	$25-40

Details not known. (Produced after normal production had stopped)

1403	Mercedes Tanker (?) and Custom Van E185-A	1982-10/1983	$25-40

Standard colors and trim.

1405	Jaguar 319-C and E72-B	1982-10/1983	$25-40

Maroon bodies, no graphics, white interior in 319-C, opaque black windows on E72-B. Other "Little and Large" combinations may exist. Please report others found using the form presented at the end of this book. Some "Little and Large" data above obtained from *The Great Book of Corgi* by Marcel R. VanCleemput.

Husky Accessories

1550	Playmat	1967-1969	$25-50

Vinyl playmat with printed play scene.

1551	Service Station & Chinese Restaurant	1967-1969	$25-50

Plastic buildings designed to be used with the playmat.

1552	Westminster Bank & Woolworth's	1967-1969	$25-50

Plastic buildings designed to be used with the playmat.

1553	Regal Cinema & Rusts Bakery	1967-1969	$25-50

Plastic buildings designed to be used with the playmat.

1554	Fisherman's Inn and Family Grocer	1967-1969	$25-50

Plastic buildings designed to be used with the playmat.

1561	Triangular Traffic Signs	1967-1969	$15-30

Six pre-painted plastic triangular traffic signs.

1562	Circular Traffic Signs	1967-1969	$15-30

Six pre-painted plastic circular traffic signs.

1571	Pedestrian Figures	1967-1969	$15-30

Five pre-painted figures. . (Made in Hong Kong.)

1572	Workmen Figures	1967-1969	$15-30

Five pre-painted figures. (Made in Hong Kong.)

1573	Garage Personnel Figures	1967-1969	$15-30

Five pre-painted figures. (Made in Hong Kong.)

1574	Public Officers Figures	1967-1969	$15-30

Six pre-painted figures. (Made in Hong Kong.)

1580	Husky Collector Case	1967-1969	$25-50

Red vinyl carry case with black handle, 4 yellow 12 car trays for total storage of 48 models, dock scene showing Husky models on lid.

1585	Husky Traveler Case		$30-60

Red vinyl carry case with fold-out plastic ramps and service station scene, hidden storage in rear section.

Corgi Rockets Accessories

1928	Rocketlube Tune-up Kit	1970-1971	$10-25

Pouch containing lubricant and applicator. Instructions printed on face of pouch.

1929	Pitstop Kit A	1970-1971	$10-25

Bare type "A" sub-chassis, spare axle sets, spare Tune-Up Key.

1931	Superloop	1970-1971	$10-25

Yellow loop pole with red base.

1933	Pitstop Kit C	1970-1971	$10-25

Bare type "C" sub-chassis, spare axle sets, spare Tune-Up Key.

1934	Autofinish	1970-1971	$10-25

Yellow finish line track connector with pivoting checkered flag.

1935	Track Connectors	1970-1971	$10-25

Yellow track connectors.

1936	Spaceleap	1970-1971	$10-25

Yellow jump-over track section.

1937	Autostart	1970-1971	$10-25

Yellow start track section with lifting start gate.

1938	Super Crossover	1970-1971	$10-25

Yellow crossover track section.

1945	Track Adaptors	1970-1971	$10-25

Yellow track adapters (to connect to "another brand".)

1951	Support Collars and Track Links	1970-1971	$10-25

Red Support collars with yellow track links.

1952	Superloop	1970-1971	$10-25

Yellow track accessories.

1953	Hairpin Tunnel/ Turret Spacehanger Bend	1970-1971	$10-25

Yellow track accessories.

1954	Cloverleaf/Crossroads Kit	1970-1971	$10-25

Yellow track supports of progressive height.

1963	New Super Track	1970-1971	$10-25

Coil of 12 feet of red track with two track connectors.

1970	Super Booster	1970-1971	$10-25

Long black spring powered car booster that fits over a section of track.

1971	Hairpin Tunnel	1970-1971	$10-25

Yellow hairpin track section with provision to be supported on post.

1972	Pit-stop and Lube Kit	1970-1971	$5-8

Six wheel / axle assemblies, wheel lube pen.

1976	Quickfire Start	1970-1971	$10-25

Yellow rapid fire start track section that supports multiple cars.

1977	Lap Counter	1970-1971	$10-25

Yellow plastic booth-like structure through which Rockets track can be routed.

1979	Spacehanger Bend	1970-1971	$10-25

Yellow track accessories.

Husky Majors (1964-1969)
Corgi Super Juniors (1970-1983)

2001-A	Four Car Garage	1968-1969, 1970-1978	$20-35

Building framework, roof with skylights, four overhead doors.

1. Yellow framework, transparent blue roof, medium blue doors, "COLLECT HUSKY MODELS" labels.
2. Yellow framework, transparent blue roof, medium blue doors, "COLLECT CORGI JUNIORS" labels.
3. Yellow framework, transparent clear roof, red doors, no side labels. (May be from late 1970s set.)
4. Red framework, transparent blue tinted roof, medium blue doors, no side labels. (From late 1970s set.)

2002-A	Hoynor Mark 11 Car Transporter	119mm 1967-1969, 1970-1976	$30-40

Cab body and base-grille castings, semi-trailer upper and lower decks, tailgate, rear base and two unpainted hinge bar castings, yellow plastic blocks, cast-in lettering.

1. White cab, blue tinted windows, orange upper deck, blue lower deck and tailgate, gray baseplates, white dog's head and "HUSKY: name, smooth diecast wheels with black tires.

2. White cab, blue tinted windows, orange upper deck, blue lower deck and tailgate, gray baseplates, white dog's head and "HUSKY: name, shaped diecast wheels with slots and black tires.

3. White cab, blue tinted windows, orange upper deck, blue lower deck and tailgate, gray baseplates, white "CORGI JUNIORS" name, shaped diecast wheels with slots and black tires.

4. Yellow cab, blue tinted windows, orange upper deck, bright blue lower deck and tailgate, white cab base, blue semi base, white "Corgi Juniors" lettering, Whizzwheels.

5. Yellow cab, clear windows, orange upper deck, bright blue lower deck and tailgate, white cab base, blue semi base, white "Corgi Juniors" lettering, Whizzwheels.

6. Red cab, clear windows, orange upper deck, bright blue lower deck and tailgate, white cab base, blue semi base, white "Corgi Juniors" lettering, Whizzwheels. (Also found in set E3025-A.)

2003-A Ford Low Loader With 140mm 1968-1969, 1970-1973Loadmaster Shovel $30-40

Cab body and base castings, blue tinted windows, semi-trailer body and tailgate castings, blue sheet metal rear base, yellow 23-A Loadmaster Shovel. (Shown in 1970 Corgi Juniors catalog with blue cab, but not produced in that color scheme.)

1. Red cab, blue trailer, metal wheels with tires, Husky base.

2. Red cab, blue trailer, metal wheels with tires, Corgi Juniors base.

3. Red cab, blue trailer, Whizzwheels, Corgi Juniors base.

2004-A Ford Removals Van 145mm 1968-1969, 1970-1973 $30-40

Cab body and white base castings, blue tinted windows, semi-trailer chassis and tailgate castings, red sheet metal rear base, vacuum plated plastic semi-trailer body with red cast-in lettering. (Shown in 1970 Corgi Juniors catalog with red cab, but not produced in that color scheme.)

1. Blue cab, red trailer chassis and tailgate, "Husky Removals" logo, Husky base, metal wheels with 5 perimeter slots with black tires.

2. Blue cab, red trailer chassis and tailgate, "Corgi Removals" logo, Corgi Juniors base, metal wheels with 5 perimeter slots with black tires.

2006-A Mack Esso Tanker 180mm 1970-1979 $30-40

Cab body, opening hood and metallic dark gray base castings, blue tinted windows, silver engine, black exhaust stack, metallic dark gray semi-trailer chassis casting with white plastic tank, chrome catwalk, red-white-blue Esso and red stripe labels, Whizzwheels.

1. White cab and tank.

2007-A Ford Low Loader and Shovel Loader140mm 1975-1978 $30-40

Same cab, base, semi-trailer and tailgate castings as 2003-A, clear windows, blue rear base casting, Whizzwheels.

1. Yellow cab with white base, blue semi-trailer (darker than 2003,) red and yellow 48-B Shovel Loader.

2. Red cab with white base, blue semi-trailer (darker than 2003,) orange and yellow 48-B Shovel Loader.

2008-A Greyhound Bus 169mm 1976-1979 $30-40

Single body casting, white interior, amber tinted windows, black plastic base, Whizzwheels.

1. White body, red-white-blue-black Greyhound Americruiser labels.

2009-A Aerocar 150mm 1976-1978 $50-75

Car body casting, clear windows, black interior and base, red upper wing casting, yellow lower wing-twin boom-tail connector, black propeller, red and yellow stripe and white N846 labels, Whizzwheels; made in Hong Kong. (Believed to have been intended as a tie-in to a James Bond movie, but rejected by the license owner.)

1. Yellow car.

2010-A Mack Exxon Tanker NOT PRODUCED N/A

Was to be Exxon version of 2006-A for USA market. Not produced.

2011-A Mack U.S. Army Tanker 180mm 1976-1978 $35-45

Same castings as 2006-A, dark olive-brown tank and catwalk, white star and U.S. Army labels, black Whizzwheels.

1. Olive drab cab and semi-trailer chassis.

2012-A Ford U.S. Army Low Loader and 140mm 1976-1980 $35-45
Armored Car

Same castings as 2007-A, white star labels, 83-A Commando Armored Car, black Whizzwheels.

1. Olive drab cab and semi-trailer.

2014-A Mercedes-Benz Car Transporter 215mm 1977-1979 $20-30

Cab body and chassis-fenders castings, amber tinted windows, yellow upper deck, red lower deck and tailgate, and two unpainted hinge bar castings, black plastic cab and semi bases and tow hook, Whizzwheels, grille-headlight label, rear stripe label.

1. White cab body, red cab chassis, lower semi deck and tailgate.

2015-A Mercedes-Benz Car Transporter 415mm 1976-1978 $30-40
and Trailer

Upper and lower decks, tailgate and two unpainted hinge bar castings, black plastic tongue, base and tow hook, yellow blocks, Whizzwheels, pulled by 2014-A.

1. White cab on red chassis, yellow upper decks, red lower decks and tailgates.

2017-A Scania Dump Truck 147mm 1977-1979 $15-25

Chassis-cab and black hydraulic cylinder and exhaust stack castings, plastic tipper, green tinted windows, black plastic front base, Whizzwheels, grille label. (Note: Prototype shown in 1977 Corgi Juniors catalog with orange chassis-cab and yellow dump body, but not released in that color scheme.)

1. Yellow chassis-cab, red tipper.

2018-A Scania Container Truck 138mm 1977-1979 $15-25

Chassis-cab and black exhaust stack castings, plastic flatbed, white plastic container with gray top and red rear doors, blue and black Seatrain labels, black plastic cab base, amber tinted windows, Whizzwheels, grille label. (Note: Prototype shown in 1977 Corgi Juniors catalog with orange chassis-cab and red flatbed body carrying black container box with white sides. Different prototype shown in 1977 Corgi catalog with blue chassis-cab and red flatbed body carrying white container box with white side labels. Third prototype shown in 1978 Corgi catalog with dark blue cab-chassis and gray flatbed body. Not released in any of these color schemes.)

1. Red chassis-cab, light gray flatbed.

2019-A Scania Silo Truck 144mm 1977-1979 $15-25

Chassis-cab and black exhaust stack castings, brown, tan and white bulk containers and framework, amber tinted windows, black plastic cab base, British Grain and grille labels, Whizzwheels.

1. Orange chassis-cab.

2020-A Mercedes-Benz Refrigerator Van 207mm 1977-1979 $20-30

Cab body, chassis and semi-trailer chassis castings, amber tinted windows, white plastic refrigerator van body with red rear doors, red-white-blue Birdseye logo, grille and rear end labels, black plastic cab base, Whizzwheels.

1. White cab, medium blue chassis under cab and trailer.

2. White cab, dark blue chassis under cab and trailer.

3. White cab, metallic blue chassis under cab and trailer.

4. White cab, dark blue chassis under cab and trailer, tan trailer body. (Possible factory error.)

2025-A Swiss P.T.T. Bus 169mm 1977-1978 $50-60

Same casting as 2008-A, white interior, amber tinted windows, black plastic base, Whizzwheels, red-yellow-black P.T.T. labels.

1. Yellow body, white roof.

2027-A Mack Ryder Rentals Van ?mm 1979-???? $30-40

Same cab as 2006-A with added yellow airdam, same semi-trailer as 2020-A without refrigerator, Whizzwheels. (Shown in 1978 Corgi catalog with red body and Kellogg's graphics, but not produced in this color scheme.)

1. Yellow cab and semi-trailer, red trailer doors, both with black chassis, Ryder Truck Rental logo.

2028-A Mercedes-Benz Refrigerator Truck 125mm 1977-1978 $20-30

Same cab and semi-trailer as 2020-A, amber tinted windows, red rear doors, black plastic cab base, grille, logo and rear end labels, Gervais logo label on left, Danone logo label on right side of semi-trailer, Whizzwheels.

1. White cab and semi-trailer, both with light blue chassis.

2. White cab and semi-trailer, both with metallic blue chassis.

2029-A Mack Fire Pumper 143mm 1979-10/1983 $20-30

Cab and unpainted chassis-grille-footboard castings, red dome light, chrome sirens, blue tinted windows, red interior and rear body, yellow ladders and hose racks, black suction hose and hose reels, number 3, "Hammond Fire Dept." and control panel labels, black plastic base, four-spoke chrome wheels.

1. Red cab and rear body, white roof panel.

Rockets Track Sets

2051 Action Speedset 1970-1971 $100-150+

Details not known at time of publication.

2052 Super Autobatics Speedset 1970-1971 $100-150+

Single track set with Autostart, Superloop and Spaceleap. Packaged with The Saint's Volvo P1800.

2053	Clover Leaf Special	1970-1971	$100-150+

Set with track, Super Booster, and multiple special track sections.

2058	Super Race-abatic Speedset	1970-1971	$100-150+

Details not known at time of publication.

2060	Skypark Tower Garage	1970-1971	$100-150+

Tall multi-level parking garage with lifting elevator and track connectors.

2062	Wall of Death Special	1970-1971	$100-150+

Set contains white Juniors Capri with "WALL OF DEATH" graphics, racing motorcycle on Rockets platform chassis, unique track accessories including multi-loop spiral and crash wall.

2063	Tom and Jerry Crazy Chase	1970-1971	$100-150+

Details not known at time of publication.

2070	Alpine Ski-set	1970-1971	$100-150+

Similar to 2052-A but with added support towers and unique blue alpine skier figure with white skis and tan poles on red Rockets chassis, Rockets track with loop and jump. (Skier figure not available separately.)

2071	Jetspeed Circuit	1970-1971	$100-150+

Set contains loop of track, Power Booster, two towers, speed bump and one car.

2074	Triple Loop Speedcircuit	1970-1971	$100-150+

Details not known at time of publication.

2075	Grand Canyon Speedcircuit	1970-1971	$100-150+

Set with track, Super Booster, and multiple special track sections.

2079	World Champion Racing Speedset	1970-1971	$100-150+

Set with track, two Rockets cars, two Super Boosters and multiple special track sections.

Twin Packs

2501-A	Zetor Tractor (4-C) &Farm Trailer (33-A)	1977?-1975	$15-20

Orange and red tractor, yellow and red trailer. (Also see E2516-A.)

2501-B	Double-decker Bus (81-A) & Austin Taxi (71-B)	1980-1981	$8-12

Standard colors and trim.

2502-A	Tractor with Blade (43-A) & Tipping Trailer (8-C)	1977?-1975	$15-20

Standard colors and trim.

2502-B	Land Rover Wrecker (31-B) & Jaguar XJS 72-B)	1980- 10/1983	$8-12

1. Medium blue Land Rover, copper Jaguar with yellow interior.
2. Medium blue Land Rover, red Jaguar with yellow interior.

2503-A	Land Rover Pickup (16-B) & Horse Trailer (38-A)	1977?-1978	$15-20

Green Land Rover, metallic copper trailer.

2503-B	Rover Police Car (16-C) & Helicopter (98-C)	1980-10/1983	$8-12

Standard colors and trim.

2504-A	Land Rover Wrecker (31-B) &Volkswagen (17-C)	1977?-1976	$15-20

Red Land Rover, green Volkswagen with flower labels.

2504-B	Land Rover Wrecker (31-B) &Jaguar E-type (39-B)	1977-1978	$15-20

Standard colors and trim.

2504-C	Land Rover Wrecker (31-B) & AMC Pacer (62-B)	1978-1979	$15-20

Standard colors and trim.

2505-A	Jaguar XJ6 (39-A) &Boat Trailer (19-B)	1977?-1975	$15-20

Standard colors and trim.

2505-B	Daily Planet Van (50-B) &Helicopter (6-D)	1979	$40-60

Standard colors and trim.

2506-A	A.M.F. Ski-Daddler (18-D) & Trailer	1977?-1975	$20-30

Orange and black Snowmobile with blue suited driver, red and orange non-standard trailer with tan suited passenger.

2506-B	Supermobile (11-C) &Super Van (47-B)	1979-1981	$50-70

Standard colors and trim.

2507-A	Tom (1213-A) & Jerry (1214-A)	1977?-1975	$100-150

Standard colors and trim.

2507-B	Tom (58-B) & Jerry (38-B)	1980-1981	$50-70

Standard colors and trim.
1. White chassis on Tom car.
2. Yellow chassis on Tom car.

2508-A	Army Jeep (76-B) & Field Gun (96-A)	1976-1977	$15-20

Standard colors and trim.

2508-B	Popeye's Tugboat (67-C) & Olive's Plane (79-B)	1980-1981	$50-70

Standard colors and trim.

2509-A	Bucket Truck (54-A) & Loadmaster Shovel (23-B)	1977?-1974	$15-20

Standard colors and trim.

2510-A	Formula 1 (22-C) & Formula 5000 (27-B) Racers	1973-1978	$15-20

Standard colors and trim.

2511-A	Scout Car (84-A) & Army Helicopter (34-B)	1974-1978	$15-20

Standard colors and trim.

2512-A	Space Shuttle (5-C) & Starship Liberator (44-B)	1979-1981	$40-50

NASA version of Space Shuttle, Silver and Yellow Liberator.

2513-A	Police Range Rover (9-C) & Healer Wheeler (36-B)	1973-1976	$15-20

Standard colors and trim.

2513-B	ERF Fire Engine (26-C) & Healer Wheeler (36-B)	1977-1978	$15-20

Standard colors and trim.

2513-C	ERF Fire Engine (26-C) &Mercedes Ambulance (1-E)	1979-1980	$8-12

Standard colors and trim.

2514-A	Skip Dumper (85-A) & Cement Mixer (20-C)	1976-1977	$12-15

Standard colors and trim.

2515-A	Citroen Dyane (89-A) & Boat Trailer (19-B)	1976-1980	$8-12

1. Yellow Dyane, standard boat colors and trim.
2. Orange Dyane, standard boat colors and trim.

2516-A	Zetor Tractor (4-C) & Tipping Trailer (8-C)	1976-1978	$18-22

Green and white tractor, yellow and green trailer. (Also see E2501-A.)

2518-A	Volvo Estate Car (51-B) & Caravan Trailer (65-B)	1976-1976	$8-12

Standard colors and trim.

2518-B	Mercedes 240D (59-C) & Caravan Trailer (65-B)	1977-1980	$8-12

1. Light blue Mercedes with clear windows, white caravan with light blue door.
2. Metallic blue Mercedes with amber tinted windows, white caravan with light blue door.
3. Red Mercedes with clear windows, Cream caravan with butterscotch door.

2519-A	Batmobile (69-A) & Batboat (1003-A)	1977- 10/1983	$80-100

1. Standard decorations, trailer hitch on Batmobile, gold trailer.
2. Same as A1 except white trailer.

2520-A	Rough Terrain Truck (13-B) &Dinghy on Trailer	1977-????	$15-20

Blue truck with white cab, red and yellow Dinghy on blue trailer.

2521-A	Army Ambulance (79-A) & Helicopter (40-B)	1977-1979	$18-22

Standard colors and trim.

2521-B	James Bond Shuttle (41-B) & Drax Copter (73-B)	1980-1981	$50-60

Yellow and White Helicopter and Space Shuttle.

2522-A	Centurion Tank (66-A) & Armored Car (83-A)	1977-????	$18-22

Standard colors and trim.

2523-A	Porsche Police Car (37-B) & Helicopter (46-B)	1977-1979	$15-20

1. White Porsche with "POLICE" side labels, white Helicopter with light blue skis and rotors and "POLICE" side labels.
2. White Porsche with "POLICE" side labels, metallic blue Helicopter with white skis and rotors and "POLICE" side labels.

2524-A	Fire Ball (90-A) & Golden Eagle (91-A) Vans	1978-1980	$8-12

Standard colors and trim.

2525-A	Triumph TR7 (10-C) & Dinghy on Trailer	1979-1980	$15-20

1. Red and blue TR7 with "BRITISH AIRWAYS 8" labels, red and yellow dinghy on light blue trailer.
2. White and black TR7 with "3" hood labels, red and yellow dinghy on dark metallic blue trailer.

2526-A	Dump Truck (7-C) & Shovel Loader (48-B)	1977-1980	$15-20

Blue and yellow Dump Truck, Red and yellow Shovel Loader.

2527-A	Kojack's Buick (68-A) & Police Helicopter (46-B)	1978-1979	$40-60

Standard Kojak Buick, metallic blue helicopter with white rotors and skis.

2528-A	Starsky & Hutch Torino (45-B) & Police Car (28-C)	1978-1980	$40-60

Standard colors and trim.

2529-A	Bond Lotus (60-B) &Stromberg Copter (3-D)	1978-1979	$40-60

Standard colors and trim.

2530-A	Range Rover (42-C) and Helicopter	1978-????	$15-20

Red Range Rover with yellow side stripe and black "RESCUE TEAM" text, White Helicopter with blue rotors and skis.

2531-A Spidervan (56-B) & Spidercopter (75-B) 1978?-???? $40-50
Standard colors and trim.

2532-A Ford Capri (61-C) & Ford Transit Wrecker (103-A)
1981-???? $8-12
Standard colors and trim.

2534-A Locomotive (108-A) & Goods Wagon (112-A) 1981-???? $8-12
Standard colors and trim.

2534-B Locomotive (108-A) & Passenger Coach (111-A)
1982-10/1983 $8-12
Standard colors and trim.

2535-A Magnum P.I. Ferrari (131-A) & Buick Police (133-A)
1980-???? $40-60
Ferrari 308GTS and Buick Police in standard colors and trim.

2536-A Professionals Capri (64-B) & Police Car (16-C) 1980-???? $50-70
Standard colors and trim.

2537-A Capri (141-A) &Mustang (140-A) 1980-???? $8-12
Standard colors and trim.

2538-A Space Shuttle (5-C) & Buck Rogers Starfighter (13-C)
1980-???? $15-20
Standard colors and trim.

2542-A Enterprise (148-A) & Klingon Warship (149-A)
1982-10/1983 $75-125
Standard colors and trim.

2550-A Matra Rancho (76-C) & Horse Box (38-A?) 1983-10/1983 $8-12
Bright green Matra and horse box trailer.

2551-A Rover 3500 (8-D) & Dinghy on Trailer 1983-1983 $8-12
Maroon Rover, black and yellow dinghy on black trailer.

2551-B Ford Sierra (129-A) & Dinghy on Trailer 1983-10/1983 $8-12
Silver Sierra with gray base and yellow interior / taillamps, black and yellow dinghy on black trailer.

2553-A Mustang Cobra (104-A) & Boat / Trailer (19-B?)
1983-10/1983 $8-12
Standard colors and trim.

2553-B Range Rover (184-A) & Boat / Trailer (19-B?)
1983-10/1983 $8-12
1. Maroon open top Range Rover, red and white boat on white trailer.
2. Red open top Range Rover, red and white boat on white trailer.

2554-A Mercedes 240D (59-C) & Caravan Trailer (65-B)
1982-1983 $8-12
Red Mercedes, tan trailer with red door.

2554-B Volvo Wagon (51-B) & Caravan Trailer (65-B) 1983-10/1983 $8-12
Tan Volvo, tan trailer with red door.

2555-A Ford Wrecker (103-A) & Jaguar XJ-S (72—B)
1983-10/1983 $8-12
White wrecker in standard trim, maroon Jaguar.

2595-A Rover Triplex (138-A) & Metro Datapost (135-A)
1983-10/1983 $8-12
Standard colors and trim.

Triple Packs

2601-A Batmobile (69-A), Batboat (1003-A) & Batcopter (78-B)
1977-1978 $AUCTION

Standard trim and colors.

Gift Sets

3001-A Garage & three vehicles (Husky) 196?-196? $60-75
Garage 2001-A & three Husky vehicles.

3001-B Garage & three vehicles (Corgi Jr.) 1975-10/1983 $35-55
Garage 2001-A & three Corgi Jr. vehicles. Standard colors on vehicles that vary per issue date.
1. Yellow garage walls, blue doors, no end labels. (1975-78.)
2. Red garage walls, blue doors, no end labels. (1979-83.)

3002-A Batmobile & Batboat (Husky) 196?-1969 $400+
Husky Batmobile 1002-A & Batboat 1003-A.

3002-B Batmobile & Batboat (Corgi Jr.) 1970-197? $250+
Corgi Jr. Batmobile 1002-A & Batboat 1003-A.

3002-C Garage Centre 1982- 10/1983 $20-30
Garage building with lift, gas pumps, accessories.

3003-A Car Transporter & five cars (Husky) 196?-1969 $125-175
Transporter 2002-A & five Husky cars.

3003-B Car Transporter & five cars (Corgi Jr.) 1970-1971? $80-100
Transporter 2002-A & five Corgi Jr. cars.

3003-C Garage Forecourt Set 1982- 10/1983 $25-35
Garage with gas pumps, lift, etc.

3004-A Garage & two cars (Husky) 196?-196? $50-60
Garage (2001-A) & two Husky cars.

3004-B O.H.M.S.S. Set 1970-1971? $AUCTION
James Bond 1010-A, 1011-A & 1012-A.

3005-A Holiday Time Set 196?-1969 $175-225
Eight Husky vehicles including non-standard Studebaker Wagonaire.

3005-B Leisure Time Set 1970-197? $125-150
Eight Corgi Jr. vehicles, all standard colors and trim.

3006-A Service Station Set 196?-196? $70-90
Building with three Husky vehicles.

3006-B Playmat 1983-10/1983 $20-30
Vinyl playmat with printed street scene.

3007-A Multi-Story Car Park (Husky) 1968?-1969? $100-120
Car park building with four Husky vehicles.

3007-B Multi-Story Car Park (Corgi Jr.) 197?-197? $50-75
Car park building with three Corgi Jr. vehicles.

3007-C Wild West Set 1981-10/1983 $40-60
Stage coach, steam locomotive, "Union Pacific" coach, standard "BUFFALO BILL'S" baggage cars and non-standard "WILD WEST" baggage car.

3008-A Crime Busters Set 1967-1969 $400++
Four superhero vehicles.

3009-A Service Station Set 1970-1971? $60-80
Station building, three vehicles, gas pumps.
1. Ford F-350 Wrecker, Guy Esso Tanker, Aston-Martin DB6.
2. Land Rover Wrecker, Guy Esso Tanker, NSU RO-80.

3010-A Farm Buildings and Six Vehicles 1968?-1969? $AUCTION
Two brown plastic farm buildings, yellow Jaguar XJ6, metallic green Horse Trailer, red Tractor, red and yellow Tipping Trailer, mint green Livestock Trailer, metallic green Willys Jeep. (One MOC example known to author at time of publication.)

3011-A Road Construction Set 1970-197? $60-75
Flatbed 2003-A with red cab, five construction vehicles in standard colors.

3013-A Emergency Rescue Set 1977-1980 $30-50
Building with three vehicles.

3015-A Transporter Set 1980-10/1983 $40-60
Transporter 2014-A & four vehicles.

3015-B Off-Road Set 1983? $???
Maroon open Range Rover with white interior, tan Volvo 245DL with tan Caravan trailer, blue Renault 5 Turbo with red base, red Mercedes-Benz 500SL coupe with tan interior, yellow open top Jeep with red roll cage. (May have been issued about the time of Mettoy's closure.)

3019-A Agricultural Set 197?-197? $50-75
Two buildings with six vehicles in standard colors.

3019-B James Bond Octopussy Set 1983- 10/1983 $400+
1. Maroon open Range Rover with tan interior, tan horsebox trailer, white aircraft with dark cockpit cover and red and blue wing stripes.
2. Maroon open Range Rover with white interior, tan horsebox trailer, white aircraft with dark cockpit cover and red and blue wing stripes.
3. Red open Range Rover with white interior, tan horsebox trailer, white aircraft with dark cockpit cover and red and blue wing stripes.

3020-A Club Racing Set 1971-197? $100-140
1. Non-standard dark blue Escort Mk I with "8" labels, non-standard dark blue car trailer, yellow Morgan Plus-8, purple Land Rover Breakdown, red Austin-Healey Sprite, maroon Ferrari 312, white Porsche Carrera 6, purple BVRT Mini, figures and traffic cones.
2. Non-standard metallic teal Capri with white base and "8" labels, non-standard metallic teal car trailer, metallic light blue Escort Mk I with "32" labels, purple Land Rover Breakdown, red Austin-Healey Sprite, maroon Ferrari 312, white Porsche Carrera 6, purple BVRT Mini, figures and traffic cones.
3. Non-standard red Capri with white base and "8" labels, non-standard dark blue car trailer, red Morgan Plus-8 with "20" labels, red Land Rover Breakdown, red Austin-Healey Sprite, maroon Ferrari 312, white Porsche Carrera 6, purple BVRT Mini, figures and traffic cones.

3021-A   Emergency 999 Set   1972-1974

                                      Holmes Wrecker $150-175

                                      Land Rover Wrecker $60-75

Non-standard Duple-Vista or Mercedes bus with added flat black scorch marks (model color varies with release date) on body and roof, Wrecker, white Studebaker Ambulance, red and white Ford Capri Fire Chief, VW Police, fire engine, figures, traffic signs, traffic cones.

1. Red and yellow Ford Holmes wrecker, purple and white Duple-Vista .
2. Red and yellow Ford Holmes wrecker, orange and white Duple-Vista .
3. Purple Land Rover wrecker, orange and white Duple-Vista.
4. Red Land Rover wrecker, metallic blue Mercedes bus without labels.

3021-B   Trucking Set   1983-10/1983 $40-60

Five vehicles.

3022-A   Rescue Set   197?-1977 $75-100

Building, playmat, standard Porsche Police Car, nonstandard Land Rover   Range Rover Ambulance, Coast Guard Range Rover, Rough Terrain Truck and Dinghy on Trailer.

3023-A   Transporter Set   1977-1979 $40-60

Transporter 2014-A & four vehicles. Vehicles and colors vary per production date.

3024-A   Road Construction Set   197?-1977 $50-75

Flatbed 2003-A, Road Roller, Scammell Cement Truck, Massey Ferguson Tractor, Terex Dumper, Ford Container truck, Front Loader, All in Standard Colors with Figures and Accessories.

3024-B   Road Construction Set   1978-1979 $50-75

Revised version of above (six different vehicles?).

3025-A   Transporter Set   197?-1976 $50-75

Transporter 2002-A & five vehicles. Vehicles and colors vary per production date and may be without standard labels or other graphics.

3026-A   Leisure Time Set   1971-1972 $50-60

Eight vehicles & accessories, standard colors and trim.

3026-B   Emergency Set   1976-1979 $50-60

Snorkel, ERF Fire Tender, Ambulance, Mercury Fire Chief, Range Rover Ambulance, Police Helicopter, signs and figures.

3028-A   Race Track Special Set 197?-197? $60-70

Seven vehicles including non-standard red Range Rover.

3029-A   Military Set   1976-1977 $40-60

Seven vehicles including nonstandard Army Land Rover Wrecker, Stinger Helicopter, Armored Car, Land Rover Military Ambulance, Commando Car, Military Jeep, Field Gun and figures.

3030-A   James Bond "Spy Who Loved Me" Set   1976-1978 $500++

Five vehicles including nonstandard Jaws Telephone Van,Stromberg's black Mercedes 240D with gray paint splatter, and Speedboat on Trailer.

3036-A   Garage and Four Car Set 1983-10/1983 $30-50

Red 2001-A garage with blue doors, four vehicles. Vehicles vary per production date.

3050-A   Concorde Set   1978-???? $40-60

650 Concorde, building, nonstandard Mercedes Bus, Leyland Van and Helicopter.

3051-A   Filling Station Set   1977-1980 $30-50

Building and three vehicles.

3052-A   Police Station Set   1977-1980 $30-50

Building, police Range Rover, police Porsche 911, police helicopter.

3053-A   Fire Station Set   1977-1980 $30-50

Building and three fire vehicles including Torino "FIRE DEPT" model.

3071-A   Growler Set   1975?-1976 $50-60

Six Growlers vehicles, standard colors and trim.

3073-A   Steer Gear-Single Pack 1977-197? $???

Details not known.

3074-A   Steer Gear-Double Pack 1977-197? $???

Details not known.

3080-A   Batman Set   1980-1981 $300-500+

Five Batman vehicles with standard graphics.

3081-A   Superman Set   1980-1981 $300-500+

Supermobile, Metropolis Police car, Supervan, red Metropolis Newspaper Van, Police Helicopter, all with standard graphics.

1. Silver Supervan.
2. Red Supervan.

3082-A   James Bond Set   1980-1981 $300-500+

James Bond Aston Martin DB6, Lotus Esprit, white and yellow Helicopter, Space Shuttle, and non-standard Jaws telephone van.

3084-A   Cartoon Characters Set 1980-1981 $200-250+

Pink Panther, Tom & Jerry, Popeye and Olive Oyl vehicles.

3100-A   Construction Set   1980-10/1983 $40-60

Orange Ford Cement Truck with black barrel, yellow Tipper Truck with black tipper, yellow Crane with vacuum plated boom, orange Front Loader with vacuum plated scoop, yellow Digger with green base and vacuum plated scoop, orange Massey-Ferguson Tractor with black scoop, green Skip Dumper with yellow tipper. Colors may vary with production date.

3101-A   Fire Set   1980-198? $50-60

Six vehicles and figures including non-standard orange Range Rover with yellow "RESCUE" door label, Rover 3500 "POLICE" car, Ford Torino "FIRE CHIEF" car, Simon Snorkel, ERF Fire Tender and Helicopter.

3103-A   Emergency Set   1980-198? $50-60

Six vehicles including non-standard yellow Chevrolet "AA" van, non-standard gold VW Polo, blue Land Rover Wrecker, Range Rover, white Mercedes ambulance, Porsche 911, with unpainted figures.

1. White Range Rover Police, white Porsche 911 Police.
2. Red Range Rover with non-standard yellow "RESCUE" door label, white and red Porsche 911 Rijkspolitie.

3105-A   Transporter Set   1982-10/1983 $40-60

Transporter 2014-A and four vehicles, vehicles vary with production date.

3107-A   Sports Car Set – 5 Vehicles   1982-10/1983 $30-50

Known with metallic blue Jaguar XJS, red 1957 Thunderbird, metallic green Mercedes-Benz 350SL, black Porsche 911, yellow-green Fiat X1/9. Cars may vary in specification and color.

3108-A   Flintstone's Set   1982-10/1983 $150-200

Five Flintstone's vehicles.

3109-A   Best of British Set   1983-10/1983 $40-60

Seven British vehicles.

3110-A   Emergency Set   1982-10/1983 $30-50

1. Ford Transit tow truck, Airport Fire Tender, Helicopter, Mercedes Ambulance, Buick police car.
2. Ford Transit tow truck, Airport Fire Tender, Paramedic Van, Mercedes Ambulance, Snorkel fire truck.

3111-A   Wild West Railroad Set 1982-10/1983 $30-50

Three vehicles and buildings.

3112-A   Wild West Frontier Set 1982-10/1983 $30-50

Three vehicles, including nonstandard horse-drawn flat wagon, and buildings.

3113-A   Wild West Set   1982-10/1983 $40-60

Locomotive, Union Pacific Coach, Stage Coach, Covered Wagon, River Boat.

3114-A   Superheroes Set   1982-10/1983 $125-175

Standard trim on Batmobile, Batbike, Batboat, Supermobile and Metropolis Buick Police Car.

3115-A   Off-road Set   1982-10/1983 $50-70

Yellow Jeep with red interior and roll bar, blue Jeep with white interior, yellow Baja Van, Safari Park Matra Rancho, yellow Renault R5-T16 without labels, maroon open top Range Rover, orange Mustang Cobra, black and red Dinghy on black trailer.

3116-A   Crimefighters Set   1982-10/1983 $100-150

1. Star Trek Enterprise, Buck Rogers Starship, Spiderbike, James Bond Lotus Esprit, Buick Police.
2. NASA Enterprise, Buck Rogers Starship, Dan Tanna T-Bird, James Bond Lotus Esprit, James Bond Aston-Martin.

3118-A   Commando Set   1982-10/1983 $30-50

Olive green buildings, Commando vehicle, army Jeep, and tank.

3121-A   Super Sports Car   1983-10/1983 $40-60

Triplex Rover, Alitalia Capri, Datapost Mini Metro, cream and red VW Polo, orange Fiat X1/9, black Porsche Carrera, Elf Renault5-T16.

3122-A   Turbochargers Set   1983-10/1983 $30-40

Three vehicles, pit, Dunlop bridge.

3123-A   Truckers Set   1983-10/1983 $30-40

Three vehicles and buildings.

ElectroRockets

Similar to Rockets except equipped with rechargeable Ni-Cad battery and motor. Part or all motor components may have been supplied by another company.

4000   Bizzarini Manta ElectroRockets   1970-1971

                                      Undamaged finish $100-150

                                      Typical damaged finish $30-40

Purple chrome-effect vacuum plated body like 918-A, gold to silver vacuum plated windows. (Warning: The battery and styrofoam packaging react with the finish of the car upon aging. The car must be stored in an open space out of the packaging with the battery removed to preserve it.)

1. Purple chrome-effect vacuum plated body.

2. Silver chrome-effect vacuum plated body.

4001   Bizzarini Manta ElectroRocket

with Auto Charger   1970-1971 $150-250

Purple chrome-effect vacuum plated body like 918-A, gold to silver vacuum plated windows Same battery warning applies.)

1. Car (4000) with Auto Charger.

4002   Alfa Romeo Montreal ElectroRockets   1970-1971

Undamaged finish $100-150

Typical damaged finish $30-40

Gold vacuum plated body, opaque black windows. (Same battery warning applies.)

4200   ElectroRockets Stunt Power Set   1970-1971 $150-300

Set Contains car, charger, and triple loop Rockets track combination.

4203   ElectroRockets Double 8 Raceway   1970-1971 $???

Details not known. Possibly packaged with both types of cars and charger.

Corgi Toys Ltd. - The Independent Years 1984 Transitional Era - 1990 Renumbering

This section contains the variation listing for models produced from the time of the October 30, 1983 Mettoy receivership up to the 1990 general re-numbering resulting from the Mattel buyout. Some of the information from the chaotic time surrounding the collapse of Mettoy is derived from the 1984 catalog issued by the factory. Information on released models from this period is confusing and contradictory, since the factory was also selling off excess Mettoy inventory at this time. Please note: A separate 5 digit stock number was also used at this time, but is not referenced in this section unless a unique model number was not assigned.

Note: values shown are in US dollars ($US) for mint-in-mint package condition as of may 2003. As a general rule, subtract 35-40% for mint loose, 50-60% for excellent, 60-70% for vg/chipped.

J 1 A   Juniors - NASA Shuttle   Apr-84 $8-12

White Upper and Black Lower Body, White Cargo Bay Doors, NASA and American Flag Graphics.

J 1 B   Juniors - Ford Capri Racer   1986? $3-5

a. White Body, Cream Interior, Blue/Yellow Stripes, "DUCKHAMS 9" Graphics.

b. White Body, Black Interior, Blue/Yellow Stripes, "DUCKHAMS 9" Graphics.

c. Black Body, White Interior, Gold Stripes, "Homefire 1" Graphics. (BP service station promotion.)

d. Orange Body, White Interior, Black Flame-like Graphics, Clear Windows, Ivory Interior, Black "38" Graphics.

J 1/ 02   Juniors - Ford Capri Racer   Jan-88 $3-5

Magenta Body with Yellow Front, Black Nose Spoiler, Clear Windows, White Interior, Yellow "12" Graphics.

J 2   Juniors - Dump Truck   Apr-84 $3-5

a. Yellow Cab, Red Dump Body and Baseplate, Black Wheels, No Windows or Front Label. (old # E7-C, possibly a transitional period model.)

b. Yellow Cab and Dump Body, Yellow Baseplate, Black "LAING" on Dump Body, No Windows or Front Label. (Jan-85)

c. Yellow Cab and Dump Body, Yellow Baseplate, No Graphics, No Windows or Front Label.

J 2/ 01   Juniors - Iveco Tanker   Jan-88 $3-5

Red Cab, White Tank, "Esso" Logo.

J 3 A   Juniors - Triumph TR7   Apr-84 $3-5

a. Brown Body, White Interior, White "TRIUMPH" Graphics. (old # E10-C.)

b. Brown Body, Tan Interior, No Graphics.

c. Red Upper and Blue Lower Body with White Divider Stripe, Tan Interior, White Box with "8" Graphics. (Jan-85)

d. Black Body, No Graphics, Yellow Interior, Clear Windows. (Possibly a transition era model.)

J 3 B   Juniors – Renault Trafic Van   1985 $3-5

Red Body, Black Chassis with "RENAULT TRAFIC" on base, 5spkWW, Clear Windows, White "DYNO-ROD 1st" Graphics. (also issued in USA as JB-3.)

J 4 A   Juniors - Starfighter   Apr-84 $3-5

White Body, Blue Canopy & Engines, Yellow Winglets. (old # E13-C.)

J 4 B   Juniors - Ford Transit Van   Jan-88 $3-5

White Body, Red and Blue Stripes on Lower Sides, Porsche Crest and "PORSCHE KREMER RACING" on Upper Sides, No Roof Rack. (Later identical 90010 made in China.)

a. "CORGI" on Base, Made in Great Britain.

b. Base Logo Blanked, Made in Great Britain.

c. "CORGI" on Base, Made in China.

J 4/ 01   Juniors - Ford Transit Van   1988? $5-8

Dark Blue Body, "White Arrow" on Sides with White Arrow Logo. (Promotional for White Arrow.)

a. Base Logo Blanked.

J 4/ 02   Juniors - Ford Transit Van   1988? $3-5

Red Body, White "FIRE CHIEF" and Segmented Side Stripe, Gold Crest on Upper Sides.

a. "CORGI" on Base.

J 4/ 03   Juniors - Ford Transit Van   1988? $8-12

Red Body, White Side Stripe, Silver Windows Panel, White "BRANDWEER ALARM 0011" Graphics.

a. Base Logo Blanked.

J 4/ 04   Juniors - Ford Transit Van   1988? $5-8

White Body, Script "Kay's: " Graphics. (Promotional for Kay's. Part of Set J3167/06.)

a. Base Logo Blanked.

J 4/ 05   Juniors - Ford Transit Van   Jan-89 $3-5

Red Body, White "FIRE CHIEF" on Sides with Crest & Diagonally divided Stripe, 4div Wheels,

J 4/ 06   Juniors - Ford Transit Van   Jan-90 $3-5

Red Body, Yellow "Royal Mail Parcels" Graphics. (1990 Re# of J63.)

a. "CORGI" on Base, Made in Great Britain.

b. Base Logo Blanked, Made in Great Britain.

c. "CORGI" on Base, Made in China.

J 4/ 07   Juniors - Ford Transit Van   1990? $3-5

Yellow Body, "AA" and "Service" in Black Rectangles, Black Outlined White Side Stripes.

a. "CORGI" on Base, Made in Great Britain.

b. "CORGI" on Base, Made in China.

J 4/ 08   Juniors - Ford Transit Van   1990? $3-5

White Body with Blue Outlined Red Side Stripe "POLICE" Graphics.

a. "CORGI" on Base, Made in Great Britain.

b. "CORGI" on Base, Made in China.

J 4/ 09   Juniors - Ford Transit Van   1990? $8-12

Red Body, "Falck Redningskorp" Graphics. (Produced for the German Market.)

J 4/ 10   Juniors - Ford Transit Van   1990? $3-5

Red Body, "Parcelforce" Graphics.

a. "CORGI" on Base, Made in China.

J 4/ ??   Juniors - Ford Transit Van   1990? $8-12

Dark Blue Body, Thin White Side Stripe with "POLIISI" Graphics. (Produced for the Finnish market. May be from later period with 900xx number.)

J 4/ ??   Juniors - Ford Transit Van   1990? $3-5

Dark Blue Body, Dark Yellow Side Stripe with "POLICE" Graphics.

a. "CORGI" on Base, Made in China.

J 4/ ??   Juniors - Ford Transit Van   1986? $3-5

White Body, No Graphics. (Found in Mothercare Bumper Car Set J3035. Not officially assigned a model number.)

a. Base Logo Blanked, Made in Great Britain.

J 4/ ??   Juniors - Ford Transit Van   1986? $3-5

Yellow Body, No Graphics. (Found in various sets. Not officially assigned a model number.)

a. Base Logo Blanked, Made in Great Britain.

J 4/ ??   Juniors - Ford Transit Van   1986? $3-5

Red Body, No Graphics. (Found in various sets. Not officially assigned a model number.)

a. Base Logo Blanked, Made in Great Britain.

J 4/ ?? Juniors - Ford Transit Van 1986? $3-5
Red Body, "POINTERS" Graphics. (Promotional for BP Service Stations. Red box. Not officially assigned a model number.)

a. "CORGI" on Base, Made in Great Britain.

J 4/ ?? Juniors - Ford Transit Van 1990? $5-8
White Body, Blue "Thames Water Leak Detection Unit" and "Customer Service 0645 200800" Graphics. (Promotional model for Thames Water.)

a. "CORGI" on Base, Made in China.

J 4/ ?? Juniors - Ford Transit Van 1990? $8-12
Red Body, Yellow "SERVICE VOGN" Graphics. (May be from later era.)

J 4/ ?? Juniors - Ford Transit Van 1990? $5-8
Red Body, "Maltesers" Graphics. (Possibly a promotional model. May be from later era.)

a. Base Logo Blanked, Made in Great Britain.

J 4/ ?? Juniors - Ford Transit Van 1990? $5-8
Dark Green or Black Body (unsure), Gold "Harrods" Graphics. (Promotional for Harrods.)

J 4/ ?? Juniors - Ford Transit Van 1990? $5-8
White Body, "COMBI" and "FOTO-VIDEO-AUDIO" Graphics. (Promotional for Combi.)

J 5 Juniors - Mercedes-Benz Bus Apr-84
Standard release $3-5
Promotional $10-15
a. Green Body , Opaque Black Windows, Two White Stripes and White "Holiday Inn" on Sides. (Same casting as old # E15-C.)
b. Yellow Body with "SCHOOL BUS" on Sides, Opaque Black Windows. (Found in Set E(J)3035.)
c. White Body, Blue Below Belt Line on Sides, Black "HOLIDAY TOURS" on Sides. (Jan-85)
d. White Body, Blue Below Belt Line on Sides, Blue "HOLIDAY TOURS" on Sides, Clear Windows, Yellow Interior. (1985?)
e. White Body, Blue and Aqua Graphics with Aqua "HOLIDAY TOURS" on Sides. (Found in Airport Set J3125.)
f. Yellow Body with "HEATHROW" on Sides, Opaque Black Windows. (See J105. Also found in Soldat Jumbo Set and Airport Set J3125.)
g. Yellow Body with "HEATHROW" on Sides, Dark Blue Tinted Windows.
h. Yellow Body with "NuBus" and Texas Instruments Logo on Sides, Opaque Black Windows. (Promotional model for Texas Instruments.)

J 5/ 02 Juniors - Mercedes-Benz Bus Jul-88 $5-8
White Body and Interior, Clear Windows, "SAS" Logo on Sides.

J 5/ 03 Juniors - Mercedes-Benz Bus Jul-88 $5-8
White Body, Air France Striping, Blue "AIR FRANCE" on Sides.

J 5/ 04 Juniors - Mercedes-Benz Bus Jun-89 $5-8
Yellow Body, Clear Windows, White Interior, Red Side Stripe, Black "PTT" Graphics. (Produced for the French & Swiss Markets. Similar to J214 which has opaque black windows.)

J 6 Juniors - Rover Police Apr-84 $3-5
a. White Body, Blue Lightbar on Roof, Tan Interior, Black Outlined Red Side Stripe "POLICE" text. (old # E16-C.)
b. White Body, Blue Lightbar on Roof, Cream Interior, Narrow Red Side Label with Black "POLICE" text. (found in reverse-window card c. 1984.)
c. White Body, Red Interior, Blue Lightbar on Roof, Red Side Stripe with Black "POLICE," Red Forward Hood with Black "POLICE" near Windshield, Black "H587" on Roof. (Jan-85)
d. White Body, Blue Lightbar on Roof, Ivory Interior, Black Diecast Base, Black Outlined Yellow Side Stripe, Black "POLICE" on Hood, "E129" on Roof, Blue Box without J Number. (Part of BP Service Station Promotion.)

J 7 Juniors - ERF Fire Engine Apr-84 $3-5
a. Red Body, Silver Access Doors, Yellow Ladder. (old # E26-C.)
b. Red/ Silver Body, Yellow Ladder, White "FIRE" Over Cab. (Jan-85, Also found as JB-7.)
c. Red/ Silver Body, Yellow Ladder, White "FIRE SERVICE 999" Over Cab. (Renumbered 90030 in 1990.)

J 8 Juniors - Simon Snorkel Fire Engine Apr-84 $3-5
a. Red Body, Dark Yellow Base & Booms. (old # E29-D.)
b. Red Body, Light Yellow Base & Booms. (1985?)
c. Red Body, White Base, Light Yellow Booms. (1985. Found in green card, possibly a factory error.)
d. Red Body, White Base & Booms, Black "SNORKEL" on Upper Boom Left Side. (Jan-85. Also found as JB-8.)

e. Red Body, White Base & Booms, Black "SNORKEL" on Upper Boom Right Side, Base Text Blanked. (1988).

J 9 A Juniors - Cement Mixer Apr-84 $3-5
a. Yellow Body, Red-Orange Drum & Holder. (old # E30-D.)
b. Brick Red Body, Cream Drum & Holder. (Found in Set E(J)3035.)
c. Orange Body, White Drum & Holder. (Found in green French card 1985.)
d. White Body with Black Side Stripes & "RMC" on Roof, Red Drum & Holder, Red Base. (Jan-85)
e. Blue Body, White Drum & Holder, White Baseplate, Opaque Black Windows. (Found in Knorr promotional set, possibly elsewhere.)
f. Light Tan Body, White Drum & Holder. (Found in set J3035.)
g. White Body, Orange Drum & Holder. (Found in set J3035.)

J 9 B Juniors - Buick Track Car 1985? $6-10
Black Body with Gold Striping, High Rear Axle, Vacuum Plated Side Exhaust Pipes, Otherwise Like J60.

J 9 C Juniors - Iveco Container Truck 1987? $3-5
White Body, "Dunlop" Graphics. (may have different number.)

J 9/ 01 Juniors - Iveco Container Truck Jan-88 $3-5
Black Cab and Box Body, "Mars Helps you Work, Rest and Play" Graphics.

J 9/ 02 Juniors - Iveco Container Truck Sep-88 $3-5
Black Cab and Box Body, "Mars" Graphics. (Revised Side Labels)

J 9/ 03 Juniors - Iveco Container Truck Sep-88 $5-8
Red Cab, Green Chassis, White Box with Red "Batchelors Peas For Quality" on Sides.

J 9/ 05 Juniors - Iveco Container Truck Jan-89 $3-5
Yellow Cab and Box Body, "British TELECOM" on Sides, 4div Wheels.

R 9/ 09 Juniors - Iveco Container Truck Jan-91 $5-8
"Tesco," Weetabix premium offer

J 9/ 12 Juniors - Iveco Container Truck 1991 $5-8
White Body, Red "TESCO" and Swish Stripe on Sides, 8div Wheels.

J 9/ ?? Juniors - Iveco Container Truck 1989? $5-8
Yellow Body, "Fyffes" Graphics on Sides, 4div Wheels.

J 9/ ?? Juniors - Iveco Container Truck 1989? $10-15
White Body, "HET VOLK" Graphics on Sides, 4div Wheels. (Belgian promotional model for Het Volk television guide magazine.)

J 9/ 02? Juniors - Iveco Container Truck 1989? $5-8
Red Cab with White Side Stripe, Black Base and Interior, White Box Body with Red Rear Doors and "Kwik Save" Logo. (Promotional for Kwik Save. May actually be different version number.)

J 10 Juniors - Aston Martin DB6 Apr-84
Standard Released Versions $3-5
Weetabix Version with Logo Graphics $10-15
a. Maroon Body without Graphics, Opaque Black Windows. (old # E22-B.)
b. Yellow Body with Black "DB6" Side Trim, Tinted Windows. (Jan-85)
c. Yellow Body with Black "DB6" Side Trim, Opaque Black Windows.
d. Yellow Body with Red "DB6" Side Trim, Clear Windows, White Interior.
e. Yellow Body with Red "DB6" Side Trim, Opaque Black Windows.
f. Yellow Body without Graphics, Clear Windows, White Interior.
g. Yellow Body without Graphics, Opaque Black Windows.
h. Darker Yellow Body without Graphics, Opaque Black Windows, Modified Base with Keyhole Slot.
i. Yellow Body with Black Side Stripe and Red / White Weetabix Logo on Doors, Opaque Black Windows. (Promotional for Weetabix, only found in set with Routemaster and Container Truck.)
j. Blue Body with Black "DB6" Side Trim, Tinted Windows.
k. Blue Body without Graphics, Opaque Black Windows. (Found in Set J3109 and elsewhere.)
l. Red Body without Graphics, Clear Windows, White Interior.
m. Red Body without Graphics, Opaque Black Windows.
n. Green Body without Graphics, Amber Tinted Windows.
o. Green Body without Graphics, Opaque Black Windows. (Found in Set J3114.)
p. Metallic Gray Body without Graphics, Opaque Black Windows.
q. White Body without Graphics, Opaque Black Windows.

J 11 A Juniors - Volvo Wagon Apr-84 $3-5
a. White Body, Red Interior.
b. Beige Body, Red Interior.
c. Yellow Body, Cream Interior. (Found in set J3124.)
d. Blue Body, ??? Interior. (Packaged on green card as B111 for Italian market after end of normal production.)
e. Dark Blue Body, Black Interior.
f. Red Body, White Interior. (May be transitional era model.)

J 11 B   Juniors - Volvo Support Car (Wagon)   Jan-85 $3-5
a. White Body with Black Roof Rack, Cream Interior, Red/ Green Stripes and "Castrol" Logo.
b. White Body with Black Roof Rack, Red Interior, Red/ Green Stripes and "Castrol" Logo.
c. White Body with Black Roof Rack, Brown Interior, Red/ Green Stripes and "Castrol" Logo.
d. Red Body with Black Roof Rack, No Graphics. (From unknown set. Clarification needed.)

J 12 A   Juniors - Ford Container Truck   Apr-84 $3-5
a. Red Body, White Container. (old # E54-A.)
b. Red Body, Tan Container. (1984.)

J 12 B   Juniors - Iveco Tanker   1987? $3-5
a. Red Cab, White Tank, "TOTAL" Graphics. (Also found in Set J3097.)
b. Red Cab, White Tank, "Esso" Graphics.
c. White Cab, Silver Vacuum Plated Tank, "Shell" Graphics. (Also found as JB12.)
d. White Cab, Silver Vacuum Plated Tank, "BP Oil" Graphics. (Also found as JB12.)
e. Green Cab, Silver Vacuum Plated Tank, "BP Oil" Graphics. (Also found as JB12.)

J 12/ 01 Juniors - Iveco Tanker   Jan-88 $3-5
Green Cab, White Tank, "BP Oil" Graphics.

J 12/ 02 Juniors - Iveco Tanker   Jul-88 $8-12
a. Green Cab, White Tank, "BP C'est Super!" on Tank. (Produced for the French Market.)
b. White Cab, White Tank, "BP C'est Super!" on Tank. (Produced for the French Market.)

J 13 A   Juniors - Refuse Truck   Apr-84 $3-5
a. Orange Cab & Chassis, Gray Refuse Body. (old # E55-B.)
b. Orange Cab & Chassis, White Refuse Body. (Found in reverse window card, 1984.)

J 13/ 01 Juniors - Iveco Beverage Truck   Jan-88 $3-5
Red Cab, White Beverage Body with Blue Cases, "PEPSI" Graphics.

J 13/ 02 Juniors - Iveco Beverage Truck   Jul-88 $5-8
Red Cab, Orange Beverage Body with Yellow Cases, "Fruite' c'est plus muscle'" Graphics. (Produced for the French Market.)

J 13/ 0? Juniors - Iveco Beverage Truck   Jul-87 $3-5
Red Cab, White Body with Red Cases, "Coca-Cola" Graphics. (Only issued in various "Coca-Cola" sets. Set usage pre-dates release in general product line.)

J 14   Juniors - Mercedes-Benz 240D Saloon   Apr-84 $3-5
a. Red Body, Tan Interior. (old # E59-C.)
b. Red Body, White Interior.
c. Blue Body, Red Interior.
d. Cream Body, Red Interior. (Found in Set E(J)3035, or packaged as (J)B-114.)
e. Green Body, Red Interior, No Graphics. (Used in sets.)
f. White Body with Black Roof Rack, Black Interior, Green Hood & Side Stripe, Black Circle with White "6" Graphics. (Jan-85)
g. Red Body with Black Roof Rack, Black Interior, White Checkered Side Tampo, "TEAM car" Graphics. (1986, also issued as JB-14.)

J 15 A   Juniors - Lotus Esprit   Apr-84 $5-8
a. Yellow Body without graphics, Opaque Black Slatted Windows. (Rework of James Bond Esprit E60-B to Standard Car.)
b. White Body, Red Side Stripe "TURBO," Opaque Black Slatted Windows. (Also found in Set E(J)3035 and packaged as JB-115.)
c. White Body without graphics, Opaque Black Slatted Windows. (Found in J3109 Best of British Set.)
d. Medium Blue Body without graphics, Opaque Black Slatted Windows. (Found in Soldat Jumbo Set.)
e. Dark Blue Body without graphics, Opaque Black Slatted Windows. (Probably from set.)
f. Red Body without graphics, Opaque Black Slatted Windows. (Probably from set.)
(**Author's note:** At no time was the open wheel road version of the Lotus Esprit produced with the "007" James Bond graphics. The label required is available as a restoration item, but is only authentic for the Mettoy era James Bond Lotus Esprit with under-water fins.)

J 15 B   Juniors - Ford Transit Pick-up (with Tire Load)   1985 $4-6
a. Yellow Body, Black Tire Load, "BTS Tyre Services" Text, Black Opaque Windows, Black Plastic Chassis, 5dblspk Wheels. (JB15, Former E146-A with added tire load.)
b. Yellow Body, Opaque Black Windows, No Graphics, No Load in Rear, Black Plastic Chassis, 4-div Wheels. (Found in French red card.)
c. Dark Blue Body, Opaque Black Windows, No Graphics, No Load in Rear, Black Plastic Chassis, 4-div Wheels. (May be from unknown set.)

d. Red Body, Opaque Black Windows, No Graphics, No Load in Rear, Black Plastic Chassis. (Found in green card. May be leftover Mettoy stock.)

J 15 C   Juniors - Ford Transit Pick-up (Covered)   1986 $4-6
a. Blue Body, White Cargo Canopy with "HILL FARM PICK YOUR OWN" Text, Black Opaque Windows, Black Plastic Chassis, 5dblspk Wheels. (JB15, Former E146-A with added cover.)
b. Yellow Body, White Cargo Canopy with "HILL FARM PICK YOUR OWN" Text, Red Tinted Windows, Black Plastic Chassis, 5dblspk Wheels.

J 15 D   Juniors - Ford Transit Van   Feb-88 $3-5
White Body, Blue "Police" on Hood, Blue Edged Red Side Stripe with White "POLICE" Text, 4div Wheels.
a. Corgi Logo on Base, Made in Great Britain.

J 16 A   Juniors - Ford Capri   Apr-84 $3-5
a. Silver Body, Black Segmented Side Stripe. (old # E61-C.)
b. White Body, Red Interior, Black Segmented Side Stripe. (Found in reverse-window card 1984.)
c. Blue Body, Gold Segmented Side Stripe. (Jan-85)
d. Yellow Body, Red Interior, Black Segmented Side Stripe. (Possibly left over from Mettoy Little-Large set.)
e. Tan Body, Black Interior, No Graphics. (Possibly from a set.)
f. White Body, Black Interior, No Graphics. (Possibly from a set.)
g. Blue Body, Red Interior, Silver "POWER" Lower Side Graphics. (Jan-85)

J 16/ 01 Juniors - BMW 325i   Jan-88 $3-5
Red Body, Thin Black Trim Stripe on Sides.
a. Flat Black Baseplate.
b. Gloss Black Baseplate.

J 16/ 02(?) Juniors - BMW 325i   Jan-88 $3-5
White Body, Thin Black Trim Stripe on Sides.

J 17   Juniors - London Taxi   Apr-84 $3-5
a. Black Body, White Interior, Clear Windows, No Markings or Trim. (old # E71-B with different window and interior colors.)
b. Black Body, cream Interior, Clear Windows, No Markings or Trim.
c. Black Body, Yellow Interior, Clear Windows, No Markings or Trim.

J 17/ 01 Juniors - London Taxi   Jan-89 $3-5
a. Black Body, Red Interior, No Markings or Trim. (Continued as 90085 in 1991.)
b. Black Body, Red Interior, "272 0 272" in Yellow Circle on Doors, 5dblspk Wheels. (Shown in catalog. Does it exist?)

J 18 A   Juniors - Jaguar XJS   Apr-84
                       Standard Released Versions $3-5
                       Promotional Versions $5-8
a. White Body, Clear Windows, White Interior, Thin Green Side Stripe with Black "JAGUAR" Graphics, Leaping Jaguar Logo and "JAGUAR" on Hood.
b. White Body, Opaque Black Windows, No Interior, Thin Green Side Stripe with Black "JAGUAR" Graphics, Leaping Jaguar Logo and "JAGUAR" on Hood. (1984. Also found in reverse window card.)
c. White Body, Clear Windows, Black Interior, Thin Black Side Stripe with "JAGUAR" Graphics, Leaping Jaguar Logo and "JAGUAR" on Hood.
d. Green Body, Clear Windows, White Interior, Thin White Side Stripe with White "JAGUAR" Graphics without Racing Number, White Leaping Jaguar Logo and "JAGUAR" on Hood. (1985. Also found as JB-18.)
e. Green Body, Clear Windows, Black Interior, Thin White Side Stripe with White "JAGUAR" Graphics without Racing Number, White Leaping Jaguar Logo and "JAGUAR" on Hood. (1985. Also found as JB-18.)
f. Green Body, Clear Windows, White Interior, Thin White Side Stripe, "6 JAGUAR" on Sides & Hood. (Found in Set E(J)3035 Apr-84.)
g. Green Body, Clear Windows, Cream Interior, Wider White Side Stripe, "6 JAGUAR" on Sides & Hood.
h. Green Body, Thin White Side Stripe with "6 MOTUL" on Sides & Hood. (Jan-85)
i. Silver Body, Opaque Black Windows, No Graphics.
j. Pearlescent Silver Body, Orange and Black Tiger Stripes on Hood, sides and Roof, Black Interior, 4div Wheels. (1990 Kellogg's Promotional, UK Only.)
k. Pearlescent Silver Body, Orange Square Label with Arabic Lettering on Hood, Opaque Black Windows, 5-dblspk Wheels. (Saudi Arabian promotional model for unknown company.)
l. Yellow Body, Black Opaque Windows, No Graphics. (Found in Transporter Set J3124 and others.)
m. Orange Body, Black Opaque Windows, No Graphics. (Found in Transporter Set J3124 and others.)
n. Red Body, Black Opaque Windows, No Graphics. (Found in Transporter Set J3124 and others.)

o. Red Body, Clear Windows, White Interior, Silver Hood And Roof Stripe-like Graphics.

p. Light Blue Body, Black Opaque Windows, No Graphics. (Found in Transporter Set J3124 and others.)

q. Medium Blue Body, Black Opaque Windows, No Graphics. (Found in Weetabix promotional box.)

r. Dark Blue Body, Black Opaque Windows, No Graphics. (Found on French red card.)

s. White Body, Black Opaque Windows, No Graphics. (Found in Garage Set J3114 and Mothercare Bumper Car Set J3035. Not assigned separate model number.)

J 19   Juniors - Matra Rancho   Apr-84 $3-5
"MADE IN ENGLAND" Base Text. (Most other Juniors have "Made in Great Britain" on Base.)

a. Green Body, Black Chassis, White Interior, Black Painted Diecast Hinge Plate, No Graphics. (old # E76-C.)

b. Green Body, Black Chassis, Red Interior, Unpainted Diecast Hinge Plate, No Graphics. (old # E76-C, also found in J200-A.)

c. Dark Blue Body, Black Chassis, White Interior, Unpainted Diecast Hinge Plate, No Roof Rack or Graphics. (1984, found in reverse window card.)

d. Medium Blue Body, Black Chassis, White Interior, Unpainted Diecast Hinge Plate, No Roof Rack or Graphics. (1984, found in red Hamleys reverse window card.)

e. Light Blue Body, Black Chassis, Red Interior, Unpainted Diecast Hinge Plate, 2 Yellow Surf Boards on Black Roof Rack, Red/ Yellow Side Stripes, Yellow "mistral" on Doors with Red Dot, Yellow "m" on Hood with Red Dot. (Jan-85)

f. Light Blue Body, Black Chassis, Red Interior, Unpainted Diecast Hinge Plate, 2 Yellow Surf Boards on Black Roof Rack, Red/ White Side Stripes, White "mistral" on Doors with Red Dot, White "m" on Hood with Red Dot. (Jan-85)

g. Light Blue Body, Black Chassis, White Interior, Unpainted Diecast Hinge Plate, 2 Yellow Surf Boards on Black Roof Rack, Red/ White Side Stripes, White "mistral" on Doors with Red Dot, White "m" on Hood with Red Dot. (Jan-85)

h. Light Blue Body, Black Chassis, Red Interior, Unpainted Diecast Hinge Plate, No Surf Boards on Black Roof Rack, Red/ Yellow Side Stripes, Yellow "mistral" on Doors with Red Dot, Yellow "m" on Hood with Red Dot. (Jan-85)

i. Dark Blue Body, Black Chassis, White Interior, Unpainted Diecast Hinge Plate, 2 Surf Boards on Black Roof Rack, No Stripes, White "mistral" with Yellow Dot on Doors, White "m" with Yellow Dot on Hood. (1986?)

j. Dark Blue Body, Black Chassis, White Interior, Unpainted Diecast Hinge Plate, No Roof Rack, No Stripes, White "mistral" with Yellow Dot on Doors, White "m" with Yellow Dot on Hood. (1986?)

k. Medium Blue Body, Black Chassis, White Interior, Unpainted Diecast Hinge Plate, No Roof Rack, No Stripes, White "mistral" with Yellow Dot on Doors, White "m" with Yellow Dot on Hood. (1986?)

l. White Body, Unpainted Diecast Hinge Plate, Rainbow Tampo on Hood, Red/ Green Stripes on Sides, Red Interior, 5-dblspk Wheels, (Box has no number, 1985, originally released as BP service station promotional, later in general product line.)

m. Pale Green Body, Black Chassis, Red Interior, Unpainted Diecast Hinge Plate, No Roof Rack or Graphics. (Found in Sets.)

n. Blue Body, Black Chassis, Unpainted Diecast Hinge Plate, Red Interior, No Roof Rack, 8div Wheels, Eagle on Hood, Red/ Yellow Graphics with "MATRA" on Doors. (May be J19/ 01. Corgi Hong Kong Ltd. 1988 on card.)

o. Black Body, Black Chassis, ??? Interior, Unpainted Diecast Hinge Plate, No Roof Rack or Graphics.

p. Orange Body, Black Chassis, White Interior, Unpainted Diecast Hinge Plate, No Roof Rack or Graphics.

J 19/ 01 Juniors – Matra Rancho   1988 $3-5
White Body, Revised Casting Eliminating Upper Tailgate, Rainbow Tampo on Hood, Red/ Green Stripes on Sides, Red Interior, 8-div Wheels, (Similar to J19, but made in China. 1990.)

J 19/ 02 Juniors - Matra Rancho   Jul-88 $8-12
Red Body and Interior, Black Base and Bumpers, "SAUPERS POMPIERS 18" Graphics. (Produced for the French market.)

J 19/ 0X Juniors – Matra Rancho   1988 $3-5
Blue Body, Black Chassis, Revised Casting Eliminating Upper Tailgate, Red Interior, No Roof Rack, 8div Wheels, Eagle on Hood, Red/ Yellow Graphics with "MATRA" on Doors. (Actual J19/ version number not known.)

J 20   Juniors - London DD Bus (Daimler Fleetline)   Apr-84 $3-5
a. Red Body, Large Union Jack on Sides. (old # E81-A.)
b. Red Body, "SEE MORE LONDON" Graphics. (Jan-85)
c. Red Body, No Graphics. (Found in set J3035.)
d. Blue Body, No Graphics. (Possibly a transitional era model.)

J 20/ 01 Juniors - London DD Bus (Daimler Fleetline)   Jan-89 $3-5
Red Body, "The LONDON STANDARD" on Sides, 4div Wheels.

J 20/ ?? Juniors - London DD Bus (Daimler Fleetline)   Sep-88 $5-8
Red Front and Forward Sides, Green Bumpers and Lower Sides, White Roof & Rear Sides with Red "Batchelors Peas No1 IN PEAS" on Sides.

J 21   Juniors - Fiat X1/9   Apr-84
Standard Released Versions $3-5
Promotional Versions $5-8
a. White Body, Yellow Red Side Stripe at Sill with Black "FIAT X1/9" Graphics. (old # E86-A.)
b. Yellow Body, No Graphics. (Found in yellow 2-pack card, liquidation of old Mettoy stock.)
c. Orange Body, No Graphics. (Found in yellow 2-pack card, liquidation of old Mettoy stock.)
d. Orange Body, Blue / Red Label with "9" on Sides. (Found in reverse window card, 1984.)
e. Orange Body, Blue Stripe Over Hood Onto Sides, White Square with Black "2" Graphics. (Jan-85)
f. White Body, Black Diecast Base, Black Roof, Red Interior, Yellow and Black "6 FIAT HELLER" Graphics. (1987?, also issued as JB-21.)
g. Black Body, Black Diecast Base, Black Interior, No Graphics. (Packaged in green card as B121 for French market.)
h. Orange Body, Black Diecast Base, ??? Interior, No Graphics. (Packaged in green card as B121 for French market.)
i. White Body, Black Diecast Base, Red Interior, No Graphics. (1985?, Found in Transporter Set J3124.)
j. White Body, Black Diecast Base, Red Interior, Light Blue and Aqua Side Stripes with Blue "X1/9" on Rear Corners of Sides. (Toothpaste promotional model.)

J 22 A   Juniors - Petrol Tanker   Apr-84 $3-5
a. White Body, Black Chassis, "BP Oil" Graphics. (old # E97-B.)
b. Blue Body, Black Chassis, Orange/ White Tank Graphic "Gulf" Graphics. (Jan-85)

J 22/ 01 Juniors - BMW 325i Track Car   Jan-88 $3-5
White Body, Black Interior, Yellow Roof, Yellow / Green Rally Trim "56" on Hood and Sides.

J 22/ 02(?) Juniors - BMW 325i Track Car   1988? $5-8
White Body, Black Interior, Red Trim, Fina Logos on Roof and Hood, Blue "FINA" and Black "74" on Doors. (Possibly a promotional model for Fina. Need clarification.)

J 23   Juniors - Renault 5 Turbo   Apr-84 $3-5
Black Baseplate and Tow Hook, Clear Windows, Vacuum Plated Rear View Mirrors.
a. Medium Blue Body, Red Bumpers and Interior, White "TURBO" on Sides, Plastic Baseplate. (Similar to E204-A but with added graphics. Also released as JB123.)
b. Medium Blue Body, White Bumpers and Interior, White "TURBO" on Sides, Plastic Baseplate
c. Medium Blue Body, White Bumpers and Interior, No Graphics, Plastic Baseplate
d. Dark Blue Body, White Bumpers and Interior, White Roof, "elf 18" on Sides with "elf" forward, Metal Baseplate without Keyhole Slot. (Jan-85)
e. Dark Blue Body, White Bumpers and Interior, White Roof, "elf 18" on Sides with "18" forward, Metal Baseplate without Keyhole Slot. (Jan-85)
f. Dark Blue Body, Red Bumpers and Interior, White Roof, "elf 18" on Sides with "elf" forward, Metal Baseplate with Keyhole Slot. (Jan-88)
g. Black (?) Body, Red Bumpers and Interior, White Roof, "elf 18" on Sides with "elf" forward, Metal Baseplate with Keyhole Slot. (May not exist.)

J 24   Juniors - Ford Transit Wrecker Truck   Apr-84 $3-5
a. White Body, Red Boom & Lightbar, Black Hook, Blue Tinted Windows, Blue Edged Red Side Stripe, Blue "RAC" and Red "RESCUE" Graphics. (old # E103-A.)
b. White Body, Red Boom & Lightbar, Black Hook, Blue Tinted Windows, Blue Edged Red Side Stripe, Blue "POLICE" on Hood, Blue "RESCUE 108" Graphics. (Jan-85)
c. White Body, Red Boom & Lightbar, Black Hook, Clear Windows, Blue Edged Red Side Stripe, Blue "POLICE" on Hood, Blue "RESCUE 108" Graphics. (Jan-85)

J 24/ 01 Juniors - Ford Transit Wrecker Truck   Jan-89 $3-5
White Body, Red Boom & Lightbar, Black Hook, Blue and Red Side Stripes, Blue "RACE" on Hood, Blue "RACE SUPPORT" on Sides, 4div Wheels.

J 24/ 02 Juniors - Ford Transit Wrecker Truck   Jul-88 $8-12
White Body, Red Boom and Lightbar, Black Hook, Red / Blue Stripes with "Europ Assistance" Graphics.

J 24/ 03 Juniors - Ford Transit Wrecker Truck   Jan-89 $3-5
Yellow Body, Boom & Lightbar, Black Hook, Clear Windows, Black Outlined White Side Stripe, Black "AA Service" on Hood, Black "AA Relay" on Sides, 4div Wheels.

J 24/ ?? Juniors - Ford Transit Wrecker Truck   1985 $3-5

Yellow Body, Black Base & Tow Hook, Red Boom & Roof Lightbar, Clear Windows, "RESCUE" on Hood, "BP" and "RESCUE" on Sides, 5dblspk Wheels, Blue Box without J Number. (BP Promotional)

J 24/ ?? Juniors - Ford Transit Wrecker Truck   1986 $3-5
White Body, Black Base & Tow Hook, Red Boom & Roof Lightbar, Clear Windows, "BP" Offset on Hood, "BP Service" on Sides, 5dblspk Wheels, Red Box without J Number. (BP Promotional)

J 25 A   Juniors - Ford Escort   Apr-84 $3-5
a. Blue Body, White "ESCORT XR3i" on Lower Sides. (old # E105-A)
b. Red Body, White "ESCORT XR3i" on Lower Sides. (Found in Weetabix promotional box.)
c. Red Body, Black Interior, No Graphics. (Jan-85)
d. Red Body, Black Interior, Divided White Side Stripes. (1986?)
e. Red Body, Black Interior, White / Black / White Side Stripes with "XR3i" on Doors.
f. Red Body, Gray LHD Interior, Yellow "Royal Mail" Graphics on Doors. (Not racing version, possibly from set.)
g. Red Body, Plastic Base, White Interior, White "77" hood & Sides, Yellow "Royal Mail Datapost" on Hood, Yellow "Datapost" on Sides. (1985?)
h. Red Body, Plastic Base, Black Interior, White "77" hood & Sides, Yellow "Royal Mail Datapost" on Hood, Yellow "Datapost" on Sides. (1986?)
i. Red Body, Black Metal Base, Gray Interior, White "77" hood only, Yellow "Royal Mail Datapost" on Hood, Yellow "Datapost" on Sides. (1986?)
j. Red Body, Black Plastic Base, Black Interior, White "66" hood & Sides, Yellow "Royal Mail Datapost" on Hood, Yellow "Datapost" on Sides. (1987?)
k. Red Body, Black Plastic Base, White Interior, White "66" hood & Sides, Yellow "Royal Mail Datapost" on Hood, Yellow "Datapost" on Sides. (1987?)
l. Dark Blue Body, Black Diecast Base, Gray LHD Interior, "DUCKHAMS QXR 38" and Other Markings. (BP Promotional, May Be Different Number than J25.)
m. Dark Blue Body, Black Diecast Base, Ivory LHD Interior, "DUCKHAMS QXR 38" and Other Markings . (BP Promotional, May Be Different Number than J25.)
n. White Body, Black Diecast Base, Gray LHD Interior, Tri-color Stripes, "100 ILFORD" Graphics. (May be repackaging of leftover Little & Large Set vehicles.)
o. White Body, ??? Interior, No Graphics. (Found in set J3035.)

J 25 B   Juniors - Renault Trafic Van   Jan-88 $3-5
White Body, "AVIS VAN RENTAL" Graphics.
a. White Body, Red Stripe, "AVIS" Logo and Red Side Stripe, "UNLIMITED MILAGE" toward Rear and "ONE WAY RENTAL" toward Front on Both Sides, Black Seats, "RENAULT TRAFIC" on base.
b. White Body, Red Stripe, "AVIS" Logo and Red Side Stripe, "UNLIMITED MILAGE" toward Front and "ONE WAY RENTAL" toward Rear, Black Seats, "RENAULT TRAFIC" on base.
c. White Body, Red Stripe, "AVIS" Logo and Red Side Stripe, "UNLIMITED MILAGE" toward Front and "ONE WAY RENTAL" toward Rear, Black Seats, "VAN" on base.

J 25/ 01 Juniors - Renault Trafic Van   Mar-89 $8-12
White Body, Black Base, "Consumers Gas" and Gas Flame Logo on Sides. (Produced for the Canadian Market.)
a. "VAN" on base

J 26   Juniors - Austin Mini Metro   Apr-84

Standard Released Versions	$3-5
Promotional Versions	$8-12

a. White Body with Red and Gold Graphics, Red "5" in Circle, Black Base & Interior, 5spk Wheels. (also issued as JB-26)
b. Black Body with Silver Lower Sides and Black "TURBO" Graphics, Tan Seats, 5dblspk Wheels. (found in 1984 reverse bubble window card.)
c. White Body with Red and Orange Stripes and Black "8" Graphics, Black Interior.
d. Red Body, Black Interior, White "66" on Hood, Yellow "Royal Mail" on Hood, Yellow "Datapost" on Sides. (1983? Initially produced during the last days of Mettoy.)
e. White Body, Black Base & Interior, 5spk Wheels, Red "TURBO" Stripe on Lower Sides. (Same graphic as used on sides of J15 Lotus Esprit. Possibly from Set.)
f. Red Body, Black Interior, White "66" on Hood & Sides, Yellow "Datapost" on Sides. (1985?)
g. Red Body, Black Interior, White "77" on Hood & Sides, Yellow "Datapost" on Sides. (1985?)
h. Black Body, Red "MG" side Graphics, ??? Seats, 5dblspk Wheels. (Shown in 1984 catalog as J26 MG Metro, but possibly not produced.)

J 26/ 02 Juniors - Austin Mini Metro Van   1983? $3-5
Red Body, Tan Interior, Red Panels in Rear Windows with Yellow "Royal Mail," Yellow Logo on Sides. (Initially produced during the last days of Mettoy.)

J 27   Juniors - Citroen 2CV   Apr-84 $3-5

a. White Body, Flowing Blue Side and Roof Stripes. (old # E115-A.)
b. Lighter Yellow Body with Black Top, Duck Graphic on Hood & Doors. (Jan-85)
c. Darker Yellow Body with Black Top, Duck Graphic on Hood only. (1986?)
d. Red Body and Top, Flowers on Front Doors and Rear, White Seats. (Jan-88)

J 27/ 01 Juniors - Citroen 2CV   1988? $6-12
Red Body, Red / White / Blue / Yellow Naval Flag Design on Roof, White Seats. (Promotional for P&O.)

J 28 A   Juniors - Airport Rescue Truck   Apr-84 $3-5
a. Red Body, Yellow Nozzle, Black/ White Segmented Side Stripe, "AIRPORT RESCUE 8" Graphics. (old # E123-A.)
b. Red Body, White Nozzle, Black/ White Segmented Side Stripe, "AIRPORT RESCUE 8" Graphics. (1985)

J 28 B   Juniors - Ford Wrecker Truck   1986? $6-12
White Body, Red Boom & Lightbar, Black Hook, Light Blue Side Stripes, Red "HOME RESCUE" on Hood, Black "AVON" and Red "ROAD RESCUE" on Sides, 5 Spoke Wheels, otherwise as J24. (Promotional produced for Avon Insurance PLC.)

J 29   Juniors - Mercedes-Benz 500SL   Apr-84 $3-5
a. Silver Body, Tan Interior. (old # E124-A.)
b. Dark Red Body, No Trim or Graphics. (Found in 1984 reverse window bubble card.)
c. Red Body, Silver Below Belt Line on Sides. (Jan-85)
d. Red Body, White Interior, Black Plastic Base with Tow Hook, No Trim or Graphics. (1986?)
e. Red Body, Cream Interior, Black Plastic Base with Tow Hook, No Trim or Graphics. (1986?)
f. White Body, Red Interior, Black Plastic Base with Tow Hook. (1988 Freeway Card.)
g. Maroon Body, Cream Interior, Silver Below Belt Line on Sides.

J 29/ 01 Juniors - Mercedes-Benz 500SL   Jan-89 $3-5
Black Body, Red Seats, Silver Below Belt Line on Sides and Across Grill and Headlamps, Black Plastic Base with Tow Hook.

J 30 A   Juniors - Ford Dropside Truck   Apr-84 $3-5
a. Bright Yellow Body, Black "Whimpey" on Doors. (old # E125-A.)
b. Bright Yellow Body, Black "BTS TYRE SERVICES" on Bed Sides. (Found in Set E(J)3035. Apr-84)
c. Bright Yellow Body, Black "BTS TYRE SERVICES" on Bed Sides, Black Plastic Tire Cargo. (Jan-85)

J 30 B   Juniors - BMW M3   Jan-88 $3-5
a. Yellow Body, Black Interior, "Silverstone 5" Markings, 4-div Wheels. (From BP Service Station Promotion.)
b. White Body, Black Interior, Thin Red Stripe, "11 TOTAL PIONEER" Graphics, 4-div Wheels. (Also found in Set J3102.)

J 30/ 01 Juniors – BMW M3   1990? $3-5
Orange Body, "Canon 44" Markings, 5-dblspk or 4-div Wheels.

J 30/ 0X(?) Juniors – BMW M3   1990? $3-5
Black Body and Interior, "Castrol 44" Graphics, 4-div Wheels.

J 31   Juniors - Ford Sierra Saloon   Apr-84 $3-5
a. Blue Body, red interior, Black Base. (old # E129-A.)
b. Blue Body, yellow interior, Gray Base. (1984, Found in reverse window card.)
c. Red Body, No Graphics. (Jan-85)
d. Red Body, Red Interior Black Base, Yellow "Post Office" in Oval on Hood, Yellow "Royal Mail" & Logo on Doors. (1986?)
e. Blue Body, Red Interior, Black Base, "ICS Shell Oils 1" Graphics. (Jan-88)
f. Black Body & Base, Red Interior, Gold "Homefire 1" Graphics, 8div Wheels, Red Box without Number. (BP Service Station promotional.)
g. White Body, Red Interior, Red "Golden Wonder" Graphics, 5-dblspk Wheels, Blue Box without Number. (BP Service Station promotional.)
h. Metallic Brown Body, Red(?) Interior, Gold Lower Side Stripe. (Possibly from J201 or Little-Large Set.)
i. Metallic Dark Blue Body, Black Interior, Black Base.

J 31/ 01 Juniors - Ford Sierra Saloon   1989 $3-5
Red Body, Red Interior Black Base, Yellow "Post Office" in Oval on Hood, Yellow "Royal Mail" & Logo on Hood. (Same as J31/ 03?)

J 31/ 03 Juniors - Ford Sierra Saloon   1989? $3-5
Red Body, Red Interior Black Base, Yellow "Post Office" in Oval on Hood, Yellow "Royal Mail" & Logo on Hood. (Same as J31/ 01?)

J 32   Juniors - Ferrari 308 GTS   Apr-84 $3-5
a. Black Body. (Continuation of Mettoy Era E131-A.)
b. Red Body, White "Ferrari" on Sides, Ferrari Logo & Italian Flag on Hood, White Seats, 5dblspk Wheels. (Jan-85), (Also found as JB32.)
c. Red Body, Black Seats, No Graphics. (Jan-88)

d. Red Body, Red Seats, No Graphics. (1988)

J 32/01   Juniors - Ferrari 308 GTS   1988 $3-5
Red Body, Black Interior. (Continuation of Mettoy Era E131-A.)

J 33   Juniors - VW Polo Turbo   Apr-84 $3-5
a. White Body, Yellow Interior, Green/ Blue Side Stripes "6" Graphics. (old # E92-A.)
b. White Body, Black Interior, Green/ Blue Side Stripes "6" Graphics. (1984.)
c. Yellow Body, Black Interior, Red Stripes & Blue "Turbo" Below Belt Line on Sides. (Jan-85)
d. Black Body, Red and Silver Blue Stripes "4" on Hood & Below Belt Line on Doors, "WEBER" Behind Doors, Black Interior, 5dblspk Wheels. (also issued as JB33.)
e. Silver Body, Tan Interior, No Graphics. (old # E92-A. May be Transitional Era model.)

J 34   Juniors - Rover Sterling 3500 Saloon   Apr-84 $3-5
a. White Body, Red Interior, "12 Triplex" Graphics. (old # E138-A.)
b. White Body, Yellow Interior, "12 Triplex" Graphics.
c. Red Body, Red Interior, Black Diecast Base, White / Yellow / Orange Side Stripes with White "13 ESSO DAILY MIRROR" Text. (also issued as JB34.)
d. Red Body, Black Interior, Black Diecast Base, White / Yellow / Orange Side Stripes with White "13 ESSO DAILY MIRROR" Text. (also issued as JB34.)
e. White Body, Red Interior, No Graphics. (Used in sets.)
f. Yellow Body, Yellow Interior, No Graphics. (Used in sets.)
g. Red Body, Cream Interior, No Graphics. (Used in sets. Also found on Hamleys reverse window card.)
h. Green Body, Red Interior, No Graphics. (Used in sets.)

J 35   Juniors - Porsche 911 Carrera   Apr-84
                 Standard Released Versions $3-5
                 Promotional Versions $5-8
                 Arabic Version $15-20
(Note: J35 models have diecast baseplate while earlier E139-A / E205-A have plastic baseplate.)
a. Black Body, 2 Thin Gold Side Stripes on Sides. (old E139-A / E205-A.)
b. White Body, Blue/ Green Stripes with Red "18" Graphics. (Jan-85)
c. Black Body, Gold Trim with White "Shell 18" Graphics. (Jan-88, Also found as JB-35.)
d. Black Body, Black Interior, 2 Gold Stripes on Hood, Gold "PORSCHE" on Lower Doors, Black Metal Base. (Jan-88)
e. Black Body, Black Interior, 2 Gold Stripes and "turbo" on Hood Label, Black Metal Base. (JB135?)
f. Black Body, Black Interior, No Graphics, Black Metal Base. (Found on red card, 1985.)
g. Red Body, Black Porsche Crest on Hood, Black "TURBO" on Lower Doors, White Interior, Black Metal Base. (1989.)
h. Red Body, Black Porsche Crest on Hood, Black "TURBO" on Lower Doors, Light Tan Interior, Black Metal Base. (1989.)
i. Yellow Body, Black Interior, No Graphics. (Found in Sets. Not assigned separate model number.)
j. White Body, Black Interior, No Graphics. (Found in Sets. Not assigned separate model number.)
k. Red Body, Black Interior, No Graphics. (Found in Sets. Not assigned separate model number.)
l. Blue Body, Black Interior, No Graphics. (Found in Sets. Not assigned separate model number.)
m. Black Body, Black Interior, "1 BLAUPUNKT" Graphics, Black Metal Base. (Possible promotional model for Blaupunkt. Background information needed.)
n. Yellow Body, Black Interior, "7 Taka-Q" Graphics, Black Metal Base. (From unknown set. Background information needed.)
o. Brick Red Body, Cream Interior, Arabic Graphics. (Promotional for Arabian market. May have different model number.)

J 35/ 02   Juniors - Porsche 911   1988 $3-5
Black Body, Gold Porsche Logo on Hood, Gold "TURBO" on Lower Doors, Clear Windows, White Interior, Black Metal Base.

J 35/ ??   Juniors - Porsche 911   Sep-88 $5-8
Red Front and Forward Sides, Green Bumpers and Lower Sides, White Roof & Rear Sides with White "Batchelors Peas" on Sides and Hood, Clear Windows, Cream Interior.

J 36 A   Juniors - Ford Mustang   Apr-84 $3-5
a. White Body, Blue Base, White Interior, Thin Red Side Stripe with Blue Ford Logo with "MUSTANG" Text. (old # E140-A.)
b. Yellow Body, Blue Base, No Graphics. (Yellow 2-pack card. Liquidation of old Mettoy stock. May be Hockey Series car without tampo printing. Other colors may exist in same packaging.)
c. White Body, Blue Base, White Interior, Red Stripes on Hood, Blue Square with Stars on Roof, Red/ Blue Stripe on Sides with "MUSTANG" Text. (Jan-85)

d. White Body, Black Base, Red Interior, Red Stripes on Hood, Blue Square with Stars on Roof, Red/ Blue Stripe on Sides with "MUSTANG" Text. (1985?)
e. White Body, Black Base, White Interior, Red Stripes on Hood, Blue Square with Stars on Roof, Red/ Blue Stripe on Sides with "MUSTANG" Text. (1985?)
f. White Body, Black Base, White Interior, Blue Panel with White Star on Hood, Blue Triangle with White Star on Roof, No Graphics on Sides. (1986?)
g. White Body, Black Base and Interior, Thin Red Stripes on Hood and Sides, Thin Red Stripe on Roof with Black "7" in Center. (1989?)
h. Dark Blue Body, Black Base and Interior, No Graphics. (Found in J3124 Transporter Set.)
i. Dark Blue Body, Black Base, White Interior, Blue Tinted Windows, No Graphics. (Found in J3124 Transporter Set.)
j. Metallic Green Body, Black Base, Yellow Interior, Green Tinted Windows, No Graphics. (From unknown set.)
k. Yellow Body, Black Base, Light Blue Interior, Clear Windows, No Graphics. (Found on French red card without model number. May be J(B)136.)

J 36 B   Juniors - Ferrari Testarossa   Apr-88 $3-5
Red Body, 4div Wheels.

J 37   Juniors - British Gas Van   Apr-84 $3-5
a. White Body, Medium Blue Roof, Tampo Printed Dark Blue Lower Sides with Small "British Gas" and Flame Symbol along Bottom, Progressive Medium and Light Blue Stripes Above, Light Blue "Gas" in Upper Rear Corners of Sides, Opaque Black Windows. (old # E144-A.)
b. White Body, Dark Blue Roof, Tampo Printed Dark Blue Stripe on Lower Sides with two Light Aqua Blue Stripes Above, Light Aqua Blue "Gas" on Upper Corner of Sides, Clear Windows. (1985.)
c. White Body, Dark Blue Roof, Tampo Printed Dark Blue Stripe on Lower Sides with two Light Aqua Blue Stripes Above, Light Aqua Blue "Gas" on Upper Corner of Sides, Amber Tinted Windows. (1985.)
d. White Body Including Roof, Tampo Printed Dark Blue Stripe on Lower Sides with two Light Aqua Blue Stripes Above, Light Aqua Blue "Gas" on Upper Corner of Sides, Clear Windows, Blank Base. (1985.)

J 38   Juniors - British Telecom Van   Apr-84 $3-5
a. Yellow Body with Heavy Roof Ribs, Opaque Black Windows, Blank Base, "British TELECOM" Tampo Printed with Coiled Line Logo. (old # E145-A.)
b. Yellow Body with Thin Roof Ribs, Opaque Black Windows, Blank Base, "British TELECOM" Tampo Printed with Coiled Line Logo. (old # E145-A.)
c. Yellow Body with Thin Roof Ribs, Opaque Black Windows, "U.S. VAN" Base, "British TELECOM" Tampo Printed without Coiled Line Logo.
d. Yellow Body with Thin Roof Ribs, Opaque Black Windows, "U.S. VAN" Base, "OPAL FRUITS" Tampo Printed on Sides. (Found in set J3045, also as a promotional separately for Opal Fruits.)
e. Yellow Body with Thin Roof Ribs, Opaque Black Windows, Blank Base, "OPAL FRUITS" Tampo Printed on Sides. (Found in set J3045, also as a promotional separately for Opal Fruits.)
f. Yellow Body, Opaque Black Windows, "AA Service" Logo and Black Outlined White Side Stripe. (May have different number.)
g. Yellow Body, Opaque Black Windows, No Graphics. (Found in set J3002, possibly elsewhere.)

J 39   Juniors - Royal Mail Van   Apr-84 $3-5
a. Red Body, Yellow "Royal Mail PARCELS" graphics, Blank Text Base, Blue tinted Windows.
b. Red Body, Yellow "Royal Mail PARCELS" graphics, "U.S. Van" Base, Clear Windows.
c. Red Body, Yellow "Royal Mail PARCELS" graphics, Blank Text Base, Clear Windows.
d. Red Body, Yellow "Royal Mail PARCELS" graphics, Blank Text Base, Opaque Black Windows.
e. Red Body, Yellow "Royal Mail PARCELS" graphics, Blank Text Base, Amber Tinted Windows.
f. Red Body, White "FIRE SALVAGE" Graphics, "U.S. Van" or Blank Text Base, Opaque Black Windows. (Found in set J3142.)
g. Red Body, White "FIRE SALVAGE" Graphics, Blank Base, Clear Windows. (Found in set J3142.)

J 40   Juniors - Opel Corsa/ Vauxhall Nova   Apr-84 $3-5
a. Red Body, Black Base, Yellow "CORSA" Graphics. (old # E170-A as Vauxhall Nova.)
b. Yellow Body, Black Base, Ivory Interior, Thin Red Stripe on Sides at Belt Line. (Jan-85)
c. White Body, Black Base, Ivory Interior, Yellow/Silver/ Black Stripes, Black "OPEL" on Hood, Opel Logo on Roof. (Jan-88)

d. White Body, Black Base, White Interior, Orange Fade to Black Graphics on Hood.

e. White Body, Dark Gray Base, Cream Interior, Orange Fade to Black Graphics on Hood.

f. Silver Body, Black Base, White Seats, Yellow Side Stripe with "BP" Crest on Doors, Crest and "VISCO NOVA" on Hood. (BP Promotional, excess stock sold-off in standard packaging.)

J 41 A   Juniors - Quarry Truck Apr-84 $3-5
a. Yellow Cab, Orange Dump Body. (old # E174-A. Also see JB141.)
b. White Cab, Red Dump Body. (Found in Bumper set J3035.)

J 41 B   Juniors - Jaguar XJS Police 1985 $3-5
White Body, Opaque Blue Lightbar on Roof, Blue Outlined Red Side Stripe, Red "POLICE" on Hood & Doors, Clear Windows, Black Interior, Black Metal Base. (Also part of Set J3158, and found as JB41.)

J 42 A   Juniors - Pipe Truck Apr-84 $3-5
a. Green Cab, Yellow Flat Bed, Gray Pipes. (old # E175-A.)
b. Green Cab, Yellow Flat Bed, White Pipes. (1984.)
c. Green Cab, White Flat Bed, Gray Pipes. (Also found in Set E(J)3035.)
d. Red Cab, Yellow Flat Bed, Gray Pipes.

J 42 B   Juniors - Iveco Container Truck 1985? $6-9
Yellow Cab, Black Base and Interior, Red Box Body with "Knorr" Logo. (Promotional found in 2-packs offered by Knorr during promotion, later as J42.)

J 43   Juniors - Tanker Truck Apr-84 $3-5
a. Dark Blue Cab and Flat Bed, Medium Blue Tank with "corgi CHEMCO" Graphics. (old # E177-A.)
b. Yellow Cab, Yellow Flat Bed, White Tank with Red "SHELL" Graphics. (old # E177-A.)
c. Yellow Cab, White Flat Bed, White Tank with Red "SHELL" Graphics. (Also released as (J)B-143.)

J 44 A   Juniors - Container Truck Apr-84 $3-5
a. Black Cab, Yellow Platform, White Box, "DUNLOP" Graphics on Box Sides. (old # E178-A.)
b. Red Cab, Platform and Box, "Coca-Cola" Graphics on Box Sides.
c. White Cab and Platform, White Box, "DUNLOP" Graphics on Box Sides. (Found as (J)B-144.)

J 44 B   Juniors - Renault Trafic Bus Jan-85 $3-5
White Body with Red "Thomas Cook" and Lower Stripe, Black Interior and Baseplate, Clear Windows.
a. "VAN" on base

J 45   Juniors - Chevrolet Corvette Apr-84
    (Standard) $3-5
    (With Advertising) $5-8
Red Interior, Black Dashboard, Clear Windows, otherwise as Mettoy era E179-A.
a. White Body, Black Underlined Red Side Stripe, "CHEVY 84" on Sides. (old # E179-A.)
b. White Body, Red Side Stripe without Underline, "CHEVY 84" on Sides. (1984.)
c. White Body, Closely Spaced Red over Blue Side Stripes, Red Chevrolet Logo on Hood, Red " 'VETTE" and Blue "85" on lower sides. (Jan-85)
d. White Body, Widely Spaced Blue over Red Side Stripes, Red Chevrolet Logo on Hood, Blue " 'VETTE" and Red "85" on lower sides. (1986)
e. Light Blue Body, No Graphics. (used in various Gift Sets, not released separately.)
f. Black Body, No Graphics. (Found in J3124 Transporter Set, not released separately.)
g. Red Body, White Panel on Hood and "7 Coca-Cola" Graphics. (used in Sets J3100-C and J3600-C, not released separately.)

J 45/ 01 Juniors - Chevrolet Corvette Jan-88 $3-5
Black Body with Red / Yellow Flames on Hood and Rear Fenders, "Flame" on Doors, Red Interior, Clear Windows, 8-div Wheels.

J 45/ 02 Juniors - Chevrolet Corvette 1988 $3-5
Red and White Body with Contrasting Body Graphics, Red Interior, Clear Windows, 8-div Wheels.

J 46   Juniors - Pontiac Firebird Apr-84
    (Standard) $3-5
    (With Advertising) $5-8
a. White Body, Blue Pinstripes "Yankees" (Repackaged Baseball Cars.) (old # 180-A & 500-525-A.)
b. Orange Body, Black Seats and Spoiler, Black Diecast Base, No Graphics. (Yellow 2-pack card. Liquidation of old Mettoy stock. Probably Baseball Series car without tampo printing. Other colors probably exist in similar packaging.)
c. Red Body, Black Seats and Spoiler, Black Diecast Base, No Graphics. (Released as B146 in France on red card, Italy on green card, 1985.)

d. Blue Body, Black Seats and Spoiler, Black Diecast Base, No Graphics. (Found in sets, 1985.)

e. Black Body, Seats, Spoiler, Black Diecast Base. (1985?)

f. Black Body with Red Panel Between Headlight Doors, Seats, Spoiler, Black Diecast Base. (Possibly U.S. Market Only. Jan-85)

g. Blue Body, Silver Stars on Sides, Silver/ White/ Red "Schweppes" Logo on Roof, White "Soft Drinks" with Silver Stars on Hood, Black Seats, Spoiler, Black Diecast Base. (53342)

h. White Body with Red Hood, White "12" on Hood, Red "Coca-Cola 12" on Sides, Black Seats, Spoiler, Black Diecast Base. (Part of Set C3700C & Others, Not Available Separately. Apr-87)

i. Brown Body with Orange/ White Stripe, White "HERSHEY'S MILK CHOCOLATE 4," Black Seats, Spoiler, Black Diecast Base. (Part of Set C3200H, Not Available Separately. Apr-87)

J 46/ 01 Juniors - Pontiac Firebird Jan-88 $3-5
Silver Body with Thin Red Side Stripe, Black Seats, Spoiler, Black Diecast Base.

J 46/ 02 Juniors - Pontiac Firebird Jan-88 $3-5
Yellow Body with Black Stripes "Fire Bird" (sic.) & White "11," Black Seats, Spoiler, Black Diecast Base. (Also found on "Freeway" card.)

J 47 A   Juniors - '54 Mercedes-Benz 300SL Apr-84 $3-5
(old # E181-A. Also see J122/01 which is silver.)
a. Red Body, Clear Windows, Yellow Interior, No Graphics.
b. Red Body, Clear Windows, White Interior, Black "1" in White Circle Under Doors and on Hood.

J 47 B   Juniors - Volvo 760 Jan-88 $8-12
White Body, Blue Lightbar on Roof, "POLIS" Graphics.

J 47/ 01 Juniors - Volvo 760 Feb-88 $3-5
Police (Other details not known at time of publication.)

J 47/ 11 Juniors - Volvo 760 1989? $8-12
White Body, Opaque Black Windows, Opaque Blue Lightbar on Roof, Black "POLITI" on Doors and Trunk Lid, "47-11" on Roof. (Made for the Scandinavian market. Only known instance where model refers to its own number.)

J 48 A   Juniors - Jeep, Open Top, No Roll Bar Apr-84 $3-5
a. Red Body, White Interior and Pusher Bar, No Graphics, Black 4X4 Wheels. (Apr-84)
b. Tan Body, Red Interior and Pusher Bar, Red Sweeping Stripe on Sides, Arched Text on Hood, Black 4X4 Wheels. (Very similar to J48-B Graphics.)
c. Orange Body, White Seats, Black Base, Untrimmed Wheels, Blue Horse on Hood, Blue Stars on Sides. (1985 BP Service Station Promotional.)

J 48 B   Juniors - Jeep, Closed Top (a.k.a. 4x4 Jeep) Jan-85 $3-5
a. White Body, Black Top, Red/ Yellow Side Graphics, Black/ Yellow Hood Graphics.
b. Tan Body, Tan Top, White Interior and Pusher Bar, Diagonal Tire Tread Pattern and "Shell 50" on Hood, Brown and Yellow Side Trim with Black "DUNLOP" and Red "50" on Sides. (Feb-88)
c. White Body, Tan Top, Red Interior and Pusher Bar, Diagonal Tire Tread Pattern and "Shell 50" on Hood, Brown and Yellow Side Trim with Black "DUNLOP" and Red "50" on Sides. (Feb-88)
d. White Body, Tan Top, Red Interior and Pusher Bar, Diagonal Tire Tread Pattern and "Shell 50" on Hood, Brown and Yellow Side Trim with Black "DUNLOP" on Sides without Red "50". (Feb-88)
e. Tan Body, Tan Top, Red Interior and Pusher Bar, Brown Sweeping Stripe on Sides, Arched "SHERIFF" on Hood, Black 4X4 Wheels. (May be J49-B. Graphics similar to tan J48-A.)
f. Tan Body, Brown Top, Red Interior and Pusher Bar, Brown Sweeping Stripe on Sides, Arched "SHERIFF" on Hood, Black 4X4 Wheels. (May be J49-B. Graphics similar to tan J48-A.)
g. Tan Body, Brown Top, White Interior and Pusher Bar, Brown and Yellow Sweeping Stripes on Sides, Arched "SHERIFF" on Hood, 4X4 Wheels with Thin Chrome Foiled Ring. (May be J49-B.)

J 48/ 02 Juniors - Jeep, Sapeurs Pompiers Jul-88 $8-12
Red Body without Top, White Interior and Pusher Bar, White "SAPEURS POMPIERS" on Hood. (Produced for French market. Possibly used in a set.)

J 49 A   Juniors - Jeep, Open Top with Roll Bar Apr-84 $3-5
a. White Body, Red Roll Bar, Red Seats. (1984. Found in reverse window card.)
b. Red Body, Red Roll Bar, White Seats. (1984. Found in reverse window card.)
c. Dark Blue Body, Red Roll Bar, White Seats, Red and White Eagle on Hood. (Jan-85)
d. Blue Body, Red Roll Bar, White Seats. (Found on red card.)
e. Blue Body, Red Roll Bar, Red Seats.

J 49 B   Juniors - Jeep, Closed Top Feb-88 $3-5
a. Olive Drab Body with White Star on Hood and Sides, Tan Roof, White Seats and Push Bar, Black Plastic Chassis, Large Black Wheels.

b. Shiny Olive Drab Body with White Star on Hood and Sides, White "U.S.A." on Front Edge of Hood, Tan Roof, White Seats and Push Bar, Black Plastic Chassis, Large Black Wheels.

c. Shiny Olive Drab Body with White Star on Hood and Sides, White "U.S.A." on Front Edge of Hood, Black Roof, White Seats and Push Bar, Black Plastic Chassis, Large Black Wheels.

d. Shiny Olive Drab Body with White Star on Hood and Sides, White "U.S.A." on Front Edge of Hood, Brown Roof, White Seats and Push Bar, Black Plastic Chassis, Large Black Wheels.

e. Shiny Olive Drab Body with White Star on Hood and Sides, White "U.S.A." on Front Edge of Hood, Brown Roof, White Seats and Push Bar, Black Plastic Chassis, Large Wheels with Vacuum Plated Centers.

J 50 A   Juniors - Range Rover, Open Top   Apr-84 $3-5
a. Maroon Body, White Interior, No Graphics.
b. Maroon Body, White Interior, White Stripe & "RANGE ROVER" Graphics.
c. Maroon Body, White Interior, Tan Stripe & "RANGE ROVER" Graphics.
d. Maroon Body, Tan Interior, Tan Stripe & "RANGE ROVER" Graphics.
e. Black Body, Red/ Orange Stripe. (Jan-85)
f. Black Body, Gold Side Stripe over White Stripe, Cream Interior.

J 50 B   Juniors - BMW M3   Jan-88 $3-5
White Body, Black Interior, "PIONEER 11" Graphics.

J 51   Juniors - Swissair Van   Apr-84 $3-5
White Body with Black Lower Sides, "swissair" with Red/ White Logo. (old # E216-A.)

J 51/ 01 Juniors - Ford Transit Van   Jan-87 $3-5
Yellow Body, White Side Stripe with Black Edge, "AA" & "Service" on Sides, 4div Wheels.
a. Corgi Logo on Base, Made in Great Britain.

J 51/ 02 Juniors - Ford Transit Van   Jan-87 $5-8
Red Front and Forward Sides, Green Bumpers and Lower Sides, White Roof & Rear Sides with Red "Batchelors Taste the difference" on Sides.
a. Base Logo Blanked, Made in Great Britain.

J 52   Juniors - Iveco Refuse Truck   Jan-85 $3-5
Black Plastic Baseplate and Interior, Clear Windows.
a. Orange Cab and Refuse Body, Black/ White Shield.
b. Orange Cab and Refuse Body, Black "NBC" on Sides. (Aug-85)
c. Yellow Cab, Gray Refuse Body, White Recycle Symbols on Sides, White "CITY SANITATION" on Front of Refuse Body. (May have different model number.)

J 52/ 02 Juniors - Iveco Refuse Truck   Jan-88 $8-12
Green Cab and Refuse Body, White "Proprete' de Paris" Graphics. (Produced for the French market.)

J 53   Juniors - Iveco Container Truck   Aug-85 $5-8
a. Yellow Body with Blue Stripes "Fyffes" on Sides.
b. White Body and Box, "IVECO PARTS" on Sides. (Jan-88)
c. Yellow Cab, Black Base and Interior, Red Box Body with "Knorr" Logo. (Promotional found in 2-packs offered by Knorr during promotion, later as J42.)
d. Red Cab, Black Base and Interior, Gray Box Body without Graphics. (found in 2-packs for unknown promotion.)
e. White Body and Box, Brown Labels with "HERSHEY'S MILK CHOCOLATE KISSES" on Sides. (Found in set J3020H.)

J 53/ 02 Juniors - Iveco Container Truck   Jun-89 $8-12
a. Red Cab / Chassis, Gray Box Body, Smoked Black Windows, "Cargo Domicile" and "Le chemin de fer de porte a porte" Graphics. (Produced for the Swiss Market.)
b. Red Cab / Chassis, Gray Box Body, Opaque Black Windows, No Graphics. (Found in UK 2-pack.)

J 53/ 04 Juniors - Iveco Container Truck   Jul-90 $8-12
White Cab and Box, "Van Gend & Loos" Labels on Sides. (Produced for the Dutch Market.)

J 54   Juniors - Renault Trafic Van   Jan-85
                              (Standard) $3-5
                              (With Advertising) $5-8
a. White Body, Clear Windows, Black/ Yellow Stripes, "RENAULT Parts and Service" Graphics, "RENAULT TRAFIC" Text on Gt. Britain Base. (Jan-88)
b. White Body, Clear Windows, Black/ Yellow Stripes, "RENAULT Parts and Service" Graphics, "VAN" Text on Gt. Britain Base. (Jan-88)
c. White Body, Clear Windows, Black/ Orange Stripes, "RENAULT Parts and Service" Graphics, "VAN" Text on China Base. (1990)
d. White Body, Clear Windows, Aircraft Profile Graphics. (Found in Swiss Version of Airport Set J3125.)
e. White Body, Clear Windows, No Graphics, "VAN" Text on Gt. Britain Base. (Found in sets.)

f. Dark Yellow Body, Clear Windows, No Graphics, "VAN" Text on Gt. Britain Base. (Found in sets.)
g. Orange Body, Clear Windows, "Reese's MILK CHOCOLATE PEANUT BUTTER CUPS" Graphics, "VAN" Text on Gt. Britain Base. (Found in Set J3020H.)

J 54/ 02 Juniors - Renault Trafic Van   Jul-88 $8-12
Yellow Body, Clear Windows, Black Interior, Blue "LA POSTE" Graphics, "VAN" Text on Gt. Britain Base. (Produced for the French Market.)

J 54/ 03 Juniors - Renault Trafic Van   Jul-88 $8-12
Red Body with Yellow Side Stripe, "ADP Aerosports de Paris" Graphics, "VAN" Text on Gt. Britain Base. (Produced for the French Market.)

J 54/ 04 Juniors - Renault Trafic Van   Jan-89 $8-12
Red Body, Clear Windows, Black Interior, White "ptt post" Graphics. (Produced for the Dutch Market.)

J 54/ 15 Juniors, Renault Trafic Van   Jul-90 $8-12
Green Body, Clear Windows, Black Interior, White "ptt telecom" Graphics. (Produced for the Dutch Market.)

J 54/ ?? Juniors - Renault Trafic Van   ??? $5-8
Yellow Body, Black Seats & Base, "LOCTITE Strength at work" on Sides, Blue Box without Number. (BP Service Station Promotional.)
a. "RENAULT TRAFIC" Text on Gt. Britain Base
b. "VAN" Text on Gt. Britain Base

J 54/ ?? Juniors - Renault Trafic Van   ??? $5-8
Red Body, Black Base, Clear Windows, White "Coca-Cola" and Swish Logo, 4 Div Wheels. (May be later era model.)
a. "VAN" Text on Gt. Britain Base

J 54/ ?? Juniors - Renault Trafic Van   ??? $8-12
White over Dark Blue Body, Black Seats & Base, "SWISS OLYMPIC" on Sides with Red and Gold Crest and Gold Accent Striping, 5Dblspk Wheels. (Promotional model for the Swiss market, found on 2-pack with a standard production model.)

J 55   Juniors - Renault Trafic Bus   Jan-85 $3-5
Black Interior, Clear Windows, Black Base. (Also see J44-B.)
a. Blue Body, "Grand Hotel" on Sides, "RENAULT TRAFIC" Text on Gt. Britain Base.
b. Blue Body, Gold Sunburst on Sides, "RENAULT TRAFIC" Text on Gt. Britain Base. (JB55)
c. White Body with Green Stripe, "Holiday Inn" on Sides, "VAN" on Gt. Britain Base. (Jan-88)
d. Red Body, No Graphics, "VAN" on Gt. Britain Base. (Jan-88)

J 55/ 02 Juniors - Renault Trafic Bus   Jul-88 $8-12
"Gendarmerie" Graphics, Other Details Not Known. (Produced for the French Market.)

(J 55/ 99)Juniors - Renault Trafic Bus   1994 $8-12
Green Body with White Roof, White Plastic Base, Black Interior, "POLIZEI" and "171" Graphics, China Base. (Produced for the German Market. Actually produced after this time period, but does not have unique model number in the Mattel sequence. Found in set 93416.)
a. Corgi Logo on Baseplate.
b. Hot Wheels Logo on Baseplate.

J 56   Juniors - Ford Escort Rally   Jan-85 $3-5
a. White Body, Black Diecast Base, Black LHD Interior, "TOTAL 84" Graphics.
b. White Body, Black Diecast Base, Black LHD Interior, "ILFORD 100" Graphics.

J 57   Juniors - Zakspeed Capri   Jan-85 $3-5
a. White Body, Off-White interior, Light Blue/ Dark Blue/ Yellow Trim, "9 DUCKHAMS" Graphics, 5dblspk Wheels. (1985, Packaged as JB1 for Hartoy in USA.)
b. Black Body, Off-White Interior, Gold/ Red Trim, "52" Graphics, 5dblspk Wheels. (Jan-88, NOT the same as the J1 Homefire Version.)

J 58 a   Juniors - Ford Sierra Pace Car   Jan-85 $3-5
a. White Body, Red/ White/ Blue Lightbar on Roof, Black / Yellow Checkered Graphics.
b. White Body, Red/ White/ Red Lightbar on Roof, Green / Yellow Checkered Graphics.
c. White Body, Opaque Red Lightbar on Roof, Green / Yellow Checkered Graphics.

J 58 b   Juniors - Ford Sierra Police Car   1985? $3-5
White Body, Red Interior, Blue Lightbar on Roof, Blue Outlined Red Side Stripe, Black "POLICE" on Hood and Doors.

J 58/ 03 Juniors - Ford Sierra Rijkspolitie   1985? $8-12
White Body, ??? Interior, Blue Lightbar on Roof, Red Chevrons and Dashes on Sides with Seal on Front Doors, "RIJKSPOLITIE" Graphics. (Produced for Dutch market.)

J 59   Juniors - Range Rover Rescue   Jan-85 $3-5

Red Body with Flat Roof, Black Roof Rack, Red Cross & Yellow Side Stripe with Black "MOUNTAIN RESCUE" Graphics.

a. Blue Tinted Windows.

b. Amber Tinted Windows.

J 59/ ?? Juniors - Range Rover (Civilian)　1986?　$5-8

Flat Roof Version of Range Rover Casting, Black Plastic Base. (Not released individually. Separate model number not assigned. Reference number used for organizational purposes.)

a. Green Body, Clear Windows, No Roof Rack, No Graphics. (Found in Bumper Set J3035 and possibly Horsebox Set J200.)

b. White Body, Clear Windows, No Roof Rack, No Graphics. (Found in Bumper Set J3035.)

c. White Body, Amber Tinted Windows, No Roof Rack, No Graphics. (Found in Bumper Set J3035.)

d. Yellow Body, Clear Windows, No Roof Rack, No Graphics, White Interior. (Probably from Bumper Set J3035. Same yellow color as AA vans but without graphics.)

J 60　Juniors - Buick Police　Apr-84　$3-5

(Note: Corgi Toys Ltd. era models do not have the working suspension feature in their baseplate.)

a. White Center Body, Black Ends, Transparent Amber Lightbar on Roof, "POLICE" in Black area on doors. Low Rear Axle, No Suspension. (Continuation of Mettoy Era E150, Which Had an Offset Round Red Roof Light and "POLICE" Side Labels.)

b. White Center Body, Black Ends, Opaque Amber Lightbar on Roof, "POLICE" in Black area on doors, High Rear Axle, No Suspension. (1986?)

c. White Center Body, Black Ends, Opaque Blue Lightbar on Roof, "POLICE" in Black area on doors, High Rear Axle, No Suspension. (Known in At Least 2 Wheel Patterns. Jan-88)

J 60/ ?? Juniors - Buick Regal Sedan　1986?　$3-5

(Note: Corgi Toys Ltd. era models all have the 3 rivet baseplate design. They do not have the working suspension feature in their baseplate.)

a. White Body, Chromed Interior, High Rear Axle, Generic Red/ Yellow Corgi Card without Number or Model Name. (May Actually Have Different Catalog Number Not Presently Known.)

b. Yellow Body, Chromed Interior, Low Rear Axle, 5-dblspk Wheels, No Markings or Graphics. (1985.)

c. Blue Body, Chromed Interior, Low Rear Axle, 5-dblspk Wheels, No Markings or Graphics. (1985.)

d. Yellow Body, Chromed Interior, High Rear Axle, 5-dblspk or 4-Div Wheels, No Markings or Graphics. (Possibly only packaged in sets.)

e. Red Body, Chromed Interior, High Rear Axle, No Markings or Graphics. (Found on red card or packaged in sets.)

f. Black Body with Gold Striping on Hood, Roof & Trunk Lid, Chromed Interior, High Rear Axle. (Does not have side exhaust pipes, otherwise identical to J9-B Buick Track Car.)

g. Green Body, Chromed Interior, High Rear Axle, Generic Red/ Yellow Corgi Card without Number or Model Name. (May Actually Have Different Catalog Number Not Presently Known.)

h. Green Body, Opaque Black Windows, Interior Not Visible, High Rear Axle, 4-Div Wheels, No Markings or Graphics. (Possibly only packaged in sets.)

i. Green Body, Clear Windows, Black Interior and Bumpers, High Rear Axle, 4-Div Wheels, No Markings or Graphics. (Possibly only packaged in sets.)

j. Orange Body, Chromed Interior, High Rear Axle, 5-Spoke Wheels, No Markings or Graphics. (Found on red card or packaged in sets.)

J 61　Juniors - U.S. Custom Van　Jan-85

(Standard)　$3-5

(With Advertising)　$5-8

a. Black Body with 2 Red Side Stripes, Opaque Black Windows, Plated Diecast Baseplate. (Continuation of Mettoy Era E-185.)

b. Black Body with 2 Pink Side Stripes, Opaque Black Windows, Plated Diecast Baseplate.

c. White Body, American and British Flag graphics, Opaque Black Windows, Plated Diecast Baseplate.

d. White Body, American and British Flag graphics, Blue Tinted Windows, Plated Diecast Baseplate.

e. Red Body, White "Coca-Cola TURBO RACING TEAM" graphics, Opaque Black Windows, Plated Diecast Baseplate. (Only found in sets J3010-C and J3600-C.)

f. Red Body, White "Coca-Cola TURBO RACING TEAM" graphics, Blue Tinted Windows, Plated Diecast Baseplate. (Only found in sets J3010-C and J3600-C.)

J 61/ 01 Juniors - U.S. Custom Van　1989　$3-5

Blue/ White Body, "TEAM RACING 15" Graphics, Diecast Baseplate, 8Div Wheels. (Same Graphics as Later 90260, which had Plastic Baseplate.)

J 61/ 02 Juniors - U.S. Custom Van　1989　$3-5

Yellow Body, Black Stripe Graphics, Opaque Black Windows, Diecast Baseplate.

J 62　Juniors - Mercedes-Benz Mini Shop　Jan-85

(Standard)　$3-5

(With Advertising)　$5-8

a. White Body, Blue Roof, Red Stripe Below Belt Line with "MINI SHOP" Text, Grocery Scene Card in Rear. (Continuation of Mettoy Era E98.)

b. White Body, Green Roof, Red Stripe Below Belt Line with "PIZZA" Text, Pizzeria Scene Card in Rear. (May be different number, need confirmation.)

c. White Body, Brown Stripe Below Belt Line with "HERSHEY'S" Text, Chocolate Shop Scene Card in Rear. (Found in set J3020H.)

J 63　Juniors - Ford Transit Van, Royal Mail Parcels　1985?　$3-5

a. Red Body, Yellow "Royal Mail Parcels" on Sides, Silver Headlights, "Corgi" Text on Base.

b. Red Body, Yellow "Royal Mail Parcels" on Sides, Red Headlights, Corgi Text on Base. (1986?)

c. Red Body, Yellow "Royal Mail Parcels" on Sides, Red Headlights, Blank Base. (1987?, Re# J4/06 in 1990.)

J 64　Juniors - Land Rover ONE-TEN　Jan-89　$3-5

Yellow Body with Closed Rear Quarter Windows, Black Edged White Stripe on Sides, Black "AA Service" on Upper Sides, 4div Wheels.

J 64/ 04 Juniors - Land Rover ONE-TEN　1990?　$3-5

White Body, Blue / Yellow Diagonal Stripes and BP Logo on Sides, Black "Safari Rally" on Upper Sides, Black "65" on Doors, 4div Wheels.

J 64/ ?? Juniors - Land Rover ONE-TEN　1986?　$3-5

Yellow Body with ??? Rear Quarter Windows, No Graphics, 4div Wheels. (Found in Mothercare Bumper Car Set J3035. Not assigned separate model number.)

J 65　Juniors - Land Rover ONE-TEN　1985?　$3-5

Red Body, Black Interior, Yellow "Royal Mail" & Logo.

a. "Corgi" Text on Base.

b. Blank Base. (1987?)

J 66　Juniors - Land Rover ONE-TEN　Jan-88　$3-5

White Body, Blue Edged Red Stripe on Sides with White "POLICE," Blue "POLICE" on Upper Sides.

a. "Corgi" Text on Base, Open Rear Quarter Windows.

b. Blank Base, Open Rear Quarter Windows.

c. Blank Base, Closed Rear Quarter Windows.

J 69　Juniors - Porsche 911 Polizei　Jan-88　$8-12

White Body without Roof Lights, Green Doors & Hood with White "POLIZEI" Graphics, Black Interior.

J 73　Juniors - Ford Escort XR3　Jan-88　$3-5

a. Red Body, White Interior, Silver "XR3i" on Lower Sides.

b. Red Body, Black Interior, Silver "XR3i" on Lower Sides.

c. Blue Body, Black Interior, Silver "ESCORT XR3i" on Lower Sides. (May be Mettoy era model.)

J 74　Juniors - Land Rover ONE-TEN　Feb-88　$3-5

a. White Body, "Safari Rally 65" Markings.

b. Dark Blue Body with Open Rear Quarter Windows, "DUCKHAMS QXR RACE SUPPORT" Markings, Black Seats, 5-dblspk Wheels. (From BP service station promotion.)

J 77　Juniors - Ferrari Testarossa　May-88　$3-5

White Body, Black Interior, 4div Wheels.

J 77/ 01 Juniors - Ferrari Testarossa　1989　$3-5

White Body, Black Interior, 4div Wheels.(Renumbering of J77 without change.)

J 77/ ?? Juniors - Ferrari Testarossa　1989　$6-9

White Body, Orange and Black Tiger Stripes on Hood and Roof, Black Interior, 4div Wheels (Kellogg's Promotional, UK Only.)

J 79　Juniors - Mercedes-Benz 300TD Ambulance　Jan-88　$3-5

White Body, Clear Windows, Blue Lightbar on Roof, Red Stripe "AMBULANCE" on Sides, Red Cross "AMBULANCE" on Hood.

a. Black Interior.

b. White Interior.

J 80　Juniors - Mini Metro　Jun-86　$10-15

White Body. (Austin Rover Promotional.)

J 81　Juniors - Buick Regal, Police NYPD　Feb-88　$3-5

Light Aqua-Blue Body, Black Bumpers and Interior, Blue Lightbar on Roof, Black/ White Checkered Side Stripe, "NYPD," "POLICE" Graphics, High Rear Axle. (Note: Corgi Toys Ltd. era models do not have the working suspension feature in their baseplate.)

a. "GT. BRITAIN" Baseplate Text.

b. "CHINA" Baseplate Text.

J 81/ 01 Juniors - Buick Regal, Police   1990? $3-5
Black/ White/ Black Body with "POLICE" Graphics, Opaque Blue Lightbar on Roof, Clear Windows, Vacuum Plated Interior, High Rear Axle, Plastic "CHINA" Base.

J 81/ 02 Juniors - Buick Regal, Fire Chief   1990? $3-5
Red/ White Body "FIRE CHIEF" with Stars, Opaque Blue Lightbar on Roof, Black Interior, High Rear Axle, Plastic "CHINA" Base.

J 82   Juniors - Volvo 760 Ambulance   Jan-87 $3-5
White Body, Black Interior, Red Cross on Hood, Red Stripe and "AMBULANCE" on Sides.

J 83   Juniors - Volvo 760 Racer   Jan-87 $3-5
White Body, Black Interior, Blue and Yellow Striping, "21 Gillanders MOTORS" Graphics.

J 84   Juniors - Volvo 760 Saloon   Jan-88 $3-5
a. White Body, Black Interior, Thin Black Trim Stripe on Sides.

b. Silver Body, Black Interior, Thin Black Trim Stripe on Sides. (BP Service Station Promotional. Overstock later sold in standard packaging.)

c. Silver Body, Black Interior, No Stripe on Sides. (Also Found in Set J3103/ 01.)

J 85   Juniors - Porsche 935 Racer   Jan-88 $3-5
White Body, Black/ Orange/ Yellow Hood Stripe, "NUMERO RESERVE philippe salvet 41" Graphics.

J 85 /03 Juniors - Porsche 935 Racer   Jan-88 $3-5
Red Body, No Graphics, Black Interior, 4div Wheels.

J 86   Juniors - Porsche 935 Racer   Jan-88 $3-5
a. Sky Blue Body, Black Interior, Yellow Stripes, "Lucas 74" Graphics, 5dblspk Wheels.

b. Green Body, Black Interior, Blue and White Stripes, "POLO" Graphics, 5dblspk Wheels. (Promotional for BP Service Stations.)

c. ??? Body, Opaque Windows, Non-standard Wheels, Pull-back Motor (Two Speed Action Die-Cast series, item #53407, not packaged as J86.)

J 87   Juniors - Porsche 935   Jan-88 $3-5
Red Body, "33" Graphics, Black Interior, 4div Wheels. (May be different model number.)

J 89   Juniors - Mercedes Benz 2.3/16 Rally   Jan-88 $3-5
White Body, Black Interior, Thin Red/ Blue Stripe, Blue "SERVIS 17" Graphics, 4div or 5-dblspk Wheels.

J 90   Juniors - Mercedes Benz 2.3/16 Saloon   Jan-88 $3-5
Red Body, Black Interior.

J 90/ ?? Juniors - Mercedes Benz 2.3/16 Saloon   ??? $3-5
Maroon Body with Gold Pinstripe, Black Interior & Base, 4div Wheels. (Red Box without Number, 1985?.)

J 91   Juniors - Jaguar XJ40 Police   Jan-88 $3-5
a. White Body, Blue Lightbar on Roof, Black Edged Yellow Side Stripe with Black "POLICE," Black "POLICE" on Hood. (Later renumbered 90393 when production moved to China with lower darker blue lightbar.)

b. White Body, Blue Lightbar on Roof, Blue Edged Yellow Side Stripe with Blue "POLICE," Blue "POLICE" on Hood.

J 91/ 01 Juniors - Jaguar XJ40 Police   Jan-89 $3-5
White Body, Blue Lightbar on Roof, Blue Edged Yellow Side Stripe with Blue "POLICE," Blue "POLICE" on Hood. (Renumbering of J91.)

J 91/ 02 Juniors - Jaguar XJ40 Saloon   Jan-89 $3-5
Light Metallic Blue Body, 4div Wheels.

J 92   Juniors - Jaguar XJ40 Saloon   Jan-88 $3-5
Dark Green Body with White Side Stripe, Leaping Jaguar Logo on Hood, Black Seats, Silver Grill, 5-dblspk Wheels.

J 93   Juniors - Jaguar XJ40 Saloon   Jan-88 $3-5
a. Silver Body with Black Side Stripe.

b. Dark Green Body with Light Green Side Stripe, Black Seats, Silver Grill, 5-dblspk Wheels. (May Be Other Number than J93.)

c. Dark Green Body with Yellow Side Stripe, Black Seats, Silver Grill, 4-div Wheels. (BP Promotional, May Be Other Number than J93.)

J 94   Juniors - Mercedes-Benz 300TD Wagon   Mar-88 $3-5
Red Body, Clear Windows, Black Interior.

J 94/ 02 Juniors - Mercedes-Benz 300TD Wagon   Jan-89 $3-5
a. White Body, Clear Windows, Black Interior.

b. Silver Body, Clear Windows, Black Interior.

J 95   Juniors - Mercedes-Benz 300TD Taxi   Apr-88 $3-5
Black Interior and Base, Clear Windows.

a. Grayish Green Body, Black "TAXI" on Doors.

b. Tan Body, Black "TAXI" on Doors with Thin Black Side Stripe.

J 96   Juniors - Helicopter   1986?
                                                    (Standard) $3-5
                                                    (Swiss) $8-12

a. Red Body, Black Rotor Blades & Base, Clear Windows. (Also Used in Royal Mail Sets.)

b. Orange Body, Black Rotor Blades & Base White "Flughaffen" Graphics. (Found in Swiss version of Airport Set J3125.)

c. White Body, Black Rotor Blades & Base, Clear Windows. (Found in set J3035 and others.)

d. Green Body, Black Rotor Blades & Base, Clear Windows. (Found in set J3035 and others.)

J 96/ 01 Juniors - Helicopter   Jan-89 $3-5
a. White Body, Black Rotor Blades & Base, Clear Windows, White "POLICE" in Blue Side Stripe.

b. White Body, Black Rotor Blades & Base, Blue Tinted Windows, White "POLICE" in Blue Side Stripe.

J 96/ 02 Juniors - Helicopter   Jan-89 $3-5
Red Body, Black Rotor Blades & Base, Yellow Tinted Windows. (described as "Fire" in catalog.)

J 97   Juniors - Land Rover ONE TEN   Jan-88 $3-5
Red Body with Open Rear Quarter Windows, Black Interior, Diagonal White Side Stripes, White "FIRE SALVAGE" with Black/ White Crest.

J 98   Juniors - Porsche Targa   Mar-88 $3-5
Red Body, Black Interior, No Graphics.

J 98/ 02 Juniors - Porsche Targa   Jan-89 $3-5
Black Body, 4-div Wheels.

J 98/ ?? Juniors - Porsche Targa   1989? $5-8
Black Body, 4-div Wheels, Orange Tiger Stripe Graphics on Hood and Sides "Tony" Graphics. (Kellogg's Promotional, UK Only.)

J 98/ ?? Juniors - Porsche Targa   1989? $8-12
Gold Vacuum Plated Body, 5-Dblspk Wheels, Black Interior, Clear Windows, No Graphics. (Promotional for unknown purpose, UK Only.)

J 99   Juniors - Porsche Targa Turbo   Mar-88 $3-5
White Body, Black "TURBO" on Sides.

J 99/ 02 Juniors - Porsche Targa Turbo   1989? $8-12
White Body, Black Interior, 4-div Wheels, Red Panels on Doors, "RIJKSPOLITIE" in Red Panel on Hood, "16" on White Part of Hood. (Produced for the Dutch market.)

J 1?? Juniors - Land Rover Wrecker   1985 $3-5
a. Red Body, Blue Tinted Windows, Silver Hook, No Graphics. (Former E31-B. Found on short red card. Possibly left-over Mettoy-era stock. Actual model number may not have been assigned.

b. Red Body, Blue Tinted Windows, Silver Hook, "M1 MOTORWAY" Graphics on Doors. (From unknown set.)

c. White Body with Blue Outlined Red Side Stripes, Blue Tinted Windows, Silver Hook, "RESCUE SERVICE" Graphics. (From unknown set.)

J 102   Juniors - Chevrolet Van, Wimpy   Apr-86 $5-8
White Body with Thin Roof Ribs, Opaque Black Windows, "Wimpy" Side Labels on Clear Plastic Backing.

J 105   Juniors - Mercedes-Benz Bus (B105)   1985 $3-5
a. Bright Yellow Body, Opaque Black Windows, Black "HEATHROW" Graphics on Sides, 5-dblspk Wheels.

b. Bright Yellow Body, Opaque Black Windows, Black "SCHOOL BUS" Labels on Sides, 5-spoke Wheels.

J 108   Juniors - Simon Snorkel (B108)   1985 $3-5
a. Red Body with Silver Deck, Yellow Booms and Bucket on White Turntable, White Plastic Base.

b. Red Body with Silver Deck, Yellow Booms and Bucket on Yellow Turntable, Yellow Plastic Base. (Possibly left-over Mettoy era stock. Later released as J8.)

J 109   Juniors - Cement Mixer (B109)   1985 $3-5
(Possibly left-over Mettoy era stock. Later released as J9.)

a. Orange Body, Ivory Drum and Holder, Opaque Black Windows.

b. Tan Body, White Drum and Holder, Opaque Black Windows.

J 110 A Juniors - Aston Martin DB6 (B110)   1985 $3-5
(Possibly left-over Mettoy era stock. Later released as J10.)

a. Yellow Body, Opaque Black Windows, No Graphics.

b. Maroon Body, Opaque Black Windows, No Graphics.

J 110 B Juniors - Renault Trafic Van   Aug-87
                                          With Crayon Package Complete $15-20
                                          Stand-alone Packaging $5-8

a. Yellow Body, Green "Crayola" on Sides, "VAN" Text on Base. (Packaged with 64 Crayons as a promotional model for Binney and Smith.)

b. Yellow Body, Green "Crayola" on Sides, "VAN" Text on Base. (Packaged individually on unmarked red Corgi card.)

J 111   Juniors - Volvo Estate Wagon (B111)   1985 $3-5
(Possibly a release of left-over Mettoy E 51-B stock, otherwise like J 11-A.)
a. Red Body, No Graphics.
b. Blue Body, No Graphics.
c. Light Blue Body, No Graphics.
d. Light Blue Body, Black Interior, No Graphics.

J 112   Juniors - Ford Skip Truck (B112)   1984 $3-5
No Windows or Interior, 5 Dblspk Wheels. (Continuation of Mettoy Era E-54A. Also packaged as JB112.)
a. Red Body, White Plastic Bucket and Base.
b. Red Body, Ivory Plastic Bucket and Base.

J 113   Juniors - Refuse Truck (B113)   1985 $3-5
(Possibly a release of left-over Mettoy E 55-B stock. Also released as J13.)
Orange Cab / Chassis, Gray Refuse Body.

J 114   Juniors - Mercedes-Benz 240D (B114)   1985 $3-5
Standard Body without Roof Sign, 5-dblspk Wheels. (Packaged as Taxi on box but produced as standard version.)
a. Black or Very Dark Maroon Body.
b. Tan Body.
c. White Body, Opaque Black Windows.

J 115   Juniors - Lotus (B115)   1985 $3-5
a. White Body, Black Louvered Windows (from Earlier James Bond Issue), Red Side Stripe with "TURBO" Text, Exposed 5-Dblspk Wheels. (Rework of E60B to normal vehicle. Also packaged as J-15.)
b. White Body, Black Louvered Windows (from Earlier James Bond Issue), No Side Stripe or Graphics, Exposed 5-Dblspk Wheels. (Found in Best of British Set J3109.)

J 118   Juniors - Jaguar XJS (B118)   1985 $3-5
(Former E72-B. Probably left-over Mettoy era stock. Later released as J18-A.)
a. Yellow Body without Graphics, Clear Windows, White Interior.

J 119   Juniors - Matra Rancho (B119)   1985 $3-5
(Former E76-C. Probably left-over Mettoy stock. Later released as J19.)
a. Green Body, No Graphics.

J 120   Juniors - London Bus (B120)   1985 $3-5
Red Body, Opaque Black Windows, No Graphics. (Possibly left-over Mettoy era stock. Also released as J20.)

J 121   Juniors - Fiat X1/9 (B121)   1985 $3-5
(Possibly left-over Mettoy era stock. Later released as J21.)
a. White Body, Black Interior and Engine Cover, No Graphics.
b. Orange Body, Black Interior and Engine Cover, No Graphics.
c. Black Body, Black Interior and Engine Cover, No Graphics.

J 121/ 01 Juniors - Ford Thunderbird   1988 $3-5
a. Red Body without White Trimmed Fins, Black Interior, 8-div Wheels. (Continuation of Mettoy Era E-96B.)
b. Red Body with White Fins, Black Interior, 8-Div Wheels.

J 121/ 02 Juniors - Ford Thunderbird   1989 $3-5
Black Body with Silver Fins, Black Interior, 8-Div Wheels. (Also used in Little/Large Set.)

J 122/ 01 Juniors - Mercedes-Benz 300SL Gullwing   1988 $3-5
Silver Body, Red Interior, 8-Div Wheels. (Continuation of Mettoy Era E-181. Also see J-47 which is red. Can be found on "Freeway" card.)

J 123   Juniors - Renault Turbo (B123)   1985 $3-5
Blue Body, Red Bumpers and Interior, Black Plastic Base, Vacuum Plated Mirrors, Clear Windows, White "TURBO" on Sides. (Possibly left-over Mettoy era stock. Later released as J23.)

J 123/ 01 Juniors - Ford Mustang   1988 $3-5
Blue Body, Dark Gray to Black Base, Red Wedge with Black and White Body Graphics, "77" on Roof and "GOODYEAR" on Doors.

J 123/ 02 Juniors - Ford Mustang   1988 $3-5
White Upper Body, Red Hatch, Black Lower Body / Base and Interior, "77 FORD COBRA" Graphics, 8 Div Wheels.

J 136   Juniors - Ford Mustang (B136)   1985 $3-5
White Upper Body, Black Lower Body / Base, White Interior, Clear Windows and Headlamps, No Graphics. (Possibly left-over Mettoy era stock. Later released as J36.)

J 141   Juniors - Quarry Truck (B141)   1985 $3-5
Yellow Cab / Chassis, Red Dump Body. (Possibly left-over Mettoy era stock. Later released as J41.)

J 143   Juniors - Tanker Truck (B143)   1985 $3-5
Yellow Cab / Chassis, White Tank Body with Red "Shell" Graphics. (Possibly left-over Mettoy era stock. Later released as J43.)

J 144   Juniors - Container Truck (B144)   1985 $3-5
a. White Cab and Platform, White Box, "DUNLOP" Graphics on Box Sides. (Also see J-44A.)
b. Black Cab, White Platform, White Box, "DUNLOP" Graphics on Box Sides. (Also see J-44A.)

J 145   Juniors - Chevrolet Corvette (B145)   1985 $3-5
White Body, Black Interior and Baseplate, Clear Windows, Red Side Stripe with Black "CHEVY 84" Graphics. (Possibly left-over Mettoy era stock. Later released as J46.)

J 146   Juniors - Pontiac Firebird (B146)   1985 $3-5
Red Body, Black Interior and Baseplate, Black Spoiler, Clear Windows, No Graphics. (Possibly left-over Mettoy era stock. Later released as J46.)

J 148   Juniors - Jeep, Covered (B148)   1985 $3-5
White Body and Plastic Cover, Red Interior and Push Bar, Black Chassis, Black Off-Road Tires including Spare on Rear, No Graphics. (Possibly left-over Mettoy era stock. Later released as J48.)

J 149   Juniors - Jeep Renegade (B149)   1985 $3-5
a. White Body, Black Rollbar, Black Interior and Push Bar, Black Chassis, Black Off-Road Tires, No Graphics. (Possibly left-over Mettoy era stock. Later issued as J49.)
b. Red Body, Red Rollbar, White Interior and Push Bar, Black Chassis, Black Off-Road Tires, No Graphics. (Possibly left-over Mettoy era stock. Later issued as J49.)

J 155/ 01 Juniors - Police Twin Set   1989 $6-10
Juniors Police J91 Jaguar XJ40 Police & J66 Land Rover.

J 156/ 01 Juniors - Fire Twin Set   1989 $6-10
Juniors J8 Snorkel & J97 Land Rover.

J 157/ 01 Juniors - Breakdown Twin Set   1989 $6-10
a. Juniors AA Service J51 Ford Transit Van & J64 Land Rover.
b. Juniors AA Service J51 Ford Transit Van & J24/03 Ford Transit Wrecker.

J 158   Juniors - Datapost Twin Set   1985? $6-10
Juniors Royal Mail J63 Ford Transit Van & J65 Land Rover.

J 158/ 01 Juniors - Datapost Twin Set   1989 $6-10
Juniors Royal Mail J63 Ford Transit Van & J65 Land Rover. (Renumbering of J158.)

J 159   Juniors – Range Rover, Open (B159)   1985 $3-5
Green Body, Black Push Bar and Base, White Interior, Clear Windshield, No Graphics. (Possibly left-over Mettoy era stock. Later released as J50.)

J 159/ 01 Juniors - Rally Twin Set   1989 $6-10
Juniors J4 Ford Transit Van & J85 Porsche.

J 160/ 01 Juniors - Great Britain Themed Card   Jun-89 $5-8
Juniors J20 Daimler Fleetline Bus "SEE MORE LONDON," J17 London Taxi.

J 163   Juniors - Chevrolet Van, Coca-Cola (B163)   1985 $3-5
a. Red Body, Opaque Black Windows, White "Coca-Cola" and Logo on Red Side Labels. (Former E36-C. Probably left-over Mettoy stock.)
b. Red Body, Clear Windows, White "FIRE SALVAGE" on Sides. (Found in Set J3142.)
c. Dark Blue Body, Clear Windows, No Graphics. (Found in Bumper Set J3035. No separate model number assigned. Same color as darker versions of Mettoy era Spider-Van.)
d. Yellow Body, No Graphics. (Found in red card and in some sets. Possibly Telecom van without graphics. No separate model number assigned.)

J 164   Juniors - Chevrolet Van, Adidas (B164)   1985 $3-5
(Former E94-B. Probably left-over Mettoy stock.)
Medium Blue Body, white "adidas" and Logo Printed on Sides.

J 165   Juniors - Helicopter (B165)   1985 $3-5
(Former E46-B. Probably left-over Mettoy era stock.)
a. Yellow Body, Black Rotors, No Graphics.
b. White Body, Black Rotors, "POLICE" Graphics.
c. White Body, Black Rotors, "POLICE STOP" Graphics.

J 166   Juniors - Digger (B166)   1985 $3-5
Yellow Upper Body, Black Lower Body / Base, White Scoop Arm and Engine, No Graphics. (old Mettoy Era E77-B Excavator.)

J 167   Juniors - Mercedes-Benz Bonna Ambulance (B167)1986? $3-5
a. White Body, No Graphics, Opaque Light Blue Windows.
b. White Body, Red Cross on Front doors, Opaque Light Blue Windows. (Released in sets J3140 and J3142. May not have been released separately.)

J 167/ 01 Juniors - Mercedes-Benz Bonna Ambulance   Jun-89 $8-12
White Body, Red Stripe and Cross on Sides, Red Stripe on Front and Sides of Roof, "NOTRUF 144" Graphics. (Produced for the Swiss Market.)

J 167/ 0? Juniors - Mercedes-Benz Bonna Ambulance   198? $3-5
White Body, Red Stripe and Blue Medical Symbol on Sides, Red Stripe on Front and Sides of Roof.

J 167/ 0? Juniors - Mercedes-Benz Bonna Ambulance   198? $3-5
White Body, Red Stripe and Cross on Lower Sides, Red Stripe on Sides of Roof, Dark Blue Tinted Windows.

J 173   Juniors - Racing Car (B173)   1985 $3-5
Black Body, No Graphics, White Driver. (Former E53-B, Probably left-over Mettoy era stock.)

B 176   Juniors - Porsche 911 Turbo (B176)   Sep-85 $15-20
Orange Body, "Crush" Logo on Hood in Arabic. (Produced for the Market in Oman.)

B 177   Juniors - Jaguar XJS (B177)   1984? $15-20
Silver Body, "7 Up" Logo on Hood in Arabic. (Produced for the Market in Oman.)

B 178   Juniors - Aston Martin DB6 (B178)   1984? $15-20
Yellow Body, "Sun Top" Logo on Hood in Arabic. (Produced for the Market in Oman.)

B 179   Juniors - Rover Sterling 3500 (B179)   1984? $15-20
White/ Blue Body, "RC Cola" Logo on Hood in Arabic. (Produced for the Market in Oman.)

J 200   Juniors - Matra Rancho & Horsebox   Apr-84 $6-10
a. Red Range Rover or Matra Rancho, Green Horse Trailer. (old# E2550), (Catalog Photo & Description do not Match.)
b. Green Matra Rancho with Black Base and Red Interior, Green Horsebox Trailer. (Jan-85)
c. Green Range Rover with Black Base and White Interior, Green Horsebox Trailer. (Need verification, individual Range Rover found unpackaged.)

J 201   Juniors - Ford Sierra & Dinghy   Apr-84 $6-10
a. Yellow Ford Sierra, Black and Yellow Plastic Dinghy on Black Trailer. (old# E2551. Dinghy also found in Off-Road Set J3015.)
b. Blue Ford Sierra with White Interior, Black and Yellow Plastic Dinghy on Black Trailer. (Found on double reverse window card, 1984.)
c. Red Ford Sierra with Gold Trim and Red Interior, Black and Yellow Plastic Dinghy on Black Trailer. (Dinghy may also be orange and black, need verification.) (Jan-85)

J 202 A   Juniors - Ford Mustang & Powerboat   Apr-84 $6-10
a. Red Mustang with Black Chassis, Red and White Boat with Black Outboard Motor, White Trailer. (old# E2553)
b. White Mustang with Black Chassis, Red and White Boat with Black Outboard Motor, White Trailer. (Found in reverse window 2-pack card 1984.)
c. White Mustang with Green Chassis, Red and White Boat with Black Outboard Motor, White Trailer. (Found in reverse window 2-pack card 1984.)

J 202 B   Juniors - Mercedes-Benz & Powerboat   Jan-85 $6-10
a. Red Mercedes with Silver Sides Below Belt Line, Red and White Boat with Black Outboard Motor, White Trailer.
b. Red Mercedes without Silver Sides Below Belt Line, Red and White Boat with Black Outboard Motor, White Trailer.
c. Red Mercedes with Silver Sides Below Belt Line, Yellow and Black Dinghy with Black Outboard Motor, Black Trailer. (Known factory packaging error.)

J 203   Juniors - Volvo & Caravan   Apr-84 $6-10
a. White Volvo Wagon, White Caravan with Blue Door. (old# E2554)
b. Ivory Volvo Wagon, Ivory Caravan with Red Door. (Jan-85)
c. Brick Red Volvo Wagon, Brick Red Caravan with Tan Door and Interior. (found in Off-Road Set J3015.)

J 204 A   Juniors - Ford Transit Wrecker & Jaguar   Apr-84 $6-10
a. White Ford Wrecker "24 hour service," Red Jaguar XJS. (old# E2555)
b. White Ford Wrecker "RESCUE 108," Red Jaguar XJS with Opaque Black Windows.

J 204 B   Juniors - Ford Transit Wrecker & Triumph TR7   Jan-85 $6-10
White Ford Wrecker with Blue Outlined Red Stripe "POLICE," "RESCUE," Red Triumph TR7.

J 205   Juniors - Container Truck & Trailer   Apr-84 $6-10
a. Black Truck with Yellow Flatbed and White Container with "DUNLOP" Graphics, Matching Unnumbered Trailer.
b. White Truck with White Flatbed and Off-white Container with "DUNLOP" Graphics, Matching Unnumbered Trailer.

J 206   Juniors - Tanker Truck & Trailer   Apr-84 $6-10
a. Red Truck with White Tank and "TOTAL" Graphics, Matching Unnumbered Trailer.
b. Yellow Truck with White Tank and "Shell" Graphics, Matching Unnumbered Trailer. (Jan-85)

J 207   Juniors - Pipe Truck & Trailer   Apr-84 $6-10
a. Red Truck with White Flatbed & Gray Pipes, Matching Unnumbered Trailer.
b. Red Truck with Yellow Flatbed & White Pipes, Matching Unnumbered Trailer.

c. Red Truck with Yellow Flatbed & Gray Pipes, Matching Unnumbered Trailer. (Jan-85)
d. Green Truck with Yellow Flatbed & Gray Pipes, Matching Unnumbered Trailer. (Jan-85)

J 214   Juniors – Mercedes-Benz PTT Bus   Apr-84 $8-12
Yellow Body with Red Side Stripe, Opaque Black Windows, Yellow "PTT" Label on Sides. (Produced for the Swiss Market. Continuation of Mettoy era E214.)

J 219   Juniors - Ford Sierra Polizei   Apr-84 $8-12
White Body, 2 Blue Roof Lights, Red Stripe on Sides and Hood, Black "POLIZEI" and "OW 21" Graphics. (Produced for the Swiss Market. Continuation of Mettoy era E219.)

J 219/ 01   Juniors - Ford Sierra Polizei   Jun-89 $8-12
White Body, 2 Blue Roof Lights, Red Stripe on Sides and Hood, Blue "POLIZEI" and "OW 21" Graphics. (Produced for the Swiss Market.)

J 228   Juniors - Austin Mini-Metro Mini-Cab   Apr-84 $8-12
White Body with Orange and Black Side Stripe, Tan Interior, Green "mini-cab" Graphics. (Produced for the Swiss Market. Possibly continuation of Mettoy era E228 if it existed.)

J 229   Juniors - Ford Escort Fahrschule   Apr-84 $8-12
Red Body, Tan LHD Interior, Triangular Black Graphics on Hood. (Produced for the Swiss Market. Possibly continuation of Mettoy era E229 if it existed.)

J 230   Juniors - U. S. Van Derendinger   Apr-84 $8-12
White Body with Red and Black Side Stripes, Opaque Black Windows, Blank Base, Red "Derendinger" on Sides. (Produced for the Swiss Market. Possibly continuation of Mettoy era E230 if it existed.)

J ???   Juniors - VW Polo Swiss PTT   Apr-84 $8-12
Yellow Body, Swiss PTT Logo on Doors. (Produced for the Swiss Market. Model number not known.)

J 239   Juniors - Datapost Twin Pack   1987? $6-10
Juniors Royal Mail J63 Ford Transit Van & J65 Land Rover.

J 240   Juniors - Police 2 pc. Set   May-87 $6-10
White Jaguar XJ6 with Blue Lightbar on Roof, Blue/ Yellow Side Stripe "POLICE," White Land Rover with Red/ Blue Side Stripe, White "POLICE" in Stripe, Blue "POLICE" on Upper Side.

C 1365   London Bus & Taxi Set   Apr-84 $15-25
C469 Routemaster Bus & Juniors J17 London Taxi. (Continuation of Mettoy Era 1365, which had Different Destination Panels on Routemaster. May also be found as C1365/ 01.)

C 1365/ 02   London Bus & Taxi Set   1989 $15-25
C469 Routemaster Bus & Juniors J17 London Taxi. (Continuation of C1365, which had Different Destination Panels on Routemaster.)

A 2411   Juniors Display Rack with 144 Juniors Vehicles   Jan-88 $???
144 Juniors in One-sided Display Rack.

A 2412   Juniors Display Rack with 192 Juniors Vehicles   Jan-88 $???
192 Juniors in One-sided Display Rack.

A 2415   Juniors Self Adhesive Shelf Display Tape   1988? $???
Roll of Preprinted Blue Shelf Tape with Corgi Logo.

A 2473   Juniors Display Carousel with 192 Juniors Vehicles   Jan-88 $???
192 Juniors in 4-sided Display Carousel.

A 2474   Juniors Display Carousel with 384 Juniors Vehicles   Jan-88 $???
384 Juniors in 4-sided Display Carousel.

A 2475   Juniors PVC Shelf Display Strip   1988? $???
Preprinted Red Shelf Strip with Corgi Logo.

A 2478   Header Board for A2411   1988? $???
Blue Header Board with Corgi Logo.

A 2479   Header Board for A2412   1988? $???
Blue Header Board with Corgi Logo.

A 2487   Corgi/ Turbos/ Juniors/ Display Carousel   Jan-88 $???
192 Juniors, 20 Turbos, 32 Corgi in 4-sided Display Carousel.

J 2880/ 01   Juniors - Police Triple Set   1989 $9-15
Juniors Police J91 Jaguar XJ40 Police, J96/01 Helicopter & J66 Land Rover.

J 2881/ 01   Juniors - Fire Triple Set   1989 $9-15
Juniors J8 Snorkel, J7 ERF Pumper & J97 Land Rover.

J 2882/ 01   Juniors - Breakdown Triple Set   1989 $9-15
Juniors AA Service J51 Ford Transit Van, J24/03 Ford Transit Wrecker & J64 Land Rover.

J 2883   Juniors 3 pc. Datapost Set   1988? $9-15
Juniors Royal Mail J63 Ford Transit Van, J65 Land Rover, J96 Helicopter.

J 2883/ 01   Juniors 3 pc. Datapost Set   1989 $9-15
Juniors Royal Mail J63 Ford Transit Van, J65 Land Rover, J96 Helicopter. (1989 Renumbering of J2883.)

J 2884/ 01 Juniors - Rally Triple Set — 1989 — $9-15
Juniors J4 Ford Transit Van, J30 BMW & J85 Porsche.

J 2885/ 01 Juniors- Great Britain Triple Set — Jun-89 — $9-15
Juniors Daimler Fleetline Bus "SEE MORE LONDON," London Taxi, White Jaguar XJ6 "POLICE" Graphics.

J 2897/ 01 Juniors - 4 pc. Teddy Bear Christmas Tree Set — Jun-89 — $12-18
Juniors J12 Iveco BP Tanker, J98/2 Porsche, J36 Ferrari, J89 Mercedes.

J 2898/ 01 Juniors - 4 pc. Teddy Bear Snow Teddy Set — Jun-89 — $12-18
Juniors J30 BMW, J91/02 Jaguar, J64 Land Rover, J86 Porsche.

J 2899/ 01 Juniors - 4 pc. Teddy Bear Father Christmas Set — Jun-89 — $12-18
Juniors J27 Citroen, J94 Mercedes, J77 Ferrari, J66 Land Rover

J 2900/ 01 Juniors - 4 pc. Teddy Bear Police Set — Jun-89 — $12-18
Juniors J15 Ford Transit Van, J91 Jaguar, J66 Land Rover, J96/01 Helicopter.

J 2901/ 01 Juniors - 4 pc. Teddy Bear Fire Set — Jun-89 — $12-18
Juniors J7 ERF Fire Engine, J8 Snorkel, J97 Land Rover, J96/02 Helicopter.

J 2902/ 01 Juniors - 4 pc. Teddy Bear Breakdown Set (AA) — Jun-89 — $12-18
Juniors J24/03 Ford Wrecker, J64 Land Rover, J91 Jaguar, J51 Ford Transit Van.

J 2903 Juniors - 4 pc. Teddy Bear Post Office Set — 1988? — $12-18
Juniors J65 Land Rover, J63 Ford Transit Van, J31/03 Ford Sierra, and J96 Helicopter, All Decorated "Royal Mail"

J 2903/ 01 Juniors - 4 pc. Teddy Bear Post Office Set — 1989 — $12-18
1989 Renumbering of J2903, Contents Identical.

J 2904/ 01 Juniors - 4 pc. Teddy Bear Race Set — Jun-89 — $12-18
Juniors J4 Ford Transit Van, J89 Mercedes, J30 BMW, J36 Ferrari.

J 2904/ 02 Juniors - 4 pc. Teddy Bear Race Set — 1989 — $12-18
Juniors J4 Ford Transit Van, Hot Rod Van, J30 BMW, Porsche.

J 2905/ 01 Juniors - 4 pc. Teddy Bear Great Britain Set — Jun-89 — $12-18
Juniors J20 Daimler Fleetline Bus "SEE MORE LONDON," J17 London Taxi, White J91 Jaguar XJ6 "POLICE," and Red J63 Ford Transit Van "Royal Mail" Graphics.

J 2909 Juniors 32 Vehicle Dealer Assortment — Jan-88 — $60-80
32 Juniors Vehicles in Dealer Display Box.

J 2910 Juniors 32 Vehicle Dealer Assortment — Jan-88 — $60-80
32 Juniors Vehicles in Dealer Display Box.

J 2935/ 01 Juniors 24 Vehicle City Scene Assortment — Jan-89 — $45-60
24 Juniors Vehicles in Dealer Display Box.

J 2936/ 01 Juniors 24 Vehicle Rally Assortment — Jan-89 — $45-60
24 Juniors Vehicles in Dealer Display Box.

J 2937/ 01 Juniors 24 Vehicle Emergency Assortment — Jan-89 — $45-60
24 Juniors Vehicles in Dealer Display Box.

J 2938/ 01 Juniors 24 Vehicle Great Britain Assortment — Jan-89 — $45-60
24 Juniors Vehicles in Dealer Display Box.

J 2946/ 01 Juniors Twin Set Assortment — Jan-89 — $???
Juniors Twin Sets in Dealer Display Box.

J 2959/ 01 Juniors Triple Set Assortment — Jan-89 — $???
Juniors Triple Sets in Dealer Display Box.

J 2971/ 01 Juniors Teddy Character Set Assortment — Jan-89 — $???
Juniors Teddy Sets in Dealer Display Box.

J 2974/ 01 Juniors Teddy Christmas Set Assortment — Jan-89 — $???
Juniors Teddy Christmas Sets in Dealer Display Box.

J 3001 Juniors - Garage with 3 Cars — Apr-84 — $18-20
Plastic 4 Bay Garage with Juniors Ford Mustang, Mercedes 240D, Jaguar XJS. (Continuation of Mettoy Era E3001, Using Leftover Stock Vehicles.)
a. Cream Garage walls, Clear Roof, Red Doors.
b. White Garage walls, Clear Roof, Red Doors.

J 3002 Juniors - 24 Hour Services Set — 1984 — $20-30
Plastic Service Station Building with Three Juniors Vehicles (Vehicles vary.)
a. Vehicles are Non-standard Yellow US Van without Graphics, Non-standard Yellow Ford Transit Pick-up without Graphics, Non-standard White Mercedes-Benz Ambulance without Graphics.
b. Other Vehicle Combinations are Possible.

J 3006 Juniors - Playmat — Apr-84 — $15-20
Polyester Fabric, 36"x24," Printed Roadways & Buildings. (Continuation of Mettoy Era E3006.)

J 3010C Juniors - 3 pc. Coca-Cola Set — Apr-84 — $15-20
Juniors Iveco Box Truck, Iveco Beverage Truck, and Van all with "Coca-Cola" Decorations. (USA Market, Hartoy Coca-Cola Card.)

J 3014 Juniors 6 pc. Emergency Squad Set — Apr-84 — $20-25
Juniors Airport Fire Tender, Blue Helicopter, Ford Transit Breakdown, Mercedes Ambulance, ERF Fire Tender, Buick Police Car.

J 3015 Juniors - Off Road Set — Apr-84 — $30-35

a. 8 Juniors Vehicles Using Leftover Stock Mettoy Era Vehicles. (Apr-84.)
b. Brick Red Volvo 240 Wagon, Brick Red Caravan with Tan Door and Interior, Green Matra Rancho, Green Horsebox, Yellow and Black Dinghy on Black Trailer, Tan and Brown Closed Jeep, Black Open Jeep with White Interior, Red Range Rover with "Mountain Rescue" Graphics. (1985-onward.)

J 3019 Juniors - James Bond "Octopussy" Set — Apr-84 — $AUCTION
Maroon Range Rover (Top Down), Gray Trailer, White Mini Airplane. (Continuation of Mettoy Era E3019, Trailer May Also Be Tan.)

J 3020 H Juniors - Hershey's Delivery Team — 1985 — $9-15
White Iveco Container Truck with Brown "HERSHEY'S MILK CHOCOLATE KISSES" Side Labels, With Mercedes-Benz Mini Shop Truck with Brown Side Stripe and "HERSHEY'S" Graphics, Orange Renault Trafic Van with "Reese's MILK CHOCOLATE PEANUT BUTTER CUPS" Graphics.

J 3035 Juniors 12 pc. Bumper Set — Apr-84 — $40-65
12 Juniors Vehicles, Some May Be in Non-standard Finishes or Using Leftover Mettoy Era Stock.

J 3035/ 0(?) Juniors 12 pc. Bumper Set - Mothercare — 1986? — $40-65
12 Juniors Vehicles, Some May Be in Non-standard Finishes or Using Leftover Mettoy Era Stock. (Special Mothercare packaging with carry handle. Known non-standard models listed as variations of released versions.)

J 3036 Juniors - Garage with 4 Cars — Apr-84 — $20-35
Plastic 4 Bay Garage with Juniors Ford Capri, Citroen 2CV, Ford Escort, Matra Rancho. (Continuation of Mettoy Era E3036, Using Leftover Stock Vehicles.)

J 3045 Juniors - Mars 4 pc. Gift Set — Sep-88 — $15-25
Red Renault Trafic "Maltesers," Black Iveco Box Truck "Mars," White Iveco Box Van "Bounty," Yellow Chevy Van "Opal Fruits" Graphics.

J 3097 Juniors - Garage with 3 Vehicles — Jan-88 — $15-25
L-Shaped Plastic Service Station, J12 "TOTAL," J4 "AA," J66 "POLICE" Graphics.

J 3097/ 02 Juniors - Garage with 3 Vehicles — Jan-89 — $15-25
L-Shaped Plastic Service Station, J32 Ferrari, E125 Pick-up, J91 "POLICE" Graphics.

J 3100C Juniors / Turbos Coca-Cola Racing Team — Apr-84 — $15-20
Red Juniors Corvette with White "7 Coca-Cola" Graphics, Red Turbos Porsche 935 with White "4 Coca-Cola" Graphics. (Imported by Hartoy Inc. for the American market.)

J 3102 Juniors 3 pc. Set — Apr-84 — $9-12
Red Ferrari Testarossa, White BMW M3 with Thin Red Stripe and Black "11 TOTAL" Graphics, unknown Porsche model.

J 3103/ 01 Juniors 3 pc. Set — 1985? — $9-12
White Vauxhall / Opel Nova with Yellow / Silver / Black Stripes, Orange BMW M3 with "44" Graphics, Silver Porsche 760 without usual Black Side Stripe.

J 3103/ 02 Juniors 3 pc. Set — 1985? — $9-12
Yellow Firebird with Black "FIRE BIRD" Graphics, White Matra Rancho with Red and Green Graphics, Black Porsche Carrera with Gold "TURBO" Graphics.

J 3109 Juniors 7 pc. Best of British Set — Apr-84 — $20-30
7 British Juniors Vehicles Usually Including London Taxi & London Bus. (Continuation of Mettoy Era E3109 Using Leftover Stock Vehicles.)

J 3114 Juniors 4 pc. Set with Garage — 1985? — $20-30
a. White Ferrari Testarossa, unidentified black coupe, Light Blue Porsche 935, Buick Police, Unassembled White Garage with Red Trim.
b. White Jaguar XJS without Graphics, Black Porsche Targa without Graphics, Red Porsche 935 without Graphics, Green Aston Martin without Graphics, Unassembled White Garage with Red Trim.
c. Many other vehicle combinations were issued at random from existing production stock.

J 3121 Juniors 7 pc. Super Sports Cars Set — Apr-84 — $20-30
7 Juniors Vehicles in Rally Trim. (Continuation of Mettoy Era E3121 Using Leftover Stock Vehicles.)

J 3124 Juniors Car Transporter with 4 Cars — Apr-84 — $25-35
a. Blue Superhaulers Car Transporter with White Upper Deck, Single Axle Mercedes Truck, 4 Juniors Cars with Standard Graphics. (Continuation of Mettoy Era E3105 Using Different Cars.)
b. Red Superhaulers Car Transporter with Silver Upper Deck, Red Volvo Globetrotter Truck, 4 Juniors Cars with Standard Graphics.
c. Red Superhaulers Car Transporter with White Upper Deck, Red Volvo Globetrotter Truck, 4 Juniors Cars with Standard Graphics.
d. Red Superhaulers Car Transporter with Gray Upper Deck, Red Volvo Globetrotter Truck, 4 Juniors Cars with Non-Standard Colors.

J 3125 Juniors 5 pc. Airport Set — Apr-84
(Standard UK) — $20-30
(European) — $25-35

a. Concord with "BRITISH AIRWAYS" Graphics, Iveco BP Tanker, Airport Fire Tender, Chevy Van with "Swissair" Graphics, Helicopter.

b. Concord with "BRITISH AIRWAYS" Graphics, Yellow "HEATHROW" Mercedes Bus, Sierra with "POLICE" Graphics, London Taxi, Police Helicopter.

c. Concord with "BRITISH AIRWAYS" Graphics, White Mercedes Bus with Blue and Green "HOLIDAY TOURS" Graphics, Renault Trafic Bus with "Grand Hotel" Graphics, London Taxi, London Bus.

d. Concord with "BRITISH AIRWAYS" Graphics, Non-standard White Renault Trafic Van with Aircraft Graphics on Sides, Sierra with "POLIZEI" Graphics, Airport Fire Tender with "Flughaffen-Feurweir" Graphics, Non-standard Orange "Flughaffen" Helicopter. (Produced for the Swiss market.)

e. Concord with "BRITISH AIRWAYS" Graphics, Non-standard White Renault Trafic Van with Aircraft Graphics on Sides, J51 Swissair Van, Airport Fire Tender with "Flughaffen-Feurweir" Graphics, Non-standard Orange "Flughaffen" Helicopter. (Produced for the Swiss market.)

J 3125/ 01 Juniors 5 pc. Airport Set   Jan-88 $20-30
Concord with "BRITISH AIRWAYS" Graphics, Juniors DD Bus, Juniors London Taxi, Renault Trafic with "Grand Hotel" Graphics, Ford Transit Van with "AA" Graphics.

J 3126 Juniors 7 pc. Holiday Set   Apr-84 $20-30
Juniors Mercedes-Benz 500 SL, Caravan Trailer, Ford Transit Breakdown, Jaguar XJS, Range Rover (Top Down) with Horsebox, Corgi Plaxton Coach.

J 3128 Juniors 13 pc. Motorway Services Set   Apr-84 $60-80
10 Juniors Vehicles (Some May Be in Non-standard Finishes), Superhaulers Mercedes Articulated Truck "YORKIE," GMC Bus "EUROEXPRESS," Mercedes Articulated Tanker "DUCKHAMS" Graphics.

J 3135/ 01 Juniors 6 pc. City Scene Set   Jun-89 $18-25
Juniors J52 Refuse Truck, J27 Citroen, J20 London Bus, J17 London Taxi, J12 Iveco Tanker, J98/02 Porsche.

J 3136/ 01 Juniors 6 pc. Emergency Set   Jun-89 $18-25
Juniors Yellow Ford Transit Van "AA," White Ford Transit Van with Red Stripe "POLICE," Red Land Rover "FIRE SALVAGE," Red Simon Snorkel with White Boom "SNORKEL," White Tow Truck with Red Stripe "RESCUE," Jaguar XJ6 "POLICE"

J 3137/ 01 Juniors 6 pc. Rally Set   Jun-89 $18-25
Juniors J4 Ford Transit Van, J30 BMW, J85 Porsche, J23 Renault, J89 Mercedes, J36 Ferrari.

J 3138/ 01 Juniors 6 pc. Great Britain Set   Jun-89 $18-25
Juniors White Land Rover "POLICE," London Taxi, Daimler Fleetline Bus "SEE MORE LONDON," White Jaguar XJ6 "POLICE," Red Ford Transit Van "Royal Mail," Yellow Ford Transit Van "AA" Graphics.

J 3140 Juniors Police 999 3 pc. Set   1986 $8-12
a. Former E1-E Mercedes-Benz Bonna Ambulance with Opaque Light Blue Windows, J24 Ford Transit Wrecker, J31 Ford Sierra Police.
b. Police Helicopter, J24 Ford Transit Wrecker, Jaguar XJS Police. (1988?)

J 3141 Juniors Delivery Service 3 pc. Set   1985? $8-12
Juniors Royal Mail J25 Ford Escort with "77" Graphics, J26 Austin Mini Metro with "66" Graphics, J39 U.S. Van with "Royal Mail Parcels" Graphics.

J 3141/ 01 Juniors Delivery Service 4 pc. Set   Jan-89 $12-16
Juniors Royal Mail J25 Ford Escort (2X), J26 Austin Mini Metro (2X).

J 3141/ 02 Juniors Delivery Service 3 pc. Set   1989? $8-12
Juniors Royal Mail J25 Ford Escort, J26 Austin Mini Metro, J39 U.S. Van.

J 3142 Juniors Emergency 999 3 pc. Set   1986 $8-12
Former E1-E Mercedes-Benz Bonna Ambulance with Non-standard Opaque Light Blue Windows, Non-standard Red US Van with White "FIRE SALVAGE" Graphics, Former E29-D Snorkel Fire Truck.

J 3155 Carry Car with 1 Juniors Vehicle   Jan-88 $15-30
Large Opening Red Body with Yellow Rear Spoiler, Juniors Vehicle with Modified Key Slot Base. (Plastic Carry Case, vehicle is usually Aston-Martin DB6 or Renault Turbo.)

J 3155/ 03 Carry Car with 1 Juniors Vehicle   Jul-89 $25-35
Yellow Body and Rear Spoiler. (Produced for Mothercare Stores, not to be confused with later Auto-City version.)

J 3156 Carry Car with 5 Juniors Vehicles   Jan-86 $30-40
Red J3155 with Additional Vehicles included.

J 3156/ 01 Carry Car with 5 Juniors Vehicles   Jan-88 $30-40
(Same as J3156, Models Updated.)

J 3158 Juniors 3 pc. London Scene Themed Card   1986? $8-12
a. Juniors Daimler Fleetline Bus "SEE MORE LONDON," London Taxi, White Jaguar XJ6 with "POLICE" Graphics.
b. Juniors Daimler Fleetline Bus "SEE MORE LONDON," London Taxi, White Helicopter with Black Rotors and Blue "POLICE" Graphics.

J 3159 Juniors Super Sport 3 pc. Set   1986 $8-12

Three Random Sports Cars.

J 3161/ 01 Advent Calendar   Jan-88 $50-60
SET INCLUDING 24 Vehicles

J 3167/ 02 Juniors Superhaulers 6 pc. Set   Jan-88 $30-40
C1231/02 "WIMPY," C1238/03 "SECURICOR EXPRESS," J97/?? "Royal Mail," J4 "KREMER," J25 "AVIS," J24 "POLICE" Graphics.

J 3167/ 05 Juniors Superhaulers 6 pc. Set   Jan-89 $30-40
C1238/04 "RADIO 1 ROADSHOW," C1231/17 "Mars," J66 "POLICE," J4 "KREMER," J51 "AA," J24 "POLICE" Graphics.

J 3167/ 06 Kays Delivery Set   Jul-89 $20-30
2X Superhaulers Volvo Container Truck "Kays," 4X Juniors Ford Transit Van "Kays"

J 3168 Juniors Transporter Set with 6 Cars   1986 $35-45
C1222 Red/ Silver Car Transporter, Matching Car Transporter Trailer with Tandem Bogie Wheels, J23 "elf," J32 Ferrari, J22 BMW, J84 Volvo 760, J90 Red.

J 3168/ 03 Juniors Transporter Set with 6 Cars   Jan-88 $35-45
C1222 Red/ Silver Car Transporter, Matching Car Transporter Trailer with Tandem Bogie Wheels, J23 "elf," J32 Red, J91 "POLICE," J83 "Gillanders," J90 Red, J93 "JAGUAR" Graphics.

J 3168/ 07 Juniors Transporter Set with 6 Cars   Jan-89 $35-45
C1222 Blue/ Silver Car Transporter, Matching Car Transporter Trailer with Tandem Bogie Wheels, J23 "elf," J87 Red, J91 "POLICE," J83 "Gillanders," J94 Red, J31 Blue.

J 3169 Juniors Bumper Set with 10 Vehicles   1986 $30-40
Ten Juniors Vehicles. (Vehicles vary, many from left-over Mettoy stock.)

J 3169/ 02 Juniors Bumper Set with 10 Vehicles   Jan-88 $30-40
J73 Red, J4 "AA," J66 "POLICE," J93 "JAGUAR," J50 "PIONEER," J18 Silver, J30 "Canon," J65 "Royal Mail," J4 "KREMER," J84 Silver.

J 3169/ 06 Juniors Bumper Set with 10 Vehicles   Jan-89 $30-40
Juniors White J18 Jaguar XJS, Yellow J10 Aston Martin, Blue J14 Mercedes, E125 Ford Transit Pick-up, J12/01 Iveco Tanker, E55 Refuse Truck, J9/01 Iveco Container Truck, J15 Lotus Esprit, E??? US Van, Green J96 Helicopter.

J 3170/ 02 Juniors Jumbo Set with 20 Vehicles   Jan-88 $60-80
J65 "Royal Mail," J19 "mistral," J46 "Schweppes," J54 "RENAULT," J32 Red, J49 Olive with Tan Roof & Red Cross Symbol, J27 Yellow, J73 "Duckhams," J4 "KREMER," J93 Green Body, J17 Taxi, J86 "74," etc.

J 3171 Juniors - Transporter Set with 3 Cars   Jan-88 $20-30
C1222 Red/ Silver Car Transporter, J83 "Gillanders," J30 "Canon," J73 "36" Graphics. (Note: Many other car combinations exist.)

J 3174 Juniors Garage Set with 4 Cars   1986 $12-15
Yellow 4-stall Garage with Red Doors, J23 "elf Renault, J24 Ford Transit Wrecker, Former E1-E Mercedes-Benz Bonna Ambulance with Non-standard Light Blue Opaque Windows, Silver Vauxhall Nova.

J 3176 Juniors Snowman Xmas Card Set   1987? $12-15
Four Juniors Civilian Vehicles. (Contents vary.)

J 3177 Juniors Bobbie Xmas Card Set   1987? $12-15
Four Juniors Police Vehicles. (Contents vary.)

J 3178 Juniors Father Christmas (Santa) Xmas Card Set 1987? $12-15
Four Juniors Civilian Vehicles. (Contents vary.)

J 3179 Juniors Postman Xmas Card Set   1987? $12-15
Juniors Royal Mail J39 U.S. Van, J63 Ford Transit Van, J65 Land Rover, J96 Helicopter.

J 3180 Juniors Fireman Xmas Card Set   1987? $12-15
Four Juniors Fire Vehicles. (Contents vary.)

J 3184 Juniors Datapost Dispatch Center   1986? $30-45
Royal Mail Superhaulers (2X), Juniors Royal Mail J39 U.S. Van, J63 Ford Transit Van, J65 Land Rover, J96 Helicopter.

J 3186 Juniors Datapost Gift Set   1986? $20-30
Royal Mail Superhauler, Juniors Royal Mail J63 Ford Transit Van, J 65 Land Rover, J96 Helicopter.

J 3189 Juniors British Telecom Gift Set   1986? $25-35
(2x) British Telecom Superhauler , (3x) Juniors British Telecom US Van.

J 3200 H Hershey's Milk Chocolate Turbo Racing Team Set Apr-87 $12-15
Brown "HERSHEY'S MILK CHOCOLATE" C150 Turbos Chevrolet Camaro Racer "6" & J46 Juniors Firebird "4" Graphics.

J 3214/ 01 Juniors, Parcelforce Set   Sep-90 $20-30
Red Juniors Iveco Box Truck, (2x) Red Juniors Ford Transit Van, (3x) Red Haulers Ford Cargo Box Truck with Trailer Hitch on at least one, Non-Standard Red Haulers Box Trailer, All with "PARCELFORCE" Graphics.

J 3215 Juniors, Transporter Set   Sep-90 $35-45
Red /Silver Auto Transporter, Red /Silver Tandem Auto Transporter Trailer, 6 Random Cars.

| J 3216 | Juniors, City Life Set | Sep-90 | $30-40 |

4 Cars, 3 Trucks, 2 Haulers.

| J 3217 | Juniors, Rally Sport Jumbo Set | Sep-90 | $40-50 |

12 Cars in Rally Trim, 2 Trucks, 2 Haulers.

| J 3219 | Juniors, Airport Set | Sep-90 | $25-30 |

Concord, London Taxi, 2 Trucks, 1 Hauler.

| J 3500 | Coca-Cola 4 pc. Truck Set | Apr-87 | $20-30 |

Red Superhaulers Scammell Articulated Truck, Red Juniors Iveco Box Van, Red Juniors Iveco Beverage Truck with White Beverage Rack Carrying Red Cases, Red Juniors Renault Trafic Van, All Decorated "Coca-Cola" Graphics. (Produced for the U.S. Market.)

| J 3600 | Coca-Cola 4 pc. Racing Set | Apr-87 | $25-35 |

Red Superhaulers Scammell Articulated Truck "TURBO RACING TEAM," Red Juniors Custom Van, Red Juniors Corvette with White Hood "7," White Juniors Firebird with Red Hood "12," All Decorated "Coca-Cola" Graphics. (Produced for the U.S. Market.)

| J 3700 | Juniors - Coca Cola Race Team Car & Transporter | May-87 | $20-30 |

Red Scammell with White 3 Axle Chassis & "Coca-Cola" on Doors, Red Single Deck Trailer with White Chassis, White/ Red Juniors Firebird "Coca-Cola 12" (3 Wheel Types), Tan Plastic Crate with Red "Coca-Cola RACING TEAM" Graphics. (Produced for the U.S. Market.)

| K 5055 | Powerplay Alarm Flashers | May-90 | $5-8 (ea.) |

12 Pack with 5 Different Liveries, Siren and Flashing Lights Activate by Squeezing Rear Wheels. (Manufactured by Maisto in China but with Corgi logo on baseplate. Models are identical to Maisto branded products sold outside European market. Value does not apply to models with Maisto logo on base.)

| Q ? | Weetabix Special Edition Collection | Mar-89 | $50-60 |

Yellow Superhaulers Container Truck, C638 Routemaster Bus, and Juniors Aston-Martin DB6, All Decorated with "Weetabix" Graphics. (Catalog Number Not Known.)

Corgi Toys Ltd. - The Mattel Years 1990 Renumbering - 1995 Management Buy-out

This section contains the variation listing for models produced from the time of the 1990 general renumbering resulting from the Mattel buyout to the 1995 management buyout. All models from this period were made in China. Note that items produced during this time would be considered Mattel products. Corgi was always maintained as a separate entity within the corporation. A bit of cross-over did occur between the former Juniors line and Mattel's Hot Wheels (in both directions), but these will be described individually. Auto-City (Juniors) items later released by Mattel as Hot Wheels Auto-City after the 1995 corporate split are also listed in the next Section.

Note: values shown are in US dollars ($US) for mint-in-mint boxed condition as of July 2002. Subtract 35-40% for mint unboxed, 50-60% for excellent, 60-70% for vg/chipped.

| 90010 | Auto-City (Juniors) - Ford Transit Van, Kremer | 1991 | $1.25-1.50 |

White Body, Red and Blue Stripes on Lower Sides, Porsche Crest and "PORSCHE KREMER RACING" on Upper Sides, No Roof Rack. (Identical to J4B, packages possibly relabeled.)

| 90011 | Auto-City (Juniors) - Ford Transit Van, Royal Mail | 1991 | $1.25-1.50 |

Red Body, Clear Windows, Black Seats and Base, "Royal Mail" Logo with Two Yellow Angled Stripes, 4-Div Wheels. (Identical to J63 except for Updated Graphics.)
a. Corgi Logo on Base.
b. Hot Wheels Logo on Base.

| 90012 | Auto-City (Juniors) - Ford Transit Van, AA | 1991 | $1.25-1.50 |

a. Yellow Body, Blue Tinted Windows, Black Seats and Base, Black Outlined White Stripe and "AA Service" on Sides, Yellow Lightbar toward Rear on Roof, 4-Div Wheels. (Identical to J51 except for Window Color.)
b. Yellow Body, Clear Windows, Black Seats and Base, Black Outlined White Stripe and "AA Service" on Sides, No Lightbar on Roof, 4-Div Wheels. (May be from Set.)
c. Yellow Body with Black Lower Sides, Blue Tinted or Smoked Windows, Black Seats and Base, Black Checkered Area Between Colors, Black Rectangle with Yellow "AA" on Sides and Hood, Yellow Lightbar toward Rear on Roof, 4-Div Wheels. (1994)

| 90013 | Auto-City (Juniors) - Ford Transit Van, Police | Jan-91 | $1.25-1.50 |

a. White Body w/ Yellow Lower Sides, Black Checkered Pattern Dividing Colors, Dark Blue Tinted Windows, Opaque Blue Roof Light, Black "POLICE" & Shield on Sides, "POLICE" on Hood, Red Dot and Black "99" on Roof, 4-Div. Wheels, Corgi Logo on Base.
b. White Body w/ Yellow Lower Sides, Black Checkered Pattern Dividing Colors, Dark Blue Tinted Windows, No Roof Light, Black "POLICE" & Shield on Sides, "POLICE" on Hood, Plain White Roof, 4-Div. Wheels, Corgi Logo on Base. (1994)
c. White Body w/ Yellow Lower Sides, Black Checkered Pattern Dividing Colors, Dark Blue Tinted Windows, No Roof Light, Black "POLICE" & Shield on Sides, "POLICE" on Hood, Plain White Roof, 4-Div. Wheels, Hot Wheels Logo on Base. (1995)

| 90015 | Auto-City (Juniors) - Ford Transit Van, RAC | Jan-91 | $1.25-1.50 |

White Body, RAC Graphics, Other Details Not Known.

| 90018 | Auto-City (Juniors) - Ford Transit Van, Het Belgische Rode Kruis | Mar-91 | $3-5 |

White Body, Tinted Windows, Silver Fake Side Windows, Red Side Stripe and Red Cross, Red "HET BELGISCH RODE KRUIS" and Reversed "AMBULANCE" Text, Corgi Logo on Base. (Produced for the Belgian market.)

| 90020 | Auto-City (Juniors) – Ford Transit Van, British Gas | 1991 | $1.25-1.50 |

Blue / White Body, Clear Windows, Black Interior and Base, Blue "Gas" and White "British Gas" on Sides, 4-Div Wheels, Corgi Logo on Base.

900XX	Auto-City (Juniors) – Ford Transit Van, (from sets)	1991-95	
	Standard Releases		$1.25-1.50
	European Regional Releases		$3-5

Various Ford Transit vans only available in sets listed here for cross-reference purposes. Set numbers as listed below:
a. Black Body, Red Lower Side Stripe, Red "TEXACO" and Logo, White "RACE SUPPORT" on Sides. (From set 92400.)
b. Red Body, "PARCEL FORCE" Graphics. (From set 92610 and others.)
c. Yellow Body, Red "WOLF" Logo on Front and Sides. (From set 93115.)
d. White Body, Yellow Side Stripe with Black "Lufthansa" Graphics. (From set 93415.)
e. Red Body, Black Roof Rack, Black Side Stripe with Black Horse behind Doors, Yellow "Ferrari" and other Graphics, Corgi Logo on Base. (From set 93425 and others.)
f. Red Body, No Roof Rack, Black Side Stripe with Black Horse behind Doors, Yellow "Ferrari" and other Graphics, Corgi Logo on Base. (From set 93151 and others.)
g. Red Body, No Roof Rack, Black Side Stripe with Black Horse behind Doors, Yellow "Ferrari" and other Graphics, Hot Wheels Logo on Base. (From set 93151 and others.)
h. Pale Gray and Navy Blue Body with Red Divider Stripe, "BRITISH AIRWAYS" Graphics. (From Set 93???. Actual number not known.)
i. White Upper and Green Lower Body, Yellow Lightbar toward Rear of Roof, "EDDIE STOWBART LTD." Graphics. (From set 91356.)
j. Red Body, White Diagonal Side Stripes with White "FIRE CHIEF" on Sides, Gold Crest Graphics. (From sets and sold individually.)
k. Dark Blue Body, White Side Stripe with "POLIISI" Graphics. (Produced for the Finnish market. May be from later period with J4-xx number.)
l. Red Body, Silver(?) Side Stripe with Silver Side Window Panel, White "ALARM" on Sides, White Panel on Front. (Produced for Dutch market. May be from earlier era.)

| 90030 | Auto-City (Juniors) - ERF Fire Engine | 1991 | $1.25-1.50 |

a. Red Body w/ Silver Sides, White "FIRE SERVICE 999" on Sides over Windows, Black Plastic Base, Blue Tinted Windows, Yellow Removable Ladder, 8-Div. Wheels.
b. Red Body w/ Silver Sides, White "FIRE" on Sides over Windows, Black Plastic Base, Blue Tinted Windows, Yellow Removable Ladder, 8-Div. Wheels.
c. Red Body w/ Silver Sides with Checkered Pattern, White "FIRE SERVICE 999" on Sides over Windows, Black Plastic Base, Blue Tinted Windows, White Removable Ladder, 8-Div. Wheels.

| 90035 | Auto-City (Juniors) - Simon Snorkel, Fire | 1991 | $1.25-1.50 |

a. Red Body w/ White Cab Roof, Silver Deck & Trim, Yellow Plastic Base & Boom, Blue Tinted Windows, Black "FIRE DEPT 07" on Cab Roof, Black "SIMON SNORKEL" on Boom, 4-Div. Wheels.

b. Red Body w/ White Cab Roof, Silver Deck & Trim, Gray Plastic Base & Boom, Blue Tinted Windows, Black "FIRE DEPT" on Cab Roof, 4-Div. Wheels. (1992)

90036? Auto-City (Juniors) - Simon Snorkel, Utility Service   1994, 1995 $1.25-1.50
Orange Body w/ Green Roof & Deck, Green Plastic Base & Boom, Blue Tinted Windows, White "S-24" on Roof and Sides, 4-Div. Wheels.
a. Corgi Logo on Base.
b. Hot Wheels Logo on Base.

90040   Auto-City (Juniors) - Iveco Container Truck, Wispa   Jan-91 $1.25-1.50
Dark Blue Cab and Chassis, Dark Blue Box with "Cadbury's Wispa" Graphics, Black Plastic Base & Interior, Clear Windows, 8-Div. Wheels.

90041   Auto-City (Juniors) - Iveco Container Truck, Royal Mail Parcel Force   1991 $1.25-1.50
Red Cab/ Chassis, Red Box with "PARCEL FORCE" and "Royal Mail" Graphics, Black Plastic Base & Interior, Clear Windows, 8-Div. Wheels.

90042   Auto-City (Juniors) - Iveco Container Truck, Mars1992 $1.25-1.50
Dark Brown Cab/ Chassis, Dark Brown Box w/ "Mars" Labels, Black Plastic Base & Interior, Clear Windows, 8-Div. Wheels.
a. Corgi Logo on Base.
b. Hot Wheels Logo on Base.

90044   Auto-City (Juniors) - Iveco Container Truck, The Sweater Shop   Dec-93 $3-5
White Cab, Chassis and Box, Black interior, Clear Windows, Black "THE SWEATER SHOP ENGLAND-SCOTLAND-WALES" Tampo on Sides, 8-Div Wheels. (Promotional model for The Sweater Shop.)

90045   Auto-City (Juniors) - Iveco Soda Truck, Pepsi   1994? $1.25-1.50
Red Cab and Chassis, White open body with Blue Bottle Load, "PEPSI" Logo on Top Panel. (Same as earlier J13/01.)

9004X   Auto-City (Juniors) – Iveco Container Truck, Lufthansa   1993? $3-5
White Cab and Chassis, Clear Windows, Black Interior, White Box Body with Yellow Stripe and Black "Lufthansa" Graphics. (From Set 93415.)

90050   Auto-City (Juniors) - Earth Mover   1992 $1.25-1.50
Yellow Body, Dark Gray to Black Scoop & Chassis, Hot Wheels Heavyweights Style Wheels with Yellow Centers. (Former E48B Shovel Loader Casting.)

90065a Auto-City (Juniors) - Iveco Tanker Truck, Shell Jan-91 $1.25-1.50
Yellow/ White Cab/ Chassis, Gray Tank w/ "Shell" & Stripes, Black Plastic Chassis & Interior, Clear Windows, 8-Div. Wheels.

90065b Auto-City (Juniors) - Iveco Tanker Truck, BP   1992 $1.25-1.50
Green Cab/ Chassis, White Tank w/ "BP" in Sash Style Green Area on Sides, Black Plastic Chassis & Interior, Clear Windows, 4-Div. Wheels. (Similar to J12 except for Tank Graphics.)
a. Corgi Logo on Base.
b. Hot Wheels Logo on Base.

90076   Auto-City (Juniors) - BMW 325i (M3)   Jan-91 $1.25-1.50
a. White Body with Thin Black Side Stripe, Black Interior, 8-Div. Wheels, No Graphics.
b. Metallic Blue Body.

90085   Auto-City (Juniors) - London Taxi, Black   1991 $1.25-1.50
Black Body, Plated Base, Red Interior, No Logo on Doors. (Continuation of J17/01.)

90086   Auto-City (Juniors) - London Taxi, Cutty Sark   May-92 $3-5
Yellow Body w/ Black Roof, Plated Base, Red Interior, "Cutty Sark Scots Whisky" Logo on Hood & Doors, 4-Div. Wheels.

90089   Auto-City (Juniors) - London Taxi, Hamley's   Jul-94 $3-5
Black Body, Plated Base, Red Interior, Gold "Hamley's" Logo on Doors, 4div Wheels.

90100   Auto-City (Juniors) – Matra Rancho   1990 $1.25-1.50
Yellow Body, White Interior, Red "m" on Hood with Black Dot, Black Base, 8div Wheels.

901101? Auto-City (Juniors) – Matra Rancho   1990 $1.25-1.50
Black Body, ??? Interior, Black Base, 8div Wheels.

90110   Auto-City (Juniors) - London Bus, Ev. Standard 1991? $1.25-1.50
Red Body, Opaque Black Windows, "The LONDON STANDARD" Side Panels, 8div Wheels. (Identical to J20/02 except for Wheel Type.)
a. Corgi Logo on Base.
b. Hot Wheels Logo on Base.

90111   Auto-City (Juniors) - London Bus, Hamley's   Jul-94 $3-5
Red Body, Opaque Black Windows, "Hamley's" Side Panels, Destination End Panels, 8div Wheels.

90125   Auto-City (Juniors) - Ford Transit Wrecker - Rescue1991 $1.25-1.50
White Body, Blue Outlined Red Lower Body Stripes, Blue "RESCUE" with "100" Crest on Sides, Red Boom and Lightbar, Black Hook, 8 Div Wheels.

90126   Auto-City (Juniors) - Ford Transit Wrecker - Kremer1991 $1.25-1.50
White Body, Red / Blue Lower Body Stripes, Blue "RACE SUPPORT" with Full Color Porsche Crest on Sides, Red Boom and Lightbar, 8 Div Wheels. (Similar decoration to J4B / 90010, also used in sets.)

90127   Auto-City (Juniors) - Ford Transit Wrecker   1991 $1.25-1.50
a. Yellow Body, Black Outlined White Stripe on Sides, "AA Relay" on Hood, "AA Service" on Sides, Yellow Boom & Lightbar, Black Hook, Black Plastic Base, Blue Tinted Windows, 4-Div. Or 8 Div. Wheels. (Identical to J24/03 except for window color.)
b. Green Body w/ White Lower Sides & Yellow Stripe, "BP" Logos on Hood & Behind Doors, Yellow Boom & Lightbar, Black Hook, Black Plastic Base with Corgi Logo, Clear Windows, 8-Div. Wheels. (1994)
c. Green Body w/ White Lower Sides & Yellow Stripe, "BP" Logos on Hood & Behind Doors, Yellow Boom & Lightbar, Black Hook, Black Plastic Base with Hot Wheels Logo, Clear Windows, 8-Div. Wheels. (1995)

9012X   Auto-City (Juniors) - Ford Transit Wrecker - Shell1993? $1.25-1.50
White Body, Red / Yellow Lower Body Stripes, "Shell" Graphics, Yellow Boom and Lightbar, Black Hook, 8 Div Wheels. (From Shell racing sets.)
a. Corgi Logo on Base.
b. Hot Wheels Logo on Base.

90160   Auto-City (Juniors) - Ford Sierra   Jan-91 $1.25-1.50
a. Tasman Blue Body (A metallic dark blue color believed to be an actual Ford color.)
b. Red Body (1992)

9016X   Auto-City (Juniors) - Ford Sierra, Shell   1994, 1995 $1.25-1.50
White Body with Yellow Chassis and Red Interior, Clear Windows, "Shell 11 GEMINI" Graphics. (From Shell Racing sets.)
a. Corgi Logo on Base.
b. Hot Wheels Logo on Base.

90165? Auto-City (Juniors) - Ford Sierra, Police   1993? $1.25-1.50
White Body with Yellow Lower Sides and Black Checkered Pattern, Opaque Black Windows, "POLICE" Graphics. (From Set 93414.)

90190   Auto-City (Juniors) - Ferrari Testarossa   1992 $1.25-1.50
a. Yellow Body, Black Interior & Base, Red / Black Stripes on Hood & Roof, Ferrari Logo on Hood, Clear Windows, 4div Wheels.
b. White Body, Black Interior & Base, Red / Black Stripes on Hood & Roof, Ferrari Logo on Hood, Clear Windows, 4div Wheels.
c. Red Body, Black Interior & Base, Red / Black Stripes on Hood Only, Black Ferrari Horse and White "Ferrari" on Hood, Clear Windows, 4div Wheels.
d. Red Body, Black Interior & Base, Black Ferrari Horse on Hood only, Clear Windows, 4div Wheels.
e. Red Body, Black Interior & Base, No Graphics, Clear Windows, 4div Wheels.

90200   Auto-City (Juniors) – Chevrolet Corvette   1991 $1.25-1.50
Black Body, Clear Windows, Red Interior, Red / Yellow Flames on Hood, "Flame" Script on Doors. (Identical to J45/ 01.)

9020X   Auto-City (Juniors) – Chevrolet Corvette   1991? $1.25-1.50
Black Body, Clear Windows, ??? Interior, Red "TEXACO" Script on Doors. (No individual number assigned. From set 92400.)

90215   Auto City (Juniors) – F1 Racing Car   1991 $1.25-1.50
White and Green Body, Black Driver, 6-spoke Wheels. (This is **not** the HW Thunderstreak, which is 90317.)
a. Car with "FUJIFILM 2" Graphics.
b. Car with "FUJIFILM 5" Graphics. (Usually found in sets where other car is "2".)

9021X   Auto City (Juniors) – F1 Racing Car   1991? $1.25-1.50
Red Body, "Ferrari" Graphics. (From set 93151 and others.)
a. Corgi Logo on Base.
b. Hot Wheels Logo on Base.

90260   Auto-City (Juniors) - Custom Van, Team Racing 15 (No Logo)   1994? $1.25-1.50
White Body w/ Blue Sides, Gray Plastic Base, Smoked Windows, "15" & "TEAM RACING" Logos, 8-Div. Wheels. (Identical Graphics to J61/02, which had a Diecast Baseplate.)

9026X   Auto-City (Juniors) - Custom Van, From Sets   1992?
Standard Releases $1.25-1.50
Promotional and European Regional Releases $3-5
a. Red and Yellow Body, Gray Plastic Base, Smoked Windows, Green Stripe, Yellow "Ferrari" and Black Ferrari Logo. (From set 93151.)

b. Dark Purple Body, Gray Plastic Base, Smoked Windows, Gold and White Flowing Checkered Flag Graphic with Red "'92" and Gold "AUTOSPORT" Text. (From set 93036.)

c. Red and Black Body, Plated Diecast Base, Smoked Windows, White Stripe, White "30 TEAM RACING" Graphics. (From unknown set.)

d. Blue Body with White Nose Spoiler and Side Panel, Gray Plastic Base, Smoked Windows, 8-Div. Wheels, Large "Hot Wheels Team Racing" Side Graphics, Corgi Logo on Base. (From set 93417.)

e. Blue Body with White Nose Spoiler and Side Panel, Gray Plastic Base, Smoked Windows, 8-Div. Wheels, Large "Hot Wheels Team Racing" Side Graphics, Hot Wheels Logo on Base. (From set 93417.)

f. Black Body with White Nose Spoiler and Side Panel, Gray Plastic Base, Smoked Windows, 8-Div. Wheels, Large "Hot Wheels Team Racing" Side Graphics, Hot Wheels Logo on Base. (From later Hot Wheels Sto-n-Go set. Same graphics used.)

g. Red Body, Gray Plastic Base, Smoked Windows, White "Van Toy Convention Race Winner" Side Graphics. (Promotional model. Other details not known.)

h. White Body with Blue Wheel Arches, Gray Plastic Base, Smoked Windows, Colorful Side Graphics with Red / White / Blue Outline of the USA and Convention Text. (Promotional model. Other details not known.)

90270   Auto-City (Juniors) - Formula 1 Ferrari   1994, 1995 $1.25-1.50
Red Body, Black Diecast Base, Black Plastic Driver, Ferrari Logo, "28," "FIAT," "PIONEER," & "WEBER" Logos, 5-Spoke Wheels.
a. Corgi Logo on Base.
b. Hot Wheels Logo on Base.

90310   Auto City (Juniors) – Jeep, U. S. Army   1993? $1.25-1.50
Olive Green Body, Black Plastic Base, Olive Plastic Cover, White Interior and Push Bumper, Large Tires with Silver 4-Lug Pattern, White Star and "USA" Graphics.

90317   Auto-City (Juniors) - Fuji Racing Car   Aug-92
**   Hot Wheels Thunderstreak Casting $30-60**
**   Corgi F1 Casting $1.25-1.50**
Green and White Body, Green Driver, Hot Wheels Pro Circuit Wheels, "FUJI FILM 2" Graphics. (Promotional for Fuji. The model described is the Hot Wheels Thunderstreak repackaged as a Corgi for a Fuji promotion in Europe. Note: Some models released under this number *may* use the Corgi F1 Casting as per 90215 rather than the Hot Wheels Thunderstreak casting. Check carefully due to the great difference in value.)

90320   Auto-City (Juniors) - Iveco Garbage Truck, Orange1992 $1.25-1.50
a. Yellow Cab/ Chassis, Gray Garbage Body, Black Plastic Chassis and Interior, White "CITY SANITATION" and Recycle Symbols on Body Sides, Blue Tinted Windows, 8-Div. Wheels, Corgi Logo on Base.
b. Orange Cab/ Chassis w/ Green Roof, Orange Garbage Body, Black Plastic Chassis & Interior, White "A-10" on Cab Roof, Recycle Symbols on Body Sides, Clear Windows, 8-Div. Wheels, Corgi Logo on Base.
c. Orange Cab/ Chassis w/ Green Roof, Orange Garbage Body, Black Plastic Chassis & Interior, White "A-10" on Cab Roof, Recycle Symbols on Body Sides, Clear Windows, 8-Div. Wheels, Hot Wheels Logo on Base.

90360   Auto-City (Juniors) - US Custom Van   Jan-91 $1.25-1.50
Data not available at time of publication.

90361   Auto-City (Juniors) - US Custom Van, Fuji FilmAug-92 $2-4
Green / White Body with Red Divider Stripe, Red "FUJI" Logos and White "RACING TEAM FUJI FILM" Text, Smoked Windows, Gray Plastic Base. (Promotional for Fuji.)

90371   Auto-City (Juniors) - Land Rover, HM CoastguardJan-91 $1.25-1.50
Data not available at time of publication.

9037?   Auto-City (Juniors) – Land Rover, BP Safari Rally1991? $1.25-1.50
White Body, Yellow, Blue and Black Side Stripes with "BP" Shield and Black "65 SAFARI RALLY" Graphics, 4div Wheels.

9037?   Auto-City (Juniors) – Land Rover, Civilian   1991? $1.25-1.50
Dark Metallic Blue-Green Body with White Roof, No Graphics, 4div Wheels.

90374   Auto-City (Juniors) - Land Rover, Emergency Fire1991 $1.25-1.50
Red Body with Closed Rear Quarter Windows, China Base, White Diagonal Stripes on Sides with "EMERGENCY FIRE" Graphics. (Similar to J97 which reads "FIRE SALVAGE.")

9037X   Auto-City (Juniors) - Land Rover, Royal Mail   1991 $1.25-1.50
Red Body, Yellow "Royal Mail" Graphics. (From Royal Mail Dispatch Set. Similar to J65.)

9037X   Auto-City (Juniors) - Land Rover, AA   1991 $1.25-1.50
Yellow Body, Black Outlined White Body Stripe, Black "AA Service" Graphics. (Similar to J64.)

90390   Auto City (Juniors) - Mercedes-Benz Ambulance   1992 $1.25-1.50
a. White Body, Red Stripe Along Sides and Along Roof Sides, Blue Tinted Windows, Black Base, Red Cross Low on Front Doors, 8-Div. Wheels, Corgi Logo on Base.

b. White Body w/ Orange Sash over Hood, Sides & up to Top Rear Corners, Blue Tinted Windows, Black Base, Blue "AMBULANCE DIAL 999" and Medical Symbols, 8-Div. Wheels, Corgi Logo on Base.

c. White Body w/ Orange Sash over Hood, Sides & up to Top Rear Corners, Blue Tinted Windows, Black Base, Blue "AMBULANCE DIAL 999" and Medical Symbols, 8-Div. Wheels, Hot Wheels Logo on Base.

90393   Auto-City (Juniors) - Jaguar XJ40, Police   1991? $1.25-1.50
White Body, Yellow Side Stripe w/ Black Upper & Lower Outline, Clear Windows, Low Opaque Dark Blue Roof Light, Black "POLICE" on Hood & Doors, Black Seats, 4-Div. Wheels.(Weetabix Premium, made in China. Box Marked 90393-9994)

90420   Auto City (Juniors) - Buick Police   1994, 1995 $1.25-1.50
Black/ White Body, Opaque Blue Lightbar, Black Plastic Base, Vacuum Plated Interior & Bumpers, Clear Windows, Orange Dot w/ Black "P.D.9" & "POLICE" on Roof, Black "POLICE" & Shield on Doors, Silver "POLICE" & "911" on Rear, Silver Shield on Hood, 8-Div. Wheels.
a. Corgi Logo on Base.
b. Hot Wheels Logo on Base.

90430   Auto-City (Juniors) - Volvo 760   Jan-91 $1.25-1.50
Dark Green Body

90440   Auto-City (Juniors) - Porsche 935   1992 $1.25-1.50
a. Red Body, Black Interior, Clear Windows, Black Plastic Base, White Stripe Graphics, Black "33" on Hood and Doors, 4-Div. Wheels.
b. White Body, Vacuum Plated Interior, Clear Windows, Black Plastic Base, Red & Yellow Stripe Graphics, Porsche Logo on Hood, 4-Div. Wheels.
c. Orange Body, Vacuum Plated Interior, Clear Windows, Black Plastic Base, Deep Blue/ White Graphics, "PORSCHE" on Hood, "935" on Doors, 4-Div. Wheels.
d. Red/ Black Body, Other Details Not Known.

90460   Auto-City (Juniors) -
**   Mercedes-Benz 2.3/16 Racer   Jan-91 $1.25-1.50**
Light Blue Body, Clear Windows, Black Interior, 4-div. Wheels, "Mobil" on Hood, Yellow Side Stripe and "55" Graphics.

90470   Auto-City (Juniors) - Jaguar XJ40, Police   1991 $1.25-1.50
a. White Body, Dark windows, Opaque Blue Lightbar on Roof, Yellow Side Stripe with Black Outlining, Black "POLICE" on Hood and Doors, 4-Div. Wheels.
b. White Body w/ Yellow Lower Sides, Black Checkered Pattern Dividing Colors, Dark Blue Tinted Windows, Opaque Blue Roof Light, Black "POLICE" & Shield on Hood, "POLICE" on Trunk Lid, 4-Div. Wheels.

90471   Auto-City (Juniors) - Jaguar XJ40, Gold   Jan-91 $1.25-1.50
Metallic Gold Body, 4-div Wheels.

90500   Auto City (Juniors) - Police Helicopter   1992 $1.25-1.50
a. White Body, Dark Blue Tinted Windows, White "POLICE" in Blue Rectangle on Sides, Black Rotors and Skis.
b. White Body w/ Yellow Lower Sides, Black Checkered Pattern Dividing Colors, Dark Blue Tinted Windows, Black "POLICE" & Shield on Sides, Red Dot and Black "42" on Tail, Yellow Rotors and Skis.

90505   Auto City (Juniors) - Rescue Helicopter   1994, 1995 $1.25-1.50
Turquoise/ White Body w/ "R" Logo, Clear Windows, Yellow Plastic Base & Blades. (Base still has 007 in recessed area from earlier James Bond Drax Helicopter usage.)
a. Corgi Logo on Base.
b. Hot Wheels Logo on Base.

9050X   Auto-City (Juniors) – Lufthansa Helicopter   1993? $3-5
a. White Body, Yellow Rotors and Skis, Blue Tinted Windows, Yellow Stripe with Black "Lufthansa" Graphics. (From set 93415.)
b. Red Body, Black Rotors and Skis, Clear Windows, White Checkered Stripe with "FIRE CHIEF" Graphics. (From sets and individually.)
c. White Body, Orange Rotors and Skis, Blue Tinted Windows, Orange Stripe with Blue "AMBULANCE" Graphics. (From set 93414.)

90520   Auto-City (Juniors) – '57 T-Bird   1991 $1.25-1.50
Black Body and Interior, Clear Windshield, 8-Div Wheels.

90540   Auto-City (Juniors) - Ford Mustang   Jan-91 $1.25-1.50
Light Blue Body, Black Base and Interior, Black and White Stripes on Hood and Sides, Black "77" on Roof, Clear Windows, 8div Wheels. (Same as late J36-A.)

90541   Auto-City (Juniors) - Ford Mustang   1991 $1.25-1.50
White Body, Black Base and Interior, Thin Red Stripe on Hood, Roof and Sides, Black "7" on Roof, Clear Windows, 8div Wheels.

90550   Auto-City (Juniors) - BMW 850csi   Apr-91
**   Standard Releases $1.25-1.50**
**   European Regional Releases $3-5**
a. Gold Body, Black Interior, Black Plastic Base, 4-Div. Wheels.

b. Black Body with Small BMW Logo on Hood, Black Interior, Black Plastic Base, 4-Div. Wheels.

c. White Body with Small BMW Logo on Hood, Black Interior, Black Plastic Base, 4-Div. Wheels. (1994?)

d. White Body with Green Hood and Trunk Lid, Green Side Stripe, White "POLIZEI" Graphics, Opaque Blue Lightbar on Roof, "878" on Roof, Black Interior, Black Plastic Base, 4-Div. Wheels. (Found in German Police Set 93416.)

90560   Auto-City (Juniors) - Ferrari 348TB, Red   Apr-91 $1.25-1.50
Red Body w/ Crest on Hood, Black Plastic Base, Tan Seats, Clear Windows, 4-Div. Wheels.

9056X   Auto-City (Juniors) - Ferrari 348TB,
Red with Tampo   1991? $1.25-1.50
Red Body, Black Plastic Base, Black Seats, Clear Windows, 4-Div. Wheels, Ferrari Logo and Yellow Checkered Flag Graphics. (From set 93151.)

90570a   Auto-City (Juniors) - Mercedes-Benz
500SL Conv., Pink   Jan-91 $1.25-1.50
Day-Glow Pink Body, Crest on Hood, Black Pinstripe on Sides, Black Diecast Base, Gray Interior, Clear Windshield w/ Pink Edge Trim, 4-Div. Wheels.

90570b   Auto-City (Juniors) - Mercedes-Benz
500SL Coupe   1992 $1.25-1.50
a. Dark Blue Body and Roof, Silver Grill, Black Diecast Base, Gray Interior, Clear Windows, 4-Div. Wheels.
b. Silver Body with Black Roof, Silver Grill, Black Diecast Base, Gray Interior, Clear Windows, 4-Div. Wheels.

90571   Auto-City (Juniors) - Mercedes-Benz
500SL Conv.   1994, 1995 $1.25-1.50
Day-Glow Yellow Body, Silver Crest on Hood, Black Pinstripe on Sides, Black Diecast Base, Gray Interior, Clear Windshield w/ Black Edge Trim, 4-Div. Wheels.
a. Corgi Logo on Base.
b. Hot Wheels Logo on Base.

90580   Auto-City (Juniors) - Jaguar XJR9,
Works Team   Jan-91 $1.25-1.50
a. Metallic Purple Body, Blue Rear Spoiler, Black Plastic Base & Interior, Clear Windows, White "6 JAGUAR" & Gold Trim, 8-Div. Wheels.
b. White Body, White Rear Spoiler, Black Plastic Base & Interior, Clear Windows, Purple Side and Nose Graphics with "52" and "Jaguar" Lettering, 8-Div. Wheels.

90800   Auto-City (Juniors) - Emergency Set, 24 pcs   Jan-91 $25-30
Data not available at time of publication.

90820   Auto-City (Juniors) - Race Rally Set, 24 pcs   Jan-91 $25-30
Data not available at time of publication.

90840   Auto-City (Juniors) - City Scene Set, 24 pcs   Jan-91 $25-30
Data not available at time of publication.

90860   Juniors Great Britain Assortment   1991   ???
48 British Vehicles (mainly supplied to Tourist Shops.)

90880   Auto-City (Juniors) - USA Set, 24 pcs   Jan-91 $25-30
Data not available at time of publication.

90930   Auto-City (Juniors) "Best Sellers" Assortment 1992?   ???
144 Vehicle Assortment. (6 Each of 24 Models.)

90940   Themed Twin Pack Assortment,
(6 Variants)   1994, 1995 $3-5
Two related vehicles plus accessories grouped around Police, Fire, Street Maintenance, Rescue, Race and City themes.
a. Corgi Logo on Bases.
b. Mixed Hot Wheels and Corgi Logos on Bases
c. Hot Wheels Logo on Bases.

90941   Themed Triple Pack Assortment, (4 Variants) Aug-94 $5-8
Data not available at time of publication.

90942   Juniors – 20 Piece set – Asda   Sep-94 $25-35
Twenty Juniors with accessories, other details not known. Produced for Asda Stores.

91250   Auto-City (Juniors) – Police 3-piece Set   1991? $5-8
Jaguar XJ40, Helicopter, and Transit Van all Decorated Yellow / White with Black Checker and "POLICE" Graphics, Traffic Cones, Stop Sign and Standing Police Officer Figure.

91352   Auto-City (Juniors) - Ford Transit Van - Eddie   1994? $2-3
Stobart Ltd.
Green and White Body, Yellow Tinted Lightbar on Roof toward Rear, "EDDIE STOBART LTD." and "ROADSIDE MAINTENANCE" Graphics, Corgi Logo on Base. (Promotional model for Eddie Stobart Ltd.)

92207a   Junior Police Squad Twin Set   1991? $3-5

Set Contains 90420 Buick Police Car and 93236 SWAT Van on Common Card.

92207b   Junior Police Squad Twin Set   1991? $3-5
Set Contains 90011 Royal Mail Ford Transit and 90041 Royal Mail Iveco Truck on Common Card.

92270   Junior GB Twin Set   1991 $3-5
Identical to J160/01 including Packaging. Supplied to Shops in Packs of 24.

92275   Junior GB Triple Set   1991 $3-5
Identical to J2885/01 including Packaging except for added Telephone Booth. Supplied to Shops in Packs of 12.

92325   Junior Tourist Teddy Set   1991 $5-8
(Identical to J2885/01 except for Packaging.) Supplied to Shops in Packs of 12.

92400   Auto-City (Juniors) - Texaco Race Set   1991? $15-18
Black "Juniors" Corvette, Black "Juniors" Ford Transit Van, Black "Haulers" Kenworth Box Truck, Black "Haulers" Kenworth Flatbed Truck, all with "Texaco" Graphics. Set Includes Signs and Figure.

92401   Auto-City Themed Sets Assortment   1992   N/A
Assortment of 12 Themed Sets (3 each of 4 themes) Not Otherwise Numbered. Individual Sets Listed Below.

92401a   Auto-City Race Set   1992 $15-18
"Juniors" 90580 Jaguar XJR9, Non-Standard White "Juniors" Ford Transit Wrecker "Shell RACE SUPPORT" with Yellow Boom, Non-Standard White/ Yellow/ Gray Haulers Ford Cargo "Shell" Tanker, Non-Standard Metallic Magenta Haulers Kenworth Flatbed Truck with "Jaguar" on Deck Top, Figure and Accessories.

92401b   Auto-City Rescue Set   1992 $15-18
"Juniors" 90013 Ford Transit Police Van, "Juniors" 90500 Police Helicopter, Non-Standard "Juniors" Black/ Yellow Matra Rancho with Yellow "CG" Logo on Hood, Black Boat Trailer with Black/ Yellow Pontoon Boat, Non-Standard White/ Yellow Haulers Ford Cargo Flatbed Truck with "POLICE 733" on Deck Top, Figure and Accessories.

92401c   Auto-City Fire Set   1992 $15-18
"Juniors" 90390 Mercedes Ambulance, Non-Standard Red/ White "Juniors" Mercedes 300TD Wagon "FIRE CHIEF" with Blue Lightbar, Non-Standard Red Haulers Ford Cargo Flatbed Truck with "FIRE SERVICE" on Cab, Haulers 91490 MAN Fire Engine, Figure and Accessories.

92401d   Auto-City Construction Set   1992 $15-18
"Juniors" 90050 Earth Mover (former E48B) with Hot Wheels "Workhorses" Style Wheels, Non-Standard Yellow/ Dark Gray "Juniors" Excavator (former E77B) with Dark Gray Boom, Non-Standard White/ Black Haulers Ford Cargo Flatbed Truck, Haulers 91470 Kenworth Crane Truck with Crate, Figure and Accessories.

92430   Auto-City (Juniors) – Parcel Force Dispatch Set 1991 $10-12
Contains Auto-City Ford Transit Van, (2x) Ford Cargo Container Truck, and Auto-City Land Rover 110, all with "PARCEL FORCE" Graphics.

92445   Auto-City (Juniors) - City Set   Aug-91 $10-12
Six Standard Auto-City Vehicles with Plastic Fuel Pumps and Signs.

92460   Auto-City (Juniors) - Race Set   Aug-91 $10-12
Six Standard Race Related Auto-City Vehicles with Plastic Power Launcher.

92475   Auto-City (Juniors) - Emergency Set   Aug-91 $10-12
Six Auto-City (Juniors) Vehicles including 90470 Jaguar XJ40 Police, 90390 Mercedes Ambulance, 90030 ERF Fire Tender, 90035 Fire Snorkel, 90013 Blue Transit Police Van and 90127 Yellow AA Transit Wrecker, Power Launcher, Traffic Cones and Road Signs.

92490   Juniors 6 pc. GB Set   1991 $15-18
Contains 90470 Jaguar Police, 90085 London Taxi, 90030 Fire Engine, 90110 London Bus, 90011 Royal Mail Van, 90012 AA Service Van.

92565   Tourist Bumper Set   1991 $15-18
Contains 90470 Jaguar Police, 90085 London Taxi, 90030 Fire Engine, 91760 Routemaster Bus, Telephone Booth, Two Figures.

92610   Auto-City (Juniors) - Parcelforce Set   Aug-91 $10-12
Contains (2x) Ford Transit Van, (2x) Ford Cargo Container Truck, and Volvo or Seddon Semi, all with "PARCEL FORCE" Graphics.

92623   Auto-City (Juniors) – Carry Car and Driver   1994? $10-15
Yellow and Blue Carry Case in F1 Racer Shape, Molded Race Driver Head, Can Carry up to Six Vehicles, "AUTO-CITY Team Racing" and "5" Graphics. (Vehicles not included.)

92625   Auto-City (Juniors) - Transporter Set   Aug-91 $10-12
Volvo Globetrotter with Matching Transporter Trailer and Tandem Trailer, 90550 BMW, 90560 Ferrari, 90570 Mercedes, 90440 Porsche, Figures and Accessories. (Cars may vary.)
a. Dark Blue / White Truck and Trailer.
b. Red / White Truck and Trailer.

c. Red / Silver Truck and Trailer.

92630   Auto-City (Juniors) – Jaguar Racing Team Set   1991? $10-12
Two 90580 Jaguar XJR9 Team Works Racers in Standard Colors and Graphics, Non-standard Auto-City Ford Cargo Flatbed Truck with Matching Flatbed Trailer in Team Jaguar Purple with White Flatbed Bodies, Jaguar Logo on Both Flatbed Decks.

93010   Auto-City Auto Tuning Centre   1992 $20-30
Molded Garage Base with Electronic Lights and Engine Sound, Car Launching Mechanism.

93015   Auto-City Bumper Construction Set   1992 $20-30
Non-Standard Large Plastic Crane, Non-Standard Yellow/ White/ Black Volvo Globetrotter with Yellow Single Deck Transporter Trailer, "Juniors" 90050 Earth Mover (former E48B) with Hot Wheels "Workhorses" Style Wheels, Non-Standard Yellow/ Dark Gray "Juniors" Excavator (former E77B) with Dark Gray Boom, Non-Standard White/ Black Haulers Ford Cargo Flatbed Truck, Figures and Accessories.

93016   Auto-City Bumper Race Set   1992 $20-30
Non-Standard Kenworth Race Transporter with White Cab and Green/ White Trailer with "FUJI FILM RACING TEAM" Graphics, Two Non-Standard "Juniors" Green/ White F1 Racers "FUJIFILM 2" and "FUJIFILM 5" with Green Drivers, Non-Standard Green/ White "Juniors" Custom Van "FUJIFILM RACING TEAM" (former E91B), Non-Standard "Juniors" Green/ White Ford Transit Wrecker "FUJIFILM RACING TEAM" with Red Boom, Figures and Accessories.

93017   Auto-City Bumper Emergency Set   1992 $30-40
"Juniors" 90390 Mercedes Ambulance, "Juniors" 90470 Jaguar XJ40 "POLICE" with Blue Lightbar, "Juniors" 90500 Police Helicopter with Yellow Rotors and Skis, Non-Standard "Juniors" Black/ Yellow Matra Rancho with Yellow "CG" Logo on Hood, Black Boat Trailer with Black/ Yellow Pontoon Boat, Non-Standard White "Juniors" Ford Transit Wrecker with Blue Lightbar and Boom, Non-Standard Red Haulers Ford Cargo Flatbed Truck with "FIRE SERVICE" on Cab, Haulers 91490 MAN Fire Engine, Plastic Launcher and Hydrant, Figure and Accessories.

93020   Auto-City Auto Repair Centre   1992 $20-30
Molded Garage Base with Electronic Lights and Welding Sound, Car Launching Mechanism.

93025   Auto-City Grid Start   1992 $20-30
Molded Pit Stop Base with Electronic Lights and Engine Sound, Car Launching Mechanism.

93036   Auto-City (Juniors) Jaguar Race Team Set   1992? $15-18
Two Identical Jaguar XJ-R Racers with "Jaguar 6" Graphics, Non-Standard Hot Rod Van with Purple Body and Checkered Flag Graphics on Sides, traffic cones, race driver figure.

93040   Auto-City Fire Station   1992 $20-30
Molded Fire Station with Electronic Lights and Sound, Car Launching Mechanism.

93050   Auto-City Electronic Garage   1992 $35-50
Multi-Level Garage with Electronic Lights and Sound, Playmat with Road Signs. Packaged with one Vehicle.

93070   Auto-City Medium Road Layout   1992 $30-40
Two-way Road System with Road Signs, Police Station with Launcher, Lights and Sound. Vehicle Not Included.

93080   Auto-City Super Electronic Garage   Mar-92 $40-60
Multi-Level Garage with Electronic Lights and Sound, Two-way Road System with Road Signs. Packaged with one Vehicle.

93085   Auto-City Crusher   1992 $30-40
Molded Base with Electronic Engine Sound, Pivoting Crane with Magnet on End of Cable. Packaged with one Vehicle and Magnetic Self Adhesive Strips.

93101   Auto-City – Racing 2-Vehicle Set   1993 $3-5
Maroon Jaguar XJ12R, White Porsche 935, Figure, Sign and 4 Traffic Cones.

93310?   Auto-City – Police 2-Vehicle Set   1993 $3-5
Yellow / White Transit Van "POLICE," Yellow / White Helicopter "POLICE," Figure, Sign and 4 Traffic Cones.

93310?   Auto-City – Breakdown 2-Vehicle Set   1993 $3-5
White / Red / Yellow Transit Wrecker with Yellow Boom, Red Ford Sierra, Figure, Sign and 4 Traffic Cones.

93310?   Auto-City – Fire 2-Vehicle Set   1993 $3-5
Red / Silver ERF Fire Tender, Red / White Simon Snorkel with Yellow Boom, Figure, Sign and 4 Traffic Cones.

93310?   Auto-City – Construction 2-Vehicle Set   1993 $3-5
Yellow / Red / Gray Road Roller, Yellow / Gray Front Loader, Figure, Sign and 4 Traffic Cones.

93310?   Auto-City – Rescue 2-Vehicle Set   1993 $3-5
White / Orange Mercedes-Benz Binz Ambulance, White / Orange Helicopter, Figure, Sign and 4 Traffic Cones.

93115   Auto City – Construction Super Set   1993? $25-45
Non-Standard "Juniors" 90050 Shovel Loader (former E48B) with Hot Wheels "Workhorses" Style Wheels, Non-Standard "Juniors" Yellow/ Dark Gray Excavator (former E77B) with Dark Gray Boom, Non-Standard "Juniors" Ford Transit Van with Yellow Body and Red "Wolf" Logo on Sides, Non-Standard "Juniors" Skip Dump (former E85A) with Yellow Chassis and Gray Dump Body, Non-Standard "Juniors" Raygo Roller (former E44A) with Yellow Rear Body and Red Roller Holder, "Haulers" 91200 Kenworth Open Back Tipper with "Wolf" Graphics, "Haulers" 91470 Kenworth Crane Truck with Crate, Figure and Accessories.

93130   Auto-City – Motorway Services Set   1994? $25-45
Large Playmat with Burger Bar and Emergency Services Buildings, 7 Auto-City Vehicles in Standard Trim, Road Signs and Street Lamps.

93135   Auto-City - Ferry Port Playset   Jun-94 $???
Large Fold-out Playmat with Car Ferry and Loading Crane.

93147   Auto-City (HW) BP Service Set   1995? $5-8
Ford Transit Wrecker, Ford Transit Van, and Iveco Tank Truck, All with Green/ White/ Yellow "BP" Graphics, All with Corgi or HW Baseplates in Hot Wheels Auto-City Card, Includes Figure, Sign, and 4 Traffic Cones.
a. Corgi Logo on Bases.
b. Mixed Corgi and Hot Wheels Logos on Bases.
c. Hot Wheels Logo on Bases.

93???   Auto-City British Airways Super Set   1995? $20-40
Contains Non-standard Ford Transit Van, Mercedes Bus, Iveco Box Van, and Helicopter All w/ "British Airways" Markings, White M.A.N. Tanker w/ "TEXACO" Markings, Red M.A.N. (Hauler) w/ White Roof & Two Blue Roof Lights, Non-standard Red Fire Service Body w/ Gray Ladder, Two Figures, Stop Sign, Four Traffic Cones. Other Details and Set Number Not Known.

93151   Auto-City Ferrari Racing Set   1995? $20-30
Contains Non-standard Red Hot Rod Van "Ferrari," Non-standard Red Ford Transit Van "Ferrari," Non-standard Red Ferrari 348TB with Ferrari Logos and Yellow Checkered Pattern, Red Ferrari 308 GTS, Red F1 Racer "Ferrari," Figure, Barrel and Road Sign.

93???   Auto-City Fuji Film Racing Team Super Set   1995? $20-40
Contains Non-standard Race Transporter (Superhauler), Ford Transit Wrecker, Custom Van and Two F1 Racers All w/ "FUJI FILM RACING TEAM" Markings. Other Details and Set Number Not Known.

93160   Auto-City Emergency Super Set   1995? $20-40
Set Includes Standard 90390 Mercedes Ambulance, 90470 Jaguar XJ40 Police, 90013(?) Ford Transit Van "POLICE" w/ Same Decoration as Jaguar, Non-standard Red Mercedes 300TD Wagon w/ White Roof and "FIRE CHIEF" Markings including Checkered Side Stripe, Opaque Blue Roof Lightbar & Circle w/ Black "03" Text, Red Helicopter w/ "FIRE CHIEF" Markings, Red Ford Cargo (Hauler) w/ Non-standard White Flatbed Body & "FIRE 05" Markings, Red M.A.N. (Hauler) w/ White Roof & Two Blue Roof Lights, Non-standard Red Fire Service Body w/ Gray Ladder, Two Figures, Stop Sign, Four Traffic Cones.

93177   Auto-City Assortment - 6 ea. of 24 Vehicles   1994? $150-175
Data not available at time of publication.

93179   Auto-City (Juniors) - Mercedes-Benz 2.3 Taxi   1994? $1.25-1.50
Yellow Body w/ Black Doors & Hood, Black Roof Sign "TAXI," Black Plastic Base & Interior, "TAXI" over Triangle on Hood & Doors, Clear Windows, 4-Div. Wheels.

93181   Auto-City (Juniors) - Mercedes-Benz Bus, Hertz 1994? $1.25-1.50
Data not available at time of publication.

93182   Auto-City (Juniors) - Miniatures Assortment, 144   1995? $200-250
   Vehicles
Data not available at time of publication.

93200   Auto-City (Juniors) - 10pc Set (Hot Wheels Box) 1996? $13-15
Data not available at time of publication.

93230   Auto-City (Juniors) - 6pc Set "Hot Wheels Team   1994? $9-12
   Racing"
Data not available at time of publication.

93231   Auto-City (Juniors) - 6pc Rescue Service Set w/   1994? $9-12
   Figures.
Data not available at time of publication.

93233   Auto-City (Juniors) - 6pc Construction Set w/ Figures.   1994?
$9-12
Data not available at time of publication.

93234   Auto-City (Juniors) - Ford Transit Van, BP 1994, 1995 $1.25-1.50
Green Body w/ White Lower Sides & Yellow Divider Stripe, "BP" on Hood & Sides, Black Plastic Base & Interior, Clear Windows, 4-Div. Wheels.

a. Corgi Logo on Base, Black Roof Rack.
b. Corgi Logo on Base, No Roof Rack.
c. Hot Wheels Logo on Base, No Roof Rack.

93235   Auto-City (Juniors) - Tipper Truck, Wolf   1994, 1995 $1.25-1.50
Yellow Body w/ Red "WOLF" on Roof, Gray Plastic Tipper Body w/ Yellow "5 WOLF" on Sides, Yellow Rear Gate, Clear Windows, Black Plastic Base, 8-Div. Wheels.
a. Corgi Logo on Base.
b. Hot Wheels Logo on Base.

93236   Auto-City (Juniors) - S.W.A.T. Vehicle   1994, 1995 $1.25-1.50
Black Body w/ White Roof, Gray Plastic Base, Smoked Windows, Silver "SWAT" and Shield on Sides, Orange Dots w/ Black "N.Y.P.D." & "60" on Roof, 8-Div. Wheels.
a. With Yellow Lightbar on Roof, Corgi Logo on Base.
b. With Opaque Blue Lightbar on Roof, Corgi Logo on Base.
c. Without Lightbar on Roof, Corgi Logo on Base.
d. Without Lightbar on Roof, Hot Wheels Logo on Base.

93237   Auto-City (Juniors) - Jeep Rescue 4x4   1994, 1995 $1.25-1.50
Turquoise/ White Body w/ "R" Logo & "RESCUE," Yellow Seats & Grill Guard, Black Plastic Base & Roll Cage, Off-Road 4-Crown Wheels.
a. Corgi Logo on Base.
b. Hot Wheels Logo on Base.

93414   Auto-City (Juniors) – Police and Fire Set   1995? $12-15
Ford Sierra "Police," Ford Transit Van "Police," Helicopter "Ambulance," Mercedes-Benz Binz "Ambulance," Simon Snorkel "Dial 999," Mercedes-Benz 300TD Fire Chief "Dial 999," ERF Fire Tender "Dial 999," Traffic Cones, 2 Figures, Road Block Sign.

93415   Auto-City (Juniors) – German Airport Set   1995? $15-25
White Mercedes-Benz Bus "Lufthansa Airport Bus," White Iveco Box Truck "Lufthansa," White Ford Transit Van "Lufthansa," White Helicopter "Lufthansa," Red Simon Snorkel Fire Truck with Yellow Diagonal Stripes and Yellow Roof, Yellow Booms with Red Diagonal Stripes, Figure, Road Sign and Traffic Cones. (All vehicles non-standard graphics)

93416   Auto-City (Juniors) - German Police Set   Jan-95 $13-15
White / Green BMW 825 with Blue Lightbar on Roof and "POLIZEI" Graphics, Green / White Renault Trafic Bus with Blue Lightbar on Roof and "POLIZEI" Graphics, 4 Traffic Cones, Sign, and Police Figure. (Also Found in Hot-Wheels Auto-City Packaging.)
a. Corgi Logo on Bases.
b. Hot Wheels Logo on Bases.

93417   Auto-City (Juniors) – 3pc Sets   Jan-95 $5-8
Three related vehicles plus accessories grouped around Roadworks, Race, Fire and Garage themes.

93417b   Auto-City (Hot Wheels) - 3pc Set "Hot Wheels   Jan-96 $5-8
Team Racing"
Hot Rod Custom Van w/ Gray Base, Jaguar XJR & F1 Racer w/ Black Base, all w/ Dark Blue Bodies, White Trim, "Hot Wheels" and "1" Logos, Oversize Race Driver Figure, Traffic Sign, 4 Traffic Cones, Hot Wheels Auto-City Card.
a. Corgi Logo on Bases.
b. Hot Wheels Logo on Bases.

93419   Auto-City (Juniors) – NATO Military Set   1995? $10-15
Chieftain Tank Sikorsky and Stinger Helicopters, Armored Car with Trailer, Covered Jeep CJ7 and Haulers Flat Bed Kenworth Truck, All with 2-Tone Green Camouflage Graphics, Two Green Plastic Soldier Figures.

93425   Auto-City (Juniors) – 6pc Sets   Jan-95 $9-12
Six related vehicles plus accessories grouped around Roadworks, Race, Fire and Polizei themes.

93425a   Auto-City (Juniors) - 6 pc. Racing Set   Jan-95 $9-12
Blue Jaguar XJ9R with "Hot Wheels" Logo Graphics, Blue Hot Rod Van with "Hot Wheels" Logo Graphics, White Ford Sierra with Yellow Base and "11 Shell" Graphics, White Ford Transit Wrecker with Red and Yellow "Shell" Graphics, Red F1 Racer with Ferrari Graphics, Red Ford Transit Van with Black Roof Rack and "Ferrari" Graphics, Signs, Figure, Traffic Cones. (All vehicles in non-standard colors.)
a. Corgi Logo on Bases.
b. Mixed Corgi and Hot Wheels Logos on Bases.
c. Hot Wheels Logo on Bases.

93700   Auto-City (Juniors) - 3 pc. Sets   1991? $5-8
Sets of 3 Themed Auto-City (Juniors) Vehicles on a Common Display Card.

9370x   Auto-City (Juniors) - 3 pc. Rally+ Set, Texaco   1991? $5-8
900xx "TEXACO RACE SUPPORT" Ford Transit, 9020x Black "TEXACO" Corvette, Non-standard "TEXACO" Kenworth Flatbed Truck with Black Cab and Chassis and Black Flatbed Body.

93703   Auto-City (Juniors) - 3 pc. Rally+ Set, Police   1991? $5-8

90013 Ford Transit Police, 90393 Jaguar XJ40 Police, Non-standard Ford Cargo Flatbed Truck with Black Cab and Chassis and White Flatbed Body.

94360c   Hot Wheels (former Auto-City), BMW 850csi, White1997 $2-4
1997 Mattel Hot Wheels (UK) Product that duplicates number. See Next Section.

94470   Auto City BMW 850csi Set   1994? $8-10
Set with one Juniors and one Turbos BMW 850csi models in standard colors.

94540b   Auto-City (Juniors) - Porsche 911   1994, 1995 $1.25-1.50
Metallic Bluish-Gray Body w/ Porsche Crest on Hood, Clear Windows, Black Plastic Base & Interior, 4-Div. Wheels.
a. Corgi Logo on Base.
b. Hot Wheels Logo on Base.

955XX   Mattel Hot Wheels Number Series   1996-97   N/A
(Post Mattel Split Number Series for Former Auto-City Models. See Later Section.)

Corgi Classics Ltd. - New Independence 1995 Management Buy-Out - 2001 Series Prefix Addition

This section contains the known or announced variations of models produced from the time of the January 1, 1996 new numbering system implementation onward to the January 1, 2001 addition of a series prefix. Models produced by Corgi Classics Ltd. are presented here.

56501   Leyland Terrier Box Truck (1/64) - Weetabix   1999 $2-4
Yellow Body Similar to 1970s Corgi Juniors Model, Not Made from Old Dies but New Dies Partly Based Upon Old Design, "Weetabix" Graphics. (Promotional model for Weetabix for on-pack offer.)

56502   Leyland Terrier Box Truck (1/64) – Eddie Stobart 1999 $2-4
Dark Green Upper Body, Red Lower Body, White Upper Cab and Front Bumper, "EDDIE STOBART LTD" and "EXPRESS ROAD HAULAGE SPECIALIST" Graphics. (Promotional model for Eddie Stobart Ltd.)

660026   Emergency Services Set   2000 $15-20
Volvo Fire Tender, Three Non-standard Ford Transit Vans in "PARAMEDIC," POLICE," and "FIRE RESCUE UNIT" Graphics.

66101   TXI London Taxi (1/64)   2000 $2-4
Black Body with Opening Rear Doors, Gray Interior, 5-Spoke Wheels, Clear Windows.

66102(?) TXI London Taxi (1/64) – Hamley's   2000 $3-5
Black Body with Opening Rear Doors, Gray Interior, 5-Spoke Wheels, Clear Windows, Red "Hamley's" Logo on Front Doors. (Promotional model for Hamley's. Also used in Gift Set 60035 when sold at Hamley's stores.)

66201   Ford Transit Van (1/64) – Eddie Stobart Ltd.   2000 $3-5
Dark Green and White Body, Black Bumpers and Base, "EDDIE STOBART LTD EXPRESS ROAD HAULAGE" Graphics. (Renumbered ES66201 in 2002.)
a. Black Outlined Lettering. (Only found in ASDA 3-pack promotion.)
b. Red Outlined Lettering. (Standard release.)

66202   Ford Transit Van (1/64) – TNT   2000 $3-5
Orange and White Body with Blue Stripe, Orange Bumpers and Base, "TNT" Graphics.

66203   Ford Transit Van (1/64) – Royal Mail   2000 $3-5
Red Body with Yellow Chevron Side Stripes, Red Bumpers and Base, "Royal Mail" Graphics.

66204   Ford Transit Van (1/64) – RAC   2000 $3-5
Orange Body, Bumpers and Base, White "RAC" Graphics.

66205   Ford Transit Van (1/64) – Pickfords   2000 $3-5
Dark Blue Body, Bumpers and Base with Roadway and "PICKFORDS The Careful Movers" Graphics.

66207   Ford Transit Van (1/64) – Transco   2000 $3-5
Light Blue Body with Red Lower Side Stripes, Black Bumpers and Base, "Transco" Graphics.

66209   Ford Transit Van (1/64) – Ford   2000 $5-8
White Body, Black Bumpers and Base, "Ford Quality" Graphics. (Promotional for Ford.)

66210   Ford Transit Van (1/64) – Ford   2000 $5-8

Red Body, Black Bumpers and Base, No Graphics. (Promotional for Ford.)

662xx(?) Ford Transit Van (1/64) – Ford   2000 $5-8
White Body, Black Bumpers and Base, "Autoteam COMPETITION 2000" Graphics
with Ford Logo. (Promotional for Ford.)

662xx(?) Ford Transit Van (1/64) – Ford   2000(?) $5-8
White Body, Black Bumpers and Base, "FordTransit" and Wedge-Over-Dots Logo
Graphics. (Promotional for Ford.)

662xx(?) Ford Transit Van (1/64) – Ford   2000(?) $5-8
White Body, Black Bumpers and Base, "Ford Credit" and "**flex**ability" Graphics.
(Promotional for Ford.) *[[Is your spelling and use of bold in "flexability"
intentional? Please advise.]]*

662xx(?) Ford Transit Van (1/64) – Avaya   2000 $5-8
White Body, Black Bumpers and Base, "AVAYA communication" Graphics.
(Promotional for Avaya.)

662xx(?) Ford Transit Van (1/64) – Elite Tail Lift   2000 $5-8
White Body, Black Bumpers and Base, "ELITE TAIL LIFT NETWORK R 24-365
SERVICE" Graphics with Internet address. (Promotional for Elite Tail Lift.)

99103   Royal Mail 4 pc. Set (1/64)   2000 $12-15
Two Different Superhaulers with "Royal Mail" Graphics , two 66203 Royal Mail
Transits.

Corgi Classics Ltd. - The Zindart Years
2001 Series Prefix Addition – Present

This section contains the known or announced
variations of models produced from the time of the
addition of a Series Prefix to the model number up
through the publication date. Please note that these
models are not organized into a series by Corgi Classics Ltd. at this point.

TY87801 Chitty-Chitty-Bang-Bang (1/64) (Jan-2002) Aug-2002   CURRENT
Model of Movie Car of Same Name Similar to 1960s Corgi Juniors Model. Not Made
from Old Dies, but New Dies Partly Based Upon Old Design, Silver Painted Hood
with Black Details, Red Interior and Side Wings, Yellow End Wings, No Figures,
Packaged in Special See-Through Sandwich-type Card. (Originally produced as a
limited release for Chitty-Chitty-Bang-Bang stage show in London. Later released
through normal outlets.)

TY81701 Ford Transit Van (1/64) – Michelin   2001   **CURRENT**
Yellow and Dark Blue Body, Black Bumpers and Base, Large White Bib Figure and
"MICHELIN" Graphics.

TY81702 Ford Transit Van (1/64) – British Telephone   2001   **CURRENT**
White Body, Gray Bumpers and Base, Large Red and Blue Figure and "BT"
Graphics.

TY81703 Ford Transit Van (1/64) – AA   2001   **CURRENT**
Yellow Body with Black Checkered Pattern along Bottom Edge, Black Bumpers and
Base, Large "AA" Graphics.

CP81705 Ford Transit Van (1/64) – Ford   2001   **CURRENT**
White Body, Black Bumpers and Base, "VAN OF THE YEAR" Graphics. (Promotional
for Ford.)

TY81706 Ford Transit Van (1/64) – James Irlam   Jan-2002   **CURRENT**
Red Body, Gray Bumpers and Base, "JAMES IRLAM" Graphics. (Note: Early
publicity photos appear to have green bumpers and base.)

TY81707 Ford Transit Van (1/64) – Tarmac   Jan-2002   **CURRENT**
White Body, Black Bumpers and Base, Large "T" Logo and "Tarmac" Graphics.

TY81708 Ford Transit Van (1/64) – Megastore NOT PRODUCED   N/A
Was to have Red Upper and Black Lower Body with White Divider Stripe, Black
Bumpers and Base, "MANCHESTER UNITED MEGASTORE" Graphics. (Pre-
production model shown in literature.)

TY81711 Ford Transit Van (1/64) – London Busses   Jan-2003   **CURRENT**
Red Body with Yellow Dashed Stripe on Sides, Black Bumpers and Base, "London
Busses Operating Services" Graphics.

TY817xx(?) Ford Transit Van (1/64) – NSVA   2001   **CURRENT**
White Body, Black Bumpers and Base, "NSVA" Graphics with Red Van Logo.
(Promotional for National Street Van Association, issued as set. May be Code 2.)

a. "Van Nationals Oxford England 2001" on Roof.
b. "http://www.nsva.uk.com" on Roof.
c. "The National Street Van Assoc." on Roof.
d. "Members Only Van" on Roof.
e. "Committee Van" on Roof.

Corgi Juniors Dies Used Elsewhere

This section contains the known variations for
models produced from the Mettoy era and later Corgi
Juniors dies either resold to other manufacturers or
used in joint ventures. In many cases, the extent of
the range offered or the variations produced on each
model is not known. The models produced as Hot
Wheels after the split between Corgi Classics Ltd. and
Mattel Inc. are also listed in this section. Values for
these models are left for experts in these other brands
to quantify.

Hot Wheels Vehicles made from Former Corgi Auto-City (Juniors) Dies

Late 1996 and onward models are considered in
the regular Hot Wheels vehicles range with 15XXX
series and upward numbers (65XXX for sets) except
where noted. Models redecorated and fitted with Hot
Wheels style wheels and sold intermixed with existing Hot Wheels models, heavily used in limited edition releases. Only models without a corresponding
Corgi Auto-City version are listed here.

A complete listing of all Hot Wheels variations
can be found in Bob Parker's book *The Complete
Book of Hot Wheels.* (Schiffer Publishing Ltd.)

15XXX series

15066   Hot Wheels Gift Pack Set - Porsche   1997
a. Five car set of Porsche models, one of which is the former Porsche 911 with
Silver Body, Red Seats, Red HW Logo on Lower Sides, HW Dished 5-Spoke Wheels
with Silver Spokes. (Similar to 15788 except wheel type.)
b. Metallic Purple Body, White Interior, No Graphics, HW Dished 5-Spoke Wheels
with Gold Spokes. (From unknown set. Listed here due to similarity.)

**15111   Hot Wheels Auto-City Action Squad Set -
          Rescue Station**   1996
Fold-out Action Scene, White/ Yellow Helicopter, Orange/ Blue Jeep 4x4, Figure &
Loose Accessories.

**15113   Hot Wheels Auto-City Action Squad Set -
          Skip Loader**   1996
Fold-out Action Scene, Yellow and Silver Skip Loader (former E85-A), Figure &
Loose Accessories.

**15114   Hot Wheels Auto-City Action Squad Set -
          Fire Station**   1996
Fold-out Action Scene, Snorkel Fire Engine (former 90035), Figure & Loose
Accessories.

**15115   Hot Wheels Auto-City Action Squad Set -
          Helicopter Squad**   1996
Fold-out Action Scene, White/ Yellow Helicopter, Figure & Loose Accessories.

**15116   Hot Wheels Auto-City Action Squad Set -
          F1 Racer Pit**   1996
Fold-out Action Scene, Red F1 Racer, Figure & Loose Accessories.

15788   Porsche Carrera, Collector #829   1998
Silver Body, Unpainted Diecast Base, Red Interior, Clear Windows, Red Hot Wheels
Logo on Lower Sides, HW Dished 3-Point Spinner Wheels with Silver Spokes.
(Same as car in set 15066 except wheel type.)

16148   Hot Wheels Action Pack - Fire Fighting   1997

Red ERF Fire Truck (95505) with Blue Tinted Windows, Silver Trim, Silver Plastic Ladder and Base, Red Snorkel Fire Engine (95506) with Gray Smoked Windows, Black and Silver Trim, Silver Plastic Booms and Base, Both with HW Dished 5-Spoke Wheels with Silver Spokes, Two Figures. (Snorkel shown on card back with silver plastic windows, but not so produced.)

16153   Hot Wheels Action Pack - Construction   1997
Yellow Ford Cement Truck (former E30-D) with Clear Windows, Black Trim, Silver Plastic Drum and Rear Support, HW Logo on Doors and Drum, Yellow Digger (former E77-B) with HW Logo and "4" on Sides, Silver Plastic Digger Arms, 2 Figures, Red Cones and Barricade.
a. HW Dished 5-Spoke Wheels on Cement Truck, Larger HW Dished 5-Spoke Wheels on Digger.

16156   Hot Wheels Action Pack - Surf Patrol   1997
White Open Top Jeep (former ?????) with Red "LIFEGUARD" Logo on Hood and Sides, Red Seats, Black Windshield & Roll Cage, Red Push Bumper, Black Base, Red & White Boat on Black Trailer, 3 Figures.
a. Jeep with Large 4-Crown Wheels, Trailer with HW Dished 5-Spoke Wheels.
b. May exist with 8-Lug Wheels on Jeep as shown on package.
c. White Jeep with Large 4-Crown Wheels, 8-Lug Wheels, Black Interior, Silver Roll Cage, Orange Flag, Red / Orange / Yellow / Black "5" Graphics. (Part of Larger F.A.O. Schwarz set with different number.)

16189   Little Debbie Collector Set - Series II   1997
Three Vehicle set, one of which is the former Open Top Jeep with White Body, Yellow Seats and Push Bumper, Black Roll Cage and Antenna, "Sunbelt Snacks" Logo on Hood and Sides.

16247-0910   Holiday Hot Wheels - Porsche 911 Targa   1996
Red Vacuum Plated Body, HW Dished 5-Spoke Wheels with Green Spokes, Green Interior, Santa Figure Driving, Blue & Green Presents on Spoiler, "Happy Holidays '96" Trim, Clear/ Green Case in Special Turntable Card.

16249-0910   Holiday Hot Wheels - Porsche 911 Targa   1996
Green Vacuum Plated Body, HW Dished 5-Spoke Wheels with Red Spokes, Red Interior, Santa Figure Driving, Red Santa's Sack on Spoiler, "Happy Holidays '96" Trim, Clear/ Red Case in Special Turntable Card.

16300   Porsche 911 Targa, Collector #493   1997
a. Yellow Body, Black Base and Interior, Black Trimmed Roll Bar and Spoiler, Silver Headlamps, Red Taillamps, HW Dished 5-Spoke Wheels with Silver Spokes.
b. Red Body, Black Base and Interior, No Trim, Corgi 4-Div Wheels with Silver Spokes. (From set packaged with black Hot Rod Van. May have different number.)

16301   Mercedes-Benz 500SL, Collector #494   1997
Metallic Gray Body, Black Base, Red Interior, Black Trimmed Windshield with HW Logo in Bottom Right Corner, HW Dished 5-Spoke Wheels with Silver Spokes, Silver Grill, Red Taillamps. (Similar to UK Version 95547.)

16303   Ferrari 308GTS, Collector #496   1997
Red Body, Black Base, Black Interior, Yellow HW Logo in Windshield, Yellow Outer Taillamps, Black Side Vents, HW Dished 5-Spoke Wheels with Silver Spokes.

16304   Ferrari Testarossa, Collector #497   1997
Pearlescent White Body, Black Base, Black Interior, Black Grill with Silver Driving Lamps, Clear Windows, HW Dished 5-Spoke Wheels with Silver Spokes, Black Taillamp area.

16305   BMW 850i, Collector #498   1997
Silver Body, Black Base, Red Interior, Opening Doors, Black Grill with Yellow Corner Lamps, Red and Yellow Taillamps, Clear Windows with Hot Wheels Logo in Rear Window, HW Dished 5-Spoke Wheels with Silver Spokes.

16306   Corvette Coupe, Collector #499   1997
a. Metallic Green Body, Black Base, Red Interior, Opening Hood, Black Roof Panel and Dashboard, Silver Grills, HW Dished 5-Spoke Wheels with Silver Spokes.
b. Metallic Green Body, Black Base, Black Interior, Opening Hood, Clear Roof Panel, Silver Grills, Auto City 8-Div Wheels with Silver Spokes. (from Target set, may have different number.)

16979   Chuck E. Cheese's Custom Van   1997
Purple Body with Side Flames and "CHUCKE.CHEESE'S" with Logo, Chrome Plastic Base, Smoked Windows, HW Dished 5-Spoke Wheels with Silver Spokes. (Promotional for Chuck E. Cheese's Restaurants.)

16980   Chuck E. Cheese's '80's Corvette   1997
Red Body with White Lower Sides "CHUCKE.CHEESE'S," Black Base and Roof Panel, Off-White Interior and Taillamps, Round Decal with Character Face on Opening Hood, Clear Windows with Hot Wheels Logo in Rear Window, HW Dished 5-Spoke Wheels with Silver Spokes. (Promotional for Chuck E. Cheese's Restaurants.)

17972   Kroger Limited Edition Set   1997

Two Vehicle set, one of which is a random 1997 HW vehicle. Some sets include one of the 16300-16306 series ex-Corgi vehicles. The other vehicle is a Kroger HW Truck.

18671   J. C. Whitney Camper (Custom Van)   1997
Aqua Body with Gold Striping and Large Side Window Tampo Printing, Small "J. C. Whitney" on Lower Sides, Metallic Gold Unplated Plastic Base, Smoked Windows, HW Dished Gold Center Wheels. (Promotional for J. C. Whitney Automotive. Same casting as 16980.)

21315   Porsche Carrera, (X-Treme Speed Series #3 of 4) 1999
Silver Body, Unpainted Diecast Base, White Interior, Smoked Windows, Brown/ Black/ White "DIRTBIKE TEAM" Graphics, Unequal Sized HW Dished 5-Spoke Wheels with Gold Spokes. (Similar to 15788 but with added graphics.)

27112   Porsche Carrera   2000
Metallic Blue Body, Unpainted Diecast Base, White Interior, Clear Windows, White HW Logo Low on Sides, Unequal Sized HW Dished 3-Spoke Spinner Wheels with Silver Spokes. (Similar to 15788.)

47084   Hot Wheels Ultimate Service Center   2001
Large Set Containing Two Former Corgi Juniors Models. Models are: Porsche Targa with Silver Body and Black Seats, Yellow Ferrari Testarossa with Black Seats and Yellow Hot Wheels Logo in Windshield, Both Cars have Dished Chrome 5-spoke Wheels.

55015   Porsche 911 Carrera   2002
Metallic Blue Body with Red and Silver Flames on Sides, Silver Painted Diecast Base, White Interior, Smoked Windows, Small Silver Porsche Logo on Hood, Unequal Sized HW Dished 3-Spoke Spinner Wheels with Silver Spokes. (Similar to 27112.)

65XXX series

65603-91   Hot Wheels Sto & Go Parking & Service Garage   1997
Versions issued in 1997 contained a 1957 T-Bird or Hot Rod Van as follows:
a. T-Bird with Red Body, Black Seats, Corgi Style 8-Division Wheels.
b. Hot Rod Van with Black Body, White Front Air Dam, Tinted Windows, Gray Plastic Base, Corgi Juniors Style 8-div. Wheels, Large Hot Wheels Logo Graphics on Sides. (Same graphics as blue Auto-City version.)

656??   Hot Wheels Sto & Go McDonald's Restaurant   1997
Versions issued in 1997 contained a 1957 T-Bird as follows:
a. Metallic Blue Body, Black Seats, Clear Windshield, Corgi Style 8-Division Wheels.
b. Red Body, Black Seats, Smoke Tinted Windshield, Corgi Style 8-Division Wheels.
c. White Body, Red Seats, Yellow Tinted Windshield, Corgi Style 8-Division Wheels.

65620   Hot Wheels Street Trax Super Highway Playset   1997
Versions issued in 1997 contained a Ferrari Testarossa (former ?????) as follows:
a. Red Body, Tan Seats, Corgi Style 4-Division Wheels.

65679   Hot Wheels Super Street Trax Set   1997
Versions issued in 1997 contained a Ferrari Testarossa (former ?????) as follows:
a. Red Body, Black Seats, Corgi Style 4-Division Wheels, other car in set is HW Toyota Celica.

65694   Hot Wheels World Gas Station   1997
Versions issued starting in 1997 contained as follows:
a. 1957 T-Bird (former ?????) with Black Body, Black Seats, Corgi Style 8-Division Wheels.
b. Ferrari Testarossa (former ?????) with Red Body, Tan Seats, Corgi Style 4-Division Wheels.

65695   Hot Wheels World Ford Dealership   1997
Versions issued in 1997 contained a 1957 T-Bird (former ?????) as follows:
a. Metallic Dark Blue Body, Black Seats, Corgi Style 8-Division Wheels.

65741   Hot Wheels World Service Center   1997
Versions issued starting in 1997 contained as follows:
a. Mercedes-Benz 500SL (former ?????) with Dark Metallic Blue Body, Black Diecast HW Base, Gray Seats, No Front or Rear Trim Detailing on Body, Yellow HW Logo on Trunk Lid, Corgi Style 4-Division Wheels.

65832   Hot Wheels World Deluxe World Set   1997
Versions issued starting in 1997 contained as follows:
a. (Set Contained 3 Vehicles, of which 2 were Former Corgi.) Mercedes-Benz 500SL (former ?????) with Dark Metallic Blue Body, Gray Seats, No Trim Detailing on Body, Corgi Style 4-Division Wheels. Metallic Dark Green Corvette (former ?????), Black Seats, Corgi Style 8-Division Wheels. (3rd Vehicle was HW Heavy Hauler Dump Truck.)

65896   Hot Wheels Oil Refinery Set   1998

Versions issued starting in 1998 contained as follows:

a. Iveco Tanker with White / Yellow Cab (similar to 90065), Red HW Logo on Cab Front, Gray Tank with Red / Yellow Stripe but No Logo, Dished Chrome Center 5 Spoke HW Wheels, Packaged with Small Oil Refinery Building.

?????   Hot Wheels - Gold Series III 16 Car Set   1996

All Former Corgi Vehicles, Black Bodies, HW Dished 5-Spoke Wheels with Gold Wheel Centers, London Taxi has FAO Schwarz, Schwarz Logo and HW Logo on Sides. All have Tan Interior unless noted. (FAO Schwarz Exclusive sold as set only. Not otherwise available) Individual vehicles are as follows:

a. Ferrari 308GTS.

b. Ferrari 348TB.

c. 1957 Thunderbird Convertible.

d. BMW 850I.

e. Porsche 911.

f. Porsche 935.

g. London Bus, Gold Vacuum-plated Windows.

h. BMW M3.

i. Mercedes-Benz 190E.

j. Mercedes-Benz 500SL.

k. Ford Mustang Cobra.

l. Ford Sierra.

m. Porsche Targa.

n. Ferrari Testarossa.

o. 1984 Corvette.

p. London Taxi with logos on sides.

9XXXX series

A series of European issue Hot Wheels from 1996-97 made from former Auto City dies were still numbered in the Corgi 9XXXX series, even though they were packaged in standard short European style Hot Wheels cards. Many later issued in USA style cards late in 1997 and afterward. All have Hot Wheels Logo's on their baseplates in place of the Corgi name. The (Double Decker) Bus is the rarest of the regular releases (just one per 72 car case.)

94360   BMW 850i (Street Racers Series, UK)   1997

a. White Body, Black Base, Red Interior, Opening Doors, Blue Tinted Windows, HW Snowflake Wheels with Silver Spokes.

b. Dark Metallic Blue Body, Black Base, Black Interior, Opening Doors, Clear Windows, Corgi 4-Div. Wheels with Silver Spokes. (possibly from a set with a different number.)

95505   Fire Eater II (#611), (former ERF Fire Tender)   1997

Red Body, Dark Blue Tinted Windows, Silver Plastic Ladder & Base, HW Dished 5-Spoke Wheels with Silver Centers, Silver HW Logo on Sides among other markings. (Also used in set 16148.)

95506   Flame Stopper II (#617),

**   (former ERF Simon Snorkel)   1997**

Red Body, Dark Blue Tinted Windows, Silver Plastic Booms & Base, HW Dished 5-Spoke Wheels with Silver Centers, Black & Silver HW Logo on Sides among other markings. (Also used in set 16148.)

95509   BMW 325i (#603}   1997

Yellow Body with Red Flame, Black Target and "5" Graphics, Black Interior, Gray Plastic Base, Snowflake Pattern Wheels.

95510   London Taxi (#619)   1997

Yellow Body, Black Interior, Silver Base, Black/ White Checkered Stripe on Sides over Black HW Logo, Black "LONDON CAB CO." And Red "SEE CITY OF HOT WHEELS" Side Text, HW Dished 5-Spoke Wheels with Silver Centers.

95512   Double Decker Bus (#613)

**   (former Daimler Fleetline)   1997**

Red Body, Opaque Black Windows & Baseplate, "The London STANDARD" Side Panels, HW Dished 5-Spoke Wheels with Silver Centers.

95514   Ford Transit Wrecker (#620)   1997

Light Blue Body, White Boom, Lightbar and Base, Black Hook, Opaque Black Windows, White Background Tampo with Red HW Logo and "KEVIN'S 24HR TOWING" Plus other Graphics, HW Dished 5-Spoke Wheels with Silver Centers.

95517   BMW M3 (Racing Series, UK)   1997

White Body, Black Base, ??? Interior, Opaque Windows, Blue/ Red Angled Stripe and "3" Graphics,, HW Snowflake Wheels with Silver Spokes.

95518   Ford Sierra XR4Ti (#615)   1997

Silver Body, Clear Windows, Red Interior & Taillamps, Orange & Blue "XR4Ti Sierra 4" Graphics, HW Dished 5-Spoke Wheels with Silver Centers.

95520   Porsche Carrera   1997

Black Body, Unpainted Diecast Base, Red Interior, Clear Windows, White "3 DYNAMIC RACING" and Orange Splash Graphics, Unequal Sized HW Dished 5-Spoke Wheels with Silver Spokes.

95522   1980 Corvette (#616)   1997

White Body, Black Roof Panels Blue Interior, Black Baseplate, Orange & Blue Side Graphics, Gold HW Logo in Rear Window.

a. Short Card, HW Dished 5-Spoke Wheels with Silver Centers. (UK)

b. Tall Card, Snowflake Pattern Wheels with Silver Centers. (USA)

95528   Land Rover Mk II (#610)   1997

Orange Body with Modified Rear Bumper Lacking Details, Clear Windows, Blue Interior, White & Blue "SMITH ELECTRIC" Graphics, Large HW Dished 5-Spoke Wheels with Silver Centers.

95530   City Police (#622), (former Buick Regal Police)   1997

Black Body with White Roof, Black Plastic Base, Gray Interior and Bumpers, Transparent Blue Lightbar on Roof, White/ Gold/ Black "POLICE INTERCEPTOR" Graphics with Small Red HW Logo on Sides, HW Snowflake Wheels without Decoration on Spokes.

95532   Porsche 935 (Racing Series, UK)   1997

a. Black Body, Black Base, Red Interior, HW Logo in Rear Window, White/ Blue/ Purple Graphics, HW Snowflake Wheels with Silver Spokes.

b. Silver Body, Black Base, White Interior, Blue Tinted Windows, Red / White / Blue / Black "935" Graphics, HW Snowflake Wheels with Gold Spokes. (From F.A.O. Schwarz History of Hot Wheels Set.)

95533   Mercedes-Benz 2.6 (#605)   1997

Metallic Gold Body, Black Interior, Silver Grill, Red Taillamps, , Gold HW Logo in Rear Window.

a. Short Card, HW Dished 5-Spoke Wheels with Silver Centers. (UK)

b. Tall Card, Snowflake Pattern Wheels with Silver Centers. (USA)

95534   Jaguar XJ40 (#609)   1997

Metallic Dark Blue Body, Blue Tinted Windows, White Interior, Black Baseplate, Silver Grill & Trim, Red Taillamps, White HW Logo in Rear Window.

a. Short Card, HW Dished 5-Spoke Wheels with Silver Centers. (UK)

b. Tall Card, Snowflake Pattern Wheels with Silver Centers. (USA)

95535   Mercedes-Benz 300TD Wagon (#606)   1997

Metallic Gray Interior & Base, Silver Grill, Red Taillamps, Clear Windows, HW Dished 5-Spoke Wheels with Silver Centers.

a. Metallic Dark Turquoise Body

b. Metallic Dark Blue Body

95537   Porsche 911 Targa (#608)   1997

Black Interior & Baseplate, Black Roll Bar & Trim, HW Dished 5-Spoke Wheels with Silver Centers, Red HW Logo in Rear Window.

95538   '57 T-Bird (#612)   1997

a. Light Aqua Body with Silver Headlamps and Red Taillamps, White Interior, Clear Windshield with Red HW Logo, Old Style HW 5-Spoke Wheels with Silver Centers, Short Card. (UK)

b. Light Aqua Body with Silver Headlamps and Red Taillamps, White Interior, Clear Windshield with Red HW Logo, Old Style HW 5-Spoke Wheels with Silver Centers, Tall Card. (USA)

c. Pink Body, Black Interior, Clear Windshield, Auto City 8-Div Wheels with Silver Centers. (from set, may have different number.)

d. Yellow Body with Silver Headlamps and Red Taillamps, Painted Body Accents, White Interior, Clear Windshield, Old Style HW 5-Spoke Wheels with Silver Centers and Whitewall Tires. (from set, may have different number.)

e. Light Aqua Body with Silver Headlamps and Red Taillamps, Painted Body Accents, White Interior, Clear Windshield, HW Dished Wheels with Silver Centers and Whitewall Tires. (from set, may have different number.)

f. Pink Body with Silver Headlamps and Red Taillamps, Painted Body Accents, Black Interior, Clear Windshield, HW Premium Wheels with Plated Spoke Centers. (from set, may have different number.)

95540   Mustang Cobra (#623)   1997

Hot Pink Body, Black Base, Black Interior, Yellow HW Logo on Front Fenders, Black "MUSTANG 5.0" Graphics, HW Snowflake Wheels with Silver Spokes.

95541   Highway Builder (Road Repair Series, UK)   1997

Yellow Body, Black Base, Black Interior, Dark Gray Scoop, "E45" Graphics on Rear Engine Cover, HW Single Silver Ring Wheels. (former Juniors E48-B Shovel Loader.)

95544   Dirt Rover (#643) (Road Repair Series, UK)   1997

Yellow Body, Dark Gray Articulated Scoop, "E32" Graphics, HW Dished 5-Spoke Wheels with Silver Centers. (former Juniors E77-B Excavator.)

95546   Ferrari 348 (Racing Series, UK)   1997

a. Red Body, Black Base, Black Interior, No Logo in Windshield, Yellow and Silver Stripes on Hood and Roof, Black "348" on Hood, HW Dished 5-Spoke Wheels with Silver Spokes.

b. Red Body, Black Base, Black Interior, Red HW Logo in Windshield, Yellow and White Stripes on Hood and Roof, Black "348" on Hood, HW Dished 5-Spoke Wheels with Silver Spokes. (Shown in literature. May have been pre-production model.)

95547   Mercedes-Benz 500SL (Cabriolet Series, UK)   1997

a. Metallic Gray Body, Black Base, Purple Interior, Black Trimmed Windshield without HW Logo in Bottom Right Corner, HW Dished 5-Spoke Wheels with Silver Spokes, Body Color Grill and Taillamps. (Similar to US Version 16301.)

b. Metallic Gray Body, Black Base, Pink Interior, Black Trimmed Windshield without HW Logo in Bottom Right Corner, HW Dished 5-Spoke Wheels with Silver Spokes, Body Color Grill and Taillamps. (Similar to US Version 16301. Shown in literature. May have been pre-production model.)

95548   Jaguar XJR9 (Racing Series, UK)   1997

Purple Body, Black Base, Black Interior, White Rear Spoiler, White/ Blue "SMOKIN' GHOST 9" Side Graphics, HW Snowflake Wheels with Silver Spokes.

95549   Sandstinger (Road Repair Series, UK)   1997

Yellow Body, Dark Gray Dump Body, Yellow Graphics, Old Style Juniors Construction Vehicle Wheels. (former Juniors E85-A Skip Dumper.)

95550   Road Roller (Road Repair Series, UK)   1997

Yellow Body, Black Base, Dark Gray Roller, "E34" Graphics on Rear Engine Cover, Old Style Juniors Construction Vehicle Wheels on Rear. (former Juniors E44-A Raygo Rascal Roller.)

95650   Tipper (#712)   1998

Dark Blue Body and Tail Gate, Silver Grill, White Articulated Tipper Body, "BD CONSTRUCTION" Graphics, Black Plastic Base, HW Dished 5-Spoke Wheels with Silver Centers. (former Juniors E49-B Tipper.)

Kiko Corgi from Brazil

Models produced or assembled in Brazil by A. Kikoler from transferred Corgi and Juniors Dies. Many used inferior wheels and had revised baseplate text. Some dies were later returned to Corgi in Great Britain, while others were later resold to third parties. Production dates and quantities uncertain. Numbering system sometimes inconsistent. Only models known to the author are listed. Many more exist. (Former Juniors E Series and J Series Dies)

C 2   Chevy Van – Captain America   1980s

a. Silver Body with Red Tinted Windows, "CAP AMERICA" Labels on Sides, "CORGI JUNIORS INDUSTRIA BRASILIERA KIKO" on Black Plastic Base. (Dies from Juniors E22D / E90A etc.)

b. Silver Body with Blue Tinted Windows, otherwise as 2a.

c. Silver Body with Yellow Tinted Windows, otherwise as 2a.

C 3   Range Rover – California Highway Patrol   1980s

a. Blue Body with Extended Roof and Two Lamps, Red Interior, Yellow Tinted Windows, "340 HIGHWAY PATROL" Hood Label, "CALIFORNIA HIGHWAY PATROL" Side Labels.

b. Blue Body with Extended Roof and Two Lamps, Red Interior, Red tinted Windows, "340 HIGHWAY PATROL" Hood Label, "CALIFORNIA HIGHWAY PATROL" Side Labels.

c. Blue Body with Flat Roof and Red Lightbar, Tan Interior, Yellow Tinted Windows, "340 HIGHWAY PATROL" Tampo Printed on Hood, "CALIFORNIA HIGHWAY PATROL" Tampo Printed on Sides.

d. Blue Body with Flat Roof and Red Lightbar, Black Interior, Smoke Tinted Windows, "340 HIGHWAY PATROL" Tampo Printed on Hood, "CALIFORNIA HIGHWAY PATROL" Tampo Printed on Sides.

C 4   Can Am Racer   1980s

a. Yellow Body, White Driver, Gray Engine, Bird Design Label on Hood, "Corgi" and "INDUSTRIA BRASILIERA KIKI" on Black Plastic Base. (Dies from Juniors E82A)

b. Yellow Body, White Driver, Yellow Engine, Bird Design Label on Hood, "Corgi" and "INDUSTRIA BRASILIERA KIKI" on Black Plastic Base. (Dies from Juniors E82A)

c. White Body, White Driver, Gray Engine, Blue "corgi and "34" Labels on Hood & Spoiler, "Corgi" and "INDUSTRIA BRASILIERA KIKI" on Black Plastic Base. (Dies from Juniors E82A)

d. Red Body, Gray Driver, Gray Engine, Blue "corgi and "34" Labels on Hood & Spoiler, "Corgi" and "INDUSTRIA BRASILIERA KIKI" on Black Plastic Base. (Dies from Juniors E82A)

e. Medium Blue Body, Gray Driver, Black Engine, Bird Design Label on Hood, "Corgi" and "INDUSTRIA BRASILIERA KIKI" on Black Plastic Base. (Dies from Juniors E82A)

f. Deep Blue Body, Tan Driver and Engine, Bird Design Label on Hood, "Corgi" and "INDUSTRIA BRASILIERA KIKO" on Black Plastic Base. (Dies from Juniors E82A)

g. Dark Green Body, White Driver and Engine, Yellow Number Label on Hood, "Corgi" and "INDUSTRIA BRASILIERA KIKO" on Black Plastic Base. (Dies from Juniors E82A)

C 6   Futura Van (Healer Wheeler) – Ambulance   1980s

a. White Body, Blue Tinted Windows, Red Label on Front with White Circled Cross, White Labels on Sides with red "AMBULANCE" and Red Circled Cross over Red Stripes.

b. White Body, Opaque Black Windows, Red "CEBOLINHA" Labels with Cartoon Child Doctor on Hood and Sides. (From Gift Set 3030.)

C 7   Guy Warrior Tank Truck – Esso   1980s

White Body with Green Tinted Windows, Red and Blue "ESSO" Graphics on Tank Sides, Modified Kiko Baseplate. (Similar to graphics on Juniors E97A except single Esso logo centered on red stripe with added blue lines above and below.)

C 8   Ford Escort – Radio Taxi   1980s

Yellow Body, Black Interior, "RADIO TAXI 2137" Labels on Hood, Roof and Sides, "CORGI JUNIORS INDUSTRIA BRASILIERA WHIZZWHEELS KIKO" on Black Diecast Base. (Dies from Juniors E63A)

a. Red Tinted Windows.

b. Green Tinted Windows.

C 8(?)   Ford Escort – Hollywood Rally   1980s

White Body, Black Interior, Black Baseplate, "Hollywood Rally" Labels, "CORGI JUNIORS INDUSTRIA BRASILIERA WHIZZWHEELS KIKO" on Black Diecast Base. (Promotional for Hollywood Cigarettes in Brazil. Dies from Juniors E63A)

C 9   Futura Van (Healer Wheeler) – Fire   1980s

Red Body, Dark Smoked Windows.

a. "FIRE" Labels with Shield.

b. Red "FIRE" Tampo Printed on Yellow Side Areas with Black Shield, Yellow Nose Area with Black "FD" Logo.

C 9(?)   Healer Wheeler (SACI)   1980s

Red Body with Smoked Windows, "FIRE" Labels on Sides, "IND BRAS" and "SACI" on Black Plastic Base. (Dies from Juniors E36B) (**Note:** SACI is a brand name used for model dies sold by Corgi / KIKO and not later returned to Corgi.)

C 10   Chevy Van – Revell   1980s

Yellow Body, "Revell PLASTIC KITS" Labels on Sides, "CORGI JUNIORS INDUSTRIA BRASILIERA KIKO" on Black Plastic Base. (Dies from Juniors E22D / E90A etc.)

a. Red Tinted Windows.

b. Blue Tinted Windows.

C 12   Range Rover - Airport Rescue   1980s

a. Red Body with Black & White Striped "Airport Rescue 88" Labels on Hood and Sides, Tan Seats, Blue Tinted Windows, "INDUSTRIA BRASILIERA KIKO" on Black Plastic Base. (Dies from Juniors E9C)

b. Red Body with Black & White Striped "Airport Rescue 88" Labels on Hood and Sides, Tan Seats, Green Tinted Windows, "INDUSTRIA BRASILIERA KIKO" on Black Plastic Base. (Dies from Juniors E9C)

c. Red Body with Black Tampo Stripes, "Airport Rescue 88" Tampo Printed on Hood and Sides, Tan Seats, "INDUSTRIA BRASILIERA KIKO" on Black Plastic Base. (Dies from Juniors E9C)

C 13   Chevy Van – Varig   1980s

Blue Body, White Side Labels with Blue "VOE VARIG" Text, "KIKO CHEVROLET VAN CORGI JUNIORS INDUSTRIA BRASILIERA" on Black Plastic Base. (Dies from Juniors E22D / E90A etc.)

a. Red Tinted Windows.

b. Yellow Tinted Windows.

c. Opaque Black Windows.

C 15   Futura Van (Healer Wheeler} - POLICE   1980s

a. Black Body with Smoked Windows, "POLICE" Labels on Sides, "PD" Label on Hood, "IND BRAS" and "KIKO" on Black Plastic Base. (Dies from Juniors E36B)

b. Blue Body with Red Tinted Windows, "POLICE" Labels on Sides, "PD" Label on Hood, "IND BRAS" and "KIKO" on Black Plastic Base. (Dies from Juniors E36B)

c. Black Body with Smoked Windows, "POLICE" Tampo Printed on Sides, "PD 8" Tampo Printed on Hood, "IND BRAS" and "KIKO" on Black Plastic Base. (Dies from Juniors E36B)

C 16   Formula 1 Racer   1980s

a. Red Body with Yellow "Shell 6" Labels, White Driver with Gray Engine and Windshield, "INDUSTRIA BRASIL" and "KIKO" on Base. (Dies from Juniors E22C)

b. Yellow Body with Red "Shell 6" Printing, White Driver with White Engine and Windshield, "INDUSTRIA BRASIL" and "KIKO" on Base. (Dies from Juniors E22C)

c. White Body with Blue "parmalat 5" Labels, White Driver with Yellow Engine and Windshield, "INDUSTRIA BRASIL" and "KIKO" on Base. (Dies from Juniors E22C)

d. Black Body with Black and White "John Player Special 7" Labels, White Driver with Gray Engine and Windshield, "INDUSTRIA BRASIL" and "KIKO" on Base. (Dies from Juniors E22C)

C 17   Chevy Van – Pepsi   1980s
White Body with Pepsi Logo and Blue Waves on Sides, "CORGI JUNIORS INDUSTRIA BRASILIERA KIKO" on Black Plastic Base. (Dies from Juniors E22D / E90A etc.)
a. Yellow Tinted Windows.
b. Red Tinted Windows.
c. Blue Tinted Windows.

C 20   Range Rover – Paramedic   1980s
White Body.
a. Raised Roof with two round lights, Yellow Tinted Windows Including Roof Lights, Red Interior, White Paper backed Labels with Red "PARAMEDIC" and Red Cross Emblem.
b. Raised Roof with two round lights, Red Tinted Windows Including Roof Lights, Red Interior, White Paper backed Labels with Red "PARAMEDIC" and Red Cross Emblem.
c. Flat roof with ridges, Red Stripes and "PARAMEDIC" Tampo Graphics, Red Lightbar on Roof, Opaque Black Windows.
d. Flat roof with ridges, Red Stripes and "PARAMEDIC" Tampo Graphics, Blank White Roof, Smoked Windows with Yellow Interior.

C 21   Land Rover Wrecker – Army   1980s
Green Body, Black Hook, White "ARMY RESCUE" Paper Labels on Hood and Sides.
a. Yellow Tinted Windows.
b. Red Tinted Windows.

C 22   Mobile Crane   1980s
a. Yellow Body with Red Tinted Windows, Tan Plastic Lower Boom and Base, Black Plastic Upper Boom and Pivot, "INDUSTRIA BRASILIERA KIKO" on Base. (Dies from Juniors E88A)
b. Green Body with Smoked Windows, Tan Plastic Upper Boom, Pivot and Base, Black Plastic Lower Boom, "INDUSTRIA BRASILIERA KIKO" on Base. (Dies from Juniors E88A)

C 23   Land Rover Wrecker – Red   1980s
Red Body, Yellow Tinted Windows and Roof Light, Black Hook, Yellow Labels on Hood and Sides with "URUBU QUEBRA GALHO REBOQUE" Text and Cartoon Character Vulture.

C 24   Mobile Crane Fire Truck   1980s
Mobile Crane Casting Slightly Modified to mount Fire Accessories, Red Body Casting, Black Base, Standard Black Wheels, Yellow Tinted Windows, Black Boom Base with White Fire Ladder of Kiko Design, White High Pressure Nozzle Behind Cab, "Corgi Juniors KIKO INDUSTRIA BRASILIERA" on Base.

C 27   Mercedes-Benz Binz Ambulance – Fire   1980s
Red Body with Yellow Tinted Windows, "FIRE CHIEF" Labels on Sides, "IND BRAS" and "KIKO" on Black Plastic Base. (Dies from Juniors E1E)

C 28   Ford Tipper Truck (Dump Truck)   1980s
a. Red Body with Clear Windows, White Corgi Dump Body with Red Tailgate, "IND BRAS" and "KIKO" on Black Plastic Base. (Dies from Juniors E49B.)
b. Red Body with Green Tinted Windows, Cream Corgi Dump Body with Red Tailgate, "IND BRAS" and "KIKO" on Black Plastic Base. (Dies from Juniors E49B.)

C 29   Mercedes-Benz Ambulance   1980s
White Body, No Interior, Dark Blue Tinted Windows, Red Cross Label on Hood, Red Side Labels with White "AMBULANCIA" Text.

C 30   Ford Van – Carreois   1980s
a. Black Cab and Chassis, Yellow Plastic Box Body, Yellow Side Labels with Black "CORREIOS TRANSPORTE DE VALORES" Graphics.
b. Red Cab and Chassis, Yellow Plastic Box Body, Yellow Side Labels with Black "CORREIOS TRANSPORTE DE VALORES" Graphics.
c. Orange Cab and Chassis, Yellow Plastic Box Body, Yellow Side Labels with Black "CORREIOS TRANSPORTE DE VALORES" Graphics.

C 30(?) Ford Box Truck
          (Tipper Truck Chassis) – Tivoli Park   1980s
Blue Cab and Chassis (as listed below,) White Kiko Box Body, Red "Tivoli Park" Labels on Sides , "IND BRAS" and "KIKO" on Black Plastic Base. (Promotional model from Tivoli Park Amusement Park in Brazil. Dies from Juniors E49B with box body of Kiko design.)
a. Medium Blue Cab and Chassis with Smoked Windows.
b. Dark Blue Cab and Chassis with Smoked Windows.

C 31   Mercedes-Benz Mobile Shop   1980s
Green Body, White Interior.

a. Salesman Printed on Rear Card Graphics, "MINI SHOP" Labels on Roof and Sides.
b. No Salesman Printed on Rear Card Graphics, "MINI SHOP" Labels on Roof and Sides.
c. No Salesman Printed on Rear Card Graphics, "MINI SHOP" Tampo Printed on Roof and Sides.

C 32   Rough Terrain Truck   1980s
a. White Upper and Brown Lower Body with Black Divider / Interior, "IND BRAS KIKO" on Base. (Dies from Juniors E13B)
b. Red Upper and Yellow Lower Body with Black Divider / Interior, otherwise as 32a.
c. Red Upper and Blue Lower Body with Black Divider / Interior, otherwise as 32a.

C 33   Ford Skip Truck   1980s
Green Tinted Windows, "IND BRAS" and "KIKO" on Black Plastic Base. (Dies from Juniors E49B except for Arms and Skip Body. Arms may be from E54A.)
a. Orange Cab and Chassis, White Plastic Loading Arms and Black Plastic Skip (Dumpster) Body.
b. Yellow Cab and Chassis, White Plastic Loading Arms and Black Plastic Skip (Dumpster) Body.
c. Yellow Cab and Chassis, Black Plastic Loading Arms and White Plastic Skip (Dumpster) Body.

C 34   Hot Rod Custom (Dodge) Van – Marvel Comics 1980s
a. Black Body with Smoked Windows, "READ MARVEL COMICS" Labels on Sides, "IND BRAS KIKO" on Black Plastic Base. (Dies from Juniors E91B)
b. Same as 34-a except Clear Windows.

C 35   Ford Cement Truck (Caminhao Betoneira)   1980s
a. Black Body with Clear Windows, Yellow and Orange Thin Plastic Cement Mixer Body of KIKO Design, "IND BRAS" and "KIKO" on Black Plastic Base. (Not from E30D Dies. Tipper Dies Used from Juniors E49B except for Cement Mixer Body.)
b. Red Body with Clear Windows, Yellow and Orange Thin Plastic Cement Mixer Body of KIKO Design, (otherwise like 35a.)
c. Orange Body with Clear Windows, Yellow Thin Plastic Cement Mixer Body of KIKO Design on Blue Plastic Base, (otherwise like 35a.)
d. Green Body with Clear Windows, Blue Thin Plastic Cement Mixer Body of KIKO Design on Yellow Plastic Base, (otherwise like 35a.)

C 36   Digger   1980s
Red Plastic Boom and Scoop, "IND BRAS" and " KIKO" on Base. (Dies from Juniors E77B)
a. Yellow Upper and Red Lower Body,
b. White Upper and Blue Lower Body,

C 37   Mercedes-Benz Mobile Shop – Ice Cream   1980s
White Body with "ICE CREAM" Labels, White Seats, Clear Windows with Cardboard Ice Cream Server Insert, "IND BRAS" and " KIKO" on Black Plastic Base. (Dies from Juniors E98B)
a. Labels on Roof and Sides.
b. Labels on Sides Only.

C 38   Hot Rod Custom (Dodge) Van – Danger   1980s
Yellow Body with Clear Windows, "DANGER" Labels with Lightning Bolt and Atomic Symbol on Sides, "IND BRAS KIKO" on Black Plastic Base. (Dies from Juniors E91B)

C 39   Ford Tipper Truck (Dump Truck)   1980s
Body with Clear Windows, Yellow Thin Plastic Dump Body of KIKO Design, "IND BRAS" and "KIKO" on Black Plastic Base. (Dies from Juniors E49B except for Dump Body.)
a. Red Body
b. Black Body

C 40   Ford GT 70   1980s
Yellow Body with Black Rear Hatch, White Seats, Black Diecast Base with "IND BRAS" and "KIKO" Text. (Dies from Juniors E12D)

C 44   Ford Torino – Black Police   1980s
Black Body with Red Roof Lamp, Opaque Black Windows and Baseplate, Yellow Side Labels with Red "POLICE" Text.

C 45   Helicopter – Blue Police   1980s
Blue Upper Body, White Lower Body and Skis, Red Rotors, Clear Windows, "POLICE" Labels on Sides.

C 46   Lotus Esprit – White   1980s
Details not available at time of publication.

C 47   Mercedes-Benz Gullwing – Black   1980s
Details not available at time of publication.

C 48   Opel Corsa – Black   1980s
Details not available at time of publication.

C 49   Ferrari 308 GTS   1980s

Red Body, Tan Seats with Black Dashboard, "IND BRAS KIKO" on Base. (Dies from Juniors E136A)

a. Black "Ferrari" on Doors

b. White "Ferrari" on Doors

C 50   Waste (Refuse) Truck   1980s

a. White Cab / Chassis, Blue Garbage Body, Opaque Black Windows.

b. Yellow Cab / Chassis, Blue Garbage Body, Dark Red Tinted Windows.

C 51   VW Polo - Red   1980s

a. Red Body, Black Interior, Blue Roof Rack with White and Yellow Surfboards on Roof.

b. Red Body, Black Interior, White Roof Rack with Blue and Yellow Surfboards on Roof.

C 52   Mercedes-Benz 500SL   1980s

a. Black Body, Tan Interior, Clear Windows, No Graphics.

b. Red Body, Yellow Interior, Clear Windows, No Graphics.

C 53   Chubb Airport Fire Tender – Red   1980s

Red Body, White Interior and Roof Nozzle, Clear Windows, Black and White Side Stripe with White "8," White "AIRPORT RESCUE" Text over Stripe.

C 54   Range Rover Open Top - Sheriff   1980s

a. Blue Body with Silver & Black "SHERIFF" on Hood, Tan Seats, "KIKO" on Black Plastic Base. (Dies from Juniors E184A)

b. Red Body with Silver & Blue "SHERIFF" on Hood, Tan Seats, "KIKO" on Black Plastic Base. (Dies from Juniors E184A)

C 55   Austin Mini-Metro – White   1980s

White Body, Black Interior, Two Red Trim Stripes Low in Sides.

C 56   Dumper Truck   1980s

Red Cab and Chassis, Yellow Dump Body, Black Wheels.

C 57   Ford Cement Truck (Caminhao de Cimento)   1980s

Orange Body with Clear Windows, Yellow Plastic Cement Mixer Drum, "IND BRAS" and "KIKO" on Yellow Plastic Base. (E30D Dies.)

C 58   Iveco Beverage Truck – Pepsi   1980s

Ford Tipper Cab and Chassis, White Beverage Body of Kiko Design, Large Opening Side Panels with Pepsi Labels, Beverage Crate Load.

C 59   Ford Transit Pick-up   1980s

a. Red Body with Black Opaque Windows, "IND BRAS KIKO" on Black Plastic Base. (Dies from Juniors E125A)

b. Same as 59a with Transparent Smoked Windows.

C 60   Citroen 2CV   1980s

a. Yellow Body with Black Roof, Red Interior, "KIKO IND BRAS" on Base. (Dies from Juniors E115A)

b. Same as 60a with Added Duck Character on Hood and Rear Doors.

C 60(?)   1957 Ford T-Bird   1980s

a. Yellow Body, Black Seats and Base, Clear Windshield. (Dies from Juniors E96B.)

b. Red Body, Black Seats and Base, Yellow Windshield. (Dies from Juniors E96B.)

C 61   Caravan (Trailer) – Red   1980s

Colors and Graphics not known at time of publication.

C 62   Rover 3500 Police   1980s

Bright Green Body with Red Lightbar and Antenna on Roof, Black Interior and Base, Clear Windows, White "POLICE" Graphics.

C 63   Rover 3500 Fire   1980s

Red Body with Blue Lightbar on Roof, Black Interior and Base, Clear Windows, Yellow "FIRE CHIEF" on Sides.

C 64   Peterbilt Dump Truck – Yellow / Red   1980s

Yellow Cab and Chassis, Red Dump Body.

C 65   Peterbilt Pipe Truck   1980s

Colors not known at time of publication.

C 66   Peterbilt Tank Truck   1980s

Colors not known at time of publication.

C 67   Peterbilt Box Truck – Dunlop   1980s

Black Cab and Chassis, Blue Flatbed with White Box Body, Vacuum-Plated Grill and Windows, "DUNLOP" Labels on Box Sides.

C 68   VW Polo – Yellow   1980s

Yellow Body, Black Interior, Orange Roof Rack with White and Red Surfboards on Roof.

C 69   Rover 3500 – Triplex   1980s

White Body with Blue Roof and Hood Panels, Black Interior, Colors and Graphics Similar to UK Produced Version.

C 70   Leyland Tank Truck – Shell   1980s

a. Dark Yellow Body, Black Base, Smoked Windows, Red "Shell" Graphics.

b. Yellow Body, Gray Base, Opaque Black Windows, Red "Shell" Graphics.

C 71   Ford Mustang Hatchback – Super America   1980s

White Body, Black Base, Gray Interior, Red Stripes on Hood, Blue Rectangle with Stars on Roof, Red and Blue Stripes on Sides with "MUSTANG" Text.

C 72   Boat and Trailer   1980s

(Dies from Boat Portion of Juniors J202-A)

a. Yellow Upper and White Lower Plastic Boat Body with Smoked Windows, Black Plastic Outboard Motor, Green Diecast Trailer without text on Base.

b. Red Upper and White Lower Plastic Boat Body with Smoked Windows, Black Plastic Outboard Motor, White Diecast Trailer without text on Base.

C 73   Dinghy and Trailer   1980s

(Dies from Dinghy Portion of Juniors J201-A)

Colors not known at time of publication. Diecast Trailer without text on Base.

C 78   Wild West Locomotive   1980s

Colors and Graphics Identical to UK Version.

C 79   Wild West Railroad Coach   1980s

Colors and Graphics Identical to UK Version.

C 80   Wild West Railroad Baggage Car   1980s

Colors and Graphics Identical to UK Version.

C 81   Wild West Steamboat   1980s

Colors and Graphics Identical to UK Version.

C 82   Wild West Stagecoach   1980s

Colors and Graphics Identical to UK Version.

C 83   Wild West Covered Wagon   1980s

Colors and Graphics Identical to UK Version.

C 91   Opel Corsa   1980s

Silver Upper Body, Black Lower Body / Base and Interior, Clear Windows, No Graphics.

C #(?)   Formula 5000   1980s

Yellow Body, Red Driver and Engine Detail, No Graphics.

C #(?)   Volvo 760 – Rally   1980s

a. Blue Body, Black Interior, Red and White "6" and Horse Graphics, Yellow Tinted Windows.

b. Blue Body, Opaque Black Windows, Red and White "6" and Horse Graphics, Gray Baseplate with "VOLVO SALOON KIKO IND BRAS" Text.

C #(?)   Citroen Dyane   1980s

Silver Body, Black Interior, No Graphics, Clear Windows.

C #(?)   VW Hot Rod   1980s

Red Body, Black Diecast Base, Silver Engines, Yellow Lightning Stripe on Sides, Yellow Circle on Roof with Red "52" Graphics.

C #(?)   Renault Trafic Van   1980s

Blue Body with Smoked Windows, "IND BRAS KIKO" on Black Plastic Base. (Dies from Juniors J25B)

C #(?)   Chevy Van – Spider-man (Homen Aranha)   1980s

Blue Body with Red Tinted Windows, White / Red / Blue "HOMEN ARANHA" Labels on Sides, "CORGI JUNIORS INDUSTRIA BRASILIERA KIKO" on Black Plastic Base. (Dies from Juniors E22D / E90A etc.)

C #(?)   Chevy Van – Tivoli Park   1980s

Black Body with Red Tinted Windows, Red "Tivoli Park" Labels on Sides, "CORGI JUNIORS INDUSTRIA BRASILIERA KIKO" on Black Plastic Base. (Promotional model from Tivoli Park Amusement Park in Brazil. Dies from Juniors E22D / E90A etc.)

C #(?)   Chevy Van – Monica   1980s

Blue Body with Red Tinted Windows, Red "LOJINHADA MONICA" Labels on Sides, "CORGI JUNIORS INDUSTRIA BRASILIERA KIKO" on Black Plastic Base. (From Monica Gift Set C 3030.)

C 400   2 Pack – Peterbilt Pipe Truck & Matching Trailer   1980s

Colors not known at time of publication.

C 410   2 Pack – Peterbilt Tanker Truck & Matching Trailer   1980s

Colors not known at time of publication.

C 420   2 Pack – Peterbilt Box Truck & Matching Trailer   1980s

Colors not known at time of publication, Believed to have "Dunlop" Graphics.

C 430   2 Pack – Ford Mustang w/ Speedboat & Trailer   1980s

Colors and Graphics Identical to Separately Released Items.

C 440   2 Pack – Rover 3500 w/ Dinghy Trailer   1980s

Colors and Graphics Identical to Separately Released Items.

C 450   2 Pack – Austin Metro w/ Caravan Trailer   1980s

White Metro, Red Caravan.

C 460   2 Pack – Rover & Caravan – Police   1980s

Bright Green Rover with Lightbar on Roof, Black Interior and Base, White "POLICE" Graphics, Bright Green Caravan with Tan Door and Interior, Same Graphics as Car.

C 470   2 Pack – Rover & Caravan – Fire   **1980s**
Red Rover with Blue Lightbar on Roof and Clear Windows, Red Caravan with Tan
Interior and Clear Windows, Both with "FIRE CHIEF" on Sides.

C 480   2 Pack – VW Polo & Caravan – Police   **1980s**
Blue VW Polo with Red Lightbar on Roof, Blue Caravan with Tan Interior and Clear
Windows, Both with "POLICE" on Sides.

C 490   2 Pack – VW Polo & Caravan – Fire   **1980s**
Red VW Polo with Blue Lightbar on Roof, Red Caravan with Tan Interior and Clear
Windows, Both with "FIRE CHIEF" on Sides.
a. Opaque Black Windows in VW.
b. Clear Windows in VW.

C 3000   Sports Car Set   **1980s**
Red VW Polo, Yellow VW Polo, Motorboat & Trailer, White Metro, Red Caravan,
White Mustang Hatchback.

C 3010   Emergency Squad Set   **1980s**
Chubb Fire Truck, VW Polo Police, Mobile Crane, Police Helicopter, VW Polo Fire.

C 3014   Emergency Squad Set   **1980s**
Chubb Airport Crash Tender, Rover 3500, Helicopter, VW Polo, Mobil Crane, Mobil
Crane Ladder Truck.

C 3015   Construction Set   **1980s**
Digger, Dumper, Ford Transit Pick-up, Ford Cement Truck, Ford Tipper Truck,
Peterbilt Pipe Truck.

C 3016   Super Sports Car Set   **1980s**
a. Red Ferrari 308GTS, Yellow Thunderbird Convertible, Silver Mercedes Gullwing,
Unknown Black Car.
b. Ford Mustang, Rover Triplex, VW Polo, Austin Metro, Caravan Trailer, Speedboat
& Trailer.

C 3020   Construction Set   **1980s**
Ford Transit Pick-up, Yellow Faun Dump Truck, Ford Cement Truck, Ford Dump
Truck, Peterbilt Pipe Truck, Mobile Backhoe.

C 3030   Monica Set   **1980s**
Futura Van CEBOLINHA, Chevy Van MONICA, Ford Box Truck CASCAO, Ford Box
Truck MAGALI.

C 3040   Wild West Set   **1980s**
One Each of All Wild West Models, Plastic Buildings and Figures.

C 3050   Car Set   **1980s**
Motorboat & Trailer, Red VW Polo, Red Open Top Range Rover, Mustang
Hatchback.

Former Super Juniors E Series and J Series Dies

C 100 (570)   Scania Box Van   **1980s**
a. Aqua Cab / Chassis, Blue Container Box with White Side Labels and "VARIG
CARGO" Graphics.
b. Red Cab / Chassis, White Container Box with Red "CB" Graphics. (Promotional
model.)
c. Yellow Cab / Chassis with White Air Dam on Roof, Yellow Container Box with White
Side Labels and "KIBON Sempre o melkor sounte" Graphics. (Promotional model.)
d. Aqua Cab / Chassis, Blue Container Box with White Side Labels and "ESTOQUE"
Graphics. (Promotional model.)

C 110 (574)   Scania Cement Mixer   **1980s**
White Cab / Chassis, White over Blue Cement Body with "SANO" Graphics.

C 120 (571)   Scania Tipper   **1980s**
a. Blue / Yellow, other details not known.
b. Red / Yellow, other details not known.

C 200 (575)   Mercedes-Benz Low Loader with Digger   1980s
a. Mercedes Truck with White Cab and Dark Blue Fenders, Clear Windows, Blue Low
Loader Trailer (like normally found with Ford D Series,) Digger with Blue Base
Casting, Yellow Cab Casting and Red Boom.
b. Mercedes Truck with Black Cab and Yellow Fenders, Clear Windows, White Low
Loader Trailer with Black Ramp (like normally found with Ford D Series,) Digger
with Blue Base Casting, Yellow Cab Casting and Red Boom.

C 210 (572)   Mercedes-Benz Tanker – Atlantic   **1980s**
Mercedes Truck with White Cab and Red Chassis, "Atlantic" Logo on Cab Doors,
Blue Tanker Trailer with Red Chassis, White "Atlantic" Labels on Sides.

C 220 (573)   Mercedes-Benz Container Truck – Saturno   1980s
Mercedes Truck with Brown Cab and Yellow Chassis, White Box Trailer with Yellow
Chassis, Brown "SATURNO" Side Labels.

Metalbox Corgi from Eastern Europe

Models produced or assembled in Hungary by Metalbox GMK from transferred
Corgi and Juniors Dies. Many used inferior wheels and had revised baseplate text.
Production dates and quantities uncertain. Only models known to the author are
listed. Many more exist.

Juniors Size Models

???   Airport Rescue Fire Tender   **1990s**
a. Red Body, White Plastic Roof Features, Transparent Yellow Tinted Windows,
White "AIRPORT" Graphics.
b. White Body, White Plastic Roof Features, Transparent Yellow Tinted Windows,
Blue "AIR FRANCE" Graphics.
c. White Body, White Plastic Roof Features, Transparent Yellow Tinted Windows,
Blue "INTERNATIONAL" Graphics.
d. White Body, White Plastic Roof Features, Transparent Yellow Tinted Windows,
Red "AIRPORT" Graphics.
e. White Body, White Plastic Roof Features, Transparent Yellow Tinted Windows,
Blue "AIRPORT" Graphics.

???   Rover 3500 Police   **1990s**
a. Green Body with Light Green Clip-on Lightbar on Roof, White Interior, Clear
Windows, White "POLICE" in Circle on Hood.
b. Green Body with Yellow Clip-on Lightbar on Roof, Red Interior, Clear Windows,
White "POLICE" in Circle on Hood.
c. Red Body with Red Clip-on Lightbar on Roof, White Interior, Clear Windows,
White "POLICE" in Circle on Hood.
d. Red Body with Yellow Clip-on Lightbar on Roof, Yellow Interior, Clear Windows,
White "POLICE" in Circle on Hood.

???   Rover 3500 Ambulance(?)   **1990s**
White Body, Red Interior, Clear Windows, Small Red Cross on Hood.

???   Rover 3500   **1990s**
a. Metallic Red Body, White Interior, Clear Windows, No Graphics.
b. Metallic Gold Body, Red Interior, Clear Windows, No Graphics.

???   Citroen Dyane   **1990s**
Black Interior, Clear Windows.
a. Odd Pink Body, Black Chevrons on Hood.
b. Red Body, Black Chevrons on Hood.
c. Orange Body, Mickey Head on Hood.
d. Metallic Red Body, No Graphics.
e. Yellow Body, No Graphics.
f. Pale Blue Body, No Graphics.
g. Medium Blue Body, No Graphics.

???   Healer Wheeler Ambulance   **1990s**
a. White Body, Blue Tinted Windows, Blue Roof Light, Small Red Cross on
Hood.
b. Yellow Body, Blue Tinted Windows, Blue Roof Light, Blue Graphics.
c. Red Body, Blue Tinted Windows, Blue Roof Light, Small "3" on Hood.
d. Metallic Red Body, Blue Tinted Windows, Blue Roof Light, No Graphics.

???   Refuse Truck   **1990s**
Red Body, Tan Refuse Body, Opaque Black Windows.

???   Container Truck   **1990s**
Yellow Cab, Black Flatbed Body and Grill, Black Container, Opaque Black
Windows.

???   Ford Cement Truck   **1990s**
a. Red Cab and Chassis, White Drum and Holder, Opaque Black Windows.
b. Spring Green Cab and Chassis, White Drum and Holder, Clear Windows.

???   Helicopter   **1990s**
a. Green Body, Yellow Chassis and Skis, Yellow Rotors, Clear Windows, White
"nino" Graphics.
b. Green Body, Yellow Chassis and Skis, Yellow Rotors, Clear Windows, White
"POLICE" Graphics.

Far East Copies Made to Resemble Corgi Models

This section contains some variations for models produced as copies of Corgi
Juniors or smaller copies of Corgi Toys. In many cases, the extent of the range
offered or the variations produced on each model is not known.

Playart diecast models made to resemble Corgi Juniors and Corgi Toys

Diecast models made by Playart in Hong Kong which are direct copies of Corgi Juniors and Corgi Toys models. Models are to a slightly smaller scale than standard Corgi Juniors. Not authorized by Mettoy.

#?   **Massey Ferguson Tractor**   **1970s?**

No Windows, Manufactured by Playart. (Copy of E43-A.)

a. Green Cab and Engine Cover, Red Scoop and Arms, Black Base and Engine.

b. Orange Cab and Engine Cover, Red Scoop and Arms, Black Base and Engine.

c. Orange Cab and Engine Cover, Green Scoop and Arms, Black Base and Engine.

d. Other colors probably exist.

#?   **Zetor Tractor**   **1970s?**

No Windows, Manufactured by Playart. (Copy of Husky / Corgi Juniors 4-C in a slightly smaller scale.)

a. Metallic Blue Body, Black Interior.

b. Other colors probably exist.

#?   **Thrushbuster**   **1970s?**

1962 Oldsmobile with Vacuum Plated Spotlamps at Corners of Windshield, Clear Windows, "U N C L E CAR" on Base, Manufactured by Playart. (Copy of Corgi 497-A in a much smaller scale.)

a. Metallic Blue Body, Black Interior.

b. Orange Body, Black Interior.

c. Orange Body, White Interior.

d. Mint Green Body, Black Interior.

e. Lime Green Body, White Interior.

f. Blue Body, White Interior.

g. Other colors probably exist.

#?   **Batmobile**   **1970s?**

Black Body, Clear Windows, Red Interior, Manufactured by Playart. (Copy of Husky / Corgi Juniors 1002-A in a slightly smaller scale.)

a. Yellow Interior, Red Figures.

b. Gray Interior, Mint Green Figures.

c. Black Interior, No Figures.

d. Other interior colors probably exist.

#?   **Cadillac Eldorado**   **1970s?**

Clear Windows, Manufactured by Playart. (Copy of Husky / Corgi Juniors 9-B in a slightly smaller scale.)

a. Metallic Blue Body, Red Interior.

b. Light Blue Body, Blue Interior.

c. Light Blue Body, Yellow Interior.

a. Metallic Light Green Body, Ivory Interior.

d. Light Green Body, Black Interior.

e. Yellow Body, White Interior.

f. Red Body, White Interior.

g. Red Body, Black Interior.

h. Other colors probably exist.

#?   **Jensen Interceptor (FF)**   **1970s?**

Clear Windows, Manufactured by Playart. (Copy of Husky / Corgi Juniors 9-B in a slightly smaller scale.)

a. Yellow Body, Black Interior.

b. Light Blue Body with White Base, Light Blue Interior.

c. Maroon Body with White Base, Light Blue Interior.

d. Red Body with White Base, Yellow Interior.

e. Other colors probably exist.

#?   **Rover 2000 TC**   **1970s?**

Clear Windows, Manufactured by Playart. (Copy of Corgi Toys 252-A in a much smaller scale.)

a. Metallic Green Body, White Interior.

b. Other colors probably exist.

#?   **Toyota 2000 Convertible**   **1970s?**

Clear Windows, Manufactured by Playart. (Copy of Corgi Toys 375-A in a much smaller scale.)

a. Dark Purple Body, White Interior.

b. Other colors probably exist.

#?   **Porsche Carrera 6**   **1970s?**

Clear Windows, Manufactured by Playart. (Copy of Corgi Juniors 41-A in a slightly smaller scale.)

a. Green Body, Black Interior.

b. Other colors probably exist.

#?   **Chevrolet Astro 1**   **1970s?**

Clear Windows, Manufactured by Playart. (Copy of Corgi Rockets 908-A in a slightly smaller scale.)

a. Red Body, Black Interior.

b. Yellow Body, Black Interior.

c. Red Body, White Interior, White "8" Tampo Printed Graphics.

d. Other colors probably exist.

#?   **Mangusta DeTomaso**   **1970s?**

Clear Windows, Manufactured by Playart. (Copy of Husky / Corgi Juniors 6-C in a slightly smaller scale.)

a. Orange Body, Pale Blue Interior.

b. Other colors probably exist.

#?   **Mercedes C111**   **1970s?**

Clear Windows, Manufactured by Playart. (Copy of Husky / Corgi Juniors 72-A in a slightly smaller scale.)

a. Metallic Purple Body, Pale Blue Interior.

b. Other colors probably exist.

#?   **Alfa-Romeo P33**   **1970s?**

Clear Windows, Vacuum Plated Interior, Manufactured by Playart. (Copy of Corgi Juniors 73-A in a slightly smaller scale.)

a. Orange Body with Blue and White "2 ESSO" Graphics.

b. Other colors probably exist.

#?   **Beach Buggy**   **1970s?**

Clear Windshield, Manufactured by Playart. (Copy of Corgi Juniors 58-A in a slightly smaller scale.)

a. Blue Body with White Seats and two sizes of knobby wheels.

b. Other colors probably exist.

#?   **Rolls-Royce Silver Shadow Coupe**   **1970s?**

Clear Windows, Manufactured by Playart. (Copy of Corgi Toys 273-A in a much smaller scale.)

a. Pale Yellow Body, Black Interior.

b. Metallic Olive Body, White Interior.

c. Metallic Maroon Body, White Interior.

d. Orange Body, White Interior.

e. Pink Body, White Interior.

f. Mustard Yellow Body, Blue Interior.

g. Other colors probably exist.

Various Other Far East brands made to resemble Corgi models

Plastic or diecast models which are direct copies of Corgi Juniors models. Extent of product line not known. Probably issued under many different brand names over time. Definitely not authorized by Corgi.

#?   **Guy Car Transporter**   **1970s?**

Blue Cab, Orange Trailer, "GORDY CAR TRANSPORT" Labels on Sides. (Almost exact copy of Corgi Juniors Guy Car Transporter but in plastic.)

#?   **Studebaker Ambulance**   **1970s?**

White Plastic Body, Blue Tinted Windows including Window where Sliding Roof Should Be Located, Red Cross Labels on Hood and Doors.

#?   **Leyland Terrier Milk Products Truck**   **1970s?**

Red Diecast Body almost identical to Corgi Leyland Box Truck, Green and Yellow Side Labels with "DAIRY MILK PRODUCTS" Graphics, Pull-back Motor Chassis with Sze-Toy 1602 on Base. (Possibly same company that would later be known as Zee-Toy.)

#?   **Leyland Terrier Tanker**   **1970s?**

Silver Diecast Body almost identical to Corgi Leyland Tanker Truck, Silver Side Labels "Shell" Graphics almost Identical to Corgi Version, Pull-back Motor Chassis with Sze-Toy 1604 on Base unless noted. (Possibly same company that would later be known as Zee-Toy.)

a. Silver Body, "Shell" Side Labels, Pull-Back Motor.

b. Silver Body, "TEXACO" Labels, Pull-Back Motor.

c. Silver Body, "Shell" Side Labels, Free Rolling.

#?   **Thunderbolt**   **1970s?**

Green Body with "TEXACO" Label, Opaque Full Canopy, Sze-Toy on Base. (Possibly same company that would later be known as Zee-Toy.)

#?   **Oldsmobile Starfire Police**   **1970s?**

Plastic Blue 1966 Oldsmobile Starfire Coupe, Red Tinted Windows, No Interior, Blue Roof Light, "POLICE" Labels on Doors, Manufactured in Hong Kong. (Copy of Husky 31-A in a slightly smaller scale.)

Section 4
Appendix

Alphabetical Cross-Reference List

Adams Probe 16: 52-A
Aerocar: 2009-A
Air Bus Helicopter: 35-B
Alfa Romeo Montreal ElectroRocket: 4002
Alfa Romeo Pininfarina P33: 33-D, 73-A, 917-A,
AMC Pacer: 62-B
AMF Snowmobile: 18-D, 2506-A
Armored Car: 2522-A
Aston Martin - James Bond: 40-C, 1001-A, 1201-A, LL-1361
Aston Martin DB6: 22-B, 901-A, J10, J110-A, J178
Aston Martin DBS: 24-B, 913-A
Austin Healey LeMans Sprite: 11-B
Austin Mini Metro: 107-A, 135-A, 2595-A, J26, J26/02, J80, LL-1353, LL-1385, J228, Kiko 55, Kiko 450
Aveling-Barford Dump Truck: 16-A
B.V.R.T Vita-Mini 1300 Mini-Cooper S: 21-C
Batbike: 23-C
Batboat on Trailer: 1003-A, 1203-A
Batcopter: 78-B
Batman - Jokermobile: 99-A
Batman - Penguinmobile: 20-D
Batmobile: 69-A, 1002-A, 1202-A, 2519-A, 2601-A, 3002-A, 3002-B, 3080-A, LL-1360
Bedford TK 7-Ton Lorry: 27-A
Bertone Carabo: 65-A
Bertone Runabout Barchetta: 74-A, 930-A
Bizzarini Manta: 77-A, 918-A, 4000, 4001
BMW 325I: J16/01, J16/02(?), J22/01, 90076, HW 95509
BMW 850i: 90550, HW 16305, HW 94360
BMW M3: J30 B, J30/01, J50 B, HW 95517
Bobsled: 52-C, 1011-A, 1012-A
Buck Rogers Starfighter: 13-C, 2538-A, J4 A, LL-1363
Bugs Bunny GP Beach Buggy: 84-B
Buick Electra: 7-A
Buick Electra Police: 9-A
Buick Regal: 206-A, J60/??
Buick Regal - Kojak: 68-A, 2527-A
Buick Regal Fire: J81/02
Buick Regal Police: 17-D, 28-C, 133-A, 150-A, 190-A, 2528-A, 2535-A, J60, J81, J81/01, 90420, HW 95530,
Buick Regal Sheriff: 28-D, 61-B

Buick Regal Taxi: 14-D
Cadillac Eldorado: 9-B, 907-A
Cadillac Eldorado Hot Rod: 57-A
Can Am Racer: 82-A, Kiko 4
Carabo Bertone: 916-A
Caravan: 65-B, 2518-A, 2518-B, 2554-A, 2554-B, J203, Kiko 61
Cement Mixer: 20-C, 2514-A,
Centurion Tank: 66-A, 158-A, 2522-A
Chevrolet Astro 1: 908-A
Chevrolet Convertible 1957: 152-A, 156-A
Chevrolet Corvette: 179-A, 600-A through 627-A, J45, J45/01, J45/02, 90200, 9020X, HW 16306, HW 16980, HW 95522
Chevrolet Van: 21-D, 22-D, 34-C, 36-C, 39-C, 47-B, 56-B, 90-A, 91-A, 91-B, 94-B, 117-A, 121-A, 144-A, 145-A, 216-A, 222-A, 224-A, 255-A, 2506-B, 2524-A, J102, J164, J230, J37, J38, J51, Kiko 2, Kiko 10, Kiko 13, Kiko 17
Chitty Chitty Bang Bang: 1006-A, 1206-A
Chrysler Matra Rancho: 76-C (Also see Matra Rancho.)
Chubb Airport Crash Tender: 119-A, 123-A, 193-A, 225-A, J28 A, Kiko 53, Metalbox #(?)
Citroen 2CV6: 115-A, J27, J27/01, Kiko 60, LL-1358
Citroen Dyane: 89-A, 2515-A, Kiko #(?), Metalbox #(?)
Citroen Safari: 2-A, 2-B, 6-A, 22-A
Commando V100 Armored Car: 83-A, 159-A
Commer "Walk-Thru" Van: 19-A
Custom Van: 185-A, 196-A, J61, J61/01, J61/02, 90260, 90360, 90361, 93236, HW 16979, HW 18671, Kiko 34, Kiko 38, LL-1403
Daimler Fleetline London Bus: 55-A, 81-A, 2501-B, J20, J20/01, 90110, 90111, HW 95512
Daimler Scout Car: 84-A
Derek Fiske Stock Car: 920-A
DeTomaso Mangusta: 6-C
Digger: HW 95544, HW 95549, Kiko #(?)
Dinghy on Trailer: 2520-A, 2525-A
Dodge Magnum: 93-B
Dumper Truck: 7-C, 2526-A, J2, Kiko #(?)
Duple Vista 25 Coach: 7-B
Earth Mover: 90050
ERF Cement Mixer Truck: 29-A
ERF Fire Tender: 26-B, 26-C, 251-A, 2513-B, J7, 90030, HW 95505

ERF Simon Snorkel: 29-B, 29-C, 29-D, 36-A, 250-A, J8, 90035, 90036, HW 95506

ERF Tipper Truck: 48-A

Euclid 35 Ton Rear Dump Truck: 42-A

Excavator: 77-B

F1 Racing Car: 90215, 90216

Farm Livestock Trailer: 33-A

Ferrari 308 GTS: 131-A, 136-A, 2535-A, J32, J32/01, HW 16303, Kiko 49, LL-1387

Ferrari 348TB: 90560, 90561, HW 95546

Ferrari 512S: 50-A, 57-B

Ferrari Berlinetta 250GT5: 6-B

Ferrari Testarossa: J36 B, J77, J77/ 01, 90190, HW 16304

Fiat X1/9: 80-B, 86-A, 203-A, J21, LL-1356

Field Gun and Soldiers: 96-A

Fire Launch: 53-A

Flintstone's - Barney's Buggy: 134-A, 3108-A

Flintstone's - Fred's Flyer: 128-A, 3108-A

Flintstone's - Wilma's Coupe: 151-A, 3108-A

Ford Box Van: Kiko 30

Ford Capri: 2062

Ford Capri: 2532-A

Ford Capri: 2537-A

Ford Capri: 56-A

Ford Capri: 922-A

Ford Capri: 925-A

Ford Capri: J16 A

Ford Capri: LL-1373

Ford Capri 3.0 - Professionals: 2536-A, 64-B

Ford Capri 3.0 S: 141-A, 61-C

Ford Capri Dragster: 67-A

Ford Capri Racer: J1 B, J1/ 02, J57

Ford Cement Truck: 30-D, J9 A, Kiko 35 a, Kiko 35 b, Kiko 57 , Metalbox #(?)

Ford D-1000 Artic: 2002-A, 2003-A, 2004-A, 2007-A, 2012-A

Ford D-1000 Container Truck: 54-A, J12 A, 2509-A, J112, Kiko #(?) , Kiko 33

Ford Escort: 105-A, 127-A, 211-A, J229, J25 A, J56, J73, LL-1359

Ford Escort Mk-I: 63-A, 923-A, 927-A, Kiko 8

Ford F-350 Camper: 35-A

Ford F-350 Tower Truck: 12-B

Ford F-350 Wrecker: 28-A

Ford Gran Torino: 2528-A, 45-B, 70-C, 70-D, Kiko 44, LL-1376

Ford GT 70: 10-B, 12-D, Kiko 40

Ford Holmes Wrecker: 1017-A, 933-A

Ford Mustang: 90540, 90541, 104-A, 140-A, 2537-A, 2553-A, 400-A, 401-A through 425-A, 427-A, 430-A, 432-A, 433-A, 435-A, 437-A, 440-A, 441-A, 446-A, HW 95540, J123/ 01, J123/ 02, J202 A, J36 A, Kiko 71, LL-1382

Ford Sierra: 90160, 129-A, 207-A, 208-A, 2551-B, 90161, HW 95518, J201, J31, J31/ 01, J31/ 03, J58 a, LL-1389

Ford Sierra Police: J219, J219/ 01, J58 b

Ford Thames Van: 20-A

Ford Thunderbird: 90520, 96-B, HW 95538, J121, J121/ 01, J121/ 02, Kiko 60, LL-1384

Ford Thunderbird Convertible: 8-A

Ford Thunderbird Hardtop: 8-B

Ford Tipper Truck: 93235, 35-C, 49-B, HW 95650, Kiko 28

Ford Transit Caravan - Martin Walter Caravan: 40-A

Ford Transit Pickup: 125-A, 146-A, 220-A, J30 A, J15 B, J15 C, Kiko 59

Ford Transit Van: 90010, 90011, 90012, 90013, 90015, 90018, 90020, 91352, 93234, J15 D, J39, J4 B, J4/ 01 through J4/ 10, J51/ 01, J51/ 02, J63

Ford Transit Wrecker: 90125, 90126, 90127, 103-A, 126-A, 226-A, 252-A, 2555-A, HW 95514, J204 A, J204 B, J24, J24/ 01, J24/ 02, J24/ 03, J28 B

Ford Zephyr Estate Car: 24-A

Formula 1: 22-C, 2510-A, 53-B, J173, Kiko 16, LL-1354

Formula 1 - Corgi F1 Casting: 90270, 90317

Formula 5000: 2510-A, 27-B, Kiko #(?)

Futura: 59-A

Goodyear Blimp: 83-B

GP Beach Buggy: 58-A, 84-B, 910-A

Grand Prix Racer: 1-D

Guy Warrior Tanker: 14-A, 14-B, 14-C, 17-A, 17-B, 23-A, 97-A, Kiko 7

Guy Warrior Truck: 10-A, 13-A

Healer Wheeler: 2513-A, 2513-B, 36-B, 99-A, Kiko 15, Kiko 6, Kiko 9, Metalbox #(?)

Helicopter: 90500, 90505, 2503-B, 2523-A, 2530-A, 40-B, 46-B, 98-C, J165, J96, J96/ 01, J96/ 02, Kiko 45, Metalbox #(?)

Horsebox: 2503-A, 2550-A, 38-A, J200

Hot Rodder: 24-C, 28-B

Hulkcycle: 100-A

Ironside Police Van: 1007-A

Iveco Beverage Truck: 90045, J13/ 01, J13/ 02, Kiko 58

Iveco Container Truck: 90040, 90041, 90042, 90044, J42 B, J53, J53/ 02, J53/ 04, J9 B, J9/ 01, J9/ 02, J9/ 03, J9/ 05, J9/ 09, J9/ 12

Iveco Refuse Truck: 90320, J52, J52/ 02

Iveco Tanker: 90065a, 90065b, J12 B, J12/ 01, J12/ 02, J2/ 01

Jaguar E Type 2+2: 21-B, 33-B, 39-B,

Jaguar Mark X: 18-A, 18-B, 1-A, 1-B

Jaguar Mark X Fire: 4-A, 4-B

Jaguar Pace Car: 926-A

Jaguar XJ40: 90471, HW 95534, J91/ 02, J92, J93

Jaguar XJ40 Police: 90393, 90470, J91, J91/ 01

Jaguar XJ6: 2505-A, 39-A, 902-A

Jaguar XJR9: 90580, HW 95548

Jaguar XJS: 32-C, 426-A, 428-A, 429-A, 438-A, 442-

A through 445-A, 72-B, J177, J118, J18 A, J204 A, LL-1372, LL-1405, 2555-A

Jaguar XJS Police: J41 B

James Bond: 1001-A, 1010-A, 1011-A, 1012-A, 115-A, 1201-A, 2521-B, 3030-A, 3082-A, 40-C, 41-B, 60-B, J3019, LL-1361, LL-1362

Jeep - Covered: 90310, 12-E, 183-A, J48 B, J48/ 02, J49 B, LL-1357

Jeep - Open: 93237, 157-A, 182-A, 2508-A, 76-B, 82-B, HW 16189, J48 A, J49 A, LL-1393, LL-1394

Jensen Interceptor: 46-A, 906-A

Jet Ranger Helicopter: 2521-B, 3-D, 63-B, 73-B

Klingon Warship: 149-A, 2542-A

Kojak's Buick Regal: 2527-A, 68-A

Lancia Flaminia: 5-A

Land Rover Forward Control: 11-A, 21-A

Land Rover ONE TEN: 90371, 90374, HW 95528, J64, J64/ 04, J65, J66, J74, J97

Land Rover Pickup: 16-B, 2503-A, 2521-A, 79-A

Land Rover Wrecker: 2502-B, 2504-A, 2504-B, 2504-C, 31-B, Kiko 21, Kiko 23

Leyland Terrier Box Truck: 101-A, 120-B, 143-A, 147-A, 191-A, 195-A, 201-A, 202-A, 209-A, 217-A, 218-A, 221-A, 228-A, 50-B, 74-B, 80-C, 87-B, 95-A

Leyland Terrier Tanker: 97-B, J22 A, Kiko 70

Loadmaster Shovel: 23-B

London Taxi: 90085, 90086, 90089, 2501-B, 71-B, HW 95510, J17, J17/ 01, LL-1365

Lotus Esprit: 2529-A, 60-B, J115, J15 A, Kiko 46, LL-1362

Lotus Europa: 32-B

Mack Fire Pumper: 2029-A

Mack Semi Truck: 2027-A

Mack Tanker: 2011-A, 2006-A

Marcos XP: 71-A, 911-A, 98-A

Massey Ferguson 3303 Tractor with Blade: 43-A, 2502-A

Matra Rancho: 90100, 210-A, 223-A, 2550-A, 76-C, 90101, J119, J19, J19/ 02, J200, LL-1355

Mercedes-Benz 190E 2.3/16: 90460, 93179, HW 95533, J89, J90

Mercedes-Benz 220: 3-A

Mercedes-Benz 230TD: HW 95535, J79, J95, J94, J94/ 02

Mercedes-Benz 240D: 2518-B, 215-A, 254-A, 2554-A, 59-C, J14, LL-1380

Mercedes-Benz 240D Police: 219-A, 59-B

Mercedes-Benz 240D Taxi: 194-A, 52-B

Mercedes-Benz 280SL: 45-A, 903-A, 928-A

Mercedes-Benz 350SL: 124-A, 181-A, J122/ 01, J202 B, J29, J29/ 01, J47 A, Kiko 47, Kiko 52, LL-1397

Mercedes-Benz 500SL: 90570, 90571, HW 16301, HW 95547

Mercedes-Benz Ambulance: 90390, 192-A, 1-E, 227-A, 2513-B, 253-A, J167, J167/ 01, Kiko 27, Kiko 29

Mercedes-Benz Bus: 93181, 116-A, 118-A, 15-C, 214-A, J214, J5, J5/ 02, J5/ 03, J5/ 04

Mercedes-Benz C111: 72-A, 909-A

Mercedes-Benz Car Transporter: 2014-A, 2015-A

Mercedes-Benz Mobile Shop: J62, 98-B, Kiko 31, Kiko 37

Mercedes-Benz Refrigerator Truck: 2020-A, 2028-A

Mercury Cougar XR7: 61-A, 70-B, 924-A, 937-A

Mobile Crane: 88-A, Kiko 24, Kiko 60(?) , Kiko 73

Monkeemobile: 1004-A, 1204-A

Morgan Plus 8: 64-A, 921-A

NSU RO 80: 37-A

Oldsmobile Starfire: 31-A

Ole Macdonald's Truck: 78-A, 931-A

Opel Corsa / Vauxhall Nova: 161-A, 163-A, 170-A, J40, Kiko 48, Kiko 91

Pencil Eater (Hungry Hatchback) Rover 3500: 200-A

Peterbilt Container Truck: 178-A, J205, J44 A, Kiko 67, Metalbox #(?)

Peterbilt Pipe Truck: 175-A, J207, J42 A, Kiko 65

Peterbilt Quarry Truck: 174-A, J41 A, Kiko 64

Peterbilt Tanker: 177-A, J206, J43, Kiko 66

Pininfarina Modulo: 49-A

Pink Panther Motorcycle: 19-C

Pontiac Firebird: 180-A, 500-A through 525-A, J3200 H, J3700, J46, J46/ 01, J46/ 02

Popeye - Olive Oyl's Aeroplane: 79-B

Popeye - Paddle Wagon: 1008-A

Popeye - Tugboat: 2508-B

Popeye - Tugboat: 67-C

Porsche 911 Carrera: 139-A, 205-A, 431-A, 434-A, 436-A, 439-A, 80-A, 94540b, J176, HW 15788, HW 21315, HW 27112, HW 55015, HW 95520, J35, J35/02, LL-1378, LL-1390

Porsche 911 Carrera Police: 2523-A, 37-B, J69

Porsche 911 Targa: HW 16247-0910, HW 16249-0910, HW 16300, HW 95537, J98, J98/ 02, J99, J99/ 02

Porsche 917: 25-B, 51-A, 94-A

Porsche 935: 90440, HW 95532, J85, J86, J87

Porsche Carrera 6: 41-A, 904-A

Powerboat: J202 B

Range Rover: 184-A, 2513-A, 2530-A, 2553-B, 42-C, 9-C, J59, Kiko 12 b , Kiko 20, Kiko 3, Kiko 54, LL-1383, LL-1395

Range Rover Open: 3019-B, J50 A, Kiko 22

Raygo Rascal 600 Road Roller: 44-A

Refuse Truck: 55-B, J113, J13 A, Metalbox #(?)

Reliant TW9 Pickup: 1-C

Reliant-Ogle Scimitar: 12-C

Renault 5 Turbo: 102-A, 204-A, J23, LL-1352

Renault Trafic Bus: J44 B, J55, J55/ 02

Renault Trafic Van: J110 B, J25 B, J25/ 01, J3 B, J54, J54/ 02, J54/ 03, J54/ 04, J54/ 15, Kiko #(?)

Road Roller: 67-B, HW 95550

Rough Terrain Truck: 13-B, 2520-A, Kiko 32

Rover 3500: 138-A, 200-A, 2551-A, 2595-A, 8-D, J179,

J34, Kiko 460, Kiko 470, Kiko 69, Metalbox #(?)
Rover 3500 Police: 16-C, 2503-B, 2536-A, J6, Kiko #(?), Metalbox #(?)
S. & D. Refuse Wagon: 25-A
Scammell Concrete Mixer: 47-A
Scooby Doo Mystery Ghost Catcher: 52-C
Scout Car: 2511-A
Shazam Thunderbolt: 24-C
Shovel Loader: 2526-A, 48-B
Skip Dumper: 2514-A, LL-1402, 85-A
Space Shuttle: 2512-A, 2521-B, 2538-A, 41-B, 5-C, J1 A, LL-1364, LL-1396
Speedboat / Trailer: 19-B, 2553-B, Kiko #(?)
Spiderbike: 57-C
Spidercopter: 2531-A
Spidercopter: 75-B
Spidervan: 2531-A
Starship Liberator: 2512-A, 2-C, 44-B
Starship USS Enterprise: 148-A, 2542-A
Stinger Helicopter: 2511-A, 34-B
Studebaker Wagonaire: 3005-A
Studebaker Wagonaire Ambulance: 30-A, 30-B, 30-C
Studebaker Wagonaire TV Camera Car: 15-B
Sunbeam Alpine: 26-A
Super Stock Car: 75-A, 920-A, 49-C
Superman Daily Planet Helicopter: 6-D
Superman Daily Planet Van: 2505-B
Supermobile: 11-C, 2506-B
Terex R35 Rear Dump Truck: 42-B
The Man From U.N.C.L.E Car: 1005-A, 1205-A
Thunderstreak - Hot Wheels Casting: 90317
Tipping Farm Trailer: 2502-A, 8-C
Todd Sweeney Stock Car: 919-A

Tom & Jerry: 2063, 1013-A, 1014-A, 2507-A, 2507-B, 38-B, 58-B
Triumph TR7: 10-C, 2525-A, J204 B, J3 A, LL-1401
Tug Boat: 93-A
U.S. Racing Buggy: 70-A
Volkswagen 1200: 20-B
Volkswagen 1200 Police: 3-B
Volkswagen 1300: 1010-A, 17-C
Volkswagen 1300 Police: 3-C
Volkswagen Hot Rod: 160-A, 60-A, Kiko #(?)
Volkswagen Luggage Elevator Truck: 32-A
Volkswagen Pickup Truck: 15-A
Volkswagen Polo: 137-A, 212-A, 92-A, J235, J33, Kiko 480, Kiko 490, Kiko 51. Kiko 68, LL-1371
Volkswagen Tower Truck: 12-A
Volvo 245DL Wagon: 2518-A, 2554-B, 51-B, J11 A, J111, J203, J11 B
Volvo 400 Farm Tractor: 34-A
Volvo 760: 90430, J47 B, J47/ 01, J47/ 11, J82, J83, J84, Kiko #(?)
Volvo P-1800: 62-A, 905-A
Waste (Refuse) Truck: Kiko 50
Wigwam Camper Van: 18-C
Wild West - Locomotive: 108-A, 2534-A, 2534-B
Wild West - Covered Wagon: 122-A
Wild West - Paddle Steamer: 113-A
Wild West - Railroad Goods Wagon: 112-A
Wild West - Railroad Passenger Coach: 111-A
Wild West - Stage Coach: 114-A, Kiko 12 a
Willys Jeep: 5-B
Wonder Woman's Wonder Car: 33-D
Woody Woodpecker's Car: 49-C
Zetor 5511 Farm Tractor: 4-C , 2501-A, 2516-A

Bibliography

Bailey, Roger, Ed., *Classic Toys Magazine,* Vol. 2, Issues 10 & 11, Classic Toys Ltd.

Browning, Andy and Pat. *Corgi Super Junior and Super Hauler Guide.* Ashford, Kent, UK: A & P Browning, 1994.

Corgi Classics Catalog, The Original Omnibus Catalog, & The Golden Oldies Collection Catalog: Corgi Classics Ltd., 1995-2003.

Corgi Toys Catalogs, Husky Toys Catalogs, & Corgi Juniors Catalogs: The Mettoy Company Ltd. (PLC), 1960-1983.

Corgi Toys Catalogs & Corgi Classics Catalogs: Corgi Toys Ltd., 1984-1989.

Corgi Toys Catalogs, Corgi Classics Catalogs, Corgi American Classics Catalogs, Corgi The Original Omnibus Company Catalogs, & Corgi Racing Collectibles Catalogs: Corgi Sales, Mattel UK Ltd, 1990-1995.

Force, Edward. *Corgi Toys.* Atglen, Pennsylvania: Schiffer Publishing Ltd., 1984 (Revised 1997).

Hammel, Tom, Ed. or Bunte, Jim, Ed., *Collecting Toys Magazine,* Vol. 1, Issue 1 through Vol. 4, Issue 4, Kalmbach Publishing Co.

Korbeck, Sharon, Ed. or Hammel, Tom, Ed., *Toy Collector and Price Guide Magazine:* Vol. 5, Issue 3, Vol. 7, Issues 1 & 2, Krause Publications.

Korbeck, Sharon, Ed. or Hammel, Tom, Ed., *Toy Collector and Price Guide Magazine:* Vol. 5, Issue 3, Vol. 7, Issues 1 & 2, Krause Publications.

Korbeck, Sharon, Ed., *Toy Shop Magazine:* Vol. 9, Issues 6-17, Krause Publications.

Mack, Charles, Ed., *Matchbox U.S.A. Magazine:* Vol. 7, Issue 4, Matchbox U.S.A.

Manzke, Bill. *The Unauthorized Encyclopedia of Corgi Toys.* Atglen, Pennsylvania: Schiffer Publishing Ltd., 1997.

Parker, Bob. *The Complete Book of Hot Wheels.* Atglen, Pennsylvania: Schiffer Publishing Ltd., 1995.

Pownall, Susan, Ed., *Corgi Collector Magazine,* Issues 1-150: Corgi Collector Club.

Stoneback, Bruce and Diane. *Matchbox Toys.* Seacaucus, New Jersey: Chartwell Books Inc., 1993.

Van Cleemput, Marcel R. *The Great Book of Corgi.* London, UK: New Cavendish Books, 1989.

West, Richard, Ed., *Model Collector Magazine,* Vol. 10, Issues 2-10, Link House Magazines Ltd.

Wieland, James and Edward Force. *Corgi Toys - The Ones With Windows.* Osceola, Wisconsin: Motorbooks International, 1981.

Internet Resources

Apps, Stephen, April 10, 2003, "Rockets" [On-line] Available: http: //www.btinternet.com/~s.apps/rockets.htm

Curtis, Mark, March 15, 2003, "Matchbox Collectors Community Hall Discussion Forum" [On-line] Available: http: //www.mboxcommunity.com/cgi-local/dcforum/dcboard.cgi

Beckett, Steve, March 15, 2003, "Steve Beckett's Husky and Corgi Juniors Page" [On-line] Available: http: //www.dfwbeckett.net/HSKindex.html

Berridge, D. V., March 15, 2003, "X1/9 Scale Models" [On-line] Available: http: //dspace.dial.pipex.com/dberridge/x19models.htm

Falkensteiner, Christian, March 15, 2003, "Christian Falkensteiner's Citroen DS/ID Break Pictures" [On-line] Available: http: //www.mboxcommunity.com/cfalkens/CitroenToys/CitroenDSBreak/ChFCitroenDSBreak.htm

Findley, Graham, March 15, 2003, "Corgi Rockets" [On-line] Available: http: //www.btinternet.com/~viviennefindley/

Hirst, Gary, March 15, 2003, "Corgi Juniors / Husky" [On-line] Available: http: //www.home.railscene.com/garyscars/corgi/Corgi.htm

Lee, Peter, March 15, 2003, "The National Street Van Association" [On-line] Available: http: //www.nsva.uk.com/id2.htm

Teunissen, Eric, March 15, 2003, "Triumph TR7 & TR8 Scale Models" [On-line] Available: http: //www.team.net/TR8/trscale/trscale.html

Yocham, Gary and Adrienne, March 15, 2003, "Yocham's Battery Charged Cars Page" [On-line] Available: http: //www.yochams.com/yochams.htm